Fear, Loathing, and Victorian Xenophobia

Fear, Loathing, and Victorian Xenophobia

Edited By

Marlene Tromp

Maria K. Bachman

Heidi Kaufman

The Ohio State University Press | Columbus

Library of Congress Cataloging-in-Publication Data
Fear, loathing, and Victorian xenophobia / Edited by Marlene Tromp, Maria K. Bachman, and
Heidi Kaufman.
     p. cm.
Includes bibliographical references and index.
ISBN 978-0-8142-1195-3 (cloth : alk. paper)—ISBN 978-0-8142-9296-9 (cd)
  1. English literature—19th century—History and criticism. 2. Outsiders in literature. 3. Preju-
dices in literature. 4. Identity (Psychology) in literature. 5. Xenophobia—Great Britain—19th
century. I. Tromp, Marlene, 1966– II. Bachman, Maria K., 1963– III. Kaufman, Heidi, 1969–
PR468.O77F43 2013
820.9'008—dc23

                              2012017517

Cover design by Mia Risberg
Text design by Juliet Williams
Type set in Adobe Garamond Pro
Printed by Thomson-Shore, Inc.

♾ The paper used in this publication meets the minimum requirements of the American National
Standard for Information Sciences—Permanence of Paper for Printed Library Materials. ANSI
Z39.48–1992.

9   8   7   6   5   4   3   2   1

Contents

❦

Illustrations

෯ᵗ෯

Acknowledgments

The editors wish to acknowledge the Nineteenth-Century Studies Association (NCSA), whose annual conferences brought us in contact with one another and nurtured the conversation that led to this book.

Introduction

Coming to Terms with Xenophobia

Fear and Loathing in Nineteenth-Century England

❦

MARLENE TROMP
MARIA K. BACHMAN
HEIDI KAUFMAN

Why Xenophobia?

Over the last few decades, the field of nineteenth-century cultural studies has been increasingly attentive to the centrality of foreignness in the study of British culture. Without question, the work of postcolonial critics such as Edward Said, Gayatri Spivak, and Homi Bhabha laid the groundwork for profoundly important ways of reading nineteenth-century culture. Their scholarship has taught us that we simply cannot understand the Victorian age without conscientious attention to the complexities of colonial and imperial contexts and ideologies. Similarly, rich scholarly material has shaped our understanding of the cultural constructions or expressions of "race" in the Victorian period. Connected to, but distinct from, these fields, studies in Jewish literary history, Jewish discourse, or Semitic discourse have helped us to think through the relations between or among race and science, religion and race, and nation-formation and imperial culture. As this essay collection demonstrates, in the nineteenth century there were various additional expressions aimed at delineating foreigners or establishing boundaries between peoples and geographies that cannot be addressed adequately by the above critical strategies: for example, the tensions raised by a woman born to Italian immigrants living in England. Her physical appearance or even her accent may seem distinctly English. However, her cultural attachments or self-claimed identity might include a mixing of Italian and English or Catholic and Protestant. Our critical methodologies and reading strategies need to expand in order to address the unique ways in which fears about foreigners gave rise to expressions of xenophobia in the nineteenth century. We begin this project with the claim that the study of xenophobia may intersect with other more established critical fields, such as the study of race discourse, imperial culture, Jewish studies, or Irish studies, but it functions as a separable field, with its own logic, genealogy, and power.

With this point in mind, we see Victorian xenophobia as a way of interpreting the perceived foreignness of people, objects, and locations as a threat to English culture and identity. It is the possibilities—the contingencies—that drive this vision and its attendant fears, and that ultimately reflect Victorian anxieties about its own identity in a moment when it was being reshaped by powerful new forces. Thus, the image of the foreigner often grew out of concerns over changing identities, or of the fear that self and other/foreigner could or might merge. It is the possibility of merging that gives rise to intense anxieties and antipathies that define Victorian xenophobia. At the same time, these expressions illuminate a parallel phenomenon—xenodochy, the welcoming of fascination with the foreigner. Rajani Sudan's *Fair Exotics* has examined the intersections of xenodochy and xenophobia in British Romantic literature.[1] Her scholarship has helped to lay important groundwork for this collection of essays, which explores both constructions of foreignness and the contours of xenophobic discourse as it evolved during the nineteenth century, culminating in the first appearance of the word "xenophobia" in 1909.

Fear, Loathing, and Victorian Xenophobia examines how xenophobia evolved and what impulses drove it both affectively and as a cultural practice. This collection looks across the Victorian period to trace the myriad tensions that gave rise to the fear and loathing of foreigners, immigrants, aliens, and ethnic/racial/religious others. The essays included here are intended to prompt new ways of reading fear and loathing of the foreigner, and to capture in a more nuanced fashion what has fallen beyond the scope of imperial discourse analysis and critical race theory. This collection is thus a provocation to think about race, nation, and relationships involving the figure of the foreigner in more complexly inflected ways. Xenophobia speaks particularly to a fear of foreign bodies and/or the transgression of physical boundaries of

---

1. Rajani Sudan, *Fair Exotics: Xenophobic Subjects in English Literature, 1720–1850* (Philadelphia: University of Pennsylvania Press, 2002).

homeland, nation-space, community, and family. Indeed, interrogating the work of xenophobia challenges us to reassess global relationships in a way that moves beyond colonized/colonizer, Oriental/Occidental, black/white binaries, and consider those relations within the larger and complex global sphere. We see this collection contributing to the emerging field of cultural mobility studies, as many of the essays implicitly address what Stephen Greenblatt has described in *Cultural Mobility: A Manifesto* as the "vitally important dialectic of cultural persistence and change."[2] Radical mobility is not a phenomenon of the twenty-first century alone; rather, as a significant stage of modern globalization, the nineteenth century (marked by European imperial expansion and an international economic organization) experienced an unprecedented increase in mobility—the movement of people, objects, ideas, and capital across the world. It is through these processes of cultural encounter and exchange that we can see how global mobility was and continues to be constitutive of the phenomenon of xenophobia.

As a first foray into delineating a theory of Victorian xenophobia we propose several axioms. Through these, we hope to move towards a dynamic method or route of inquiry that other cultural critics will continue to flesh out.

1. Xenophobia circulates around and is produced by an ambiguous and elusive concept of "foreignness." Foreignness becomes problematic in the popular British consciousness, in part because it cannot be fixed; its boundaries are constantly shifting. While concepts such as "race" may be biologically empty, they often have definable and relatively stable material markers, and this perceived stability permits us to believe we can name, identify, and often manage it. "Foreignness" resists clarity and categorization.

A person may walk a short distance, for example, cross a real or imagined boundary, and become a foreigner—even if he was not categorized as such when setting out. Just as compelling, the walker may or may not consider himself a foreigner, regardless of what boundaries he crosses, and the people he meets may or may not agree with his assessment of himself and them. Another example is the *Titanic* disaster hearings in both the U.S. and Britain in 1912, when the term "xenophobia" had been conceptually well-established. In these hearings, American and British officials and witnesses explicitly and frequently refer to some passengers and crew as "foreign" in describing events—a term that cannot accurately mark people's identities in the middle of the ocean and in international waters. In material terms,

---

2. Stephen Greenblatt, *Cultural Mobility: A Manifesto* (Cambridge and New York: Cambridge University Press, 2010), 6–7. While mobility can, according to Greenblatt, "lead to heightened tolerance of difference and an intensified awareness of the mingled inheritances that constitute even the most tradition-bound cultural stance, [*sic*] it can also lead to an anxious, defensive, and on occasion violent policing of the boundaries" (6–7).

"foreigner" makes no sense many miles from the shore in the North Atlantic, where there are no "natives" or national landscapes by which to define who is foreign and who is not. However, if we trace the operation of xenophobia, we can discern a system to these attributions—even when they are false or mistaken in terms of the logic of their application (a British citizen defining another British citizen as "foreign" for example). That system is the xenophobia that had become nameable by the time of the *Titanic* catastrophe of 1912.

2. Xenophobia is a psychopathological condition, marked by a distrust and loathing of foreignness. More specifically, it is a response to the anxiety induced by the fear of foreign contamination from outside the self or even from within. It is a fear of impurities, an anxiety about the corruption and dissolution of Englishness, even by the English themselves. As a fear and revulsion of the foreign, xenophobia is not to be confused with "xenodochy" or "xenophilia"—a desire for and fascination with the foreign, though this may be a parallel impulse in the relation to the foreign.

3. More than just a mindset, xenophobia is a practice that results in antagonistic behavior towards the foreigner. That is, xenophobia is a phenomenon that has very real consequences and effects—politically, culturally, socially, psychologically, materially, physically. While the nineteenth century had a largely (and often deeply vexed) open-door immigration policy, Parliament passed the Alien Act in 1905—a fact that misleadingly suggests that xenophobic thinking began at this moment. While this 1905 act created an immigration control bureau and gave the government the right to expel foreigners, the discomfort with the foreign "intrusion" had already been percolating throughout the culture, sometimes manifesting as fear, sometimes as loathing. For example, anti-Lascar legislation that would have prohibited East and South Asian sailors from boarding British ships was proposed at the turn of the century, but the growing presence of East and South Asian sailors on British ships had already produced enormous anxiety long before the proposed legislation. The National Sailors' and Firemen's Union in Liverpool had "decided to refuse to coal, load, or store any ship that carried 'blackleg' [strikebreaker] labour or Chinese,"[3] complaining that ships carried too many "lascars" or "Oriental" seamen, who were "altogether useless in saving life."[4] The passage and pressure to pass legislation in the early 1900s was the product not simply of increased immigration, but also of discomfort that crystallized into an anti-foreign sentiment and anti-foreign action over the course of the Victorian era.

---

3. "Liverpool Shipping Trouble," *The Times,* 30 April 1912, 8.

4. Brotherhood of Locomotive Firemen and Engineers, "The *Titanic* Disaster," *Brotherhood of Locomotive Fireman and Engineers Magazine* (July 1912): 94.

4. Xenophobia, as both a complex mindset and a practice, must be understood through the study of the intricate matrix and intersection of relations and identities—social, cultural, political, psychological, etc.

5. Xenophobia is a cultural mechanism that has not been rendered visible by other tools of analysis in nineteenth-century studies. While pervasive in the nineteenth century, xenophobia becomes apparent once it has been articulated as a distinct strand of nineteenth-century thought and practice. Its processes are not captured fully by notions of racism, anti-Semitism, or imperialism. While xenophobia may be accentuated by "othering" on the basis of class, race, or nation, it is not this act of othering on these grounds: i.e., "We are not x; we are y."

6. Xenophobia happens, significantly, "on the street." It is not an ideology or practice that falls within the exclusive province of professionals (such as scientists, economists, government officials) or their professional products (research, studies, reports)—although xenophobia may shape the rationales of the practitioners in these fields, and their work may serve to justify those impulses in the cultural mainstream. Xenophobia is articulated in the popular sphere; it is largely owned and operated by the "masses." Xenophobia, moreover, can be embodied in the *impulse* that inspires texts and socials practices, as much as in the texts and social practices themselves.

7. Xenophobia is one consequence of mobility, and thus it produces systems of border patrol. The vulnerabilities and anxieties produced by shifting boundaries and the impossibility of cultural containment are at the heart of xenophobia. Precisely because the foreign is polymorphous, it creates anxiety about boundaries—xenophobes become attentive to, suspicious of, and hostile toward the foreign. Xenophobia emerges as a by-product of nationalism and nation-building, as ideas move across national and social boundaries and as people travel, live, and read the world in new ways. In the twenty-first century, global societies have become interconnected in complex and disparate ways, and it is these phenomena of widespread human mobility and global communication that drive xenophobic impulses in our own cultural moment. Xenophobia, therefore, often works to block mobility across a range of landscapes.

Reading Difference Anew: Xenophobia amidst Studies of Difference

A study of xenophobia enters into a rich and varied critical context. The work of postcolonial studies has been key in fleshing out this landscape. Edward Said first articulated and developed what he saw as the pervasive constructs of Orientalism in western culture that underpinned imperialism.[5] Gayatri Spivak introduced gender and taught us that we simply cannot understand the Victorian age without a keen attentiveness to the interplay of gender and empire.[6] Homi Bhabha responded with what he saw as a tendency to a flat absolutism in Said's theories which function by "disclosing the ambivalence of colonial discourse [which] also disrupts its authority."[7] Several theorists have nuanced and developed the articulations of these practitioners. Anne McClintock, Antoinette Burton, and Chandra Mohanty, for example, have followed Spivak's and Bhabha's redirections of Said, focusing on the way in which counterknowledges or resistant voices have played a key role in the development of imperial ideologies.[8] In *Imperial Leather* McClintock notes that "[T]he dynamics of colonial power are fundamentally, though not solely, the dynamics of gender."[9] Similarly, Burton draws our attention to the ways that the work of empire was not simply being played out in the colonies, in travel writing, or in colonial offices, but in middle-class English homes.[10]

Indeed, postcolonial literary analysis and historiography—particularly in the substantial work of Catherine Hall, Ann Laura Stoler, and Gauri Viswanathan—provide a dynamic heuristic for investigating the complex and shifting relations between the colonizer and the colonized. In her study on the "racing" of Englishness, *Civilizing Subjects: Colony and Metropole in the English Imagination,* for example, Hall explains how we must understand the relations between colonizer and colonized ("between colony and metropole") as a mutually constitutive hierarchy: "each was part of the making of the other, but the colonizer always exercised authority over the colonized."[11] In

---

5. Edward Said's groundbreaking *Orientalism* (New York: Pantheon, 1978) first introduced these themes, and his *Culture and Imperialism* (New York: Knopf, 1993) fleshed out the discussion and responded to critiques about the flatness of his argument, nuancing his explanations.

6. Gayatri Spivak's important essay "Can the Subaltern Speak?" opened her discussion, and *In Other Worlds* (New York: Routledge, 1988) introduced gender as a key component of empire. Her "Three Women's Texts and a Critique of Imperialism" in *Feminisms*, 798–814, made the charge that we cannot read Victorian literature without attending to imperialism.

7. Homi K. Bhabha, "Of Mimicry and Man: The Ambivalence of Colonial Discourse" in *Modern Literary Theory: A Reader,* 237. See also Homi K. Bhabha, *The Location of Culture* (New York: Routledge, 1994).

8. Chandra Talpade Mohanty, "Under Western Eyes: Feminist Scholarship and Colonial Discourse," in *Colonial Discourse and Post-Colonial Theory.* Also significant in the shaping of postcolonial theory were Mohanty's early critiques that western academics have failed to see the ways in which their work in the academy often reproduces the very structures that they claim to critique.

9. Anne McClintock, *Imperial Leather: Race, Gender, and Sexuality in the Colonial Contest* (New York: Routledge, 1995), 364.

10. Antoinette Burton, *Burdens of History: British Feminists, Indian Women, and Imperial Culture* (Chapel Hill, NC: University of North Carolina Press, 1994), and *At the Heart of Empire: Indians and the Colonial Encounter in Late-Victorian Britain* (Berkeley: University of California Press, 1998).

11. Catherine Hall, *Civilizing Subjects: Colony and Metropole in the English Imagination* (Oxford: Blackwell, 2002), 8.

challenging assumptions of homogeneity within the categories of colonizer and colonized, Hall, Stoler, and Viswanathan, among others, illustrate the ways in which race and ethnicity are constituted by gender, class, and sexuality.[12] These works have helped to frame debates about imperial ideologies, which in turn have led scholars to consider the myriad ways in which ideas about foreignness evolved through specific nineteenth-century contexts and histories. Xenophobic expressions and ideologies intersect with these contexts and histories, clearly, but they emerge through the confluence of other forces as well. The essays in this collection are therefore attentive to these critical methodologies, but they simultaneously address some of the unique arrangements and perspectives that shape xenophobic discourse in the Victorian period.

Building on the work of feminist scholarship and postcolonial studies underscores the significance of the ways in which Robert J. C. Young's work, like our own, draws together multiple methodologies in his study of colonial hybridity.[13] Similarly, Anne McClintock's analysis of the Victorian reinvention of race and the cult of domesticity were part and parcel of a similar set of methodologies that extended the work of Said by employing psychoanalysis as a model to explore the mass marketing of empire. Through this approach McClintock provocatively interrogates the ways in which imperialism and racial ideology delineated white bourgeois identity in Victorian imperial culture.[14]

While the idea that race and racism, as they were codified in the home and in the colonies, played a constitutive part in the making of English bourgeois identity (as Young, Stoler, and McClintock have shown), in *Dark Vanishings: Discourse on the Extinction of Primitive Races,* Patrick Brantlinger compelling demonstrates how extinction discourse—that idea that savages were fated to become extinct—functioned as an ideological tool to justify European expansion.[15] Other important studies of race include the work of Catherine Hall, Keith McClelland, and Jane Rendall in *Defining the Victorian Nation: Class, Race, Gender and the British Reform Act of 1867,* a study that attends to legal shifts, nationalism, and the way in which Hall explains, "Britain was increasingly conceptualized in terms that linked those of kindred race."[16]

12. Ann Laura Stoler, *Carnal Knowledge and Imperial Power: Race and the Intimate in Colonial Rule* (Berkeley and Los Angeles: University of California Press, 2002); Gauri Viswanathan, *Masks of Conquest: Literary Study and British Rule in India* (New York: Columbia University Press, 1989).

13. Robert J. C. Young, *Colonial Desire: Hybridity in Theory, Culture and Race* (New York: Routledge, 1995).

14. McClintock, *Imperial Leather,* 5.

15. Patrick Brantlinger, *Dark Vanishings: Discourse on the Extinction of Primitive Races* (Ithaca, NY: Cornell University Press, 2003).

16. Catherine Hall, "The Nation Within and Without" in *Defining the Victorian Nation: Class,*

Of course, it is impossible to consider the many cultural dimensions of racism and race consciousness in the Victorian period without considering other approaches to the field, such as those by Douglas Lorimer, George Stocking, Nancy Stepan, Jennifer DeVere Brody, and Laura Callanan,[17] in addition to Edward Beasley's recent work, *The Victorian Reinvention of Race,* which adeptly traces the development and articulation of racial ideologies in this period. Indeed, Beasley focuses his attention on how the idea of racial difference crystallized in mid-Victorian England and how the processes of racism were formed. He reminds us that "[s]lavery and xenophobia existed in the English speaking world on both sides of the Atlantic in the eighteenth century."[18] And just as Beasley sets xenophobia and racism apart, so too must we trace out its development in this period. Clearly, the work of critical race studies evokes for us the fruitfulness and potential of xenophobia as a means of developing a more nuanced understanding of how race, nation, and empire are distinctive and evolving threads operating in the period.

The work of this rich scholarly legacy not only broadens our understanding of the workings and culture of colonialism and the fear of foreigners, but points to the significance of foregrounding xenophobia as a critical lens for reading Victorian culture. Just as we can begin to articulate uncharted regions and boundaries that have gained increasing precision, these scholarly elisions have become fertile ground and fissures for xenophobia studies, in part because of the careful articulation of the landscape surrounding them by critics of race, nation, and empire. Indeed, scholars of postcolonial studies have already begun to reflect on subsequent inadequacies and misapplications of postcolonial theory. Ania Loomba, for example, has spoken of the ways in which postcolonial theory has been embraced by the academy with great vigor and enthusiasm, but has often been denuded of political and practical content and, as a result, has become distressingly far removed from the con-

---

Race, Gender and the British Reform Act of 1867, 18.

17. See Douglas Lorimer, *Colour, Class and the Victorians: English Attitudes to the Negro in the Mid-Nineteenth Century* (Leicester: Leicester University Press, 1978); George Stocking, *Victorian Anthropology* (New York: The Free Press, 1987); Jennifer DeVere Brody, *Impossible Purities: Blackness, Femininity, and Victorian Culture* (Durham, NC: Duke University Press, 1996); Nancy Stepan, *Picturing Tropical Nature* (London: Reaktion Books, 2001); and Laura Callahan, *Deciphering Race: White Anxiety, Racial Conflict, and the Turn to Fiction in Mid-Victorian English Prose* (Columbus: The Ohio State University Press, 2005). Also, without question, Frantz Fanon's foundational study *Black Skin, White Masks* (New York: Grove Press, [1952] 2008) and, more recently, David Theo Goldberg's *Racist Culture: Philosophy and the Politics of Meaning* (Oxford: Wiley-Blackwell, 1993) have become foundational texts for any investigations of racialized discourse and racist expression throughout modernity.

18. Edward Beasley, *The Victorian Reinvention of Race: New Racisms and the Problem of Grouping in the Human Sciences* (New York: Routledge, 2010), 1.

texts that it has (theoretically) been designed to study.[19] We believe this phenomenon is one reason for the overbroad application of postcolonial theory and the failure to articulate an alternative means of reading those situations in which its explanatory power is misapplied. Not only has it become the dominant critical lens for reading foreignness, race, and nation in the Victorian period, but our nearly universal application of this model in critical conversations has sometimes blinded us to other interpretive possibilities. This collection of essays begins, then, by making visible the relations among groups of people and the discourse of the "foreign" in such a way that engages with tensions and concerns that have not or cannot be addressed fully by our current critical methodologies.

New scholarship, in fact, has begun to evince a discomfort with the over-application of "imperialism." Recently, Daniel A. Novak has argued that Elizabeth Gaskell's writing on the Cagots, who were European and "white," but still marginalized, points to the limitations of postcolonial theory.[20] Novak notes that "While post-colonialist critics are right to remind us of the omnipresence of Imperialism in Victorian culture, [it is] possible that the colonial imaginary has often stood in for other theories of race, even in studies that treat forms of European otherness[.] In recent years, the colonial model has been used to read Victorian figurations of European groups such as Irish, Jews, [Gypsies], and Slavs."[21]

We propose that xenophobia is one means of comprehending why the Cagots could be identified as Gaskell's "Accursed Race," in spite of their apparent whiteness. The study of xenophobia provides one avenue through which to develop and articulate the very phenomenon that scholars have set out to explore—and can elucidate other important threads of inquiry as well. One such thread running throughout many of the essays in this collection is

---

19. Ania Loomba, *Colonialism/Postcolonialism* (New York: Routledge, 2002). Loomba further notes that the star system of the American academy has led students and critics alike to deploy the work of Said, Spivak, and Bhabha with little creativity or thought.

20. Daniel Novak, "Gaskell's 'Accursed Race': Rethinking Gaskell and Victorian Racial Theory," North American Victorian Studies Association (Montreal), November 12, 2010. Novak's presentation is part of a larger work in progress: how race and whiteness are figured inside Europe.

21. Novak notes the work of critics like Brian Cheyette, Reina Lewis, and Deborah Nord who have argued that representations of European others reproduce the tropes of Orientalism, while Andrew Hammond and Jopi Nyman have argued that such representations are in fact *derived* from colonialism. See Andrew Hammond, ed., *The Balkans and the West: Constructing the European Other, 1945–2003*, and Jopi Nyman, *Under English Eyes: Constructions of Europe in Early Twentieth-Century British Fiction* (Amsterdam: Rodopi, 2000). Novak also notes the important work of Joseph Metz's article, "Austrian Inner Colonialism," for example, which demonstrates this trend in thinking through European representations of *European* race. *PMLA* 121.5 (2006): 1475–1492. See also other recent work such as Robert J. C. Young's *The Idea of English Ethnicity* (New York: Wiley-Blackwell, 2008) and Julia Shields's "'The Races of Women: Gender, Hybridity, and National Identity in Dinah Craik's *Olive*," *Studies in the Novel* 39.3 (fall 2007): 284–300.

the construction of Englishness and its relation to an emergent discourse of xenophobia. In fact, the important discussions by Simon Gikandi, Ian Baucom, and Anthony Easthope on how Englishness was formed through the mediation of alterity implicitly inform the myriad explorations of xenophobia in this volume.[22] Gikandi's investigation of "the ways in which Englishness was itself a product of the colonial culture that it seemed to have created elsewhere," and the "notion of an English identity in crisis," are crucial factors for understanding the genesis of xenophobia.[23] Baucom also refined how we conceive of Englishness by arguing for the importance of place and location in both the formation and destabilization of English national identity. For Baucom, the entire imperial era was characterized by "serial collapses of authentic English identity" and the "dispersal" of England's "locations of identity": "as England dispersed its Gothic cathedrals, cricket fields, imperial maps, costumed bodies, and country houses across the surface of the globe," Baucom notes, "it found that these spaces, and the narratives of identity they physically embodied, were altered by the colonial subjects who came into contact with them."[24] Though Easthope does not focus particularly on imperialism's impact on national identity, he stresses that "Englishness is carried and reproduced by a specific form of discourse"[25]—in specific cultural markers or expressions, such as journalism, comedy, tragedy, poetry, and historical writing. Indeed, to see nation—and by extension English national identity—as a distinct discursive formation is crucial for understanding xenophobia as a mechanism by which English identity and fears about the dissolution of Englishness have been expressed.

No less influential in Victorian studies is the proliferation of work in recent years on Jewish writers, studies of race and anti-Semitism, and the figure of the Jew in nineteenth-century British culture. Sander Gilman's influential work has drawn important connections between race and gender or race and anti-Semitism in late Victorian culture.[26] Gilman's understanding of race and nation in relation to Jewish figures in literature and art has been foundational in its focus on Victorian science, and other discourses of authority

22. See Ian Baucom, *Out of Place: Englishness, Empire, and the Locations of Identity* (Princeton, NJ: Princeton University Press, 1999), Antony Easthope, *Englishness and National Culture* (London and New York: Routledge, 1999), and Simon Gikandi, *Maps of Englishness: Writing Identity in the Culture of Colonialism* (New York: Columbia University Press, 1996).

23. Gikandi, *Maps of Englishness,* 10.

24. Baucom, *Out of Place,* 220.

25. Easthope, *Englishness and National Culture,* 31.

26. Sander Gilman, *The Jew's Body* (New York: Routledge, 1991); "'I'm Down on Whores': Race and Gender in Victorian London" in *Anatomy of Racism;* and "Black Bodies, White Bodies: Toward an Iconography of Female Sexuality in Late Nineteenth-Century Art, Medicine, and Literature" in *"Race," Writing, and Difference.*

that helped create and solidify racial and anti-Semitic discourses in the Victorian period. Recent studies have moved on to nuance the formulation of Jewish otherness, to consider Semitic discourses or Jewish discourses equally pernicious, but nuanced differently in response to historically specific concerns. For example, in his study *Constructions of "the Jew" in English Literature and Society,* Bryan Cheyette argues persuasively that "[t]he radical emptiness and lack of a fixed meaning in the constructions of 'semitic' difference" which, he argues, "results in 'the Jew' being made to occupy an incommensurable number of subject positions which traverse a range of contradictory discourses."[27] Much like the images discussed in this collection, the foreign figure is often presented ambivalently, or as a figure whose meaning shifts to accommodate local or current anxieties about difference or the stability of English identity. Cheyette and others who focus on images of 'the Jew' in the cultural sphere recall James Shapiro's study of a previous century—which raised the question, "if even a Jew could be English, what could one point to that defined essential Englishness?"—Michael Ragussis's work considers how such national boundary markers were contextualized by fears about passing, conversion, and interracial/religious marriages in nineteenth-century literary culture.[28] While the study of xenophobia is not the same kind of interrogation as studies of anti-Semitism, the essays in this collection are similarly concerned with issues of passing, intermarriage, or purity (however such a word is defined).

Fear, Loathing, and Victorian Xenophobia, therefore, draws from and builds upon these pivotal studies to examine some of the ways in which postcolonial studies, race studies, and Jewish studies might lead us toward a fuller understanding of how xenophobia interacts with, but remains distant from, other critical methodologies and subjects.

Just as race and nation cannot be understood through the rhetoric of empire alone, so global relations must be comprehended as more than just an economic narrative, even in the context of the nineteenth century's expanding consumer capitalism. While it is true that wealth production drove English engagement with "foreigners," the more nuanced analysis we propose renders visible the broader scope of anxieties and fears guiding relationships among and between English people and foreigners: it makes clear that while profit and economic power played a role, so too did xenophobia, which under-

---

27. Bryan Cheyette, *Constructions of 'the Jew' in English Literature and Society: Racial Representations, 1875–1945* (Cambridge: Cambridge University Press, 1993), 8. Cheyette also points out that the figure of "the Jew" is more than just a degenerate other in British culture; this figure, "like all 'doubles,' is inherently ambivalent and can represent both the 'best' and the 'worst' of selves" (12).

28. Michael Ragussis, *Figures of Conversion: 'The Jewish Question" and English National Identity* (Durham, NC: Duke University Press, 1995); James Shapiro, *Shakespeare and the Jews* (New York: Columbia University Press, 1996), 199.

girded the production of many social, political, and imaginative measures to manage relations with the foreign. For example, while English relations with India were clearly driven by empire, there are discernible similarities between English-Irish relations. By considering the role of xenophobia, we can shade more finely what these two very historically and socially different relations have in common, without ignoring their differences. Legal measures from the 1829 Catholic Emancipation Act to the 1905 Aliens Act clearly signal the intentional engagement with these questions and the importance of negotiating boundaries within English culture. So, too, does the work of the science of racialization, both in popular culture and in professional venues.

Nineteenth-Century Contexts

Why focus on xenophobia in nineteenth-century culture? The Victorian age marks a pivotal moment for shifting understandings of national identity, racial ideologies, and articulations of Englishness. Indeed, "xenophobia" crystallized over the course of the nineteenth century, a period of rapid and unprecedented social transition. Improved trade, travel, and transportation created opportunities for material and cultural migrations, and unprecedented levels of exchange among and between cultures. For example, the industrial revolution which began in the previous century facilitated the mass production and affordability of objects that circulated at home and abroad; enabled the transit of people, perspectives, and ideas; and disrupted putative spatial, ideological, and national boundaries. Moreover, a class system dramatically in flux—a rising professional class, a decaying aristocracy, and an overburdened working class, not to mention the ever-widening gap between the rich and the poor—profoundly unsettled the social structure that had for so long shaped and stabilized relations among the English populace. All of these unprecedented disruptions contributed to perceptions of the foreign—including people and migrating objects—as both simultaneously omnipresent and threatening even when they were not overtly visible.

The idea of a homeland and or a sense of belonging to a place evoke some of the key tensions that helped to codify a xenophobic mindset in the Victorian period. In such images identity is construed through an essentialist lens as absolute, unchanging, and linked to blood and land. In a famous passage from George Eliot's *Daniel Deronda* (1876), for example, the narrator underscores the power that home and homeland played in the epic articulations of family, race, and nation in this period, and the related assertions of difference. If a body could not "truly" belong, it was by default deemed other. Eliot's narrator describes that form of belonging in the following way:

A human life, I think, should be well rooted in some spot of a native land, where it may get the love of tender kinship for the face of earth, for the labours men go forth to, for the sounds and accents that haunt it, for whatever will give that early home a familiar unmistakable difference amidst the future widening of knowledge: a spot where the definiteness of early memories may be inwrought with affection, and kindly acquaintance with all neighbours, even to the dogs and donkeys, may spread not by sentimental effort and reflection, but as a sweet habit of the blood. At five years old, mortals are not prepared to be citizens of the world, to be stimulated by abstract nouns, to soar above preference into impartiality; and that prejudice in favour of milk with which we blindly begin, is a type of the way body and soul must get nourished at least for a time. The best introduction to astronomy is to think of the nightly heavens as a little lot of stars belonging to one's own homestead.[29]

This passage has been read as a touchstone for the complicated politics of nationhood in the novel. What does it mean to be English? According to Eliot's narrator one must not only live within the geographical boundaries of the nation, but must have been reared on the milk from English cows, or must have been nourished in body and soul by the nightly heavens above one's home. Moreover, individuals need a filial connection with neighbors in order to absorb local perspectives, rather than being impartial "citizens of the world," who might view the values and attitudes from other landscapes with detachment. Equally significant here is the understanding that global perspectives emerge not only from the formal study of space or geography, but from the view acquired through "belonging to one's homestead." More than simply excising transnational, multidimensional, or assimilative possibilities—admittedly troubling enough—the narrator protests, or presents the idea, that one may never be at home in a land where one has not been raised. Such passages subtly articulate and reflect anxiety about the need for such delineations at this moment in Victorian history. These lines raise a number of questions addressed in the essays that follow. What do we make of Victorian culture's preoccupation with forging connections among land, body, and blood? On one level, Eliot's narrator nostalgically renders homeland as a spot of Wordsworthian time where character is formed in childhood. Yet, on another level, this passage raises the specter of crossed boundaries even as it offers a measured, calming calculation on the stability of homeland. What, after all, is this "future widening of knowledge" against which this spot of homeland will provide a buffer? And what happens to people once they become "citizens of the world" to make "the sweet habit of the blood" necessary?

---

29. George Eliot, *Daniel Deronda* (London: Penguin Books, 1995), 22.

From Mrs. Jellyby's humanitarian efforts and missionary work in Africa in Dickens's *Bleak House* to legal and political attempts to manage immigration and various aspects of enfranchisement, we can locate English efforts to regulate what social scientists have called "insider groups" and "outsider groups." Grand gestures like the Great Exhibition and the interactions among those people representing "all the nations of the world" on the streets of London are all sites to which the lens of xenophobia can be profitably employed. In doing so, we discover that xenophobia in the context of the nineteenth century was no longer an individual or isolated response to the foreign; rather, it had become an embedded cultural response to conceptions of home, abroad, nation, belonging, class, race, and numerous other identity markers undergoing extraordinary change in this period. In this volume, we begin with the concepts of "fear and loathing" in an attempt to flesh out the political, economic, legal, social, and psychological impulses that were generative of xenophobia, rather than simply identifying the effects of xenophobia. Indeed, even today we are better equipped to handle the classist assumptions of writers like Mayhew and Booth than we are to discuss the ways in which constructions of the foreigner or of the immigrant particularly intersected with discourses of race and class. Bringing together work from art history, history, literary studies, cultural studies, women's studies, Jewish studies, Irish studies, and postcolonial studies, the contributors to this volume offer a variety of new methodological and theoretical approaches to address the rich global dimensions of xenophobia in nineteenth-century England.

Xenophobia at Work

The organization of this volume underscores the centrality of the axioms we defined above in shaping xenophobic thinking and in its material manifestations in the world, or xenophobia at work. In the first part, "Epidemic Fear," we turn to xenophobia's affective structures and triggers, exposing their genealogy by teasing them apart. In the second part, "Xenophobic Panic," we turn to the fear activated by social changes and practices and the particular form of loathing that emerged in the Victorian period around "foreignness." The third part, "The Foreign Invasion" includes essays that explore ideas about the foreign figure, and the reasons why such figures were perceived to be such a threat to the alleged stability of Englishness.

PART I: EPIDEMIC FEAR

We have sought to bring a new precision to the language of xenophobia and to the varying kinds of social resistance to xenophobic ideologies and practices. Specifically, we asked what made xenophobia a path worth exploring; how xenophobia was distinct from racial hatred or the work of empire; and in what physical landscapes (at home and abroad) xenophobia might occur. The authors here speak to the questions we have raised, seeking to explore xenophobia as a new analytic tool that recalibrates our understanding of the nineteenth century. "Epidemic Fear" looks at English anxieties about the dilution, decay, or dissolution of English identity. This part examines xenophobia as a particular kind of fear rooted in the crossing (or fear of crossing) of physical boundaries and the related anxieties and hatreds of foreign contact, contagion, and contamination.

In "The Pollution of the East: Economic Contamination and Xenophobia in *Little Dorrit* and *The Mystery of Edwin Drood*," Marlene Tromp examines the ways in which economic contact was structured by xenophobia in the Victorian period. While a desire for wealth shaped and grew the nation, fear and hatred of the sources of that wealth required constant purification of financial interests. Eastern nations were perceived as a physically polluting danger to England and to intimate English relationships. Businesses supported by foreign trade "blackened" the city of London and seemed to threaten the English businessman, linking the soiled skies and buildings to an assault on the home and family. Tromp demonstrates how Dickens's *Little Dorrit* (1857) and *The Mystery of Edwin Drood* (1870) expose such anxieties about the economic and personal threat posed by the East. These novels, Tromp argues, marry debt—both personal and economic—and familial perversions to social and economic relations with foreigners. Though accruing wealth was a particularly English practice, engaging in direct contact with foreigners and the money that circulated across the empire triggered powerful xenophobic responses to wealth. Finally, Tromp suggests that as imperial desire became increasingly vexed, xenophobia became more deep-seated within the cultural psyche.

Focusing on England's long-standing suspicion of Italians, Jay D. Sloan's "Victorian Quarantines: Holding the Borders against 'Fevered' Italian Masculinity in Dante Gabriel Rossetti's 'St. Agnes of Intercession'" considers how such fears triggered xenophobic critical reactions to the work of the Anglo-Italian (an "Italian" in England) poet and painter, Dante Gabriel Rossetti. As evidenced by Robert Buchanan's infamous attack upon Rossetti as the leader of "The Fleshly School of Poetry" in 1871, English critics would employ a metaphorics of "disease" to target the pathogenic potential of Rossetti's inherently "foreign" poetry and to identify him as a threat to British national "health." Over the course of his career, English critics would attempt to "quarantine" Rossetti's work, portraying him as the embodiment of the "effeminate Italian"—transgressive on both ethnic and gender grounds—and particularly dangerous because he was freely "broadcasting" his contagions in Britain among the vulnerable native population. It is this "local urgency," Sloan argues, that distinguishes these truly xenophobic critical reactions from the "merely" racist rhetoric. That Rossetti recognized and attempted to combat this "local" critical paradigm, Sloan demonstrates, is made evident in the plot and composition history of "St. Agnes of Intercession."

Rajani Sudan's essay, "Contracting Xenophobia: Etiology, Inoculation, and the Limits of British Imperialism," discusses new attitudes towards inoculation articulated at the end of the nineteenth century, suggesting that they mark a distinct shift in Britain's imperial aims. Sudan indicates that methods of inoculation forced Britons to suspend, however theoretically, the xenophobia that structured cultural, metropolitan, and civic British identity. The introduction of foreign bodies through inoculation as a way of warding off disease appeared to be perfectly sensible, partially because these intrepid souls were open to receiving new ideas, but also because many doctors' travels placed them in contact zones where ecologies of new diseases and biomedical treatments were often patently visible. But Victorian Britain, mindful of its imperial trajectory, seemed to equate the medical practice of inoculation with a cultural one. Thus many Britons may have read inoculation as an unpatriotic act, a treasonous introjection of the elements of disease into the corpus of the metropole. Sudan suggests that inoculation became increasingly vexed as Britain professed to turn conquest and colonization into the social missionary work that characterized Victorian cultural imperialism. Domestic Victorians, fearing the palpable consequences of smallpox epidemics, were prone to locate its etiology elsewhere, in others, thus insuring their cultural immunity to the pathogen.

Drawing on Sara Ahmed's theory of how emotions, particularly hate and fear, work to shape the "surfaces" of individual and collective bodies, Maria K. Bachman uncovers the cognitive and affective processes that drive xenophobia in her essay, "Charles Dickens, Wilkie Collins, and the Perils of Imagined Others." Responding to the Indian Mutiny in 1857, an enraged Charles Dickens declared that if he were Commander in Chief in India, he would do his "utmost to exterminate the Race upon whom the stain of the late cruelties rested."[30] Rather than unleashing actual violence against the Hindu and Muslim sepoys, Dickens collaborated with his good friend Wilkie Collins on a fictive, but hardly pacifist, response to the uprising. Strategically published as the widely circulated extra Christmas number of *Household Words*, *The Perils of Certain English Prisoners*, Bachman suggests, functions as

---

30. Charles Dickens, *The Letters of Charles Dickens*, vol. 8 (New York: Oxford University Press, 1995), 459.

an affective economy that circulates, both literally and figuratively, the horror of the events at Cawnpore and the fears of subsequent assaults on England by "barbaric" foreign others. Embedded in the tale's two plotlines, Bachman argues, are competing ideologies of nation, culture, language, and history. While Dickens's two chapters may attempt to amplify the fear and loathing toward non-English others that erupted in the aftermath of Cawnpore, Collins's contribution enacts its own intratextual mutiny by mitigating Dickens's xenophobic sentiments and exposing the myth of English superiority.

In "Maudlin Profanity and Midnight Debauchery: Infanticide and the *Angelito*," Jennifer Hayward shifts our focus to Britons and Americans traveling abroad in Chile and their depiction of Chilean mourning practices. She reads accounts of Chilean *angelitos* as part of a double-edged investigation into Victorian constructions of mourning and Anglo-Chilean constructions of national identity in informal empire. Since Chile was never part of the formal empire, and since its mixture of European and indigenous peoples complicated the easy, binary racism of other sites of empire, this essay allows exploration of the distinctions between empire, racism, and xenophobia. When read against Victorian sentimental discourse—and balanced by Chilean accounts of the meaning of the *angelito* for mourning families— these descriptions of the *angelito* illuminate the fears and anxieties aroused by Chilean "debauchery" and Catholic "profanity." The body of the *angelito* terrifyingly literalizes the Victorian icon of the dying child, while the horror experienced by British and American observers underscores the anxieties underlying Victorian national and imperial identity. Read historically, these accounts help to explain the English colony's gradual isolation from Chileans—who were, as Podsnap would put it, increasingly constructed as "Not English!"

PART II: XENOPHOBIC PANIC

Moving beyond the fears about invasion and infiltration (which defined Part I), "Xenophobic Panic" explores the ways in which the English perceptions of political and cultural events outside its borders shaped and were shaped by xenophobia through the myriad narratives that emerged in response to those events. Beginning with English-Irish relations, Charlotte Boyce examines xenophobic representations of Irish identity in her essay, "Food, Famine, and the Abjection of Irish Identity in Early Victorian Representation." Boyce suggests that race is too narrow a lens through which to read the complex relations between England and Ireland immediately prior to and during the Great Famine; she argues that xenophobia offers more productive theoretical insights into these interactions because, crucially, xenophobia does not exist in isolation, but rather in a mutually constitutive relationship with xenodochy. This economy helps to explain the multifaceted and contradictory depictions of the Irish located in Victorian print culture: welcomed, contingently, as members of the Union, the Irish were also disparaged as the idle, undisciplined antitheses of their English neighbors. During the Famine, hostile presentations predominated as the English press sought to explain the disaster in terms of Irish alterity. Boyce indicates that one of the main phobic markers of this foreignness was food; Ireland's distress was consistently attributed to its over-reliance on the potato. Linking a Kristevan notion of abjection to depictions of Irishness, she argues that the supposed qualities of potatoes were conflated with the presumed traits of Irish identity. She ultimately suggests that dietetic representations of the Irish during the Famine were the result of an ideological imperative to safeguard the boundaries of English identity at a moment of historical crisis.

Exploring one of the most significant sites for understanding and articulating the foreign in the nineteenth century, Joy Sperling's essay, "'Wot is to Be': The Visual Construction of Empire at the Crystal Palace Exhibition, London, 1851," explores the physical layout and design of the Great Exhibition. Sperling argues that the exhibit emerged out of threats to the social, political, economic, and even racial instability that racked England in the 1840s, factors that all suggested an anxiety about the English concept of "self." Mounted at a time when Victorian society had not clearly articulated its views on national and imperial hegemony, and when the structure of British society and Britain's place in society and in the world was not yet inevitable, visual structure came to stand as a surrogate for the imagined purity and strength of the English and England. Both were invaded and "polluted" by the people and wares from the many "foreign" nations that were paradoxically invited to participate in the "friendly" competition of the Great Exhibition. The Exhibition, Sperling contends, helped to shape Victorian concepts of nationhood by dramatically clarifying on a visual level, who and what was considered English and normative. Xenophobia serves as a means of assessing how the palace building can be read as framing the construction of the English "self" (or body) in contrast to the invading horde of "foreign" visitors, who were simultaneously feared and eagerly anticipated.

Patrick Brantlinger, in his essay "Terrible Turks: Victorian Xenophobia and the Ottoman Empire," argues that by the start of Queen Victoria's reign, the Terrible Turk was an ancient stereotype, with roots in the anti-Islamism that inspired the Crusades. The specifically Turkish element emerged with the conquest of Constantinople in 1453 by the Ottoman forces of Mehmed II. From then until the Enlightenment, the Ottoman Empire provided a counterimage thus arousing "imperial envy" for the British Empire. In the 1800s, as the Ottoman regime disintegrated, the British Empire progressed apparently from triumph to triumph. Brantlinger suggests that the stereotype of the Terrible Turk often seemed less "racist" in orientation or emphasis than xenophobic, embodying a fear of one or more of the features commonly identified with the Ottoman Empire, its rulers, and its armies. Terribleness included rage or anger, irrationality and arbitrariness, cruelty, the practice of slavery, lust, and the near-complete domination, including erotic domination of women. Still another factor that contributed to xenophobic reactions to Ottomans or Turks is the rejection and fear of Islam as a key, expansive rival to Christianity.

In "Ethnicity as Marker in Henry Mayhew's *London Labour and the London Poor,*" Thomas Prasch examines what he terms the "bewildering range of ethnic types that strut through the pages of Henry Mayhew's classic survey of the urban underclasses of mid-Victorian London" as a sign of England's global reach through trade and travel. He argues that the presence of the foreigner was a sign not only of England's growing cosmopolitanism, but of the web of connections uniting people from home and abroad. Yet far from offering a celebration of the expanse of the empire of trade, the human varieties of street types, Prasch argues, signaled a threat to Victorians—a threat, that is, to the cultural traditions of English urban working classes. Although Prasch reads these depictions as a form of xenophobia, he also shows how Mayhew sought to transform ethnic differences into racial categories.

PART III: THE FOREIGN INVASION

Building on Parts I and II, and focusing on visual and narrative culture, this final cluster of essays show how and why Englishness is perceived to be imperiled not just because it comes into contact with the foreign other, but because the presence of the other threatened to dismantle the delineations separating one group from the next. Thus, Part III, "The Foreign Invasion," focuses on xenophobic expressions as an utterance of fear about the status and coherence of national identity at a moment when immigration and class mobility were thought to be responsible for the erosion of ancient boundaries and barriers.

In "Jewish Space and the English Foreigner in George Eliot's *Daniel Deronda,*" Heidi Kaufman carves out a distinction between expressions of anti-Semitism and xenophobia. She argues that these terms may overlap in many ways, but maintain a separate discursive structure, and emerge from distinct concerns in this novel. Kaufman demonstrates that xenophobia appears in such moments where the insider Englishman, Deronda, anticipates and fears the foreigner's power to (re)define him. Deronda's xenophobic imagination leads him to construe Judaism as a religious/racial entity situated in a glorious past which Deronda renders nostalgically; and in a degenerate, fallen present, represented in his mind by "ugly" modern Jewish bodies. Kaufman shows that while the latter expression clearly falls into the discourse of anti-Semitism, the former stems from Deronda's xenophobia, or his fear of cultural alignment with the Jewish people he meets in Frankfurt's Juden-gasse and London's East End.

In "Exile London: Anarchism, Immigration, and Xenophobia in Late-Victorian Literature," Elizabeth Carolyn Miller reads xenophobic expressions in a cluster of late-century literature about anarchism by H. G. Wells, Arthur Conan Doyle, Joseph Conrad, and Helen and Olivia Rossetti. According to Miller, anarchism posed a threat to the nation by challenging and seeking to overturn political and social structures of English culture. The texts she analyzes sought to expose the nature of this threat, and to explore the consequences of the dilution and demise of English national identity brought about by rising patterns of immigration. Rather than remaining historically specific, literature about anarchism presented all immigrants as equally threatening to the social order. Miller adds that anarchists threatened not only England, but "Englishness" as a racial and cultural category, and in this way anarchist groups were targeted as signs of the dangers of unrestricted immigration.

In "Xenophobia on the Streets of London: *Punch*'s Campaign against Italian Organ-Grinders, 1854–1864," Annemarie McAllister offers new ways of thinking about Victorian struggles to delineate racial and ethnic markers amidst the pages of one of the most popular magazines of its day. As she considers the tensions raised by comparisons between the English and Italians on the pages of *Punch,* McAllister provides an instructive and illuminating study of the interplay of visual and narrative depictions of Italians in English culture, and of the role of cartoon humor to address xenophobic tensions. Although images of Italians bore some resemblance to other immigrant groups, McAllister argues that several features made Italian organ grinders a unique form of stereotyping. Italians, she notes, had long been associated with music, which ultimately helped to build a case against them in xenophobic discourse. "Such behavior" she adds, "could be ascribed to the traditional low status of performers, and resentment at such dominance of Italian cultural capital" but in fact class distinctions were only part of what provoked these cartoons in the pages of *Punch.* Placing the figure of the organ grinder within other relevant cultural contexts, such as the Crimean war, theories about phrenology and physiognomy, and the evolution of the magazine itself, McAllister concludes that "*Punch* representations are concerned more with boundary maintenance, the construction of class and urban 'rights' to space, and an outlet for profound hostilities."

In her focus on language and silences, Minna Vuohelainen presents the problem of destabilized English identity for late Victorian culture. Her essay, "'You know not of what you speak': Language, Identity, and Xenophobia in Richard Marsh's *The Beetle: A Mystery* (1897)," makes the case for a new genre called "invasion gothic" which she defines as "a mixture of urban gothic and fashionable invasion narrative, articulated in an essentially xenophobic discourse, in which British identity, security, and superiority are placed under threat from a foreign, often supernatural, monster." The novel stands, then, not just as an example of xenophobic thinking, but of a new subgenre ushered in by the rising xenophobic tensions of late-century British culture. Vuohelainen maintains that moments of silence or failed speech acts in the novel signal anxieties about linguistic degeneration that many feared would surely follow in the wake of a rising immigrant population and the accompanied deterioration of a "pure" English identity. Thus, while the English people in the novel lose the power of speech, the intruder Beetle remains articulate, and indeed even manages to appropriate the English language as a weapon against the English.

If early Victorian readers were in any doubt about the dangers of an Eastern European nobleman moving to London, Dracula's pride in his mixed blood would have only reinforced their xenophobic impulses: so argues Thomas McLean in "Dracula's Blood of Many Brave Races." The irony, McLean points out, is that English blood is as "mixed" as Dracula's and from the same causes: war, empire, and immigration. Reading Bram Stoker's novel as a nightmare of continental immigration, McLean demonstrates how we can see Transylvania not only as a metaphor of colonial or physical desire but as a part of Europe. In doing so, McLean places the novel's eponymous character not simply in the realms of gothic literature, but also among the foreign revolutionaries settling in Britain during the second half of the nineteenth century. McLean first examines nineteenth-century immigration to Britain from other parts of Europe, in particular the increasing number of political refugees who arrived in London after the revolutions of 1848—refugees whose radical affiliations and failed uprisings encouraged xenophobic feelings among their new British neighbors. He then focuses his investigation on Stoker's text in order to place the nationalist warrior Count Dracula within this context, suggesting that the novel can be read as the threat of all that is foreign to the apparently pure blood of its protagonists.

The volume concludes with Anne J. Kershen's Afterword, which places the essays in *Fear, Loathing, and Victorian Xenophobia* within a longer historical framework. Kershen notes that the term "xenophobia," "if used precisely," does not imply racial inferiority. However, as the essays in this collection along with Kershen's essay attest, "the two can be used in tandem." The Afterword includes numerous examples from English history of the ways in which racism, anti-Semitism, Islamaphobia, and other forms of racial hatred intersected with or helped bolster xenophobic ideologies. In turn, these histories gave birth to a new language that reflected English anxieties about the so-called foreigner. Yet Kershen reminds us that words alone were not the only consequence of xenophobic thinking; they were created alongside and often in collusion with physical violence aimed at "foreigners."

Conclusion and New Beginnings

We expect that *Fear, Loathing, and Victorian Xenophobia* will begin to position, more thoroughly and particularly, the xenophobic impulse in the nineteenth century. The multi- and interdisciplinary essays in this collection argue compellingly for the uniqueness of xenophobic discourse—a uniqueness that stands apart from and yet intersects with every other form of hatred and fear in the period. In this way these essays reconsider and redefine what we understand about and how we study race, imperialism, and nation formation in Victorian culture. Moreover, by offering a theoretical and critical intervention into these established fields, the contributors to this collection demonstrate how the study of xenophobia adds a new dimension to our understanding of identity, politics, and language in this period.

Works Cited

Baucom, Ian. *Out of Place: Englishness, Empire, and the Locations of Identity.* Princeton, NJ: Princeton University Press, 1999.

Beasley, Edward. *The Victorian Reinvention of Race.* New York: Routledge, 2010.

Bhabha, Homi K. *The Location of Culture.* New York: Routledge, 1994.

———. "Of Mimicry and Man: The Ambivalence of Colonial Discourse." In *Modern Literary Theory: A Reader*, edited by Philip Rice and Patricia Waugh. 234–241. London: Edward Arnold, 1996.

Brantlinger, Patrick. *Dark Vanishings: Discourse on the Extinction of Primitive Races.* Ithaca, NY: Cornell University Press, 2003.

Brody, Jennifer DeVere. *Impossible Purities: Blackness, Femininity, and Victorian Culture.* Durham, NC: Duke University Press, 1996.

Brotherhood of Locomotive Firemen and Engineers. "The *Titanic* Disaster." *Brotherhood of Locomotive Fireman and Engineers Magazine*, July 1912.

Burton, Antoinette. *Burdens of History: British Feminists, Indian Women, and Imperial Culture.* Chapel Hill: University of North Carolina Press, 1994.

————. *At the Heart of Empire*. Berkeley: University of California Press, 1998.

Callahan, Laura. *Deciphering Race: White Anxiety, Racial Conflict, and the Turn to Fiction in Mid-Victorian English Prose*. Columbus: The Ohio State University Press, 2005.

Cheyette, Bryan. *Constructions of 'the Jew' in English Literature and Society: Racial Representations, 1875–1945*. Cambridge: Cambridge University Press, 1993.

Dickens, Charles. *The Letters of Charles Dickens. The Pilgrim Edition Volume VIII: 1856–1858*. Edited by Graham Storey and Kathleen Tillotson. New York: Oxford University Press, 1995.

Easthope, Antony. *Englishness and National Culture*. London and New York: Routledge, 1999.

Eliot, George. *Daniel Deronda*. Edited by Terrence Cave. London: Penguin Books, 1995.

Fanon, Frantz. *Black Skin, White Masks*. 1952. Reprint, New York: Grove Press, 2008.

Gikandi, Simon. *Maps of Englishness: Writing Identity in the Culture of Colonialism*. New York: Columbia University Press, 1996.

Gilman, Sander. "Black Bodies, White Bodies: Toward an Iconography of Female Sexuality in Late Nineteenth-Century Art, Medicine, and Literature." In *"Race" Writing, and Difference*, edited by Henry Louis Gates, Jr. 223–261. Chicago: University of Chicago Press, 1986.

————. "'I'm Down on Whores': Race and Gender in Victorian London." In *Anatomy of Racism*, edited by David Theo Goldberg. 146–167. Minneapolis: University of Minnesota Press, 1990.

————. *The Jew's Body*. New York: Routledge, 1981.

Goldberg, David Theo. *Racist Culture: Philosophy and the Politics of Meaning*. Oxford: Wiley-Blackwell, 1993.

Greenblatt, Stephen. *Cultural Mobility: A Manifesto*. Cambridge and New York: Cambridge University Press, 2010.

Hall, Catherine. *Civilizing Subjects: Colony and Metropole in the English Imagination*. Chicago: University of Chicago Press, 2002.

Hall, Catherine, Keith McClelland, and Jane Rendall. *Defining the Victorian Nation: Class, Race, Gender and the British Reform Act of 1867*. New York: Cambridge University Press, 2000.

Hammond, Andrew, ed. *The Balkans and the West: Constructing the European Other, 1945–2003*. New York: Ashgate, 2004.

Lewis, Reina. *Gendering Orientalism: Race, Femininity and Representation*. New York: Routledge, 1995.

"Liverpool Shipping Trouble." *The Times*, 30 April 1912, 8.

Loomba, Ania. *Colonialism/Postcolonialism*. New York: Routledge, 2002.

Lorimer, Douglas. *Colour, Class and the Victorians: English Attitudes to the Negro in the Mid-Nineteenth Century*. Leicester: Leicester University Press, 1978.

McClintock, Anne. *Imperial Leather: Race, Gender, and Sexuality in the Colonial Contest*. New York: Routledge, 1995.

Metz, Joseph. "Austrian Inner Colonialism." *PMLA* 121.5 (October 2006): 1475–1492.

Mohanty, Chandra Talpade. "Under Western Eyes: Feminist Scholarship and Colonial Discourse." In *Colonial Discourse and Post-Colonial Theory*, edited by Patrick Williams and Laura Chrisman. 196–220. New York: Columbia University Press, 1994.

Nord, Deborah Epstein. *Gypsies and the British Imagination 1807–1930*. New York: Columbia University Press, 2006.

Novak, Daniel. "Gaskell's 'Accursed Race': Rethinking Gaskell and Victorian Racial

Theory." North American Victorian Studies Association (Montreal), November 12, 2010.

Nyman, Jopi. *Under English Eyes: Constructions of Europe in Early Twentieth-Century British Fiction*. Amsterdam: Rodopi, 2000.

Ragussis, Michael. *Figures of Conversion: "The Jewish Question" and English National Identity*. Durham, NC: Duke University Press, 1995.

Said, Edward. *Culture and Imperialism*. New York: Knopf, 1993.

———. *Orientalism*. New York: Pantheon, 1978.

Shapiro, James. *Shakespeare and the Jews*. New York: Columbia University Press, 1996.

Shields, Julia. "The Races of Women: Gender, Hybridity, and National Identity in Dinah Craik's *Olive*." *Studies in the Novel* 39.3 (fall 2007): 284–300.

Spivak, Gayatri. "Can the Subaltern Speak?" In *The Post-Colonial Studies Reader*, edited by Bill Ashcroft, Gareth Griffiths, and Helen Tiffin. 24–28. London: Routledge, 1995.

———. *In Other Worlds*. New York: Routledge, 1988.

———. "Three Women's Texts and a Critique of Imperialism." In *Feminisms*, edited by Robyn R. Warhol and Diane Price Herndl. 798–814. New Brunswick, NJ: Rutgers University Press, 1991.

Stepan, Nancy. *Picturing Tropical Nature*. London: Reaktion Books, 2001.

Stocking, George. *Victorian Anthropology*. New York: The Free Press, 1987.

Stoler, Ann Laura. *Carnal Knowledge and Imperial Power: Race and the Intimate in Colonial Rule*. Berkeley and Los Angeles: University of California Press, 2002.

Sudan, Rajani. *Fair Exotics: Xenophobic Subjects in English Literature, 1720–1850*. Philadelphia: University of Pennsylvania Press, 2002.

Viswanathan, Gauri. *Masks of Conquest: Literary Study and British Rule in India*. New York: Columbia University Press, 1989.

Young, Robert J. C. *Colonial Desire: Hybridity in Theory, Culture and Race*. New York: Routledge, 1995.

———. *The Idea of English Ethnicity*. New York: Wiley-Blackwell, 2008.

PART I

Epidemic Fear

❧

Epidemics of contagious disease, real and metaphorical, were a phenomenon that evoked both fear and fascination throughout Victorian society. This section of the volume serves as a foray into the myriad ways in which Victorian xenophobia operated as a strategic defense—indeed, as a behavioral immune system—against foreign infection. The essays included here consider how the rhetoric of foreign contagion and contamination, of infiltration and infection, and of disease and death, circulated and spread throughout the nation. The discourse of xenophobia that emerged was predicated on the growing perception of an English body perpetually threatened by foreign pathogens. The narratives of foreign pollution that proliferated in literature, the popular press, as well as medical and scientific journals not only exacerbated fears about the dilution, decay, and dissolution of English identity, but also contributed to the evolution of an increasingly ethnocentric middle-class culture.

In "The Pollution of the East: Economic Contamination and Xenophobia in *Little Dorrit* and *The Mystery of Edwin Drood*," Marlene Tromp investigates the ways in which foreign investment triggers xenophobic anxieties. According to Tromp, while economic contact with foreign nations was at once a source of great wealth for Britain, these monies were perceived as importing foreign pollution, thus threatening the health and well-being of the English nation and body. For Jay D. Sloan, the dangerous carrier of foreign contagion is not "dirty" money, but rather the dissipated artist. In his essay, "Victorian Quarantines: Holding the Borders against 'Fevered' Italian Masculinity in Dante Gabriel Rossetti's

'St. Agnes of Intercession'," Sloan explores how the excessive poetic passions of Rossetti's Italian artist-protagonist come into direct conflict with longstanding English fears of "diseased" Italians. And while Victorian Britain may have been attempting to build up its cultural immunity to "diseased" foreign bodies, Rajani Sudan provocatively demonstrates how the medical practice of inoculation—the injection of foreign bodies into healthy English bodies—to prevent real epidemics of contagious disease forced Victorians to renegotiate the xenophobic attitudes that were constitutive of Englishness. Maria K. Bachman also draws our attention to the interconnectedness of cultural nationalism and xenophobia, with a particular focus on the cognitive and affective processes that underlie the behavioral immune system. In her essay, "Charles Dickens, Wilkie Collins, and the Perils of Imagined Others," she explores how the fear and loathing of foreigners are produced in textual contact zones as "effects of circulation" and how the notion of "Englishness" is thus fortified through a community of readers or "shared witnesses." Jennifer Hayward is also interested in textual contact zones—English-language newspapers and Anglo-American travel narratives, particularly—in her investigation of the nineteenth-century "infanticide epidemic" in Chile. In her essay, "Maudlin Profanity and Midnight Debauchery: Infanticide and the *Angelito*," Hayward shows how these accounts of Chilean *angelitos* perpetuated xenophobic attitudes toward that culture while at the same time they also served to strengthen an imperial Anglo identity.

1

The Pollution of the East

Economic Contamination and Xenophobia
in *Little Dorrit* and
The Mystery of Edwin Drood

❧

MARLENE TROMP

"[S]he thought she was wiser, now, than her man of business, who was not such a good man of business by this time, as he used to be . . . and she took it into her head to lay [her money] out for herself. So she took her pigs . . . to a foreign market; and a very bad market it turned out to be. First, she lost in the mining way, and then she lost in the diving way—fishing up some treasure, or some such Tom Tidler nonsense . . . and then she lost in the mining way again, and, last of all, to set the things entirely to rights, she lost in the banking way. I don't know what the bank shares were worth for a little while . . . cent per cent was the lowest of it, I believe; but the Bank was at the other end of the world, and tumbled into space, for what I know; anyhow, it fell to pieces, and never will and never can pay sixpence."

—*David Copperfield*[1]

Xenophobia, Money, and Dickens

Scholars have read Dickens's novels with an eye to both empire and race. I am interested in employing the lens supplied by a critical understanding of xenophobia to the study of two novels, *Little Dorrit* (1857) and *The Mys-*

---

1. Charles Dickens, *David Copperfield* (New York: Penguin, 1996), 473.

tery of Edwin Drood (1870), particularly with regard to the loss described by otherwise-indomitable Betsey Trotwood in the passage from *David Copperfield* above: the perceived danger of economic depletion inherent in the foreign—investments inferior even to her collapsing, alcohol-crippled, but *domestic,* man of business. Business transacted at the "other end of the world" can simply tumble one's money into "space," though, of course, as this essay will propose, the dangers might even be greater than this. I will apply the lens of xenophobia to render more fully visible the anxieties associated with even highly abstracted *economic* transactions, in which wealth circulated in and out of the "foreign" through trade, rather than with direct or personal contact with the foreign. My goal here is to point to an increasing xenophobia that can be detected in the movement of English money into the foreign and of foreign money into England. I will argue that anxieties about foreign investment emerged in fiction before they were clearly articulated in the late-century financial literature, just as this volume proposes that "xenophobia" evolved conceptually in the culture before it emerged in the language.[2]

We can see evidence of the anxiety about the danger of economic relations with the foreign explicitly articulated in 1875 by a Select Committee of the House of Commons, which produced a special report on "Loans to Foreign States." This report warned that a "petty and insolvent state" might solicit loans with disreputable agents and bilk the population, through deception and misrepresentation, out of a fortune.[3] In the most sweeping study of Victorian foreign investment patterns conducted to date, Chabot and Kurz argue that "The city of London, with its perceived propensity to funnel capital overseas rather than into domestic industry, was widely suspected of hastening the decline of British industry."[4] While Chabot and Kurz contend that the perception of such investment as harmful to the British economy was actually mistaken—a fact that makes this anxiety even more important to explore as it reveals a tenacious xenophobic belief that fails to tare with a social and economic reality—they note a "prodigious" increase in foreign investment as the century progressed.

Most scholars, however, even those studying these more explicit articulations of the anxiety about foreign investment, have focused on the ways such

---

2. In *The Private Rod,* I argue that the articulation of social shifts often takes place in fiction (and in other forms of art) before they appear in the culture's (nonfictional) self-representation or self-assessment (Marlene Tromp, *The Private Rod: Marital Violence, Sensation, and the Law in Victorian Britain* (Charlottesville: University of Virginia Press, 2000).

3. "Loans to Foreign States," *Reports from Committees,* vol. 4 (London: House of Commons, 1875): xlx.

4. Benjamin R. Chabot and Christopher J. Kurz, "That's Where the Money Was: Foreign Bias and English Investment Abroad, 1866–1907," *The Economic Journal* 120 (September 2010): 1056.

anxiety revolved around notions of empire. Cannon Schmitt, for example, who insightfully reads some fictional representations as a "broad attack on the culture of investment," identifies them as a form of economic imperialism in foreign lands.[5] Moreover, even where xenophobic anxieties are present, they often remain undetected or unanalyzed by critics. Often the most nuanced analyses, like Rutterford and Maltby's excellent study of women's investment in the nineteenth century, fail to trace patterns of economic xenophobia. Rutterford and Maltby, for example, quote a passage from Trollope's 1867 *The Last Chronicle of Barset* in which the speaker rejects the dangers of "city money"—generally associated with global/foreign investment, as Chabot and Kurz explain—calling it "always very chancy." The character instead embraces "a first-class mortgage on land" as an alternative—a thoroughly local and domestic investment.[6] The authors do not, however, discuss the anxiety about foreign investment that this novel emphasizes, perhaps because foreign investment still dominated the material practices of the age. My argument, then, does not suggest that foreign investment did not take place or that anxieties about foreignness worked to drive the English out of the global marketplace. In fact, it was their willingness to participate, in spite of sometimes catastrophic losses, that drove the creation of the select committee on foreign investment in the House of Commons.

Though such foreign investment had gone through dramatic ups and downs, with enormous gains and enormous losses (like that represented in the South Sea bubble in the eighteenth century),[7] the growth of empire in the nineteenth century made foreign investment not only commonplace, but ubiquitous. In an 1876 essay on investing fraught with xenophobic and racist language, Alexander Innes Shand notes, that "In 1866 [a year that witnessed one of major nineteenth century financial crises] and before it, many investors strongly fancied foreign stocks."[8] While the dangers of such investments were perfectly apparent to him, he indicates that, prior to several painful Victorian market collapses, there often appeared to be creditable

---

5. Cannon Schmitt, "Rumors, Shares, and Novelistic Form" in *Victorian Investments*, 192.

6. Janette Rutterford and Josephine Maltby, "'The Nesting Instinct': Women and Investment Risk in a Historical Perspective," *Accounting History* (2007): 319.

7. In 1711, the South Sea Company bought a significant portion of the British war debt incurred during the Spanish War of Succession in return for exclusive trading rights in Spain's South American colonies and the promise of government interest payments. Fueled by what people later understood were unrealistic beliefs about the potential for the company to make money and by the company's clever puffery of these expectations, investors speculated wildly on the stock and drove the value up by a multiple of ten. When the company began to fail and the owners cashed in their own stock, its collapse ruined thousands of people who had invested their money with confidence in this government-backed venture.

8. Alexander Innes Shand, "Speculative Investment," *Blackwood's Edinburgh Magazine* 120 (September 1876): 301, emphasis added.

reasons for—and great profit in—making foreign investments. His new wisdom, he explained, was partly a product of the fact that the dangers had been fully realized, but too late. He lamented that in spite of high rates of foreign investment,

> Geography and statistics are not the strong points of the average British investor; and when he is dazzled by the fascinating lights brought out in strong relief, he is apt to ignore the facts that are left in the shadows of the background. We know how freely he honored the drafts that Honduras, Costa Rica, Nicaragua, and St. Domingo drew on his credulity. He lent [i.e. invested, with hope of return] as if he believed that the swamps were solid land, studded with populous towns, and opened up by excellent highroads— as if countless cords of mahoganies and dyewoods could be cut, and hauled, and stacked *just as if they had been grown in the New Forest or the Home Park at Windsor*—as if pontoon railways, that cost a life a yard, were to carry the traffic of one of our metropolitan extensions. Judging foreigners by his experiences of our own honorable Stock Exchange, it no more struck him that there might be an easier standard of financial morality among Indians, and half-breeds, and curly-headed negroes, than that there might be a bottom to the deposits even of those innumerable sea-fowl that whiten the islands of the Peruvian seaboard.[9]

Clearly, for Shand, there *is* an inherent inferior financial morality among foreigners and, moreover, this failing creates a real danger for the English investor in the foreign. Significantly, this investor might even be outside of the central financial centers, but an ordinary, provincial Englishman.[10] The "Indians, and half-breeds, and curly-headed negroes," then, served as the foil for the "average British investor," rather than the Britons who were selling the stock or launching the schemes abroad—a xenophobic (as well as racist and imperialist) response. Though Shand warns briefly against domestic debacles like the railway shares crash, the bulk of his essay about wise investing concentrates on detailing *foreign* dangers, along with his fear that the English won't see them until it is too late. Of course, these xenophobic fears were not necessarily realities. In fact, as prominent economic historian Martin Daunton argues, the integration of Asia and Africa "into the global economy was much more destructive [to them], making them more susceptible to famine and disease," whereas "Europe and above all . . . Britain" saw "reduced food prices [and] higher wages."[11]

---

9. Shand, "Speculative Investment," 301.

10. Shand, "Speculative Investment," 299.

11. Martin Daunton, *Wealth and Welfare: An Economic and Social History of Britain 1851–1951*

Beginning with the influential Maynard Keynes in the 1930s and continuing to this day, however, economists have suggested that British investment in the foreign had displaced the domestic investment which was commonplace in the United States and Germany (the two nations that outpaced Britain in the international economic competition at the turn of the century), and precipitated the ruin of Britain's international dominance. The short-term profits that were at the heart of the desire for the foreign and foreign investment, according to these notions, may well have destroyed the long-term economic well-being of the English nation-state, as Peter Temin argues in the *Economic History Review*.[12] (Perhaps the "alarm of both contemporaries and modern histories"—which Daunton sees as overstated—was, in part, generated by the same xenophobia.) The anxieties explicitly articulated in Shand in 1876 continue to be debated by economists today, but were anticipated by Dickens's fiction (and that of many others). Whatever the political fluctuations and practices of empire, xenophobia remained deeply entrenched, complicating economic politics as much as the broadening financial networks. English Victorians, even while they constantly engaged the foreign, became increasingly suspicious of the foreign taint on their money. By the mid-nineteenth century, both the consumption of foreign goods and foreign investment seemed inevitable to most Britons. A desire for wealth (and certainly many other things as well) impelled the nation into the global marketplace, but profound fear and anxiety about the sources of that wealth emerged in the social economy of fiction.

The lack of critical attention to these tensions in Dickens, I would argue, has been due to the lack of an adequate lens to bring them into focus. In *Little Dorrit* (1857) and *The Mystery of Edwin Drood* (1870), the xenophobic response to wealth laden with the taint of the foreign meant that wealth required constant purification. Consuming foreign goods threatened, so it seemed, to transform the English body. Eastern nations were perceived as physically polluting not only to England, but to intimate English relationships. English businessmen, but also the English home and family, were defamiliarized, English normativity was disrupted, and foreignness seemed to creep in with every pound England made. Both novels expose anxieties about the economic and personal threat posed by the East. This anxiety is most significant in that it occurs in spite of the fact that Dickens, like most

(New York: Oxford, 2007), 218.

12. Peter Temin, "Capital exports, 1870–1914: an alternative model," *Economic History Review*, 2nd ser., XL 3 (1987): 453–458, 457. This argument is a response, in part, to Donald McCloskey's discussion of Victorian economics (and Craft's critique of that). Crafts agrees, for reasons different from those of Temin, that electing foreign investment over domestic was deleterious to British economic well-being in the nineteenth century. See also Daunton, 248.

of his fellow Britons, advocated for the benefits of international "communication and commerce" and saw economic protectionism as a barrier to Progress and national growth (a failure of which he accused China, a key player in his representation of foreign investment anxiety).[13] Both novels marry debt—personal and economic—and familial perversions to social and economic relations with foreigners. Though accruing wealth seemed a particularly English practice, consuming foreignness triggered powerful xenophobic responses to such wealth and threatened—at least imaginatively—to rob the English of their very identity. The two novels I will examine here, however, present very different pictures about the possibility of cleansing the domestic space of foreign taint. Whereas Arthur Clennam's poisoning foreign investments in *Little Dorrit* can be purified by a new investments in the domestic, Dickens was less sanguine about the possibility of purification thirteen years later in *The Mystery of Edwin Drood*. Here, the English homeland itself becomes a site of damage rather than healing—a result of economic contact with a polluting Eastern world. Identifying the dangers of consuming the East became a primary strategy for explaining the decline of English global power: a result of poisonous—if sometimes profitable—consumption.

I. Foreign Pollution in *Little Dorrit*

By 1857, the year in which the last installment of *Little Dorrit* was published, the English economy was booming, and "pollution" was something every Londoner understood. The city was regularly choked by the soot of "the Big Smoke," and environmental pollution served as a powerful metaphor for the introduction of foreign pollutants into the British landscape. The "great age of globalization," the era in which trade and the business economy of the nation became inextricably linked to nations the world over,[14] was also the age of urban pollution. Scholars have spoken both to anxieties about the relationship between money and filth and connections with the East and the "taint" they introduced, but little has been done to examine the ways in which specifically *economic* contact with foreign nations was perceived as a physically polluting danger to the English nation and body. In his social history of the "darkness of noon," Bill Luckin describes the way that "terrifying images of 'strangulating' smoke fog and biological or racial decline

---

13. Charles Dickens, "The Great Exhibition and the Little One," *Household Words* 5 (July 1851): 360. See Elizabeth Hope Chang's excellent discussion of this material in *Britain's Chinese Eye: Literature, Empire, and Aesthetics in Nineteenth-Century Britain* (Stanford, CA: Stanford University Press, 2010).

14. Daunton, *Wealth and Welfare*, 17.

interacted with and reinforced one another."[15] He argues that representations of literal, physically destabilizing pollution "were influenced by . . . conceptions of racial hierarchies within and between cultures."[16] Often arguments like this one point to the importation of foreign goods or the actual presence of lascars in working-class communities. In fleshing out the dangers of trading in the Far and South East, Barry Milligan remarks, "the growing colonial commerce with the Orient was plying the domestic market with ever greater quantities and kinds of exotic commodities, 'pestilent Luxuries' which some Britons feared were infiltrating and deteriorating British culture and identity, 'leav[ing] an indelible stain on our national character' (Coleridge, Collected Works 1:226) by irreversibly making it more Oriental and less British."[17] Even highly desirable objects imported from China increased the sense of China's "familiar exoticism," to use Elizabeth Chang's phrase: a concept that "conveys a sense of unbridgeable cultural and aesthetic difference that is amplified, not diffused, by increased circulation and reproduction."[18]

I venture into the interstices of these previous scholarly arguments to probe more deeply the role of the foreign, foreign money, and even English money that circulated through Eastern nations. While these monies were potentially a source of great wealth for Britain, they always carried with them the possibility of importing a much more undetectable foreign pollution than foreign goods or people. For most Britons *in* Britain contact with the East or with the "foreign" more broadly was oblique—through objects, images, and emblems. Direct contact with the *people* of a "racially degenerate" nation was much more uncommon, except for business and leisure travel (the latter of which was still in its infancy). Occident and Orient were most completely and most *invisibly* bound by trade—and not just by the tangible goods that passed across borders, but often by fiscal transactions.

In other words, while foreign figures in Dickens are fascinating, equally compelling and complex is the way that foreignness becomes a dangerous poison visible in *the English themselves*. For this reason, while this argument can easily be applied to the obviously dangerous Rigaud or the attractive and exotic Landlesses (who are unspecifiably foreign and evoke a complex array of responses), I am interested in the more subtle cases in the narrative as well: the thoroughly English Clennams, Doyces, Crisparkles, and Merdles. The English characters are ultimately at the crux of the anxiety in these novels,

---

15. Bill Luckin, "'The heart and home of horror': The Great London Fogs of the Late Nineteenth Century," *Social History* 28 (2003): 33.

16. Luckin, "'The heart and home of horror,'" 41.

17. Barry Milligan "'The Plague Spreading and Attacking Our Vitals': Opium Smoking and the Oriental Infection of the British Domestic Scene," *Victorian Literature and Culture* 20 (1992): 162.

18. Chang, *Britain's Chinese Eye*, 6.

not the foreigners alone. In this way, the dangers absorbed into the English themselves by foreign trade become visible. The churning engines of business that blackened London were fueled, in part, by foreign markets and foreign monies, and it was the latter that was perceived to pose the greatest threat to the British home and family.

Little Dorrit revolves around financial manipulations, pollution, and social and economic relations with foreigners. It begins in a foul prison, where we meet an especially dangerous villain, Rigaud, who has committed two "crimes." The first is that he "owns no particular country,"[19] marking him as eminently "foreign," though *not* of any particular race or nation, and thus triggering xenophobic anxieties about the very real threat that he poses. Second, he dabbles in and carries with him the taint of many nations economically, and—perhaps inevitably given the calculus I will discuss—he has gained his foreign wealth illegitimately. The poison that permeates him and that he helps to render visible in the narrative, however—and this is where we begin to sense the real danger—is in the economic exchange that is not just the province of the dark criminal. Yoked by circumstance *and* practice are the English Clennams and Meagleses, imprisoned in a quarantine because of their converse with the East. The curse of this foreign economic taint, then, pollutes the good and the bad, the individual and, as we shall see, the collective. The male protagonist, Arthur Clennam, ultimately provides a model for purifying England and her people. His return to London dramatizes the processes necessary to mitigate the contaminating impact of foreign economic investment with purifying *domestic* investment and its cognate, the domestic space.

ABSORBING FOREIGN POLLUTION

Arthur Clennam's family business in China leaves him a man contaminated—with a "dark face" and without "[w]ill, purpose, or hope" (20). To underscore the source of this taint, he spends his temporary quarantine in an atmosphere "foul[ed]," like he is himself, by "Hindoos, Russians, Chinese . . . who *come to trade*" there (3). Significantly, it not the presence of these foreigners alone in this foreign place that produces the pollution, but the more widely permeating threat introduced by their "trade:" the economic contamination that remains an active financial residue even when they, themselves, depart. In spite of the thoroughly practical Englishness

---

19. Charles Dickens, *Little Dorrit* (New York: Modern Library, 2002), 12. Subsequent references to this text will be cited parenthetically.

of Clennam and Mr. Meagles—a banker who had grown rich and become a globe trotter, "like Captain Cook" (23)—these men carry their financial dealings and the less visible costs of these activities across national borders. Indeed, it is absolutely clear that Mr. Meagles, though less visibly than Clennam, could not have made his fortune without foreign economic exchange, since banking investments had moved widely in and out of the foreign since the eighteenth century,[20] a fact underscored by the purchased Eastern objects that populate his thoroughly English home. When Mr. Meagles complains of the quarantine as "imprisonment," Clennam complacently remarks that they have "come from the East, and East is the country of the plague." His friend retorts, "The plague! . . . I came here as well as ever I was in my life; but to suspect me of the plague is to give me the plague. And I have had it—and I have got it" (18). Money, as Mary Poovey tells us, was (and is) a wholly symbolic and representational enterprise: the bank note standing in for gold that often didn't exist.[21] Those in quarantine may be wholly removed from physical contact with the East, but they carry a far more lasting and symbolic *financial* contamination—the "germ" of the East contaminates the homeland that profits from it.

Metaphorically, this pollution is visible on the English landscape. Just as Clennam is marked, the London to which he returns, flush with economic prosperity, is mired in filth. As Christopher Herbert has argued, London has a "thematics of disgust focused upon imagery of stains, contamination, pollution, nauseating smells, infectious disease, filth, slime, rot. . . . even in the 'gentlemanly residence' of Mr. Tite Barnacle, which seems impregnated, as the narrator delicately puts it, with 'a strong distillation of mews,' a pollution imparted by what Herbert calls filthy lucre.[22] This soul-killing and nation-crippling atmosphere is both an environmental and moral plague in *Little Dorrit:* "Melancholy streets in a penitential garb of soot, steeped the souls of the people who were condemned to look at them out of windows in dire despondency. [Bells rang] as if the Plague were in the city and the dead-carts were going round. Everything was bolted and barred that could possibly furnish relief to an overworked people" (30). These "overworked" people

---

20. The twinning and replacement by account in the Meagles's family (one good English twin by Tattycoram) suggests that this kind of account engagement will always soil the family. All the doubling (Pet's twin) [Tattycoram is "tak[en] into account" (21) and owes them] and Flintwinch's double, even Clennam's in-love/not-in-love-with-Pet self, seem significant to me with regard to the splitting caused by foreignness and money. This also appears in Pancks's gypsyness, which requires loans, and Rigaud's double foreigness, which does as well.

21. Mary Poovey, *Genres of the Credit Economy: Mediating Value in Eighteenth- and Nineteenth-Century Britain* (Chicago: University of Chicago Press, 2008).

22. Christopher Herbert, "Filthy Lucre: Victorian Ideas of Money," *Victorian Studies* 44.2 (2002): 201.

are not just the laborers whose backs are broken by the physical work in the soot, but the investors and traders, "overworked" by the foreign exchanges. The Barnacles, as financiers of the "national ship," have even become "whole colonies" (261) in and of themselves. Building on Herbert's and Gallagher's argument that money, in mid-century fiction (and in Dickens, particularly),[23] is inevitably associated with moral pollution, I'd like to *characterize* that pollution and its dangers, especially as they are figured in Britain itself, through their source. In other words, I will argue, "dirty" money is the money that moves through and accrues profit from connections with the foreign.

The economic dealings that bear the Eastern effluence finance the mortgage, but they also "pollute" the environment and even the sacred space of the home. The intensely xenophobic and anxious response to this pollution is visible in the representation of all the wealth in the novel. The businessman Casby's house seems "stifled by Mutes in the Eastern manner" (148), Clennam's mother's lodgings and countenance become nearly "Egyptian" (50), the fashionable address of the Barnacles, who were "lord[s] of the Treasury [and] Chinese consuls," is "dingy," "dark," and dirty with a foul odor (148), and even the profoundly homely Chiverys, who stock their tobacco shop with Bengal Cheroots and other foreign products, inhabit a damp and dull home, a phenomenon that suggests that this "danger" crosses class lines.

Though Mrs. Clennam, the Casbys, the domestic Barnacles, and the Chiverys have never left the country or met an Egyptian or a Chinese person—and many of them keep no foreign *object* in their homes—their money circulates through foreign lands in order to produce their profits, and this produces a xenophobic fear. The starkest example of English investment failure is Merdle. Certainly, any "extensive merchant" who was "immensely rich [and] turned all he touched to gold" (247) would have been impacted by the fact that foreign investment tripled from the 1850s to the 1870s.[24] However "empty" Merdle's wealth ultimately proves, there is no question of his engagement with the foreign in representing his riches: his home is a buzzing site for talk of Africa, the colonies, the East, and the investments one might make there (258–259).[25] Moreover, this "buzz" characterizes one way that the pollution spreads; because Merdle is "one of England's world-famed capitalists and merchant-princes," the state figureheads believe that "To extend the triumphs of such men, was to extend the triumphs and resources of the nation"

---

23. Catherine Gallagher, *The Body Economic: Life, Death, and Sensation in Political Economy and the Victorian Novel* (Princeton, NJ: Princeton University Press, 2008).

24. Daunton, *Wealth and Welfare*, 215.

25. Indeed, this investment is described as the conversion of the "root of all evils" (money) into "the root of all good" in a "commercial country" and for "Society's benefit." One investment is vaguely described as being on the "border of two of the Eastern countries," another as pertaining to "Africa" (258–259).

(258). His investment practices spread like a disease or pollution, fostered by their global reach and seeming global power. In spite of the fact that Merdle's crimes are *domestic* forgery and fraud, there is simply no way to detach his money from the global circulation of wealth and the international market that affects anyone who invests in him (a fact that is potently critiqued with the case of Daniel Doyce, as I'll explain below).

The desire to profit, whatever the investment, infects most of the characters in the novel, even Pancks and Clennam. While far-reaching investments in the foreign might make men like Merdle wealthy and others desirous to invest with them, those same investments simultaneously trigger intense xenophobic fears in the other characters (and perhaps in readers as well). Though Merdle seems "safe and genuine" (603) we later learn that this is far from true. In fact, the only response that can begin to eradicate such a deep investment in the foreign is Merdle's death and the collapse of his financial network. Yet, the same symbolic engagement with the foreign that produces his failure also takes down the countless and nameless others who speculate on him, including Clennam, who—in spite of perceiving the speculative fever focused on Merdle as a dangerous contagion—invests anyway. Thus, even after Merdle is eliminated, the taint of foreign money remains. Finally, while Clennam senses that his inheritance and wealth are soiled, it is not simply sexual sin that pollutes his wealth, as most scholars have argued. Indeed, it is just as damaging to Clennam that his mother's money and his own failed investments (like his parents' before him and many of those around him) are in China and in Merdle.

THE IDEA OF THE FOREIGN

Merdle emblematizes the most catastrophic, Bernie Madoff–like investment failure. Likewise, the contemporary short-selling of stock (the "borrowing" of a stock to sell and buy it back at a profit—in other words, betting that its price will drop in the interval) or naked short selling (the same process, but one in which the stock was never even "borrowed" in the first place), in which there never are any *goods* but only a wholly representational, materially empty economic exchange—supported the fraudulent assertion of nonexistent wealth that invited massive greed-driven investment and brought down the seemingly invincible U.S. economy in the twenty-first century. What is most striking about Merdle's investments and the danger they pose in the narrative is that the engagement with the foreign in this case is entirely symbolic and immaterial. In other words, Merdle's imaginary money—sourced in an unknowable and necessarily global investment—taints British society with an influx of foreign financial pollutants and does so regardless of the absence of value, exchange, or objects inherent in the trade. The *fact* of such circulation alone—even if the circulation doesn't actually occur in the novel's economy—is enough to produce the dramatic xenophobic reaction in the narrative.

Mrs. Merdle, the dominant social force in contemporary London, demonstrates the depth of the penetration in society and the home. She articulates the mystery of Merdle's wealth (and the means by which it becomes universally accepted) when we first meet her, ensconced on golden cushions like a Pasha—but consistently interrupted by an orientalized bird, an emblem of the kind of wealth Merdle has introduced into domestic investment and the domestic space. Indeed, foreign investment has become the very stuff of society itself, constantly penetrating domestic financial currents as the bird does Mrs. Merdle's otherwise authoritative speech: "Mr. Merdle is a most extensive merchant, his transactions are on the vastest scale, his wealth and influence are very great, but even he—," and at this climax, the bird squawks so much that Mrs. Merdle must remark, "Bird, be quiet!" The bird's interjection, in the moment at which Mrs. Merdle is about to name her husband's limitations ("but even he—"), metaphorically suggests that the foreign bird has disrupted Merdle's "wealth and influence." Moreover, as the narrator points out, this disruptive, foreign bird has been so thoroughly incorporated that it begins to seem like *Society itself.* The narrator tells us that it was "as if [the bird's] name were Society and it asserted its right to its exactions" (247). In this Merdle-warped financial and social world, "Society"/the foreign bird takes its "exactions"; it is an oppressive system to which everyone must submit and which even Mrs. Merdle herself cannot manage: "Society suppresses and dominates us—Bird, be quiet!" Following Mrs. Merdle's futile attempts to quiet the bird, the narrator expresses a xenophobic fear of this new "Society" and new means of gaining "wealth and influence" by grotesquely rendering the exotic bird as a creature who manipulates and exceeds the cage that cannot control or silence him: "The parrot broke into a violent fit of laughter, after twisting divers bars of his cage with his crooked bill, and licking them with his black tongue" (248).

Insisting that this system is inescapable, Mrs. Merdle dismisses an escape to a "simpler life" and instead underscores western greed and economic profitability in foreign lands: "A more primitive state of society would be delicious to me. There used to be a poem when I learnt lessons, something about Lo the poor Indian whose something mind [a passage from Pope's "Essay on Man"].[26] If a few thousand persons moving in Society could only go and be

---

26. Alexander Pope, "An Essay on Man" (3: 99–112).

   Lo, the poor Indian! whose untutor'd mind

Indians, I would put my name down directly; but as, moving in Society, we can't be Indians, unfortunately—Goodbye!" (250–251). While Mrs. Merdle seems to reject the self-embodiment of the foreign ("we can't be Indians"), the very jewels on her bosom are financed by Eastern investments, and her speech is interrupted, even when we don't hear the bird. Her sentence drops off, and she can only bid her guests farewell and fall into silence while the bird shrieks. Moreover, the line she absents from Pope's "Essay on Man" ("Lo the poor Indian *whose something mind*") signifies the collapse of an idyllic Eastern life through "Christians['] thirst for gold." The western desire for wealth and its reach into foreign lands "torment[s]" the natives and infects everything it touches. If we understand the impulse of economic xenophobia, this densely coded scene and the imagined foreign origins at the heart of Merdle's hollow empire become clear.

Clotting the channels of prosperity, then, with Eastern investment serves as a bar to domestic success in the novel. Clennam's inventor business partner, Daniel Doyce, in fact, can find no interest in domestic support and is treated as "an infamous rascal and a treasonable disturber of the government peace" (124). Indeed, his very failure to attract the attention of domestic investment is precisely what the novel laments. The suppression of his brilliant designs serves as a "warning [to] every ingenious British subject to be ingenious at his peril . . . as though invention were on par with felony" (532). Instead, such talent is forced to turn to "foreign countries," the sea of global investment, and, as the narrative warns, this pattern *impoverishes* the nation, even if the outcome is enormous individual financial profit (125). Doyce, who relentlessly seeks domestic investment, is the solution. Clennam's seduction by Merdle and global investment is the problem, the domestic firm collapsing at the touch of Merdle's false millions, sourced in a "virulent" "infection" of foreign investment (603). Doyce is an object lesson: the English should invest in the English. Because it is only Clennam who actively seeks the poison, he bears the entire burden of the business's failure and is locked in the debtor's prison—which reveals both the emptiness of the foreign investments as well

---

Sees God in clouds, or hears him in the wind;
His soul proud Science never taught to stray
Far as the solar walk or milky way;
Yet simple Nature to his hope has giv'n,
Behind the cloud-topp'd hill, a humbler heav'n;
Some safer world in depth of woods embrac'd,
Some happier island in the wat'ry waste,
Where slaves once more their native land behold,
No fiends torment, no Christians thirst for gold!
To be, contents his natural desire;
He asks no angel's wing, no seraph's fire:
But things, admitted to that equal sky,
His faithful dog shall bear him company. (1099)

as the site at which the debt was owed—his home and the most homely figure in the novel, Little Dorrit. In this way, *Little Dorrit* calls for the return
of investors like Doyce, condemning their forays outside the Circumlocution
Office and the country for investment, and calling for their growth through
domestic investment.

DOMESTIC INVESTMENTS

Encountering her first in the home of his *own* shattered family, which has
been broken by its failure to place money (as we later learn) in the proper
domestic place, Clennam's purest and best interest in the narrative—financially and morally—is in Little Dorrit. A woman who is at peace with modest means—even if it means eschewing the kind of "investments" that would
make her rich, Little Dorrit is the quintessential "domestic" figure. It is
through the long-deferred love of this character that Clennam is ultimately
redeemed. While she loves him persistently throughout the vicissitudes of her
fortunes, he cannot fully appreciate her *value,* though he supports efforts that
improve her financial fortunes. Born into a debtor's prison for her father's
failings, Little Dorrit's character is not, as many critics have argued, an indict-
ment of earning or of attention to money. In fact, "At thirteen, she could
read and keep accounts" and "was the head of [her own] fallen family" (75).
She arranges training and work for her siblings and herself and serves as a
counterpoint both to those in the debtor's prison *and* to those abroad when
her family comes into a fortune who are "listless" and "[fall] into a slouch-
ing way of life" (73, 530). In whatever condition Little Dorrit lives, she has
dignity and grace. She does not require foreign travel or foreign investment;
in fact, she renounces both. This serves as a lesson for an unquiet nation who
sees as its "whole duty" in a "commercial country" to "be as rich as you can,"
whatever the costs. Her talents and practices, like Doyce's, cannot be valued
by her own people and in her own land.

Through the discovery of a long lost fortune, the Dorrits are released
from debt and debtor's prison, but this change is not one that suits Little
Dorrit, who never had any debts of her own. She is unhappy in her family's
genteel travels and longs for home, England, and the domestic. Moreover,
even in the bosom of wealth, she remains "careful . . . about the expenses of
the day" (486). In an unsurprising turn, her father's seduction by the Merdle
epidemic leaves her and her siblings in poverty again. This fall, however, does
not tarnish her, because *her* investments are *not* there. And, indeed, as many
critics have pointed out, Little Dorrit is the only financial investment that

Clennam makes that does not fail. When we learn in the final pages of the novel that Clennam's bitter mother has withheld from Little Dorrit a fortune that has been channeled through the same kind of foreign investments that laid the Clennam family low, Little Dorrit rejects that wealth. She calls upon her beloved Clennam, who has engaged himself to her, to burn—unbeknownst to him—the document that could bring them both this dirty money. (This purgative fire is also applied to Mrs. Clennam who has fallen at the hands of the foreign Rigaud and her foreign investment.) Though Mrs. Clennam's fall might seem the resolution of the improper investments, the Clennam money has all been marked by its foreign taint and must be evacuated from English space. The "charm" Clennam puts in the fire with his own hand is accompanied—at Little Dorrit's request—by a confession of his love.

This is a model of the kind of financial gain that is valuable—not just the domestic space, but domestic investment. In this way, one can remove the taint of the foreign, remain free of the pollution, and tamp down xenophobic fears. As Little Dorrit describes it, she "was never rich before . . . never proud before . . . [but is] rich in being taken by" Clennam. By closing the circle on domestic investment, they cut off the polluting channel of the foreign and reproduce safely on British soil. Even if this detachment from foreign investment implies a decrease in domestic wealth, it is still preferable: "I would rather pass my life here with you, and go out daily, working for our bread, than I would have the greatest fortune that ever was told" (845). Significantly, Little Dorrit does not abandon labor or the money that can be earned. Instead, she eliminates the kinds of investments that soiled their past. This economic structure is completely clean, and, if they abide by it, Little Dorrit and Clennam can "go amongst the noise and haste and live in peace."

II. Consuming Waste and *The Mystery of Edwin Drood*

The Mystery of Edwin Drood, on the other hand, suggests the irreparably transformative damage foreign trade has caused, yoking even sacred institutions to poison, pollution, and death—while it simultaneously acknowledges *contact* with the foreign as inevitable and tantalizing. In the economy of *The Mystery of Edwin Drood,* the English themselves become opium- and Turkish Delight-eating savages: murderers, cheats, and thieves. *The Mystery of Edwin Drood* suggests that domestic investment and the domestic space can no longer ameliorate the pollution produced by foreign trade. Here, the English homeland becomes a site of contamination, rather than healing—a result of economic contact with a polluting Eastern world. Identifying the dangers of consuming the East becomes a primary strategy for explaining the decline of English global financial power: a result of poisonous—if sometimes profitable—food. In *Drood*, a woman becomes a "Chinaman" by eating opium.[27] Another woman eats Turkish Delight while she and her fiancé discuss Egypt, Arabs, and Turks—then he transforms into an "Egyptian boy" himself (47, 62).

Though *Little Dorrit* presented hope that the foreign pollution could be contained by domestic investment, Dickens's last, unfinished novel offers a far less optimistic picture of the management of xenophobic fears. In *The Mystery of Edwin Drood*, even fruits of domestic labor are tainted with the foreign because the foreign is unavoidably in circulation in the home nation; it has become impossible for British nationals to remain outside the circuit of foreign economic poisoning. Ruth Lindeborg has argued that, as the century progressed, "evolutionary theories rationalized and reinforced Victorians' sense of their difference from the 'savages' of their colonies [and elsewhere], but the growth of Empire paradoxically reduced that distance by making these supposed prehistorical peoples, and the places they inhabited, part of Britain's identity."[28] Though some characters remain exclusively on the home front in this novel, the circulation of English money into the foreign economy and back home as wealth, alters "home" itself, a pattern produced by and producing a xenophobic response. While many critics have pointed to the way that Jasper's opium addiction signals an engagement with the foreign other, even the most abstemious characters are marked by foreign economic exchange—with deadly results.

I will explore this novel by carrying over the metaphors from the previous section: pollution and economic exchange. I will also elaborate more fully the phenomenon of consumption—material and economic. In *Little Dorrit*, the introduction of the foreign was often metaphorized as "pollution." Grace Moore has developed this metaphor, arguing that the orientalized commodities in Dickens's later novels evidence a kind of accumulation of waste that becomes overwhelming, an omnipresent foreign detritus. "The colonial commodity," she suggests, "is no longer the awkward obstacle that clutters the homes of *Bleak House* or the various junk shops Dickens depicts in his novels. Rather it is something all-consuming and potentially all-engulfing. . . . The detritus of empire"—which, in her words, is "little more than garbage"—"is everywhere and Dickens's last novels attempt to make it more

27. Charles Dickens, *The Mystery of Edwin Drood* (New York: Penguin, 2002), 38. Subsequent references to this work are cited parenthetically as ED.

28. Ruth H. Lindeborg, "The 'Asiatic' and the Boundaries of Victorian Englishness," *Victorian Studies* 37 (spring 1994): 383.

visible to readers who have become accustomed to it as backdrop to their daily lives."[29] I agree, but I would suggest that this pollution is more broadly figured and rendered visible in its fullness through the lens of xenophobia. First, the pollution need not be exclusively "oriental," but merely foreign. Second, it is not stagnant, stable, and potentially avoidable, like the dust heaps in *Our Mutual Friend.*

Instead, what makes the "foreign detritus" so terribly threatening in *The Mystery of Edwin Drood* is its constant movement, circulation, and pervasiveness—not just materially, but also less visibly and more diffusely in the realm of the economic. Significantly, this is the trajectory of xenophobia. Geologist Pierre Desrochers has woven together these strands of (economic) circulation and waste in his study of Victorian environmental practices. He has argued that, by the 1870s, England began very effectively to *recycle* their waste: returning it to the market economy in order to produce additional profit. A larger and larger portion of the nation's waste and pollutants were being reprocessed and resold "[b]ecause of the profit motive."[30] Indeed, in the largely representational world of the economy, not only is the source of money uncertain—in other words, where it has traveled both physically in the form of banknotes and more abstractly in terms of investment and profits—it also became even easier to re-circulate a foreign "pollution." A bank note itself, for example, might never have been to China, but its buying power might have emerged through the very foreign trade that produced xenophobic anxieties.[31] Moreover, if the material waste to which Moore refers could be recycled into the economy, how much more easily could the wealth of the foreign landscape slip into a domestic space? This reading lends a new sense to "dirty money." Xenophobic anxieties could be provoked by the fact that wealth could never be sourced exclusively from home. If one didn't travel to or invest in the foreign, another in whom one invests might have. Moreover, the site of that investment need not be the clearly dangerous figure of a Rigaud or Merdle. It might be in the likes of ordinary Englishmen

---

29. Grace Moore, "Turkish Robbers, Lumps of Delight, and the Detritus of Empire: The East Revisited in Dickens's Late Novels," *Critical Survey* 21.1 (2009): 84–85.

30. Pierre Desrochers, "Does the invisible hand have a green thumb? Incentives, linkages, and the creation of wealth out of industrial waste in Victorian England," *Geographical Journal* 175.1 (2009): 12. I disagree with Desrochers's fundamental argument that the Victorians can provide a model for today, based on the efficacy of their business practices. He reads their effectiveness as a product of their desire for profit and suggests that we can rest assured that this will drive businesses today to reduce waste as well. He also indicates that businesses that polluted were subject to lawsuits. This argument fails to take into account the magnitude of the pollution problem and the serious cost to the poor, who were unable to launch suits against industries that produced damaging and poisonous waste.

31. Mary Poovey's work in *Genres of the Credit Economy* reminds us that there was a great deal of energy invested in trying to stabilize the banknote and situate it as socially reliable.

like Edwin Drood. This made the endless loop of foreign investment seem inevitable and inevitably toxic.

FOR ALL THE TEA IN CHINA

The target of much scholarship on *The Mystery of Edwin Drood* has been Jasper, and it is around this character that most scrutiny with regard to the taint of the East has revolved. It is not difficult to see why. Jasper's opium dreams reimagine England itself and the English gentleman in ways that bespeak narrative xenophobia. They create a vision of England's "oppressive[ly] respectab[le]" (ED, 23) "ancient Cathedral town" (ED, 7), Cloisterham, as an Eastern city, complete with Sultans, Turkish robbers, scimitars, and elephants. In the wake of the novel's opening vision, Jasper literally finds himself in bed with a "Chinaman," a Lascar (an Indian or East Asian seaman), and a haggard woman—as many investors found themselves financially "in bed" with the East and overseas trade. Jasper, who never leaves England and serves as a lay music leader in the Cloisterham cathedral, consumes Eastern pollution and becomes murderous. Critics have repeatedly noted that Jasper lies at the very heart of Englishness because of his profession and the largely seamless way in which he moves between the two worlds. David Faulkner, in fact, has argued that in *The Mystery of Edwin Drood,* "the cultural difference lies not between [the East and England], but within" England itself, which has at this point in time become "colonizable, indeed a colonized space. English culture appears highly permeable, pieced together from difference and otherness."[32] Juliet John has argued that Jasper "personifies the duality and corruption inherent in Victorian ideas of both respectability and Englishness."[33]

Following Faulkner's and John's arguments, I would suggest, in fact, that there is no clearly discernible difference between the East and the English self in *The Mystery of Edwin Drood.* The permeability Faulkner describes means that the foreign has been consumed, internalized (another means of marking a Dickensian villain, according to John), and absorbed—and that is a central tension in the narrative. Take Jasper's taint, for example, which has often been figured by critics as a "product" of his opium smoking. Barry Milligan, in one of his many studies of opium smoking in nineteenth-century

32. David Faulkner, "The Confidence Man: Empire and the Deconstruction of Muscular Christianity in *The Mystery of Edwin Drood*," in *Muscular Christianity: Embodying The Victorian Age* (New York: Cambridge University Press, 1994), 189.

33. Juliet John, *Dickens's Villains: Melodrama, Character, and Popular Culture* (Oxford: Oxford University Press, 2001), 236.

England, has deftly described the ways in which opium smoking was both dramatically overestimated due to anxieties about the foreign presence in London,[34] and productive of a profound fear that "a comprehensive infection of Chineseness that [was] not limited to the opium den [was] eating away at the very identity of the British people."[35] Indeed, it is not only Jasper's *vision* of Cloisterham in which we see the dangerous foreign poison polluting and permeating the place. Midway through the novel, Cloisterham itself becomes "half strange and half familiar" marked by the "outerworld" with which it has constant economic exchange (ED, 153). Even the traditional Victorian Christmas, has been marked by the unavoidable presence of the foreignness. The traveling Wax-Work display is not an English delight, but has circulated throughout the land and carries with it not only "foreign" images, but the mark of foreigners themselves. The Narrator describes it as "the Wax-Work which made so deep an impression on the reflective mind of the Emperor of China" (ED, 154). Timothy Carens finds a similar pattern in *Bleak House.* He argues that "imperial culture expressed [a] suspicion [of the foreign] in novels that narrate a collapse of clear distinctions between the familiarity of the English nation and character and varieties of strangeness associated with the colonial periphery."[36] He sees Dickens cynically portraying civilizing failure in African imperial outposts in the language of *Bleak House.* I would suggest that it is not only those nations in which imperial action is taking place that produce an anxiety we can trace in Dickens's work, but *any* foreignness and the "pollution" that is brought home by the circulation of the English in the foreign.

It is not simply the ingestion of opium, then, that makes Jasper—or "Princess Puffer,"[37] the woman who supplies his opium—so dangerous to themselves and those around them, but the taint that any contact with the foreign carries home. One aspect of this process that critics have often missed, however, is that opium, like any other commodity, is bought and sold for profit. There is not just an ingestion of the drug, but a *purchase* of the drug, by both the user (the final consumer) and the seller (the market point).

---

34. Barry Milligan, "The Opium Den in Victorian London," in *Smoke: A Global History of Smoking* (London: Reaktion Books, 2004), 118.

35. Milligan, "'The Plague Spreading and Attacking Our Vitals': Opium Smoking and the Oriental Infection of the British Domestic Scene," *Victorian Literature and Culture* 20 (1992): 163.

36. Timothy Carens, *Outlandish English Subjects in the Victorian Domestic Novel* (New York: Palgrave Macmillan, 2005), 3.

37. Ruth H. Lindeborg, "The 'Asiatic' and the Boundaries of Victorian Englishness," *Victorian Studies* 37 (spring 1994): 383. Lindeborg, in her study of Joseph Salter's missionary work in London among the Lascars, argues that working-class English women who married lascars seemed to lose their Englishness and their gender identity, much like Princess Puffer: "they [wore] men's clothing, smoke[d] opium, and behave[d] like male sailors" (388).

Clearly, this economic exchange puts Jasper's church salary into the pockets of the opium traders, serving as a stark metaphor for the debilitating effects of such an exchange at the level of the individual and the state. Moreover, the foreignness of opium is itself an emblem of this economic circulation that marks the English with the foreign. Most critics have only fleshed out the relationship of this drug to the Chinese because of its use there, but opium was fundamental to Victorian negotiation of foreign trade. The poppies were grown in India and the high levels of opium use in China were due to *British* transfer of the drug to rectify the English trade imbalance with China. Britain imported silk and tea from China, but British woolens, clocks, and music boxes, in addition to Indian cotton, were not enough to counterbalance the silk and tea, creating a trade deficit, which produced a "serious sterling loss."[38] A number of critical books and pamphlets published during the nineteenth century lamented British involvement in the opium trade in China. In spite of the profit produced by the opium trade, the process was seen as intensely polluting—not only because of the drug, but because of the anxiety about the polluting effects of China's foreignness. Henry Charles Sirr, writing on British involvement in China, argued that it was so dangerous that "If any man . . . have a mind to visit China, from curiosity, let him turn his time and his money to better account. If any man be allured to it by the love of gain, let him think that health is better than wealth."[39] Intimately linked to wealth and wealth production, the circulation of money through China (and of opium) makes the source of the deadly poison diffuse and abstract.

Sirr observed that "[b]y the sale of this pernicious drug Great Britain's sons *gain gold;* and earn opprob[r]ium for dealing destruction around them, bringing into derision the name of a Christian country, by enabling the Chinese to violate the laws of their own nation, in obtaining the prohibited and cursed poison; the use of which entails destruction, mentally and bodily on its infatuated devotees."[40] He further argues that this taint reflects back on the English and produces "the filthy lucre of gain" for England (ED, 221). The foreign taint in *Drood,* however, does not simply adhere to the traveling businessmen that Sirr's book concerns. Instead, this financial process, ironically initiated by a gesture that appears to keep the foreign circulating in the foreign—Britain's introduction of opium into China—the foreign doubles back through the economic circuit and emerges in the homeland and in the worlds

38. Wenying Xu, "The Opium Trade and *Little Dorrit:* A Case of Reading Silences," *Victorian Literature and Culture* 25 (1997): 55.

39. Henry Charles Sirr, *China and the Chinese: Their Religion, Character, Customs and Manufactures: The Evils Arising from the Opium Trade: With a Glance at our Religious, Moral, Political, and Commercial Intercourse with the Country,* vols. I and II (London: Orr & Co, 1849), 38–39.

40. Sirr, *China and the Chinese,* 2. Emphasis added.

of those who never leave the nation. Consider "Princess Puffer's" warning to Jasper: "Never take [opium] in your own way. It ain't good for trade and it ain't good for you" (ED, 258). Only by circulating in the economy, only by keeping the wealth increasing through the opium, does Britain *seem* to prosper. This novel warns, however, that through the economic—complexly threaded from Britain to India to China and Britain—the money and not just the drug is thoroughly saturated with foreignness. By engaging with foreignness, the English become marked and foreignness is mixed into the very stuff of Englishness. When Princess Puffer claims that she has the "true secret of mixing" (ED, 8), we can begin to imagine how much more broadly this mixing and the anxieties it produces run: provincial villagers are eyeing the same wax works as the Emperor of China, and even the most benign characters are handling money that bears the taint of the foreign economic circulation.

THE FOREIGN EXCHANGE AT HOME

When we use the lens of xenophobia, we can see the ways that an anxiety-producing foreignness need no longer be tied to a singular or particularized imperial event and, moreover, that it can infect even the most homely of English characters, crossing lines of class. For example, Durdles, whose constant presence in the Cathedral situates him, as well, at the heart of Englishness, not only becomes an unwitting party to a capital crime, but he becomes like the famed explorer Belzoni himself, tapping to sound the walls of the cathedral for bodies, just as Belzoni tapped the walls of the pyramids for Egyptian mummies (ED, 41). While plotting his nephew Edwin Drood's murder, Jasper secretly feeds Durdles opium, a metaphor for the pollution, hidden in Durdles's English wine as "payment" for walking him through the cathedral. The bottle, we are told "circulates freely;—in the sense, that is to say, that its contents enter freely into Mr. Durdle's circulation" (ED, 135). Durdles consumes the foreign in the transaction and is drawn into the pollution and Jasper's scheme. Durdles, like Princess Puffer, speaks about the "mixing of things" that would make it a "confused world" (ED, 135). While Durdles is referring, in this statement, to the mixing of the living and the dead, this is precisely the job in which he engages every day—transgressing the line between the living and the dead to locate bodies, mark graves, and sleep in the graveyard. His mixing, like Princess Puffer's, becomes an emblem of the more anxiety-producing mixing that is so profoundly evidenced in the text. Though Rosa, Edwin's fiancée and the focus of Jasper's desire, remarks coyly that Edwin's bride-to-be must "hate Arabs, Turks, and Fellahs," the

pyramids, and "tiresome old burying grounds" (ED, 31)—the truly dangerous burying grounds are the ones *in* Cloisterham, where Jasper plots Edwin's
death and Durdles will become a pawn. Even homely figures like Durdles,
then, are brought into the circulation of this foreign danger.

Similarly, Rosa, one of the most virtuous and English of characters, is
affected. Rajani Sudan describes xenophobia as a complex blend of desire
and fear, like the "fascination of repulsion" that Rosa experiences when she
interacts privately with Jasper (ED, 219). Rosa is held in thrall by a "terrible spell" that Jasper casts. What most readers have failed to explore in her
relationship with Jasper, however, is how the two characters interact on the
grounds of economic exchange. Jasper is in Rosa's employ as a paid music
master, a relationship that engages her in economic contact with him as well.
Moreover, Jasper's confession of "love" impels Rosa into the financial world in
a new way. Prior to this moment, Rosa had avoided direct engagement with
financial exchange. Her guardian Mr. Grewgious (a financial manager and
"Receiver of the Rents") had always attended to her bills himself and made
all the arrangements for her money. However, in expectation of her wed-
ding to Edwin, Grewgious arrives to talk with Rosa about "Pounds, shillings,
and pence," indicating that he has never done so before because it is a "dry
subject for a young lady" (ED, 88). When Rosa flees from Jasper, she takes,
for the first time, a more direct entry into the world of economic exchange.
She purchases a bus fare and then a train ticket to London, placing her own
hands in the market economy, rather than through an agent. It is no wonder
that while she feels "soiled" by the "impurity" of Jasper's contact with her,
Grewgious's establishment in the London to which she flees is no less "gritty
and shabby" (ED, 222).

Her former fiancé and Jasper's secret nemesis, Edwin, is tainted by the
same economic pollution. Though others have pointed out that his anticipated profession is to "wake up Egypt a little" (ED, 72) by "engineering in
the East" (ED, 21), it is not simply in anticipation that he is marked by foreign exchange. His father's wealth had come from foreign work and investment. In every moment, he's already marked by this circulation. While he
plaintively hopes that his bride will take "a sensible interest in the triumphs
of engineering skill, especially when they are to change the whole condition
of an underdeveloped country" (ED, 31), he fails to acknowledge the ways
in which the impact is not one-sided, but an exchange. His money and position emerge from foreign investment and, like Rosa and Edwin's failure to
"get along" no matter how they try (ED, 32), the foreign and the English are
joined, regardless of the wishes of the individual parties involved. In both

cases, an exchange has already been made. While Rosa and Edwin can rescind their agreement, they are marked by the barter their fathers made and by the choices that have already drawn them into this economy. Thus, Rosa too, in spite of her reluctance to go to Egypt, consumes so much Turkish delight that she's marked by what she's already consumed, covered with the sugary, sticky dust (ED, 33). Edwin, himself, becomes an "Egyptian boy" whom Rosa supposes can look into his own hand and tell the future, but he (naively) can't see the destruction awaiting him, like his father before him (ED, 35).

Not only is the cost of this match evident in the danger that befalls Edwin (and the threats made against Rosa), but it is also literally in the air. When Edwin goes to visit Grewgious in London to make the final financial arrangements and retrieve the ring with which he is to marry Rosa, he is choked by the London pollution. He enters Grewgious's chamber coughing and gagging: "It's this fog . . . and it makes my eyes smart like Cayenne pepper" (ED, 115). The eastern spice that makes Edwin's eyes smart is pollution, of course, like the pollution so omnipresent in *Little Dorrit*. In *The Mystery of Edwin Drood*, however, one of the novel's most noble characters invites Edwin to take his Cayenne with dinner instead—to ingest the spice: "You had better take your cayenne pepper here than outside." It is at this "gipsy-party" (ED, 115)—a virtual stew of foreignness and danger—that Edwin realizes how seriously wrong his relationship with Rosa is. When Grewgious produces the ring, a precious marker of Rosa's parents, of both fathers' wills, and of the exchange they are to mark, he cautions Edwin using precisely the language Durdles has used earlier: the fuzzy boundary between life and death. He "charges" him "by the living and the dead" not to make a plaything of "treasure" and to bring the ring back, if anything is amiss in their relationship. In the wake of the dinner, it is clear that Edwin himself (and Grewgious) believe something is amiss. Though the novel reminds us that "two states of consciousness which never clash" (ED, 23) can exist in a single person— "thus, if I hide my watch, when I am drunk, I must be drunk again before I can remember where"—it is clear that the line between them cannot be maintained. Just as Jasper's desire to murder his nephew cannot be separated from his role as a choirmaster in the Cathedral, so the economic gain that is produced through foreign exchange cannot be kept apart from the people in the homeland—it is breathed in from the air and consumed in the food. The British are, then, like Jasper who, though almost certainly the murderer, "devote[s] [himself] to [the] destruction" of the murderer (ED, 186). This foreign engagement, like the opium trade, cycles back on the English to pollute the home front.

THE POLLUTION WITHIN

The characters of Neville and Helena Landless, a twin brother and sister
from British Ceylon, become more potent metaphors for the circulation of
foreignness and the xenophobic response. We cannot read them as simply
figures of empire or racism: Neville and Helena are not imperial subjects
themselves nor are they definitively un-English. They are, however, clearly—
but imprecisely—foreign because they have not been reared in England
(they are, in fact, "Land-less"). Xenophobia, however, does not require that
their "land" or "race" be specified. Indeed, they might be wholly English by
descent (we have no certain indicator of their race/ethnicity), but having
been raised among foreigners has marked *them* as foreign. Their identity can
be wholly abstracted and still produce sufficient anxiety to make Neville a
murder suspect. The desire for them, like the desire for the foreign money,
does not mitigate the danger they seem to represent. Similarly the profit that
was produced by foreign investment (like the children we can imagine might
have appeared from the unions with the Landlessness and unambiguously
English characters) would enrich the individuals, but not the nation, and
would be—in spite of the more immediate pleasures—a danger.

The twins, we are told, are "An unusually handsome lithe young fellow,
and an unusually handsome lithe girl; much alike; both very dark, and very
rich in color; she of almost the gipsy type; something untamed about them
both; a certain air upon them of hunter and huntress; yet withal a certain air
of being the objects of the chase, rather than the followers. Slender, supple,
quick of eye and limb; half shy, half defiant; fierce of look, and indefinable
kind of pause coming and going on their whole expression, both of face
and form, which might be equally likened to the pause before a crouch, or
a bound" (ED, 58–59). Their darkness, though they are not "natives" themselves, suggests that they have (in Lamarckian fashion) imbibed the foreign
taint. Their "indefinable coming and going" suggests their circulation in the
social economy. Though they look "much as if they were beautiful barbaric
captives brought from some wild tropical dominion" (ED, 59), they also
immediately begin to circulate in the Cloisterham economy and seem to be
insiders as much as outsiders, paying into the local economy and playing into
the local social landscape. Helena becomes a paying pupil at the Nun's house,
like Rosa, and Neville is taken under the tutelage of Rev. Crisparkle.

Jasper frames Neville for Edwin's murder by playing on the xenophobia
the siblings "incite." While Helena and Neville are clearly not villains, their
foreignness is enough to create anxiety. Neville is supposed by Cloisterham
to have "whipped to death sundry 'Natives'"—Asians, Africans, West Indians, and even Inuits—who are "vaguely supposed in Cloisterham always to

be black" (ED, 183). This vision effectively situates Neville as a carrier of foreign danger, even if he is not of those races himself. When Jasper feeds both the newcomer and Edwin opium in their wine, he manages to provoke a fight between the two (in part because, like Jasper, Neville has also become entranced with Rosa). The young men bicker, and Edwin stingingly remarks to Neville, "You may know a black common fellow, or a black common boaster, when you see him (and no doubt you have a large acquaintance that way); but you are no judge of white men." This "insulting allusion to his dark skin infuriates Neville," who flings dregs of wine at Edwin and whose heart and head pound until he seems "like a dangerous animal" (ED, 79). Though the Landlesses might have been largely integrated into the small town (and the narrative portrays them as attractive characters), even the genial Edwin responds to Neville in a broadly xenophobic fashion rather than reading their conflict as a product of a particular and personal disagreement.

Moreover, Edwin's comments signify both Neville's own uncertain race, as well as the savagery of the foreign that Neville has *brought home*. For example, Neville expresses fears to the Reverend Crisparkle that the "natives" among whom he has grown up have something "tigerish in their blood" (ED, 63), and both Neville and Crisparkle fear that Neville may have contracted these characteristics. Simply put, contact with the foreign taints. If Neville becomes so marked, it is unclear how figures such as Edwin or Crisparkle can avoid similar marking. The poison of Neville and Edwin's quarrel, in fact, travels through the community even in the food they eat. The narrator explains that the toxic tale made its way into the homes of Cloisterham through their bread and milk: "the baker brought it kneaded into the bread, or the milkman delivered it as a part of the adulteration of his milk"; indeed, it becomes a part of the "town atmosphere" (ED, 83). No one can escape the circulation of the foreign.

It is no wonder then that Sapsea, the Mayor of Cloisterham, is depicted as such a fool for believing that he can manage the foreign and master it. As he explains, "If I have not gone to foreign countries . . . foreign countries have come to me" *through his extensive trade* (ED, 37), like all the English. He can put his finger on an object with a merchant's assuredness and say, "'Pekin, Nankin, Canton.' It is the same with Egypt and . . . the East Indies" (ED, 37–38). He calls this "an extensive knowledge of the world" (ED, 39), and believes that "Providence made a distinct mistake in originating so small a nation of hearts of oak [England], and so many other verminous peoples" (ED, 127). Sapsea foolishly believes, however, that it is possible to eliminate this verminous taint and imagines "reduc[ing] to a smashed condition all other islands but this island, and all continents, peninsulas, isthmuses, promontories, and other geographical forms of land soever" (ED, 127). His naïve belief that crushing what's outside will manage what's already been imbibed bespeaks the threat the novel seems to express and explains the futility of the weakly xenophobic response Sapsea experiences when interacting with characters like Neville. As Tim Dolin has argued, "the xenophobic Sapsea. . . . is Cloisterham's representative example of what Dickens had called 20 years earlier 'the true Tory spirit' that 'would have made a China of England, if it could.'"[41] Sapsea's ideologies and desires have failed and will fail, because he can't locate the proper object for his xenophobia, which already exists as much in the most English aspects of his (in Dolin's words) "already profoundly orientalized" home town,[42] and, as I would add, in the very economic exchanges in which he has professionally engaged as an auctioneer.

While Dolin has also argued that the more favorable characters "participate in the confusion of English and un-English . . . domestic and imperial,"[43] the confusion is much broader than the "imperial" and much broader than what is represented in Rosa or Edwin, who have had contact with Jasper. For example, we can see this tension presented in Tartar, in whom Rosa has begun to feel a romantic interest. Tartar is "sunburnt" brown from his long interaction with foreign cultures, like Neville (199). Though he has left off traveling when he came into a fortune through an uncle and is clearly a heroic character, Tartar still evokes the narrative's xenophobic attentions to the foreign as much when he is a member of the landed gentry as when he is a Navy man. In the former, he participates in the local economic circuit implicated in foreign trade just as surely as when he purchased the foreign objects that litter his apartment when he was traveling in the Navy. While he may have finally come "home," his habits are regulated by his naval and global past. He brings with him not only the perpetually sunburned skin (retained, like the mark of the foreign with which he has contact, even though he has returned to the northern climes of England), but also foreign ways of living in the world that often surprise his new friends. Rosa's attraction to him does not mitigate these facts. Once she has (innocently) entered economic circulation, she encounters Tartar, but, in spite of the apparent goodness of both characters, the uneasy presence of not just Jasper, but the foreign, pervades their interactions. English/foreign contact, like Helena Landless's attraction to Crisparkle, does not erase the anxieties foreignness invokes, in spite of its seeming inevitability. Rosa and Crisparkle, two of the most centrally English and heroic figures, imbibe the foreign through her Turkish Delight and his mother's concoctions, through the Landlesses and Tartar, indeed, through

---

41. Tim Dolin, "Race and the Social Plot in *The Mystery of Edwin Drood*," in *Race and the Victorians*, 95.

42. Dolin, "Race and the Social Plot," 94.

43. Dolin, "Race and the Social Plot," 95.

the very air. Significantly, they are marked by that contact. The presence of the foreign is not purified by them, but continues to create a sense of unease. Elizabeth Chang notes that even with the management implied in the well-ordered Chinese display cabinets that appear throughout the novel, "the misplaced commodity consumption of opium can remap the . . . physical territory of British space."[44] Indeed, the opium den itself has, in Chang's reading, become not only "a primary example of Chinese difference," but a contagion that "denot[es] corrupting iniquity in British urban space."[45] While the unease has been most often located in Jasper, I would argue that it has a much further reach: into the homeliest characters and into the most intimate personal relations in the novel.

Ultimately, there's no satisfying end in *The Mystery of Edwin Drood*—and the unfinished state of the novel, of course, doesn't even permit us the resolution about which I speculate above. We do know, however, that Dickens had explained to his illustrator, Luke Fildes, that the last chapter would have the villain unrepentant, telling of his own crimes as if they were committed by someone else.[46] Like the foolish Sapsea, who believes that the foreign other is still "outside," and not within, Jasper dedicates himself to destroying the murderer and fails to recognize (at some level) that it is he. No love matches could end the mixing of blood and money: Neville's love for Rosa; Rosa's attraction to Tartar; Helena's affection for Crisparkle don't simply introduce the foreign into the English; they help *underscore the fact that it's already there.* Even the good Englishwomen, Miss Twinkleton and Miss Billickin, who market their schooling and rooms, respectively, are deeply involved in trade and compete with one another in the drawing room the way that men might compete on the floor of the stock exchange, circulating global monies into even the single woman's home.

It is no wonder that Grewgious's assistant, Bazzard has written a play called "The Thorn of Anxiety," a play Grewgious believes is quite remarkable. The thorn of anxiety in this novel may be the fear of the foreign, the marked xenophobia that pervades the text and has thoroughly infiltrated the nation itself. We are told that Bazzard feels degraded by Grewgious's patronage, though Grewgious rescued him from a life of manual labor, because Bazzard is so superior to those around him (ED, 228). One can imagine that, if the novel had been completed, we might have seen a staging of Bazzard's play,

---

44. Chang, *Britain's Chinese Eye* (Stanford, CA: Stanford University Press, 2010), 127. Chang's excellent work on *Edwin Drood* and Dickens suggests that Dickens saw the consumption of Chinese goods as a "problem" managed by narrative (see 121–124). I would suggest that Dickens was less comfortable with the ability of narrative to resolve his anxieties, anxieties, Chang notes, which are so tellingly betrayed in his discussion of the Great Exhibition.

45. Chang, *Britain's Chinese Eye*, 111.

46. See Dolin, "Race and the Social Plot," 86.

which would bespeak the anxiety that pricks the characters, along with the happy romantic unions of several figures. Even without the play and the novel's final chapters, however, we have Dickens's narrative to point to the xenophobic anxiety that marks everyone and that locates the threat of the foreign not only in English pocketbooks, but in the English themselves.

Works Cited

Carens, Timothy. *Outlandish English Subjects in the Victorian Domestic Novel.* New York: Palgrave Macmillan, 2005.

Chabot, Benjamin R. and Christopher J. Kurz. "That's Where the Money Was: Foreign Bias and English Investment Abroad, 1866–1907." *The Economic Journal* 120 (September 2010): 1056–1079.

Chang, Elizabeth Hope. *Britain's Chinese Eye: Literature, Empire, and Aesthetics in Nineteenth-Century Britain.* Stanford, CA: Stanford University Press, 2010.

Daunton, Martin. *Wealth and Welfare: An Economic and Social History of Britain, 1851–1951.* New York: Oxford University Press, 2007.

Desrochers, Pierre. "Does the invisible hand have a green thumb? Incentives, linkages, and the creation of wealth out of industrial waste in Victorian England." *Geographical Journal* 175.1 (2009): 3–16.

Dickens, Charles. *David Copperfield.* New York: Penguin, 1996.

———. *Little Dorrit.* New York: Modern Library, 2002.

———. *The Mystery of Edwin Drood.* Edited by David Paroissien. New York: Penguin Books, 2002.

Dolin, Tim. "Race and the Social Plot in *The Mystery of Edwin Drood.*" In *Race and the Victorians,* edited by Shearer West. 84–100. Brookfield: Ashgate, 1996.

Faulkner, David. "The Confidence Man: Empire and the Deconstruction of Muscular Christianity in *The Mystery of Edwin Drood.*" In *Muscular Christianity: Embodying The Victorian Age,* edited by Donald E. Hall. 175–193. New York: Cambridge University Press, 1994.

Gallagher, Catherine. *The Body Economic: Life, Death, and Sensation in Political Economy and the Victorian Novel.* Princeton, NJ: Princeton University Press, 2008.

Hall, Catherine, Keith McClelland, and Jane Rendall. *Defining the Victorian Nation: Class, Race, and Gender.* New York: Cambridge University Press, 2000.

Herbert, Christopher. "Filthy Lucre: Victorian Ideas of Money." *Victorian Studies* 44.2 (winter 2002): 185–213.

House of Commons. "Loans to Foreign States." *Reports from Committees, Volume 4.* London: House of Commons, 1875.

Jeorde, Lynn B. and Stephen P. Wooding. "Genetic variation, classification, and 'race.'" *Nature Genetics Supplement* (November 2004): S28–S33.

John, Juliet. *Dickens's Villains: Melodrama, Character, and Popular Culture.* New York: Oxford University Press, 2001.

Lindeborg, Ruth H. "The 'Asiatic' and the Boundaries of Victorian Englishness." *Victorian Studies* (spring 1994): 381–404.

Luckin, Bill. "'The heart and home of horror': The Great London Fogs of the Late Nineteenth Century." *Social History* 28 (2003): 31–48.

Milligan, Barry. "The Opium Den in Victorian London." In *Smoke: A Global History of Smoking,* edited by Sander L. Gilman and Zhou Xun. 118–125. London: Reaktion Books, 2004.

———. "'The Plague Spreading and Attacking Our Vitals': Opium Smoking and the Oriental Infection of the British Domestic Scene." *Victorian Literature and Culture* 20 (1992): 161–177.

Moore, Grace. "Turkish Robbers, Lumps of Delight, and the Detritus of Empire: The East Revisited in Dickens's Late Novels." *Critical Survey* 21.1 (2009): 74–87.

Poovey, Mary. *Genres of the Credit Economy: Mediating Value in Eighteenth- and Nineteenth-Century Britain.* Chicago: University of Chicago Press, 2008.

Pope, Alexander. "An Essay on Man," *Norton Anthology of English Literature, Major Authors,* edited by M. H. Abrams. 1097–1103. New York: Norton, 1996.

Rutterford, Janette and Josephine Maltby. "'The Nesting Instinct': Women and Investment Risk in a Historical Perspective." *Accounting History* 12.3 (2007): 305–327.

Shmitt, Cannon. "Rumors, Shares, and Novelistic Form." In *Victorian Investments,* edited by Nancy Henry and Cannon Schmitt. 182–201. Bloomington: Indiana University Press, 2009.

Shand, Alexander Innes. "Speculative Investment." *Blackwoods Edinburgh Magazine* 120 (September 1876): 293–316.

Sirr, Henry Charles. *China and the Chinese: Their Religion, Character, Customs and Manufactures: The Evils Arising from the Opium Trade: With a Glance at our Religious, Moral, Political, and Commercial Intercourse with the Country.* Vols. I and II. London: Orr, 1849.

Sudan, Rajani. *Fair Exotics.* Philadelphia: University of Pennsylvania Press, 2002.

Temin, Peter. "Capital exports, 1870–1914: An alternative model." *Economic History Review,* 2nd ser., XL 3 (1987): 453–458.

Xu, Wenying. "The Opium Trade and *Little Dorrit:* A Case of Reading Silences." *Victorian Literature and Culture* 25.1 (1997): 53–56.

2

Victorian Quarantines

Holding the Borders against "Fevered" Italian Masculinity in Dante Gabriel Rossetti's "St. Agnes of Intercession"

❧✿❧

JAY D. SLOAN

Our other plagues were home-bred, and part of ourselves, as it were; we had a habit of looking on them with a fatal indifference, indeed, inasmuch as it led us to believe that they could be effectually subdued. But the cholera was something outlandish, unknown, monstrous; its tremendous ravages, so long foreseen and feared, so little to be explained, its insidious march over whole continents, its apparent defiance of all the known and conventional precautions against the spread of epidemic disease, invested it with a mystery and a terror which thoroughly took hold of the public mind, and seemed to recall the memory of the great epidemics of the middle ages.

—W. T. Gairdner, *Public Health in Relation to Air and Water*

Victorian England's attitudes towards foreignness were both complex and often conflicted. Generally ethnocentric, Victorian travelers, for example, typically voiced *both* their sincere admiration of the cultural heritage of other nations (their history, music, art, and literature) *and* their profound distaste for non-English peoples and ways of life. Not surprisingly, in their descriptions of *un*-English foreigners, Victorians commonly employed the language of race, characterizing foreigners as constituently uncivilized, ignorant, unhealthy, and even less-than-human. For this reason, contemporary literary scholars have for some time been interested in how this rhetoric supported and/or challenged such inherently ethnocentric and racist enter-prises as colonialism and imperialism.[1]

As interesting as the rhetoric of Victorian racism is, however, equally fascinating is the potent cultural rhetoric of Victorian xenophobia. The gen-eral thrust of racism is outwards, a projection of racial otherness upon those perceived to be both distinct from and inherently inferior to one's own racial group. It emerges from the felt safety of a collective "us" and typically utilizes culturally discriminatory and segregational practices to ensure the stability and security of that ethnocentric identity. Xenophobia, on the other hand, emerges from a different psychological and perceptual space. It is based in the belief that one's collective identity is under attack, that, in fact, the "other" is making, or indeed has perhaps already made, significant inroads against "us." The panic that underlies such a genuinely phobic response is evoked, then, by an unforeseen confrontation with the feared other, usually in a cultural space previously thought safe (i.e. in one's home/homeland). The resulting shock and horror is further compounded by a sense of failed diligence, a sense that our guard has proven insufficient and we have thereby failed to keep ourselves safe.

This essay will focus specifically on England's long-standing suspicion of Italians, and particularly on how such fears triggered xenophobic critical reac-tions to the work of the Anglo-Italian poet and painter, Dante Gabriel Ros-setti (an "Italian" *in* England). As evidenced by Robert Buchanan's infamous attack in 1871 upon Rossetti as the leader of "The Fleshly School of Poetry," xenophobic English critics would employ a metaphorics of "disease" to tar-get the pathogenic potential of Rossetti's inherently Italianate poetry and to identify him as a threat to British national health. According to Buchanan, Rossetti and his followers are, "so to speak, public offenders, because they are diligently spreading the seeds of disease broadcast wherever they are read and understood."[2] Over the course of Rossetti's career, English critics would repeatedly attempt to quarantine his work, portraying him as the embodi-ment of the "Effeminate Italian"—transgressive on both ethnic and gender grounds—and particularly dangerous because he was freely broadcasting his contagions in Britain, among the potentially vulnerable native population.[3]

---

1. I have in mind here works such as Anne McClintock's *Imperial Leather: Race, Gender, and Sexuality in the Colonial Contest* (1995); Jennifer DeVere Brody's *Impossible Purities: Blackness, Femininity, and Victorian Culture* (1998); Laura Callanan's *Deciphering Race: White Anxiety, Racial Conflict, and The Turn to Fiction in Mid-Victorian English Prose* (2005); and Radhika Mohanram's *Imperial White: Race, Diaspora, and the British Empire* (2007).

2. Thomas Maitland [Robert Buchanan], "The Fleshly School of Poetry: Mr. D. G. Rossetti," *The Contemporary Review* 18 (1871): 336. Subsequent references to this work will be cited paren-thetically.

3. In her discussion of the "historical indeterminacy of 'Pre-Raphaelitism,'" Julie F. Codell

It is this local urgency that distinguishes these truly xenophobic critical reactions from merely racist Victorian rhetoric.

That Rossetti recognized and attempted to combat this local critical paradigm is made evident in the plot and composition history of his story, "St Agnes of Intercession." Set in contemporary Victorian England, the tale reveals Rossetti's early awareness of and frustration with the limitations that Victorian society imposed upon the artist's understanding and exploration of his own artistic soul. His artist protagonist's quest for artistic authenticity, shaped by the apparent reincarnation of the artist's passionate Italian heritage, comes into direct conflict with xenophobic Victorian fears of diseased Italian passions (fevers) with predictable results. As the story illustrates, however, once reclaimed, the artist finds it impossible to import such a fevered poetic identity back into heavily guarded England. His now excessive/transgressive poetic passions mark him as a dangerous carrier of foreign contagion. That Rossetti was never able to envision a way out of this powerful critical quarantine, either in his life or his art, is evidenced by his failure to narrate a successful closure for the tale, despite repeated attempts throughout his life. His art remains ultimately silenced by Victorian England's implacable fear and loathing of the foreign, a fate that Rossetti would himself largely share.

The position held by Italy in the English cultural imagination has always been a divided, ambivalent one. Jacob Korg argues that "the tendency to attribute two distinct sides to the Italian character" constitutes what he calls an "English tradition of Italy." Throughout this tradition, "we hear that Italy is a land of ravishing art and repellent cruelty," that "the Italian character is volatile and capricious, and reaches to the limits of human capacities for good and evil."[4] In the late seventeenth and early eighteenth centuries, the English upper classes became enamored with the concept of Italy as a storehouse of classical art and origin point of the Renaissance—as a place of learning and cultural refinement. "The Grand Tour" consequently evolved as a means to take advantage of Europe as what Maura O'Connor calls a "cultural training grounds." Sending their sons abroad, parents of privilege "hoped that these impressionable fellows would learn to become refined gentlemen as a result of their travels to the Italian peninsula, their favorite destination on the

argues that, after his death, Rossetti would have to be "domesticated" by critical promoters "in order to be fully appropriated as [a] national icon," for "debates over Rossetti's role in the PRB raised issues of both national identity and masculinity." "Pre-Raphaelites from Rebels to Representatives: Masculinity, Modernity, and National Identity in British and Continental Art Histories, c. 1880–1908," in *Writing the Pre-Raphaelites: Text, Context, Subtext*, 54, 67. For a specific discussion of Rossetti's perceived violations of Victorian codes of masculinity, see my essay "Attempting 'Spheral Change': D. G. Rossetti, Victorian Masculinity, and the Failure of Passion," *The Journal of Pre-Raphaelite Studies* 13 (spring 2004): 5–20.

    4. Jacob Korg, *Browning and Italy* (Athens: Ohio University Press, 1983), 7.

European continent. These refinements combined an appreciation for classical learning and political philosophy with Renaissance manners and 'faultless grooming.'"[5]

While English parents saw the Grand Tour as the culmination of their sons' educations, they were simultaneously conflicted about the temptations that might also await their children on foreign soil. For, as O'Connor notes, the Grand Tour also presented "these adolescent sons . . . [with] the space and freedom to indulge their appetites for sensual pleasures without incurring the censure of their parents. . . ." The Grand Tour, then, "presented risks, challenges, and delights alongside of responsibility, instruction, and grooming."[6] By the mid-eighteenth-century heyday of the Grand Tour, Italian life had already long been associated in the English mind with an indulgence in sensuality and decadent passions. Even as early as the late sixteenth century, the English scholar Roger Ascham had voiced concerns about the emerging practice of sending vulnerable young English gentlemen abroad to live and study in Italy. Ascham, a scholar of Greek and Latin, tutor to the young Princess Elizabeth, Latin secretary to Edward VI, and eventually secretary to Elizabeth I, visited Italy in the early 1550's. And he would utilize those firsthand observations a decade and a half later in his famous treatise on education, *The Scholemaster*. Published in London in 1570, Ascham's treatise offered a "plaine and perfit way of teachyng children, to understand, write, and speake, the Latin tong." Of the Italy of the *past*, he says, "Time was when Italy and Rome have been, to the great good of us that now live, the best breeders and bringers up of the worthiest men, not only for wise speaking, but also for well doing in all civil affairs, that ever was in the world."[7]

But, as Ascham is quick to interject, that time is gone. If classical Italy once gave the world models of "the worthiest men," notable for their adherence to their civil duties, contemporary Italy, according to Ascham, has lapsed, has fallen to the temptations of "Circe." And Ascham worries that should some sound English youth find his way to Italy now, "some Circes shall make him, of a plain Englishman, a right Italian."[8] For those English youth already inclined to vice, Italy would be even more disastrous:

> I could point out some with my finger that never had gone out of England
> but only to serve Circe in Italy. Vanity and vice and any license to ill living

---

5. Maura O'Connor, *The Romance of Italy and the English Political Imagination* (New York: St. Martin's Press, 1998), 14.

6. O'Connor, *The Romance of Italy*, 14.

7. Roger Ascham, *The Scholemaster* (1570; repr., Menston, England: Scholar Press, 1967), 23. Spelling and punctuation modernized.

8. Ascham, *The Scholemaster*, 24.

in England was counted pale and rude unto them. And lo, being Mules and Horses before they went, returned very Foxes and Asses home again: yet everywhere very Foxes with subtle and busy heads: and where they may, very wolves with cruel malicious hearts. A marvelous monster, which, for filthiness of living, for dulness [*sic*] to learning himself, for wiliness in dealing with others, for malice in hurting without cause, should carry at once in one body, the belly of a Swine, the head of an Ass, the brain of a Fox, the womb of a Wolf.[9]

A number of elements in this passage are particularly noteworthy. First is the decidedly xenophobic movement in the text as Ascham's attention moves from young Englishmen yielding to the temptations of Circe in Italy, to their eventual return home. Their original "pale," homegrown vices—rebelliousness and obstinacy—have been twisted and compounded by the Circe of Italy into much greater evils—true deviousness and cruelty of character. Now back in England, they spread their evil "everywhere." The immediacy of the threat they pose to English life and civilization is evident in Ascham's comment that he can "point out" some of them in his immediate audience. Here again is the xenophobe's fear of failed diligence, his anxiety that his countrymen, lulled by their unsuspecting trust in these returning native sons, consistently fail to recognize the truly "monstrous," bestial changelings now residing amongst them. Further, the movement from human to beast, from plain Englishman into right Italian, signals not only an ethnic/racial transmutation, but a gendered one as well. For in surrendering to the feminized space of corrupted Italy (Circe, the sorceress who threatens the heroic travels of true English/men), these prodigal sons have lost what remained of their native manly character. The beguilements of femininity have sapped them of their virility and powers of self-control, leaving them at the mercy of their own unrestrained and animalizing passions.

Thus, Ascham must finally proclaim a wholesale ban against Italy, not only against sending English youth there, but even against allowing them to read Italian books. The "monstrous" danger of the "Englishman Italianated" is simply too great:

These be the enchantments of Circe, brought out of Italy, to mar men's manners in England: much, by example of ill life, but most by precepts of fond books, of late translated out of Italian into English, sold in every shop in London, commended by honest titles the sooner to corrupt honest manners: dedicated over boldly to virtuous and honorable personages, the easier to beguile simple and innocent wits.[10]

9. Ascham, *The Scholemaster*, 26.
10. Ascham, *The Scholemaster*, 26.

Even Italian books, then, trigger xenophobic fears of a virtuous England under cultural assault. Translated into English, now bearing apparently "honest titles" and misleadingly dedicated to local "virtuous and honorable personages," these books but conceal their truly corrupt, Italian character. Englishmen thus must be vigilant in order to avoid being beguiled.

A number of changes occurred in the final decades of the eighteenth century and the first decade of the nineteenth that would radically revise the role and experience of the Grand Tour. The English political and economic dominance over Europe that followed the British victory over France in the Seven Years' War (1756–1763) for the first time granted the middle classes real access to European travel. According to O'Connor, in the span of a few decades, "The cultural and political meaning of Italy for the English came to depend largely on the perceptions and views of the peninsula depicted by middle-class travelers in journals and guidebooks and by artists in paintings and drawings."[11] At the same time, a new generation of Romantic writers, fired by the French Revolution and its political aftermath, began to reconfigure Italy in the English popular imagination. If anything, the temporary restrictions on travel to Italy caused by the Napoleonic wars (1799–1814) only served to strengthen the hold of this "imaginary Italy" upon the English mind,[12] bringing with it both an interest in "what Italy might be politically," and an overall Romantic "recasting" of Italian character.[13] In the resulting "fictitious" travel literature of Byron's Childe Harold or Ann Radcliffe's gothic Italy, O'Connor claims, "the Italian peninsula was romantically (and metaphorically) recast as a woman in distress, a tragic figure, a country poised, in Byron's words, 'between glory and desolation.'"[14] Tossed between Austrian political domination on the one hand, and Napoleonic military invasion on the other (and back again following the Congress of Italy in 1815), the Romantic portrayal of Italy—at the time a collection of small, "unenlightened" feudal states—is still strikingly feminine. The face of the evil, all-corrupting Circe has been replaced, however, with that of a helpless and innocent victim of European male aggression.

And significantly, it is to no small degree due to this potent Romantic revision that Victorian England would later show such largesse in accepting Italian political refugees, like Dante Gabriel Rossetti's own father, Gabriele

---

11. O'Connor, *The Romance of Italy,* 18.

12. O'Connor, *The Romance of Italy,* 19. According to O'Connor, from the 1790s to 1814, Napoleon's victories severely limited British access to much of Europe, with the result that a whole "younger generation of English men and women learned about Italy secondhand; that is, by reading travel literature and histories and by following accounts of Napoleon's military adventures on the Italian peninsula" (19).

13. O'Connor, *The Romance of Italy,* 19.

14. O'Connor, *The Romance of Italy,* 20.

Rossetti. A Neapolitan exile, Gabriele Rossetti would be aided in immigrating to England in 1824 by Admiral Sir Graham Moore (in command of the English Mediterranean fleet), reportedly due to the intercession of his wife, a devotee of Rossetti's politically liberationist poetry. Interestingly, as Harry Rudman describes it, Gabriele Rossetti had to be smuggled out of Italy, brought on board *disguised* as an English naval officer.[15] In a real way, then, both political and cultural borders were lowered to allow Gabriele Rossetti entry to England via yet another act of ethnic/racial substitution. The right Italian, made sympathetic by political persecution (Rossetti advocated for the reformation of the Kingdom of Naples as a constitutional monarchy), becomes English and is welcomed to his new homeland. Gabriele's subsequent marriage to the half-English/half-Italian Frances Mary Lavinia Polidori (her brother was Byron's famous physician), and the birth of Dante Gabriel Rossetti and his three siblings, would thus be made possible by the establishment of an expatriate Italian, and then second-generation Anglo-Italian, community *within* England.

As powerful as the Romantic impulse to recast Italy was—generating English political interest in the possibility of Italian unification and a great deal of support for such radical republicans of the Risorgimento as Giuseppe Mazzini and Giuseppe Garibaldi—it also, however, set the stage for the counter-reactions of English middle-class visitors who were shocked by the realities of Italy once travel to the peninsula was restored following the fall of Napoleon. The voice of native English ethnocentrism quickly reasserted itself in volumes of Victorian travel literature that began detailing the vice, poverty, and decay of Italy and of the Italian character.

Having successfully adopted what Maria Frawley calls a "self-fashioned identity as [a] professional tourist-traveler and writer,"[16] Francis Trollope would follow up her successful *Domestic Manners of the Americans* (1832), with *A Visit to Italy* (1842). Like many English travelers of the period, Trollope is culturally ethnocentric and personally self-absorbed to the point that, as Frawley puts it, she "makes little attempt to evoke the Italian character at all." She herself remains "the central character and her impressions are the focus of interest."[17] Describing the view from her seaside hotel window in Genoa, Trollope spots a sudden "study," a "group of nine boys" so "utterly listless in their idleness" that she finds herself led to speculate on the cause: "They, one and all, looked in perfect health, and I could only suppose that

---

15. Harry W. Rudman, *Italian Nationalism and English Letters: Figures of the Risorgimento and Victorian Men of Letters* (New York: Columbia University Press, 1940), 187.

16. Maria H. Frawley, *A Wider Range: Travel Writing by Women in Victorian England* (Cranbury, NJ: Associated University Presses, 1994), 48.

17. Frawley, *A Wider Range*, 49.

habitual idleness had taught them to be content with this half-dead condition. Poor little fellows! . . . Several of them were superbly handsome, with curly locks, and eyes as black as sloes. I would have given something to have them all busily at school."[18] Trollope's position as a tourist-observer in Italy is marked emphatically in the passage, both by her physical removal from the scene—she observes from above, from her window—but also by her description of the scene as a study, just as she speaks, a few lines earlier, of a view of the Mediterranean which she enjoys from another hotel window. She writes, then, as if she had come upon a series of interesting Italian canvases while wandering through a local museum, an impression borne out by her commenting on the beauty of the Italian boys. In her puzzlement over the boy's lethargy, however, and in her initial search for a possible pathological cause to explain it, we see Trollope's distinctly xenophobic English concern with disease among foreigners. Unable to diagnose any apparent illness, she jumps to the conclusion that their weakness of character must be due to poor cultural conditioning. They've never been taught better. In wishing them "all busily at school," Trollope asserts a stolid belief in the power of rigorous (English) discipline, and her casual confidence in her ability to judge their "condition" at a glance reveals her unflappable English ethnocentrism.

Not all Victorian travelers to Italy remained quite so calm and self-possessed in the face of the so-called indolent "Italian character." Many who came seeking culture and refinement would find their long-term exposure to Italy profoundly disconcerting. In *Pictures from Italy* (1846), Charles Dickens confronts the essential cultural contradictions of Italy, also on the streets of Genoa, an area for which he eventually developed a great fondness. Strolling through "rich Palaces" and "magnificent and innumerable Churches," he is overwhelmed, however, by a sudden encounter with the squalid realities of modern Italian life:

> the rapid passage from a street of stately edifices, into a maze of the vilest squalor, steaming with unwholesome stenches, and swarming with half-naked children and whole worlds of dirty people—make up, altogether, such a scene of wonder: so lively, and yet so dead; so noisy, and yet so quiet: so obtrusive, and yet so shy and lowering: so wide awake, and yet so fast asleep: that it is a sort of intoxication to a stranger to walk on, and on, and on, and look about him.[19]

---

18. Mrs. [Francis] Trollope, *A Visit to Italy* (London: Richard Bentley, 1842), 1: 46–47.

19. Charles Dickens, *American Notes* and *Pictures from Italy* (1846; repr., London: Oxford University Press, 1957), 293. Subsequent references to this text will be cited parenthetically.

Walking *amongst* "dirty" Italians, Dickens is consumed by a "bewildering phantasmagoria" (239) that surrounds and intoxicates him. It is Dickens's immersion in this squalid Italian life that so starkly distinguishes his experience from Trollope's. He does not observe, untouched, from the heights of a hotel window. But wandering thus exposed through Italy also puts Dickens in harm's way. It is perhaps not surprising when he begins to exhibit symptoms of the same Italian indolence that so troubled Trollope. In his later visits to a series of "mouldy, dreary, God-forgotten towns," Dickens notes, "What a strange, half-sorrowful and half-delicious doze it is, to ramble through these places gone to sleep and basking in the sun!" Among these villages, he claims, "I became aware that I have never known till now, what it is to be lazy. . . . I feel I am getting rusty. That any attempt to think, would be accompanied with a creaking noise. That there is nothing, anywhere, to be done, or needing to be done" (317). Dickens's language in these passages is culturally alarming. It evokes Ascham's warnings against the enchantments of Circe, signaling the potential surrender of Dickens's own vital, manly, and English character. The confusion of sleep for life, the dissipation of thought and energy, suggests the lost capacity for focus and action that plagues the mariners of Tennyson's "The Lotus-Eaters," men similarly lost in the intoxication of foreign shores.

As he continues his travels through Italy, Dickens wakes to the growing realization that "in every stagnant town, [lies] this same Heart beating with the same monotonous pulsation, the centre of the same torpid, listless system" (320). And perhaps it is in recognition of this systemically diseased Italian character that Dickens evinces a sudden sense of xenophobic panic and revulsion in his description of one of his last stops in the country, the abhorred village of Fondi:

> A hollow-cheeked and scowling people they are! All beggars; but that's nothing. Look at them as they gather round. Some are too indolent to come downstairs, or are too wisely mistrustful of the stairs, perhaps, to venture: so stretch out their lean hands from upper windows, and howl; others, come flocking around us, fighting and jostling one another, and demanding, incessantly, charity for the love of God, charity for the love of the Blessed Virgin, charity for the love of all the Saints. A group of miserable children, almost naked, screaming forth the same petition, discover that they can see themselves reflected in the varnish of the carriage, and begin to dance and make grimaces, that they may have the pleasure of seeing their antics repeated in the mirror. . . . Surrounded by this motley concourse, we move out of Fondi: bad bright eyes glaring at us, out of the darkness of every crazy tenement, like glistening fragments of its filth and putrefaction. (410–411)

Dickens's horror as this cast of Italian grotesques "gather round" and "surround" the carriage carrying him and his wife—an encroachment of diseased foreignness upon the safe domestic (English) space of his carriage—is palpably xenophobic, as is his urgent desire to "move out of Fondi," "out of the darkness." Here the "indolent" Italian character has taken on a decidedly malevolent and malignant guise, like a grasping, beggarly embodiment of some medieval plague, its "bad bright eyes" becoming but extensions of the "filth and putrefaction" in which it resides.

The art historian and critic, John Ruskin, would also spend much of 1845 traveling extensively throughout Italy, studying, sketching, and struggling to save decaying Italian artwork and architecture from widespread national neglect. In a series of letters home to his parents—the more blunt because private—Ruskin details not only his increasing despair, but also his rapidly increasing disgust with the Italian character. Writing from Florence on June 25, 1845, he cries out in frustration to his parents:

> If you could but see, as I do, near & close, the mighty crowds of the dead that stand in countless portraiture of the walls of the Novella & the Carmine—grand, Fathers of the Church—that seem not out of place though standing among the prophets & the saints of elder time—& then, leaving the dark cloisters for the sunshine, you see in the place of these, pale, effeminate, animal eyed, listless sensualists, that have no thought, or care, or occupation, or knowledge, or energy.[20]

As in Dickens, Ruskin's language again evokes Ascham's, particularly in the attribution of "effeminate" and "animalistic" traits to Italians. And like Ascham, Ruskin considers this evidence of racial and cultural devolution: "The race of Giotto & Orcagna & Dante," he notes, "were a very different people from those of the present day."[21]

Having established a context for reading long-standing English fears of Italians in terms of their supposedly "diseased" tendencies towards indolence and dissipation, we can now turn our attention back to England and to the critical scrutiny directed towards artists such as the Anglo-Italian poet and painter, Dante Gabriel Rossetti. According to Bruce Haley in *The Healthy Body and Victorian Culture,* "no topic more occupied the Victorian mind than Health—not religion, or politics, or Improvement, or Darwinism. In the name of Health, Victorians flocked to the seaside, tramped about in the Alps or Cotswolds, dieted, took pills, sweated themselves in Turkish

---

20. John Ruskin, *Ruskin in Italy: Letters to His Parents, 1845,* ed. Harold I. Shapiro (Oxford: Oxford University Press, 1972), 129.

21. Ruskin, *Ruskin in Italy,* 128–129.

baths, adopted this 'system' of medicine or that."[22] A "working definition" of "health" for Victorians, however, Haley claims, would be remarkably comprehensive, incorporating not only physical and mental, but also "moral" and "creative" soundness:

> *Health is a state of constitutional growth and development in which the bodily systems and mental faculties interoperate harmoniously under the direct motive power of vital energy or the indirect motive power of the moral will, or both. Its signs are, subjectively recognized, a sense of wholeness and unencumbered capability, and, externally recognized, the production of useful, creative labor.*[23]

This expansion of health to include the concept of an appropriately and recognizably directed vital energy and moral will explains the antipathy so many Victorian travelers voiced for Italian listlessness; to the English mind, such a failure of "motive power" is an indicator of disease. Creatively, too, Victorians looked for a focused balance of energies. Citing such Victorian literary critics as George Brimley, Leslie Stephen, and John Stuart Mill, Haley notes a consistent and overriding belief that "the creative, healthy act must then involve a strong assertion of the will, of volitional force against emotional force."[24] To let emotion overwhelm the creative enterprise is to be undisciplined as an artist, but more importantly, it is profoundly unhealthy. For this reason, Haley claims, "The Victorian critic believed that he should diagnose a work, looking for signs of disease or soundness, and then looking further for causes of the disclosed condition."[25]

When in 1871, Robert Buchanan, using the pseudonym of Thomas Maitland, launched his infamous attack upon "The Fleshly School of Poetry" in *The Contemporary Review,* he managed to capture in the term "fleshly" the very heart of mainstream Victorian ideological concerns with Rossetti's purportedly unhealthy, sensual (Italian) poetry. Despite the excesses of his argument, for which he would be chastised,[26] Buchanan quite effectively

---

22. Bruce Haley, *The Healthy Body and Victorian Culture* (Cambridge, MA: Harvard University Press, 1978), 3.

23. Haley, *The Healthy Body,* 21; italics original.

24. Haley, *The Healthy Body,* 52.

25. Haley, *The Healthy Body,* 46.

26. Robert Buchanan, the writer of *London Poems* (1866) and several other works, including plays and novels, was quickly spotted for what he was, a man of small literary talent and great literary jealousy. When Buchanan (writing under the pseudonym Thomas Maitland) launched his attack upon Rossetti as the head of "the Fleshly School of Poetry," he garnered some substantial critical repudiation. "The fleshly gentlemen have bound themselves," Buchanan had claimed, "by solemn league and covenant to extol fleshliness as the distinct and supreme end of poetic and pictorial art; to aver that poetic expression is greater than poetic thought, and by inference that the body is greater than the soul, and sound superior to sense; and that the poet, properly to develop his poetic faculty,

delineates the Victorian era's—and specifically the literary critic's—concern with safeguarding the national health. "The fleshly school of verse-writers are," Buchanan announces, "so to speak, public offenders, because they are diligently spreading the seeds of disease broadcast wherever they are read and understood. Their complaint too is catching, and carries off many young persons" (Maitland, "The Fleshly School," 336).

While Buchanan marks the entire school as evidencing in their work dangerously unwholesome imaginations and appetites, he reserves his particular censure for Rossetti, whom he identifies as the senior member and leader of the group. Unlike the boyishly naughty verses of his follower Swinburne, the "shameless nakedness" of Rossetti's poems emerge from the pen of "a grown man, with the self-control and easy audacity of actual experience." "But it is neither poetic, nor manly, nor even human," Buchanan claims, "to obtrude such things as the themes of whole poems. It is simply nasty" (Maitland, "The Fleshly School," 338). Much of Buchanan's venom, then, is targeted at Rossetti as a willful broadcaster of disease among younger and more impressionable men, both poets and readers alike. But for the danger they represent to others, Buchanan suggests, he would simply dismiss Rossetti's poems as "silly sooth." Like Ascham, however, Buchanan perceives such literary works as particularly dangerous for those with weaker constitutions, for "young gentlemen with animal faculties morbidly developed by too much tobacco and too little exercise. Such indulgence, however, would ruin the strongest

---

must be an intellectual hermaphrodite, to whom the very facts of day and night are lost in a whirl of aesthetic terminology" (Maitland, "The Fleshly School," 335).

Though Buchanan had certainly tapped directly into central ideological concerns with Rossetti's work, his particularly personal and mean-spirited rhetoric drew immediate fire. Rossetti supporters responded with letters in *The Athenaeum* and many other literary critics also denounced Buchanan. Buxton Forman, for example, chastised Buchanan in *Tinsley's Magazine*: Buchanan's "attack" had been "covert and uncritical"; it was "full of personalities;" [Buxton Forman], "The 'Fleshly School' Scandal," *Tinsley's Magazine* 10 (1872): 102. Ten years later, months after Rossetti's death, an abashed Buchanan was still apologizing. Writing in the July 1, 1882 issue of *The Academy*, Buchanan whined, "A man who is Quixotic enough to attack windmills must expect summary and clumsy treatment." Of Rossetti specifically, he oddly announced, "Mr. Rossetti, I freely admit now, never was a fleshly poet at all; never, at any rate, fed upon the poisonous honey of French art;" Robert Buchanan, "The Martydom of Madeline," *The Academy* 22 (1882): 11.

The great irony, of course, is that despite the "summary treatment" of Buchanan, the general critical appraisal of Rossetti was *exactly* that he was a "fleshly poet." But Buchanan, by launching his attack covertly under the pseudonym of "Thomas Maitland," by referring favorably in his article to his *own* work, and by speaking too generally of a whole "school" of male "fleshly poets," had made a number of serious tactical errors. In attacking the lack of virility and manliness in Rossetti, he had clumsily brought his own weaknesses under scrutiny; in using a pseudonym, he hadn't played fair (like a true gentleman should); in covertly praising his own work, he had displayed false modesty and boastfulness; and by generalizing broadly about personalities, he had revealed an incautious and "uncritical" tendency. In other words, he had brought his own honest English "manliness" into question.

poetical constitution; and it unfortunately happens that neither masters nor pupils were naturally very healthy" (Maitland, "The Fleshly School," 349).

In analyzing Rossetti's verses carefully and closely, Buchanan goes on to render his diagnosis, citing specific evidence of the supposed disease apparent in Rossetti's poetic and painterly body:

> There is the same thinness and transparence of design, the same combination of the simple and the grotesque, the same morbid deviation from healthy forms of life, the same sense of weary, wasting, yet exquisite sensuality; nothing virile, nothing tender, nothing completely sane; a superfluity of extreme sensibility, of delight in beautiful forms, hues, and tints, and a deep-seated indifference to all agitating forces of agencies, all tumultuous griefs and sorrows, all the thunderous stress of life, and all the straining storm of speculation. (Maitland, "The Fleshly School," 337)

As would many critics of the fleshly school poets (notably John Morley and Thomas Bayne, and even the poets Browning and Tennyson), Buchanan here descries the morbidity of a consumptively sensual poetry like Rossetti's, playing its stagnant sensuality against the agitating conceptual exertions vital to any genuinely healthy and sane verse. Not subjected to any of the necessary trials and challenges of a healthy life, Rossetti's poetry festers in the exquisite, oily phosphorescence of decadence.

Given the "English tradition of Italy" described earlier, Buchanan's critical rhetoric is strikingly familiar. The same terms used to mark the diseased indolence of the Italian character are here utilized to mark the diseased indolence of Rossetti's poetry. And the xenophobic nature of the attack is also the same. Both are perceived as threats to the health and very identity of the Englishman. The implications of Buchanan's rhetoric are also startling. Sounding very much like an advocate for the Contagious Diseases Act, Buchanan suggests that a compulsory critical examination of the poetic body is not only justifiable, but culturally imperative. And by extension, so too is the critical quarantine of poets suspected of being contagious. The peddling of diseased poetic flesh, especially to the young and vulnerable, must be recognized not only as a serious threat to public health, but as a criminal act as well.

According to Rossetti's brother William, "St. Agnes of Intercession," like the better-known story "Hand and Soul," dates from 1848, from the earliest days of his literary career.[27] Yet, while "Hand and Soul" has often been read as Rossetti's artistic manifesto of the then-emerging Pre-Raphaelite

---

27. Dante Gabriel Rossetti, *The Collected Works of Dante Gabriel Rossetti*, ed. William M. Rossetti (1897; repr., St. Clair Shores, MI: Scholarly Press, n.d.), 524. Subsequent references to this text will be cited parenthetically as CW.

Brotherhood, "Saint Agnes" has received relatively little critical attention. In the notes to *The Collected Works of Dante Gabriel Rossetti* which he edited, William Rossetti, while calling "St. Agnes" "no unworthy pendant to *Hand and Soul*," adds, "It does not seem to be intended to bear an equal weight of moral and spiritual significance" (Rossetti, CW, 524). However, what makes "St. Agnes" particularly significant, at least for the purposes of this study, is that it represents a serious attempt by Rossetti to bridge the huge ideological gap—inherent in his own Anglo-Italian identity—between a disciplined, conventional English artistic identity and a passionate, unconventional Italian artistry.

Significantly, the tale was never completed. Rossetti's attempt to infuse the passionate—the Italian—into the life of his protagonist, a male English artist living a domestic, commercially promising life in contemporary Victorian England, simply comes to a sudden, indeterminate halt. This suggests a cultural impasse that Rossetti was never able to resolve. But Rossetti's continuing efforts to complete "St. Agnes," not only originally between 1848 and 1850, but again in 1869–1870, and yet once more during the final days of his life, suggests an ongoing personal investment in finding ideological closure. The tale, and its history of composition, then, serves as an illustration of Rossetti's lifelong struggle to articulate an alternative aesthetic identity in a culture frantically, xenophobically, devoted to holding the borders against him.

The tale opens with the narrator-protagonist recalling one of his earliest and strongest recollections—the memory of his father returning home from work in the evening and there "singing to us in his sweet, generous tones" (Rossetti, CW, 399). William Rossetti claims that this opening frame is directly modeled on real life: "Something in the nature of actual reminiscence may be traced in the opening details; as that of our father singing old revolutionary and other songs" (Rossetti, CW, 525). If, indeed, this scene is meant as a familial invocation, then the "father" in the tale is none other than Gabriele Rossetti, the expatriate Italian poet who had cheered the Napoleonic takeover of northern Italy as a triumph of liberty, and who after the fall of Napoleon had just as enthusiastically cheered the return of the exiled King Ferdinand IV of Naples. Finding the king insufficiently reformist, however, Gabriele Rossetti switched allegiances again, joined the rebel Carbonari, and became a popular poet of revolution. King Ferdinand, having gained the support of the Austrian army, soon reconsolidated his power by abolishing the constitution that had momentarily been forced upon him, and Gabriele consequently fled Italy.

Eventually reaching England, Gabriele had been forced to adopt a much quieter existence, entertaining fellow Italian expatriates in his home, and becoming a teacher of Italian and a recognized, though eccentric, scholar of Dante. In the moment preserved in Rossetti's tale, however, Gabriele Rossetti flares forth in his revolutionary, poetic glory yet again. And the sedate life of the English home, the domestic space itself, is quickly overwhelmed by this unleashing of Italianate poetic energies. The room becomes fervent with visions: "I used to sit on the hearth-rug, listening to him, and look between his knees into the fire till it burned my face, while the sights swarming up in it seemed changed and changed with the music: till the music and the fire and my heart burned together, and I would take paper and pencil, and try in some childish way to fix the shapes that rose within me. For my hope, even then, was to be a painter" (Rossetti, CW, 399).

Initially, then, the scenario is set, as in "Hand and Soul," with the young artist "burning" with passion and trying to translate that passion into art, art being the only means of "fix[ing] the shapes that rose within."[28] And while this young artist in England has not the advantage of living in Italy, he does have passionate Italian parents who model and encourage his every effort. In a book supplied to him by his mother, the young artist is first exposed to Italian art, there discovering a print of a work by Bucciolo d'Orli Angiolieri portraying St. Agnes in her mystical glory. Strangely, he finds this print holds "a strong and indefinable charm." He spends hours copying it and trying unsuccessfully to learn something about the artist. His father, in support of his son's growing passion for art, even removes him from school and allows him to pursue his own private "bent of study" (Rossetti, CW, 400).

Remarkably, Rossetti describes a style of artistic education, largely self-motivated and self-invented, which is guided by personal passion alone. This not only greatly parallels Rossetti's own artistic education, but also stands in sharp contrast to the realities of formal English education, a system characterized by a sharply disciplined and disciplining curriculum (such as that fancied by Francis Trollope for her Italian boys), and by the regimens thought necessary to evoke the restraint and self-discipline of a proper Victorian gentleman. But Rossetti's tale soon veers from this seemingly idyllic path of artistic self-realization as his protagonist chooses to embrace the constraints of a domestic English professional life. Emerging from the "cloud within" (Rossetti, CW, 400), the young man meets, quickly falls in love with, and then proposes to Mary Arden, his sister's friend. In choosing to marry, however, the artist recognizes the demands that both his fiancé's loftier class, and

---

28. According to his brother William's diary, Rossetti had originally titled the tale "An Auto-psychology," a title that suggests not only Rossetti's deep interest in his protagonist's psychological struggle to articulate his "Italian" artistic passions, but his close personal identification with those struggles as well. William Michael Rossetti, *Preraphaelite Diaries and Letters* (London: Hurst & Blackett Limited, 1900), 268.

English domesticity in general, place upon him. Thus, he determines that he must first acquire a secure, elevated station in life, and in order to achieve such a position as an artist, he begins a new decidedly "modern" work suited to make his fame, a painting for which his fiancé supplies the model for the principal figure.

In a great twist of irony, however, the narrator makes a startling discovery on the day his painting is finally exhibited publicly. Upon entering the exhibit hall, the artist is waylaid by a well-known critic and poet who insists upon viewing the show with him. Irritating the artist with his obvious sympathies for only the most hackneyed and sentimental works, the artist is horrified to find the critic directing his attention to the artist's own painting on a nearby wall.[29] Proclaiming it "quaint, crude, even grotesque" (Rossetti, CW, 408) —adjectives that all parallel those applied by critics to Rossetti's own early work—the critic notes: "'It is like the works of a very early man that I saw in Italy. Angioloni, Angellini, Angiolieri,—that was the name,—Bucciuolo Angiolieri. . . . The head of your woman there . . . is exactly like a St. Agnes of his at Bologna'" (Rossetti, CW, 409). The artist is first mortified to recognize in his painting the image of the oft-copied print of his childhood, but then astonished to recognize in the face of the St. Agnes the face of his fiancé. Not only has he failed in attempting a modern work, but he now realizes that his very childhood passion for the St. Agnes image had prepared his heart for young Mary Arden.

Puzzling over this startling discovery, the artist yearns to visit Italy: "I could hardly persuade myself that the idol of my childhood, and the worship I had rendered it, was not all an unreal dream; and every day the longing possessed me more strongly to look with my own eyes upon the veritable St. Agnes" (Rossetti, CW, 410). Delaying his marriage, the artist travels to Italy, and begins "ransacking" every gallery until he finds Angiolieri's "St. Agnes," a painting that overwhelms him: "As I looked, my whole life seemed to crowd about me . . . ," for in it he finds "the exact portrait of Mary, feature by feature" (Rossetti, CW, 414). The catalog tells him that the painting, "though

---

29. As Jerome McGann has pointed out in his essay, "Dante Gabriel Rossetti and the Betrayal of Truth," *Victorian Poetry* 26 (1988): 339–361, this public exhibition of the piece, like the artist's choice of a modern subject, foregrounds concerns of artistic marketability. As McGann notes, "the passage shows how the sensibility of a man who is committed to the 'intrinsic values' of art suffers a crucifixion of the imagination when he feels compelled to operate in and through the mediations 'evolved in society.'" He adds, "Rossetti's painter fears and respects his companion's power in the culture-industry of their world" (341). Interestingly, Rossetti rarely exhibited his paintings publically, preferring to paint privately for patrons. In his attack upon Rossetti, Buchanan significantly comments, "for reasons best known to himself," Rossetti "has shrunk from publicly exhibiting his pictures, and from allowing anything like a popular estimate to be formed of their qualities" (Maitland, "The Fleshly School," 336). The implication is clear that Rossetti has been "hiding," an idea that only reinforces Buchanan's xenophobic suspicions about their likely "diseased" nature.

ostensibly representing St. Agnes, is the portrait of Blanzifore dall 'Ambra, a lady to whom the painter was deeply attached, and who died early" (Rossetti, CW, 415). Struck by the story, and the pang of love for Mary that it evokes in him, the narrator is given yet a greater shock. He is led by the catalog to a second painting, a self-portrait by the artist of *St. Agnes:* "A trembling suspense, with something almost of involuntary awe, was upon me as I ran towards the spot; the picture was hung low; I stooped over the rail to look closely at it, and was face to face with *myself*!" (Rossetti, CW, 417). In these surprising turns, then, Rossetti evokes a sense of artistic fate, of the inescapability of one's true passionate nature, a nature that cannot be contained. From underneath all the merely English trappings of commercial artistic success and domestic social rituals, the artist's true Italian nature rushes forth, overwhelming both. The narrator is brought "face to face" with himself, finds his own features in those of the Italian artist who had painted the sainted glory of his love four centuries before.

Nowhere, however, is Rossetti's tale so intriguing as in its attempted conclusion. For having restored his artistic hero to his true character, Rossetti finds he must somehow return him to the domestic confines of England. But his protagonist seems to lose heart at the prospect. While he has come to accept the "truth" of his self-discovery in Italy, he is cowed by the remembered reality of an England for whom the Englishman Italianated is an unfathomable horror. He contemplates the impossibility of even trying to narrate his experience, and retreats instead to the cultural safety of silence: "The tremendous experience of that moment, the like of which has never, perhaps, been known to another man, must remain undescribed; since the description, read calmly at common leisure, could seem but fantastic raving" (Rossetti, CW, 417). The fear of having his transformative mystery marked as mere "fantastic raving" is both personally and culturally potent here; it signals a meta-narrative moment when the protagonist—and Rossetti himself—acknowledge that, in England, the articulation of a passionate Italian artistry will be disdained as unmanly, effeminate hysteria.

The night before his return to England and to Mary, the narrator has an ominous dream that foreshadows his impossibly conflicted homecoming. He once again envisions the opening exhibition of his initial painting of Mary, but this time "a crowd was before it; and I heard several say that it was against the rules to hang that picture, for that the painter (naming me) was dead" (Rossetti, CW, 419). Even his dream tells him, then, that as an artist both he and his work are as "dead" to the English public; his Italianate work is, in fact, "against the rules." Further, he envisions Mary on the arm of another man, a man who, upon turning, is revealed to be his long-dead self, Bucciuolo. When the narrator in his dream demands her release as his bride, Bucciuolo replies, "'Not mine, friend, but neither thine'" (Rossetti, CW, 420). Just as Bucciuolo's own dreams for wedded bliss had been shattered four centuries earlier, so, too, is the artist warned that his passion will not find fulfillment in conventional English domesticity.

Thoroughly alarmed, the narrator awakes, gathers his baggage, and returns to England, every step of the way "occupied by one haunting and despotic idea." Interestingly, he adds that "on the day when I left Perugia I had felt the seeds of fever already in my veins; and during the journey this oppression kept constantly on the increase. I was obliged, however, carefully to conceal it, since the panic of the cholera was again in Europe, and any sign of illness would have caused me to be left on the road" (Rossetti, CW, 421). In this metaphor of "seeds of fever" planted in his veins in Italy, the narrator thus activates the same cultural fears of unhealthy, Italianate contagion seen in Ascham and many other English writers. It is a fever that the narrator was indeed wise to conceal, for he would not have reentered Victorian England unchallenged otherwise.

Upon returning to his home, the frantic narrator is quickly assured by his startled family that Mary is well. And the narrator's relief is so great that he finally succumbs to his fever, a "raging fever" that endures for five weeks.[30] Awakening to the "health," "pillows" and "sunshine" of his own English bedroom, the narrator finds that "one constant thought" still afflicts him, a thought that had "now grown peremptory, absolute, uncompromising, and seemed to cry within me for speech, till silence became a torment" (Rossetti, CW, 422). His fever's last force has been concentrated, then, in this psychological need to speak; the narrator thus finds he must "tell the whole" to his parents. The reaction of his parents to his "extraordinary disclosure," however, both puzzles and alarms him:

> Before I had gone far with my story, however, my mother fell back in her seat, sobbing violently; then rose, and running up to me, kissed me many times, still sobbing and calling me her poor boy. She then left the room. I looked towards my father, and saw that he had turned away his face. In a few moments he rose also without looking at me, and went out as my mother had done. (Rossetti, CW, 422)

---

30. This plot of English character being tried by the fires, by the fever of wanton romanticism is, of course, commonly seen in nineteenth-century novels. However, it is most frequently applied to women who transgress the confines of a chaste and decorous femininity—hence, the chastising fever of Marianne Dashwood, which comes in response to her overweening affections for Mr. Willoughby in Jane Austen's *Sense and Sensibility.* In Rossetti's story, where the same fate falls upon the male protagonist, the larger cultural import is similar (though Rossetti turns it to different effect), yet further evidence of Rossetti's unhealthy Italian effeminacy.

In the reactions of his protagonist's parents, Rossetti foregrounds the strident Victorian cultural tenets that would have confounded the passion-haunted artist. His father reenters the room, and alone hears the rest of his son's story: "When I had finished, my father again appeared deeply affected; but soon recovering himself, endeavoured, by reasoning, to persuade me either that the circumstances I had described had no foundation save in my own diseased fancy, or else that at the time of their occurrence incipient illness had caused me to magnify very ordinary events into marvels and omens" (Rossetti, CW, 423). We discover in the parents' reactions, then, not only the absolute inability of the English to entertain the possibility of such an Italian mystery, but the gendered markers that complicate their perceptions. For in both the mother's fleeing from the room and the father's "turning away his face" and refusal to look at his son, we see not a primary parental concern for an ill child, but an absolute, horrified recoiling from a son's unmanly and diseased fancy. While the mother is too mortified even to reenter the room, the father returns manfully to wrestle mightily with his son, to endeavor to reassert proper masculine control and discipline by reasoning with his passion-addled boy.

As his father clearly tells him, what most profoundly disturbs both him and his wife, what constitutes their grief in this circumstance, is their son's steadfast adherence to his delusion. This is evidenced by his disturbing ability to talk "*connectedly* on the same wild and unreal subject" (emphasis added) long after his delirium had passed and "after they had hoped me to be on the road to recovery." For this reason, his father feels he must finally "implore" him "most earnestly at once to resist and dispel this fantastic brain sickness" (Rossetti, CW, 423). What the father foregrounds in his reaction, then, are not the inescapable consequences of an illness, but his perception of his son's very *un*-English failure to assert his own powers of masculine self-control. His fever has become self-indulgent, and further, his father now feels he must tell him, it is a dire weakness, one that "allowed to retain possession" might well end in the "endangerment" of the son's "reason" (Rossetti, CW, 423). For a Victorian male, of course, the loss of reason is tantamount to the loss of English, masculine, and even human identity itself. As did Ascham and Ruskin, the narrator's father evokes the cultural trope of undisciplined Italian passion as a form of animalizing possession. How rightfully the narrator had seen the need to conceal his fever upon reentering England. In displaying it openly, he has become culturally monstrous, even to his parents. He is truly Ascham's Englishman Italianated.

That the "father" here speaks with the appalled voice and full authority of Victorian culture, rather than as a concerned "papa," marks a shocking disparity in the tale, a disparity that reveals the enormous cultural tensions which Rossetti is struggling unsuccessfully to negotiate and close narratively. This portrayal of a staunch, restraint-enforcing father seems glaringly irreconcilable with that of the passionate, vision-evoking, and freedom-loving father seen in the tale's opening. Here, the father's speech is narrated as a particularly violent form of cultural "silencing": "My father's last words struck me like a stone in the mouth; there was no longer any answer that I could make. I was very weak at the time, and I believe I lay down in my bed and sobbed" (Rossetti, CW, 423–424). How very much this moment of fierce cultural censoring resembles similarly violent moments in Victorian portrayals of transgressive femininity, instances that feminist critics have long discussed. Here is the same sudden stripping away of all subjectivity, of agency and identity, so that the character is left unable to either speak or act. For having been measured against the cultural standards of the healthy Englishman and found wanting, marked as effeminate (which is only further verified by his subsequent "weak sobbing") the narrator here, too, finds himself denied a subject position from which to speak and act.

That Rossetti's narrator is here attempting to speak his silence, to articulate a mystery forbidden to (English)men, to voice what English society has dubbed madness, is the narrative irony that also enables a subversive reading of the tale. That Rossetti is here attempting to articulate an alternative form of passionate Italian artistry, over and against predominant Victorian models, is made plausible not only by the certainty that the narrator holds regarding his own interpretation of events, but also by the vividness with which the narrator describes his heightened fears, not of being actually mad, but of facing cultural reprisals for beliefs and behaviors that others have *termed* "mad": "From that day until I was able to leave my bed, I never in any way alluded to the same terrible subject; but I feared my father's eye as though I had been indeed a madman." So terrified is the narrator that he will reveal his madness, his Italianate disease, in public, that he refuses to see even old friends. As he phrases it, he fears "that my incubus might get the better of me" (Rossetti, CW, 424), a remark that reveals not only the narrator's acceptance, his possession, of *his* personal demon (his inner Italian character), but also his consciousness that his demon is culturally marked along gender lines. For in figuring his madness as an "incubus," the narrator echoes strident English anxieties regarding undisciplined masculine passions, passions that in their excess, in their sensual seductiveness, are the direct counterpart of the more frequently reviled succubus, or figure of transgressive female sensuality. The narrator himself, then, thus acknowledges and accepts the essential effeminacy of his own nature.

Rossetti, however, clearly cannot close his tale with the narrator suspended in such a state of inexpressible, yet thoroughly explosive, passion.

These narrative tensions must be resolved somehow. At a loss to achieve closure in any other way, Rossetti apparently pulls his narrator back into a state of repentance, a turn-around that comes so suddenly, so abruptly, that Rossetti himself must have found it dissatisfying. It was at this point, in fact, that he abandoned the entire story. We are told only that the narrator finally decides that he must see Mary, an attempt to reestablish an English domestic connection that cannot be carried forth until all trace of Italianate passion has been purged. The narrator's repentance is therefore sounded, appropriately enough early one Sunday morning, by the peal of church bells: "I cannot express the sudden refreshing joy which filled me at that moment. I rose from my bed, and kneeling down, prayed while the sound lasted" (Rossetti, CW, 425). Having heard the call of Christ, a sound, manful, English Christ, Rossetti's narrator confesses his error, pleads for forgiveness, and is raised a new "man": "shutting the door behind me, I stood once again in the living sunshine" (Rossetti, CW, 425).

For the first time since his trip to Italy, he thinks of Mary without fear, with some surety that their union is once again realizable. And as he walks to Mary's home, surrounded by old, familiar sights, and reliving the memories they evoke, he finds that "the sense of reality grew upon me at every step, and for the first time during some months I felt a man among men" (Rossetti, CW, 425). Only now, then, after exorcising his effeminizing Italian demon, can he rise from the level of the animal to stand a "man among (English) men"; only now can he be recognized as a man at all. To complete his recovery from his "fever," Rossetti's narrator must surrender his belief in the reality of Italy, and put in its place an assurance of the reality of England:

And thus now, with myself, old trains of thought and the conceptions of former years came back as I passed from one swarming resort to another, and seemed, by contrast, to wake my spirit from its wild and fantastic broodings to a consciousness of something like actual existence; as the mere reflections of objects, sunk in the vague pathless water, appear almost to strengthen it into substance. (Rossetti, CW, 426)

If only by leaving England for Italy was the narrator able to invert reality in the first place, to place the reality of Italian passion above that of stolid English domesticity, returning to England apparently necessitates a re-inversion of those realities. Thus, it would seem that "St. Agnes of Intercession" is, in the end, not primarily a story of passionate, individual artistic identity at all, but a story of culture, a story which details the ruthless power that cultural ideologies have to define and constrain livable realities.

In ill health, his eyesight failing and finding it impossible to paint, Rossetti would turn to the still unfinished, still unpublished tale of "St. Agnes" yet again in the final weeks of his life. But according to his brother, he neither revised the fragment nor even attempted to add to it. Clearly, the tale continued to confound him. His earlier attempts at a conclusion, in which he had first allowed his protagonist to indulge his expansively Italian artistic passions, only to then violently wrench him back into manful, self-disciplining English compliance, suggest the inescapability of a stark choice: embrace a transgressive artistic identity (marked as illness) and face cultural quarantine, or recant, adopt a culturally approved artistic identity, and enjoy a staid, conventional success. Rossetti couldn't face either alternative. And yet the fact that the tale was there at the end of his career, as it had been at the beginning, suggests that the dilemma at the heart of the story—the irreconcilable dualism of Anglo-Italian's identity—had proven equally inescapable. It had continued to haunt him throughout his career, even as he attempted to live, write, and paint it. This dilemma is evident not only in his work, but in the "readings" of Rossetti's character left after his death by family, friends, and foes alike.

In *Dante Gabriel Rossetti as Designer and Writer* (1889), one of the many volumes of literary history, criticism, and biography that he would write after his brother's death, William Rossetti would argue that "there was a good deal of the Englishman in Rossetti," famously portraying him as "a sort of typical John Bull in a certain unreasoned and impatient preference for Englishmen and things English to foreigners and things foreign . . . [though] for Italy and Italians he had necessarily a fellow-feeling—substantial, though by no means indiscriminate or thorough-going. . . ."[31] Interestingly, then, William suggests that Rossetti himself to a great degree manifested the same sort of English ethnocentrism that was often so evident in the criticism which plagued his work. And yet six years later, William significantly qualified his earlier claim, noting, "I must always regard my brother—in spite of some ultra-John-Bullish opinions and ways—as more an Italian than an Englishman—Italian in temper of mind, in the quasi-restriction of his interest to the beautiful and the passionate, in disregard of those prejudices and conventions that we call 'Philistine,' in general tone of moral perception. And yet he was very far from being like his Italian father, and was wholly unlike his Italian grandfather."[32] What is remarkable about the two comments are their differing contexts. In the first passage, William is describing one of his brother's few attempts at writing political verse, specifically the poem

31. William Michael Rossetti, *Dante Gabriel Rossetti as Designer and Writer* (London: Casssell & Co., Limited, 1889), 135.

32. William Michael Rossetti, *Dante Gabriel Rossetti: His Family Letters* (London: Ellis & Elvey, 1895), 1: 408.

"Wellington's Funeral," written in 1852 after the death of the Duke of Wellington. In the second passage, William is addressing his brother's artistic reputation among his friends and supportive fellow artists, noting in particular Coventry Patmore's praise for his brother's "sweet and easy courtesy," which Patmore marked as "peculiar to his nation" (i.e. Italy).[33] The implications of these two divergent descriptions seem to be that in those relatively rare moments when Rossetti did rise in his art to address commonplace English politics, his views became entirely English, even Bullish. Yet, naturally, inherently, as an artist among friends and fellow artists, he was Italian.

Indeed, unlike his patriotic father Gabriele, who had nurtured dreams of Italian unification and liberation (and even of a return home with his family) until his death in 1851, or in fact his brother William, whose lifelong devotion to Italian nationalism is captured by the epigraph on his tombstone ("Having seen the realization of Italian unity"), Dante Gabriel Rossetti harbored very little interest in politics, Italian or English. As evidenced by his early love of Italian art, his translations of Italian poetry, his love of his own namesake Dante, and his lifelong pursuit in his own work of a distinctly Italian aesthetics of passion, his affinities to Italy were fundamentally personal and artistic, not contemporary or pragmatic. As his niece, Helen Rossetti Angeli, who inherited the role of family historian from her father William, notes of her uncle: "Gabriel had no sentimental attachment to the land of his forefathers, which he never even beheld. He was too Italian for sentimentality, and too deeply absorbed in his art to be disturbed by politico-national sympathies."[34] Or as Rossetti would himself famously write in a letter to Barbara Leigh Smith Bodichon on April 24, 1870, "You see I am an inveterate southerner though I fear no particular patriot."[35]

And yet, if Rossetti's sweet and easy Italian nature dominated in his artistic and personal life, it did so to his great cost whenever its essential *un*-Englishness was detected by ethnocentric and xenophobic Britains, as can frequently be heard in Victorian responses to his art. As his niece suggests, "Gabriel, for all his love of England and things English, and his bluffish English exterior, was not English: he was the son of an exile, and an exile himself to the end. If he did not realize this—and few do realize their actual entity—his friends did, and his enemies. 'Not really an Englishman,' quoth Ruskin in retrospect summary—'A sly Italian' declared Millais's British mother."[36] For many, Rossetti was all too clearly and alarmingly Italian.

33. William Michael Rossetti, *Dante Gabriel Rossetti: His Family Letters*, I., 408.

34. Helen Rossetti Angeli, *Dante Gabriel Rossetti: His Friends & Enemies* (1949; repr., Manchester, NH: Ayer Company Publishers, 1977), 256.

35. Dante Gabriel Rossetti, *Letters of Dante Gabriel Rossetti*, ed. Oswald Doughty and John Robert Wahl (Oxford: Clarendon Press, 1965), II: 854.

36. Angeli, *Dante Gabriel Rossetti: His Friends & Enemies*, 256.

In contrasting the supposedly manageable "home-bred plaques"[37] of England with the "outlandish, unknown, monstrous" influx of the Asiatic cholera that swept into England in the 1830s, the Victorian doctor quoted in the epigraph to this chapter[38] aligns his medical rhetoric with a long-standing tradition of English xenophobia, mirroring and reinforcing the same terminology used so effectively by Victorian literary critics similarly mindful of English national "health." English critics, like their medical colleagues, were driven by fears that a foreign contagion might overwhelm all "known and conventional precautions," and they utilized similarly draconian measures to contain disease. Critically marked as both foreign and dangerous, Dante Gabriel Rossetti would struggle throughout his career to articulate an Anglo-Italian artistic identity that was both personally genuine, and culturally acceptable. Like his antagonist in "St. Agnes," however, Rossetti never quite escaped Victorian critical quarantines, facing a measure of critical scrutiny far above that leveled at his fellow fleshly poets. Viewing his art and reading his poetry in light of this critical opposition, however, one must respect Rossetti's lifelong attempts to mediate a successful closure both to his early tale of "St. Agnes" and to his own search for artistic integrity.

Works Cited

Angeli, Helen Rossetti. *Dante Gabriel Rossetti: His Friends & Enemies*. 1949. Reprint, Manchester, NH: Ayer Company Publishers, 1977.

Ascham, Roger. *The Scholemaster*. 1570. Reprint, Menston, England: Scholar Press, 1967.

Buchanan, Robert. "The Martydom of Madeline." *The Academy* 22 (1882): 11–12.

Codell, Julie F. "Pre-Raphaelites from Rebels to Representatives: Masculinity, Modernity, and National Identity in British and Continental Art Histories, c. 1880–1908." In *Writing the Pre-Raphaelites: Text, Context, Subtext*, edited by Michaela Giebelhausen and Tim Barringer. 53–79. Burlington, VT: Ashgate, 2009.

Dickens, Charles. *American Notes and Pictures from Italy*. The Oxford Illustrated Dickens. London: Oxford University Press, 1957.

[Forman, Buxton]. "The 'Fleshly School' Scandal." *Tinsley's Magazine* 10 (1872): 89–102.

Frawley, Maria H. *A Wider Range: Travel Writing by Women in Victorian England*. Madison, NJ: Fairleigh Dickenson University Press, 1994.

---

37. English writers have long addressed native, English "home-bred" diseases in literature, though usually, as described here, with a measure of (perhaps "fatal") "indifference." In his portrayals of the poverty and disease that plague such socially neglected neighborhoods as "Tom-all-Alone's" in *Bleak House,* for example, Dickens struggles to overcome the apathy of the English upper classes. But though his portrayal of Jo expresses his social outrage at the refusal of his countrymen to take responsibility for the fate of the most vulnerable classes of English society, Dickens does not evince the kind of "phobic" response towards disease that the English typically demonstrated with "foreign" contagions.

38. W. T. Gairdner, *Public Health in Relation to Air and Water* (1862; repr., New York: Routledge, 2001) 5: 15–16.

Gairdner, W. T. "Public Health in Relation to Air and Water." 1862. In *The Early Sociology of Health and Illness.* Vol. 5. Edited by Kevin White. New York: Routledge, 2001.

Haley, Bruce. *The Healthy Body and Victorian Culture.* Cambridge, MA: Harvard University Press, 1978.

Korg, Jacob. *Browning and Italy.* Athens: Ohio University Press, 1983.

Maitland, Thomas [Robert Buchanan]. "The Fleshly School of Poetry: Mr. D. G. Rossetti." *The Contemporary Review* 18 (1871): 334–350.

McGann, Jerome J. "Dante Gabriel Rossetti and the Betrayal of Truth." *Victorian Poetry* 26 (1988): 339–361.

O'Connor, Maura. *The Romance of Italy and the English Political Imagination.* New York: St. Martin's Press, 1998.

Rossetti, Dante Gabriel. *The Collected Works of Dante Gabriel Rossetti.* Edited by William M. Rossetti. 1897. 2 vols. St. Clair Shores, MI: Scholarly Press, n.d., ca. 1969.

———. *Letters of Dante Gabriel Rossetti.* Edited by Oswald Doughty and John Robert Wahl. Oxford: Clarendon Press, 1965.

Rossetti, William Michael. *Dante Gabriel Rossetti as Designer and Writer.* Notes by William Michael Rossetti, including a prose paraphrase of *The House of Life.* London: Cassell, 1889.

———. *Dante Gabriel Rossetti: His Family Letters, with a Memoir by William Michael Rossetti.* London: Ellis & Elvey, 1895.

———. *Pre-Raphaelite Diaries and Letters.* London: Hurst & Blackett Limited, 1900.

Rudman, Harry W. *Italian Nationalism and English Letters: Figures of the Risorgimento and Victorian Men of Letters.* New York: Columbia University Press, 1940.

Ruskin, John. *Ruskin in Italy: Letters to His Parents, 1845.* Edited by Harold I. Shapiro. Oxford: Oxford University Press, 1972.

Sloan, Jay D. "Attempting 'Spheral Change': D. G. Rossetti, Victorian Masculinity, and the Failure of Passion." *The Journal of Pre-Raphaelite Studies* 13 (spring 2004): 5–20.

Trollope, Mrs. [Francis]. *A Visit to Italy.* 2 vols. London: Richard Bentley, 1842.

3

Contracting Xenophobia

Etiology, Inoculation, and the
Limits of British Imperialism

ᦨᕷᦩ

RAJANI SUDAN

Buried in the pages of an 1893 issue of the popular magazine *The Woman At Home* is a small advertisement for Watkins' Cream of Tartar that offers the following recipe:

> Even the worst case of smallpox can be cured in three days. Dissolve one ounce of cream of tartar in a pint of water. Drink this at intervals when cold. It has cured thousands, never leaves a mark, never causes blindness, and avoids tedious lingering.

Quackery was, of course, not uncommon in the Victorian era when medical practices were emerging and solidifying as scientific discourse, and the advertisements for quick fixes to dread diseases had a popular, if uninformed, following. In fact, the popularity of quackery tended to reflect, often with uncanny accuracy, the development of serious medical practices.[1] Watkins' Cream of Tartar was merely continuing a marketing tradition set in mid-Victorian England.

What is remarkable about this recipe, however, is that it is directed toward this *particular* cure of smallpox. Smallpox, endemic in Britain since the seven-

---

1. See Sally Shuttleworth, "Female Circulation: Medical Discourse and Popular Advertising in the Mid-Victorian Era" in *Body Politics: Women and the Discourses of Science*, 47–66. Her work examines the parallel developments of medicine as a science and the dissemination of quackery.

teenth century, had a long, unhappy history of periodic epidemics from 1628 (before people began charting deaths) to the most recent one in 1871. Given the duration of this disease's reign, it is not surprising that an established method for preventing smallpox infection had been in place for a number of decades.

Almost a century before this advertisement appeared, Edward Jenner developed the cowpox vaccine that he then used to inoculate James Phipp and turned the tide of the disease's sway. The unimaginable success of this practice resulted in a series of laws in 1853 that made the smallpox vaccine mandatory among children. But even before this famous event, at a time of greater resistance to the idea of smallpox inoculation (the Royal College of Physicians in London was silent on the matter, the Paris Faculté de Médecine openly hostile), two London physicians successfully argued for its case to members of the Royal Society. John Arbuthnot (1665–1735) and James Jurin (1684–1750) tallied the number of deaths occurring from natural and inoculated smallpox and offered quantitative evidence that fewer people died from inoculated smallpox.[2] Quackery took many forms but it tended to replicate, albeit falsely, the common methodologies developed by medical research: the consumption of pills, for example, to ward off the effects of disease or to cure contracted infections. So why, in the last decade of the century, during the most sophisticated period of medicine Britain had ever known, would this anachronistic old wives' tale of a cure, a recipe without the remotest connection to any prophylactic practice already in place, merit even the small credence of a magazine advertisement?

To answer this question one has to look at the etiology of inoculation, both as medical practice and philosophical concept. The earliest use in English (1589) refers to the grafting of plants. Not surprisingly, then, Lady Mary Wortley Montagu, writing to Sarah Chiswell in April 1717 from Constantinople, conjures this horticultural reference to define what she observed in Turkey:

> Apropos of distempers, I am going to tell you a thing that I am sure will make you wish yourself here. The smallpox, so fatal and so general amongst us, is here entirely harmless by the invention of engrafting (which is the term they give it).[3]

---

2. See Andrea Rusnock, *Vital Accounts: Quantifying Health and Population in Eighteenth-Century England and France* (Cambridge: Cambridge University Press, 2002), 44–45.

3. *Lady Mary Wortley Montagu, Embassy to Constantinople: the Travels of Lady Mary Wortley Montagu* (New York: New Amsterdam Books, 1988), 121. Subsequent references to this text will be cited parenthetically. Whether or not Montagu was, in fact, the champion of Turkish culture she represented herself as being is debatable. What is notable, however, is the way in which she deploys empirical methods to bolster her observations. In this particular example, the French ambassador's

It is unclear whether or not the process Montagu represents was termed "engrafting" in Turkish or whether she was translating a term that had yet to exist in English, but what is clear is the emphasis Montagu places on "here." In her case, it is the town of Adrianople: a place, she assures her interlocutor, that is hardly composed of the "solitude you fancy" but is, rather, an enviable location primarily because of its cultural sophistication. Indeed, she adds, "the French ambassador says pleasantly that they take the smallpox here by way of diversion as they take waters in other countries" (Montagu, 121) offering his testimony to the refinement of the Turkish practice to her disbelieving English correspondent.

Describing the process, Montagu takes pains to emphasize the fact that it is predominantly a female practice:

> There is a set of old women who make it their business to perform the operation. Every autumn, in the month of September, when the great heat is abated, people send to one another to know if any of their family has a mind to have the smallpox. They make parties for this purpose, and when they are met (commonly fifteen or sixteen together) the old woman comes with a nutshell full of the matter of the best sort of smallpox and asks what veins you please to have opened. (Montagu, 121)

She also writes of her intent to "try it on my dear little son," and adds:

> I am patriot enough to take pains to bring this useful invention into fashion in England, and I should not fail to write to some of our doctors very particularly about it if I knew any one of 'em that I thought had virtue enough to destroy such a considerable branch of their revenue for the good of mankind, but that distemper is too beneficial to them not to expose all their resentment the hardy wight that should undertake to put an end to it. (Montagu, 121)

Montagu hardly privileges English physicians and their medical beliefs over the putatively dubious practices of Turkish women in *souks*. Her cynical representation of the British medical profession clearly positions avaricious doctors as obstructions to any kind of innovation, foreign or otherwise. Andrea Rusnock accounts for some of the deep-seated antipathy to the practice,

---

remarks are included to represent the objectivity of her truth-claim. Because his class position corresponds with her own, his opinion is validated—elevated to an articulation of a truth. In *A Social History of Truth: Civility and Science in Seventeenth-Century England* (Chicago: University of Chicago Press, 1994), Steven Shapiro argues that this is an example of the relationship between class, knowledge, and truth claims and is critical to an understanding of the production of early modern epistemology.

arguing that the homeopathic methodology was counterintuitive to the Hippocratic maxim. [4] Rusnock also argues

> Because of its non-European origins, some such as the physician William Wagstaffe, author of the influential pamphlet *A Letter to Dr. Freind Shewing the Danger and Uncertainty of Inoculating the Small Pox* (1722), disparaged inoculation because it was practiced 'by a few *ignorant women,* amongst an illiterate and unthinking People.' And finally, English nationalists raised Hippocratic objections to a practice developed in a foreign land (Turkey) for a foreign people: It could not possibly suit the needs of the Christian, meat-eating, English.[5]

Montagu's remarks challenge such logic. In the same letter to Sarah Chiswell, she dismisses the "Grecian" (Christian) method—one that marks the sign of the cross on the body instead of opening larger veins—as "superstition," noting that this method "has a very ill effect." Her comments about British doctors, then, may also be closely linked to issues of creating and opening a feminine discursive space, something that spurs her to "have courage to war with 'em," and entreat Sarah Churchill to "admire the heroism in the heart of [her] friend" (Montagu, 121–122). However critical Montagu is of the profession, she refrains from an explicit critique of their national identity; by contrast, the patriotism with which she characterizes her intentions enables her to seek foreign *techne*[6] in order to counteract smallpox. Montagu's campaign did in fact trigger important experiments with smallpox inoculation, including the public injection of six Newgate prisoners in August 1721, whose recovery from the disease induced by the inoculation in the following month encouraged Princess Caroline to endorse the practice to members of her own family.

Countering Montagu's defense of Turkish *techne,* Srinivas Aravamudan reads her peregrinations as an example of levantinization, arguing that her turn homeward in the penultimate letter to Abbé Conti and her introduction of inoculation in England together function as a critically renegotiated anglophilia.[7] Certainly the entry of the "Levant" into British cultural consciousness—incorporated as an English term when English merchants negotiated

---

4. Rusnock, *Vital Accounts: Quantifying Health and Population in Eighteenth-Century England and France* (Chicago: University of Chicago Press, 2009), 45.

5. Rusnock, *Vital Accounts,* 45.

6. By *techne,* I refer to the Greek τεχνή, meaning art or craft. The *OED* defines *techne* as both an art, skill, or craft and a principle or method by which something is produced or achieved.

7. Srinivas Aravamudan, *Tropicopolitans: Colonialism and Agency, 1688–1804* (Durham, NC: Duke University Press, 1999), 184–185.

for shipping rights with the Grand Turk in 1579—may have been perceived as a less insidious, milder capitulation to the threat of a darker, more complete fall into alterity.[8] Such "falls" occurred with an alarming frequency in the early days of Fort St. George, for example, and the first governors of Madras were challenged almost daily to keep their British factors British.[9] Montagu's own "fallen" son, Edward Wortley Montagu, Jr., claimed to be Turkish, and spent his life in a vexed relationship with England, claiming to be Muslim to his death in 1776.[10] Defoe's reference to the Levant in the opening of *A Journal of the Plague Year* (1722) may be read as similarly apotropaic. Linking Levantine commerce with the entry of the plague into the European body, Defoe makes a clear connection between trade and disease, and even if conveniently displaced onto Holland, his insouciant comment about the unimportance of the disease's etiology suggests a degree of tolerance to Levantine "goods":

> It was about the beginning of September, 1664, that I, among the rest of my neighbours, heard in ordinary discourse that the plague was returned again in Holland; for it had been very violent there, and particularly at Amsterdam and Rotterdam, in the year 1663, whither, they say, it was brought, some said from Italy, others from the Levant, among some goods which were brought home by their Turkey fleet; others said it was brought from Candia; others

---

8. Fernand Braudel, *The Mediterranean and the Mediterranean World in the Age of Philip II* (Berkeley and Los Angeles: University of California Press, 1995), 254.

9. Purchased by Francis Day in August 1639 from the reigning king, Peda Venkata Raya, Fort St. George emerged from the small strip of land as a factory and warehouse for the trading enterprises of the British East India Company who had finally obtained a *firman* from the Vijayanagara sovereign. The early governors of what came to be known as Madras were hard put to keep their soldiers from sampling the delights of "Black Town" (the indigenous Indian city) and Sir William Langhorn was forced to order the following decrees in 1678:

> 7. It is likewise ordered that both Officers and Souldiers in the Fort shall on every Sabbath day, and on every day when they exercise, weare English apparel; in respect the garb is most becoming as Souldiers, and correspondent to their profession; in penalty of forfiting one months allowance on the Officers part, and half a months allowance on the Private Souldiers part.
> 8. Whosoever he be that shall attempt to get over the walls of the Fort upon any pretence whatsoever, shall for so heinous and grievous an offence be kept in Irons till the shipps arrival; and then, his wages being suspended, be sent home for England, there to receive condigne punishment. . . . .

Henry Davison Love, *Vestiges of Old Madras, 1640–1800, Traced From the East India Company's Records Preserved at Fort St. George and the India Office and From Other Sources,* Vol. I (1913; New York: AMS Press, 1968), 381.

10. See Bernadette Andrea, *Women and Islam in Early Modern English Literature* (Cambridge: Cambridge University Press, 2007). Andrea has done extensive work on the role of Edward Wortley Montagu, Jr., as an alternative (and corrective) to the paradigm of orientalism Edward Said introduced.

from Cyprus. It mattered not from whence it came; but all agreed it was come
into Holland again.[11]

Like the gossips Montagu observed—the "ignorant women" William Wagstaffe scornfully dismissed—infection, for Defoe, travels discursively. While
Aravamudan argues that transported in Montagu's letters about her Turkish
travels is a form of inoculation that strengthens the British corpus against
foreign invasion, Defoe's fictionalized account of 1665 imagines a virulent
disease transmitted "from the letters of merchants and others who corre-
sponded abroad" to the neighborhoods of London with devastating effect.[12]
In this case, levantinization falls short of its tropicopolitan duty, but is this a
paradigmatic failure or the problem of a xenophobic archive?

It turns out the etiology of inoculation extends beyond Montagu's discoveries in early eighteenth-century Constantinople, beyond the introduction of
the practice in the *Philosophical Transactions* of the Royal Society, the Royal
College of Physicians and beyond Jenner's injections. Montagu's letters were
eagerly read by recipients who composed the best and brightest of English
literati. Her appeal to the largely aristocratic medical profession was, for better or for worse, predicated upon the idea of aristocratic privilege and British
pre-eminence.[13] European fantasies about the munificence of Levantine luxury structured the ways in which they imagined the spaces of political power:
the courts of the Grand Signior, the harem, and the hammam. Montagu's
letters—"You will be surprised," she writes to Anne Thistlethwayte in April
of 1717, "at an account [of Turkish homes] so different from what you have
been entertained with by common voyage-writers who are fond of speaking of what they don't know" (Montagu, 125)—have been variously read as
correctives to English travel writers, where she uncovers a highly politicized
feminine discursive space with her entry into the harem and hammam, or
as a replicated masculine gaze into forbidden territory, inflected by feminine
Orientalism.[14] Whatever the case, her epistolary accounts are offered to an
audience defined by the court. Dismissing English travel writers as "common," Montagu reinforces the notion that authentic travel writing is the
privilege of ambassadors who bring back new strategies for negotiating and

---

11. Daniel Defoe, *A Journal of the Plague Year* (Oxford: Oxford University Press, 2010), 3.

12. Defoe, 3.

13. The Royal College of Physicians accepted only graduates of Oxford and Cambridge into
their elite society, thus guaranteeing that the practice of medicine was the province of the nobility.
This didn't mean that others couldn't practice medicine—the field was unregulated by any governmental process—but that the formal appeal Lady Mary Wortley Montagu made was to an audience
composed of her own class.

14. In addition to Aravamudan, see Andrea's powerful argument in *Women and Islam in Early
Modern English Literature.*

countering alterity, not the labor of merchants who are more prone to spread disease and misrepresentation along with their wares.

But there were other voyagers who routinely ventured even further east than the Levant. Working under vastly different circumstances than Lady Mary Wortley Montague and her retinue, British East India Company "servants" contributed an impressive arsenal of foreign *techne* to British archives in the massive correspondence between the Court of Directors in London and their soldiers, factors, merchants, agents, writers, and ministers. These often underpaid, overworked agents, thoroughly taxed by their subordinate relation to powerful Moghul monarchs, had reported from the late seventeenth century onward of the practice of smallpox inoculation in Bengal, but it wasn't until the eighteenth century that these reports were formalized and published in the *Philosophical Transactions*. Robert Coult, for example, writes from Calcutta in 1731:

> Here follows an account of the operation of Innoculation of the Smallpox as performed here in Bengall: taken from the concurring account of Several Brahmans and physicians of this Part of India. The Operation of Innoculation Called by the Natives Tikah has been known in the Kingdom of Bengall as near as I can learn about 150 years and according to the Brahamanian Record was first performed by one Dununtary a Physician of Champanagar, a small town by the Sydes of the Ganges about halfway to Cossimbazaar whose memory is now holden in Great Esteem as being thought the Author of this Operation, which secret, say they, he had Immediately of God in a Dream.[15]

Later, in 1767, J. Z. Holwell discusses the methodology in great detail, noting that the

> Art of Medicine has, in several instances, been greatly indebted to accident; and that some of its most valuable improvements have been received from the hands of ignorance and barbarism: a truth, remarkably exemplified in the practice of inoculation of the small pox. However just *in general* this learned gentleman's remark may be, he will as to his *particular reference,* be surprised to find, that nearly the same salutary method, now so happily pursued in England, (howsoever it has been seemingly blundered upon) has the sanction of remotest antiquity. . . . If the foregoing essay on the Eastern mode of treating small pox, throws any new and beneficial lights upon this cruel and destructive disease or leads to support and confirm the present successful and happy method of inoculation, in such wise as to introduce, into *regular and universal*

---

15. British Library, European Manuscripts, Add. MSS 4432 (ff. 271–272).

practice, the cool regimen and free admission of air, (the contrary having proved
the bane of millions) I shall, in either case, think the small time and trouble
bestowed in putting these facts together most amply recompensed.[16]

Clearly, the transmission and dissemination of this practice predated Montagu and Jenner by a number of centuries, according to these writers, and had
very specific genealogies in Vedic scriptures. Holwell elaborates on Coult's
reference to Brahmin practice:

> The sagacity of this conclusion, later times and discoveries has fully verified,
> at the period in which the *Aughtorrah Bhode* scriptures of the Gentoos were
> promulgated, (according to the Brahmins three thousand three hundred and
> fifty six years ago) this disease must have been of some standing, as those
> Scriptures institute a form of divine worship, with *Poojahs* or offerings to a
> female divinity, stiled by the common people *Gootec Ke Tagooran* (the goddess
> of spots), whose aid and patronage are invoked during the continuance of the
> small pox season, also in the measles, and every cutaneous eruption that is in
> the smallest degree epidemical. Due weight being given to this circumstance,
> the long duration of the disease in Indostan will manifestly appear; and we
> may add to the sagacious conjecture just quoted, that not only the Arabians,
> but the Egyptians also, by their early commerce with India through the Red
> Sea and Gulf of Mocha, most certainly derived originally the small pox (and
> probably the measles likewise) from that country, where those diseases have
> reigned from the earliest known times. . . .[17]

Complaining that the "usual resource of the Europeans is to fly from the
settlements, and retire into the country before the return of the small pox
season,"[18] Holwell gives an eloquent defense of a medical practice that predates both Turkish or European adoption and expands its etiology to include
places that, by the Victorian era, had been dismissed as barbarous, primitive,
and, most importantly, the origins of disease.[19] The notion that methods of
preventing the transmission of smallpox may also have originated from these
sites simply did not register with Victorian cultural consciousness.

Early prophylactics to this powerful disease were transmitted by East
India Company members to London, but no one read their letters—or, if

---

16. BL, EM, Add. MSS 4432 (ff. 285–288).

17. BL, EM, Add. MSS 4432 (ff. 285–288).

18. BL, EM, Add. MSS 4432 (ff. 285–288).

19. One way of accounting for the Turkish origin of smallpox inoculation is to imagine the
transmission of *techne* via trade routes, the same way that "Arabic" numerals (including the concept
of 0) moved from India to Asia Minor via Arabic merchants.

they did, they seemed to have been dismissed as the fantasies of "common voyage-writers"—until Montagu made it her own noble cause. In a preternaturally inoculative fashion, Indian methods of smallpox inoculation had *already* been incorporated into the British corpus before it became a Levantine *cause célèbre* and was officially lodged in the scientific annals of the Royal Society. Paradigms for inoculation existed in the British scientific and medical archive, and yet they were ignored by a population of Britons whose xenophobia seemed to increase with every new Indian purchase acquired through the military contests that now characterized East India Company pursuits. The value of a British archive of scientific epistemology was thus defined by xenophobia. While one could accept and even embrace Lady Mary Wortley Montagu's letters from Constantinople, correspondence from India—a place increasingly defined by primitivism by the time of Jenner's experiments—could be safely and justifiably disregarded and forgotten. Edward Jenner, then, did not have to openly acknowledge the existence of a similar practice when he created his successful cowpox vaccine by the end of the eighteenth century. Yet the disease raged in late nineteenth-century Britain, killing as many as 50,000 people in 1871. The question is: why? The "answer" lies in a complicated ideological amalgam of class, race, gender, and imperial identity that, I argue, is driven by xenophobia.

Nadja Durbach argues that the anti-vaccination movement that started in response to the 1853 vaccination acts was a defining phenomenon for late Victorian England. Pointing out the distinction between inoculation and vaccination, she uncovers the ways in which these two practices are ideologically different:

> . . . inoculation was generally performed by paramedical personnel such as Nanny Holland, who were in direct competition with vaccinating doctors. Indeed, doctors consistently depicted inoculation as a feminine, foreign, folk practice in contrast to vaccination, which they constructed as masculine, English, and expert.[20]

These beliefs replicate William Wagstaffe's fears of consuming foreign bodies. Jenner's experiments with vaccination in the 1790s paid little attention to the practice of variolation that was common with lay practitioners who used live cultures to inoculate their patients except to highlight the dangers of this procedure. But Jenner paid *no* attention to the inoculation process defined by East India Company members. J. Z. Holwell had written to the Royal

---

20. Nadja Durbach, *Bodily Matters: The Anti-Vaccination Movement in England, 1853–1907* (Durham NC: Duke University Press, 2005), 21.

College of Physicians in London well before Jenner's experiments (1767), describing in minute detail the method used by travelling Brahmins for at least the past 150 years (according to his letter), which would fix inoculation in India in the second decade of the seventeenth century, about the time of the first round of East India Company correspondence:

> Previous to the operation the Operator takes a piece of cloth in his hand and with it gives a dry friction upon the part intended for inoculation, for the space of eight to ten minutes, then with a small instrument he wounds, by many slight touches, about the compass of a silver groat, just making the smallest appearance of blood, then opening a linen double rag (which he always keeps in a cloth around his waist) takes from hence 2 small pledgit of cotton that had been emerged with the variolous matter, which he moistens with two or three drops of the *Ganges* water, and applies it to the wound, fixing it on with a slight bandage, and ordering it to remain on for six hours without being moved, then the bandage to be taken off, and the pledgit to remain until it falls off itself. . . . from the time he begins the dry friction, to the tying of the knot of the bandage, he never ceases reciting some portion of the worship appointed, by the *Aughtorrah Bhade,* to be paid to the female divinity before-mentioned. . . . The cotton, which he preserves in a double callico rag, is saturated with matter from the inoculated pustules of the pre-ceding year, for they never inoculate with fresh matter, nor with matter from the disease caught in the natural way, however distinct and mild the species.[21]

I have quoted from Holwell's letter at length to point out that far from using live smallpox cultures that were collected from infected people, the Brah-min method emphasized the danger of such forms of inoculation. It may very well be that the cowpox vaccination that Jenner developed (although there is evidence that cowpox had been used for inoculation before Jenner's experiments) had a higher rate of success than older methods of variola-tion practiced by both Brahmins and Turks. The point is not which method ultimately prevailed. Rather, I am interested in the ideologies that underpin Jenner's complete lack of interest in any previous body of knowledge about smallpox, especially given his apprenticeship to John Hunter (1770), who was elected as Fellow of the Royal Society in 1767, the very year Holwell (who himself was a Fellow of the Royal Society) had published his observa-tions. Returning to Durbach's contention that inoculation was now repre-sented as a "feminine, foreign, folk practice," and drawing upon Wagstaffe's earlier contention that inoculation was practiced "by a few *ignorant women,*

---

21. BL, EM, Add. MSS 4432 (ff. 285–288).

amongst an illiterate and unthinking People,"[22] it would seem as if the distinction between inoculation and vaccination was predicated not as much upon empirical evidence as on ideologies of gender, race, and nationalism. Even if Jenner had had access or had acknowledged access to earlier forms of inoculation, he had to render the method English. Hence the historiographical attention paid to the milkmaids that Jenner observed in Berkeley, who were apparently immune to smallpox according to Jenner's observations. The English milkmaid, Sarah Nelmes (from whose blistered hand he extracted the cowpox "matter"), and even the cow Blossom, from whom Sarah Nelmes had contracted the disease and whose hide still resides, if that's the right word, in St. George's Hospital (where Jenner trained), rewrote both Indian and Turkish scenes of medical innovation as English.[23] Variolation and inoculation, originally either Indian or Levantine in etiology, were thus rendered the pathogenesis of British epistemology that transformed those processes into the far more constructive practice of vaccination.[24] Replacing the Brahmin prayer (*poojah*) to *Gootec Ke Tagooran,* the goddess of spots, whose patronage was sought at every outbreak of smallpox in Bengal, and the invocations to Krishna (who is famously associated with milkmaids) to whom Brahmins would also plead, with the milkmaid lore that Jenner appropriated, Jenner created the conditions in which vaccination could now be read as "masculine, English, and expert." It is, perhaps, a small irony that cowpox is indigenous to England, and that shortly after Jenner published his "discoveries," the demand for cowpox matter grew exponentially so that the proper transportation of the lymph became a powerful issue.[25] Moving from the dangerous urban topography that made it possible for smallpox (and smallpox inoculation) to be imported and interpolated into the body of the metropole, vaccination thus replaced inoculation and relocated the entire method as part of a pastoral landscape that generated its own indigenously produced agent against disease.

Nevertheless, resistance to smallpox inoculation in Victorian England found compelling voices. William Tebb, speaking at the Second International

---

22. Quoted in Rusnock, 45.

23. Smallpox inoculation was also practiced in China and Africa, although the methods varied. Most notably, George Washington ordered his army to be inoculated against smallpox; he may well have observed the African method when he was in Barbados.

24. I might add that, given its Brahmin origins and the sacred status of the cow in Hindu culture, it is a deep irony that cowpox replaced smallpox as the matter of inoculation.

25. See Andrea Rusnock, "Catching Cowpox: The Early Spread of Smallpox Vaccinations, 1798–1810," *Bulletin of the History of Medicine* 83 (2009): 17–36. I want to be very clear about the distinction between English and British. Jenner's situation in the West midlands of England is one that invokes the cultural imperialism at work in British subjectivity. The sovereign body is English. To be a British reinvention, vaccination could have multiple dangerous origins and many could claim the practice as a result of Scottish Enlightenment. But as a specifically English phenomenon, vaccination remained squarely in the domestic center of the sovereign body politic.

Congress of Anti-Vaccinators of 1881, appealed primarily to a deeply rooted sense of Englishness to promote his position, claiming, "Compulsory medicine . . . is opposed to the ancient constitution of England, and is, therefore, a gross infraction of the liberty of the Citizen and of parental rights."[26] In 1896 Walter Hadwen, a doctor and an ardent anti-vaccinator, delivered the following inflammatory speech to a crowd of passionate believers:

> It is not a question merely of the health but of the very lives of the children which are at stake in this matter; and I believe that the present century shall not close until we have placed our foot upon the dragon's neck, and plunged the sword of liberty through its heart. . . . Yes, we are going forward with the 'crazy cry' of liberty of conscience upon our unfurled banner, and we never intend to rest until we get it.[27]

The power and weight of these arguments clearly depends on a strong sense of national identity but one that conceives of Englishness as its robust center. The place of the Irish, the Scots, and the Welsh—to say nothing of South Asia—is strangely eccentric to the discourse of anti-vaccinationists, especially considering that smallpox vaccination was mandatory in colonial India.[28] Despite the rhetoric that William Tebb, for example, used to unite his cause to "the Colonies and the whole of Europe," little attention was paid to inhabitants of those colonies.[29] It seems, then, that the threat was most virulent at the domestic center of the metropole, whose susceptibility to infection needed not only state-sanctioned legislation but also a strong xenophobic voice to police its boundaries.

But what were the boundaries of imperial Britain? Anxiety over colonial borders erupted in a number of different discourses, and in particular, the arena of disease and public health was open to an especially xenophobic rhetoric.[30] Alan Bewell identifies how disease defines boundaries:

---

26. William Tebb, *Sanitation, Not Vaccination the True.* Paper read before Second International Congress of Anti-Vaccinators, October 12, 1881. http//www.whale.to/vaccine/tebb1.html. Accessed 11/15/09.

27. National Anti-Compulsory Vaccination Reporter, 1 October 1883. http://catalogue.nla.gov.au/Record/3256355. Accessed 11/13/09.

28. In *Making a Social Body: British Cultural Formation, 1830–1864* (Chicago: University of Chicago Press, 1995), Mary Poovey locates the social body as a phenomenon that allows social analysts to describe a part of the population as simultaneously problematic (from, say, a moral standpoint) and constructive (from an economic one) as part of an organic whole. This model may account for the eccentricity of other parts of imperial Britain in the debates over vaccination.

29. Durbach, 79.

30. For another reading of boundaries, disease, and "transcultural circulation" in mid-Victorian Britain, see Pamela K. Gilbert's *Disease, Desire, and the Body in Victorian Women's Popular Novels* (Cambridge: Cambridge University Press, 2005).

Cholera crossed many of the boundaries—cultural, geographical, and cli-
matic—that were thought to exist between Britain and its colonial possessions, and by so doing it challenged those boundaries and led to their
reconceptualization. It changed how the British saw themselves and their
place in the colonial world. Significantly, this new understanding emerged
in tandem with a new conception of India, which was now perceived as the
cause, the geographical locus, and the primary exporter of a modern plague.[31]

Although Bewell is referring specifically to cholera, the same arguments can
be made for smallpox's environmental footprint and its newly renegotiated
geographic locus. Victorian England seemed to have rewritten smallpox
as an environmental disease. For example, Alfred Russell Wallace believed
that certain types of environmental conditions caused smallpox: "foul air
and water, decaying organic matter, overcrowding, and other unwholesome
surroundings."[32] Many believed that even if smallpox was clearly transmitted
from person to person, under the right conditions it could spontaneously
generate.[33] For Wallace and other anti-vaccine supporters, the very idea of
integrating disease that was produced by dirty environments as a prophylactic
measure was counterintuitive and nonsensical. But more importantly vaccination signified a dangerously unpatriotic act: a willing renunciation of one's
English fairness, an enthusiastic fall into alterity. Interestingly, about this time
the idea of disease had shifted from having a mercantile mobility—Defoe's
representation of the plague travelling on ships laden with goods from the
Levant—to being fixed in the landscape, typically ones located in India. Writing for *The Lancet*, James Martin argues

> The cholera epidemics which have ravaged various parts of Hindustan since
> 1817, have always originated in and issued forth from India, but not, to my
> knowledge, been imported into India by ships from infected countries. . . . It
> may therefore be inferred, that the cause of the disease, however latent or
> submerged for a time, is never actually absent from the soil of India, or from
> some of its localities."[34]

Once again the rhetoric connecting the environmental origins of smallpox
that anti-vaccinators used to their advantage turns this specific reference to

---

31. Alan Bewell, *Romanticism and Colonial Disease* (Baltimore, MD: The Johns Hopkins University Press, 1999), 244.
32. Quoted in Bewell, *Romanticism and Colonial Disease*, 244.
33. Durbach, *Bodily Matters*, 153.
34. Quoted in Bewell, *Romanticism and Colonial Disease*, 245.

cholera into a paradigm for smallpox as well. As Durbach notes, the distinction between contagious diseases and ones with environmental derivations
was often blurred.[35] The boundaries of Britain were, therefore, continually
vexed by the very project of its imperial expansion. For Victorian Britons
caught up in the anti-vaccination movement it made sense to keep the limits
of disease at a convenient distance, if only to foreclose any possible contact
with the foreign *techne* of inoculation no matter how much it had been
recast as an English practice. As long as one attended to cleanliness and
purity, one could safely suppose to have extirpated the cause of smallpox
so that inoculation was unnecessary and superfluous.[36] Yet this was also the
moment of Britain's cultural triumph as the civilizing missionary. Figures like
Charlotte Bronte's St. John Rivers, "a more resolute, indefatigable pioneer
never wrought," who, in *Jane Eyre,* "labours for his race" and "hews down
like a giant the prejudices of creed and caste that encumber it" loomed large
in literary representation.[37] These contradictory acts may be usefully understood as driven by xenophobia. As I have argued elsewhere, xenophobia is
not simply a fear of the foreign, because how do we understand something
as distinctly foreign without recognizing it within some signifying system
that makes sense to us? Xenophobia operates, then, as a fetish: as something
in which we invest and cathect a good deal of cultural meaning in order to
organize and clarify our own culture and nation as something distinct.[38] It
was possible, then, for the anti-vaccination movement in Victorian Britain to
launch its often vitriolic invective against the Parliamentary body that made
smallpox vaccination mandatory because there was already in place, albeit
nearly invisible—certainly unread by at least one eminent Victorian physician—fragmented epistolary records of the Indian practice of inoculation.

The antipathy toward vaccination articulated at the end of the nineteenth
century marks a distinct shift of Britain's imperial aims. Methods of inoculation forced Britons to suspend, however theoretically, the xenophobia that
structured cultural, metropolitan, and civic British identity. The introduction
of foreign bodies, denatured or not, into the body as a way of warding off
disease appeared to Lady Mary Wortley Montague perfectly sensible, just as
it had to Robert Coult, J. Z. Holwell, and Helenus Scott, another doctor
working for the British East India Company, partially because these intrepid
souls were open to receiving new ideas, but also because their travels placed

---

35. Durbach, *Bodily Matters,* 153.

36. These arguments were posed by Mary Hume-Rothery, John Pickerton (who edited the *Anti-Vaccinator and Public Health Journal*), and J. J. Garth Wilkinson, all virulent anti-vaccinationists.

37. Charlotte Bronte, *Jane Eyre* (New York and London: Norton, 1993), 301.

38. See Rajani Sudan, *Fair Exotics: Xenophobic Subjects in English Literature, 1720–1850* (Phila-delphia: University of Pennsylvania Press, 2002).

them in "contact zones," to borrow Mary Louise Pratt's term, where ecologies of new diseases and biomedical treatments were often patently visible.[39]

Literary representation of smallpox reflected the perceptive shift from eighteenth- to nineteenth-century Britain. John Cleland's tour-de-force, *Memoirs of a Woman of Pleasure* (1748), is probably best remembered for its salacious fantasies of Fanny Hill's life. What's less well known about the novel is its investment in disease. Before commencing her tales of bedroom drama, Fanny Hill describes the conditions that prompted her to follow a life of "pleasure," stating the stark circumstances of her familial situation:

> I was now entering my fifteenth year, when the worst of ills befell me in the loss of my tender fond parents, who were both carried off by the smallpox, within a few days of each other; my father dying first, and thereby hastening the death of my mother, so that I was now left an unhappy friendless Orphan. . . . That cruel distemper which had proved so fatal to them had indeed seized me, but with such mild and favourable symptoms that I was presently out of danger, and what I then did not know the value of, was entirely unmarked.[40]

Cleland's perfunctory remarks about Fanny's girlhood follow a tradition established by eighteenth-century novelists in which the heroine's orphaned circumstances are hastily explained, thus leaving her open, as it were, to a series of adventures that would hardly have been sanctioned by responsible parents. It is no mystery, then, that Fanny's status is a consequence of smallpox, given the ubiquitousness of the disease. Fanny herself, however, is "seized" by this "cruel distemper" which, far from killing her or permanently imprinting her with the marks of its temporary possession, leaves her "entirely" untouched. This small detail acts as the inoculative moment: Fanny's interpolation of the disease that has had such fatal consequences for her flawed parents—her maimed father, mender of fishing nets and her beleaguered schoolmistress mother—renders her infinitely more valuable in the marketplace of social and sexual congress. Rather than remaining in Lancashire to replicate her parents' "scanty subsistence," Fanny is thus able to seek her fortune elsewhere. Having been infected, as it were, by Esther's representations of London's fine sights, she decides "all which [I] imagined grew in London, and entered for a great deal into my determination of trying to come in for my share of them." As she is "entirely" untouched by the marks of smallpox, so Fanny is

---

39. See Mary Louise Pratt, *Imperial Eyes: Travel Writing and Transculturation* (New York: Routledge, 1992).

40. John Cleland, *Fanny Hill, or Memoirs of a Woman of Pleasure* (New York: Penguin, 1985), 40.

"entirely taken up with the joy of seeing myself mistress of such an immence sum" (eight guineas, seventeen shillings in silver). The "mild and favourable symptoms" that characterize her bout of smallpox also seem to inoculate her against the immoral travails of prostitution; her sexual adventures notwith-standing, Fanny accrues a real fortune, a secure marriage, where, "in the bosom of *virtue,* [she] gathered the only uncorrupt sweets" (my italics).[41]

John Cleland's personal history attests to his proximity to the practice of smallpox inoculation. He entered the British East India Company shortly after he left school (1723) and spent 1728–1740 working for the company in Bombay, years where he may very well have known about and observed the practice. After his subsequent return to England, he was arrested in 1748 and put into the Fleet Prison for debtors where he wrote *Memoirs of a Woman of Pleasure,* which was published later that year. London's Smallpox Hospital was built in 1746 with the exclusive purpose of inoculating and treating the poor, and remained the only place where the indigent popula-tion could receive free inoculations. Surely Cleland, fresh from his tenure in Bombay, having been refused any part of the family fortune and languishing in prison over a £840 debt, would pay attention to the horrors of a danger-ous and disfiguring disease facing a young orphaned girl and would include this inoculative fantasy as part of his erotic imaginary.

Literary representation of inoculation, however, makes a definitive turn in the nineteenth century. One of the grand hysterical novels of the fin-de-siècle, Bram Stoker's *Dracula,* reflects, among other things, much of the xenophobic resistance to vaccination. Yet while I would argue that *Dracula* doesn't offer metaphorical allusions to vaccination, as Durbach contends, it is a novel that is concerned with *inoculation* and its various threats. The nov-el's concern with the generalized Victorian anxiety over women's "concealed inner recesses" harboring polluted blood reaches a frenzied climax in the killing of the vampiric Lucy Westenra.[42] Although much of the scene enacts the legitimate consummation of Lucy's "marriage" to Arthur Holmwood,[43] a ceremonial ritual that reinstates his proper place as the Victorian husband and restores sexual civility to Lucy herself, her overdetermined healing speaks to a curiously conflated set of anxieties over borders and boundaries, the environmental etiology of disease, and of the dangers of inoculation. Bewell argues that the definition of contact Britain had with India was problematic:

Spread along the main transportation and commercial arteries of the nine-

---

41. Cleland, *Fanny Hill,* 40.
42. Shuttleworth, "Female Circulation," 56.
43. Bewell, *Romanticism and Colonial Disease,* 244.

teenth century—by river, sea, road, and later by railway—cholera mapped the
many lines of communication between Britain and its colonial possessions.[44]

Cholera replicates the routes taken by smallpox in Defoe's *Journal of the
Plague Year*; the problem with colonial and commercial contact is that diseases that were represented as originating from India were now capable of
moving into the corpus of the metropole. In much the same way, Jonathan
Harker's promising voyage to Castle Dracula in Transylvania results in the
proliferation of vampiric disease that travels by "river, sea, road, and . . . railway" to the very heart of modernity.

Jonathan Harker battles the specter of disease with an arsenal of tools
that are "nineteenth-century up-to-date with a vengeance":[45] his shorthand,
his Kodak, his ordnance survey maps, and the institutions where he seeks
information (British Museum) are all used to confine the etiology of Dracula's
uncanny powers within the walls of his castle where they can remain relatively ineffective, incapable of spreading westward. But they fail. The British
Museum has no maps of Transylvania or Castle Dracula, and certainly no
maps that compare with the ones produced by the military division of the
Board of Ordnance that was first commissioned to charter the Scottish Highlands in order to control Jacobite supporters.[46] The dearth of information
available at the British Museum seems especially trenchant compared with
the wealth of British knowledge the Count commands:

> In the library I found, to my great delight, a vast number of English books,
> whole shelves full of them, and bound volumes of magazines and newspapers.
> A table in the centre was littered with English magazines and newspapers,
> though none of them of very recent date. The books were of the most varied
> kind—history, geography, politics, political economy, botany, geology, law—
> all relating to England and English life and customs and manners. There were
> even such books of reference as the London Directory, the 'Red' and 'Blue'
> books, Whitaker's Almanac, the Army and Navy Lists, and . . . the Law List.[47]

The sheer variety of texts housed in the Count's library embarrasses Harker's
position, and he is reduced to showing photographs of the Count's new
property in Carfax while the Count reads a Bradshaw, familiarizing himself
with railway timetables. Thus, Harker's tools facilitate Dracula's invasion of

---

44. Bewell, *Romanticism and Colonial Disease*, 244.

45. Bram Stoker, *Dracula* (New York: Norton, 1997), 25.

46. The borders of England's cultural imperialism had to be policed as carefully as its colonial
ones: harbored in the heart of the Scottish Highlands is the possibility of a Stuart insurrection.

47. Stoker, *Dracula*, 25.

London. Even Harker's shorthand fails as a *techne* to counter the nightmares of the past that threaten to kill "mere modernity." Dracula reads through Harker: he intercepts Harker's calls for help and replaces them with his own cryptic missives. Stripped quite literally of any suit he has—his clothes, his agency—Harker, unmanned, is left alone in the castle.

Only after Dracula has inoculated London—after he has planted himself in Carfax and opened Lucy Westenra's and Mina Harker's veins—do these tools begin to recover their use. The trains and steamships and railway carriages swiftly pursue Dracula back to his Transylvanian lair. Two knives effectively exterminate Dracula: Harker's *kukri* and Quincey Morris's Bowie. The latter knife with its characteristic cross, wielded by the intrepid Texan, obviously alludes to the promising technologies produced by new Christian "civilized" frontiers. Harker's *kukri* is a little more complicated. Curved like a scimitar, *kukris* were favored by the Nepali Gurkhas in their series of conflicts with the British East India Company that eventually culminated in a war earlier in the century (1814–1816), which is when these knives made their way into England. *Kukris* have a historical connection with the famed eleventh-century Damascus swords fashioned of *wootz,* an early form of carbon steel that was manufactured in India and exported to Damascus from the third to the seventeenth century.[48] Brandishing a weapon that was far more likely to be found in Dracula's armory than in any English store, Harker's triumphant return to the scene of his unmanning is made possible by this inoculative appropriation of older Hindu technologies.

Victorian Britain, mindful of its imperial trajectory, seemed to equate the medical practice of inoculation with a cultural one. Thus far from entertaining the introduction of foreign *techne* into British practice, as Montagu, Coult, Holwell, and Scott were willing to do, many Britons may have read inoculation as an unpatriotic act, a treasonous introjection of the elements of disease into the corpus of the metropole. Clearly as a practice, inoculation becomes increasingly vexed as Britain professes to turn commercial profit from conquest and colonization into the social missionary work that characterized Victorian cultural imperialism, domestic and otherwise. If, as Bewell has argued, the "global expansion of human travel also made possible the *globalization of disease,*" then Victorian xenophobia becomes a strategic defense against infection. Bewell notes that "new colonial disease ecologies" lacked a "uniformity of experiences" and therefore their representation was vexed by the absence of stabilizing structure.[49] Domestic Victorians, fear-

---

48. The manufacture of *wootz* is recorded by Helenus Scott in the *Philosophical Transactions* about the same time as J. Z. Holwell's treatise on smallpox inoculation.

49. Bewell, *Romanticism and Colonial Disease,* 4.

ing the palpable consequences of smallpox epidemics, were prone to locate its etiology elsewhere, in others, thus insuring their cultural immunity to the pathogen.[50] Incorporating pathogenic otherness amounted to declaring oneself the origin of (cultural) disease, and so popularly advertised cures for smallpox were as mild as cream of tartar dissolved in water.

Works Cited

Andrea, Bernadette. *Women and Islam in Early Modern English Literature.* Cambridge: Cambridge University Press, 2008.

Aravamudan, Srinivas. *Tropicopolitans: Colonialism and Agency, 1688–1804.* Durham, NC: Duke University Press, 1999.

Bewell, Alan. *Romanticism and Colonial Disease.* Baltimore, MD: The Johns Hopkins University Press, 1999.

Braudel, Fernand. *The Mediterranean and the Mediterranean World in the Age of Philip II.* Berkeley and Los Angeles: University of California Press, 1995.

British Library, European Manuscripts.

Cleland, John. *Fanny Hill, or Memoirs of a Woman of Pleasure.* Edited by Peter Wagner. New York: Penguin, 1985.

Defoe, Daniel. *A Journal of the Plague Year.* Edited by Louis Landa. Oxford: Oxford University Press, 2010.

Durbach, Nadja. *Bodily Matters: The Anti-Vaccination Movement in England, 1853–1907.* Durham, NC, and London: Duke University Press, 2005.

Gilbert, Pamela K. *Disease, Desire, and the Body in Victorian Women's Popular Novels.* Cambridge: Cambridge University Press, 2005.

Gilman, Sander. *Disease and Representation: Stereotypes of Sexuality, Race, and Madness.* Ithaca, NY: Cornell University Press, 1985.

Love, Henry Davison. *Vestiges of Old Madras, 1640–1800, Traced From the East India Company's Records Preserved at Fort St. George and the India Office and From Other Sources.* Vol. I. 1913. Reprt., New York: AMS Press, 1968.

Montagu, Lady Mary Wortley. *Embassy to Constantinople: The Travels of Lady Mary Wortley Montagu.* Introduced by Devla Murphy. Edited and compiled by Christopher Pick. New York: New Amsterdam, 1988.

National Anti-Compulsory Vaccination Reporter. 1 October 1883. http://catalogue.nla. gov.au/Record/3256355. Accessed 11/13/09.

Poovey, Mary. *Making a Social Body: British Cultural Formation, 1830–1864.* Chicago: University of Chicago Press, 1995.

Pratt, Mary Louise. *Imperial Eyes: Travel Writing and Transculturation.* New York: Routledge, 1992.

Rusnock, Andrea. "Catching Cowpox: The Early Spread of Smallpox Vaccinations, 1798–1810." *Bulletin of the History of Medicine* 83 (2009): 17–36.

———. *Vital Accounts: Quantifying Health and Population in Eighteenth-Century England and France.* Cambridge: Cambridge University Press, 2002.

---

50. See Sander Gilman, *Disease and Representation: Stereotypes of Sexuality, Race, and Madness* (Ithaca, NY: Cornell University Press, 1985).

Shapiro, Steven. *A Social History of Truth: Civility and Science in Seventeenth-Century England*. Chicago: University of Chicago Press, 1994.

Shuttleworth, Sally. "Female Circulation: Medical Discourse and Popular Advertising in the Mid-Victorian Era." In *Body Politics: Women and the Discourses of Science*, edited by Mary Jacobus, Evelyn Fox Keller, and Sally Shuttleworth. 47–66. New York and London: Routledge, 1989.

Stoker, Bram. *Dracula*. Edited by Nina Auerbach and David Skal. New York: Norton, 1997.

Sudan, Rajani. *Fair Exotics: Xenophobic Subjects in English Literature, 1720–1850*. Philadelphia: University of Pennsylvania Press, 2002.

Tebb, William. *Sanitation, Not Vaccination the True*. Paper read before Second International Congress of Anti-Vaccinators. 12 October 1881. http//www.whale.to/vaccine/tebb1.html. Accessed 11/15/09.

4

Charles Dickens, Wilkie Collins, and the Perils of Imagined Others

❦

MARIA K. BACHMAN

Responding to the Indian Mutiny in 1857,[1] an enraged Charles Dickens declared in a letter to Angela Bourdett-Coutts that if he were Commander in Chief in India, he would do his "utmost to exterminate the Race upon whom the stain of the late cruelties rested . . . [and] with all convenient dispatch and merciful swiftness of execution, to blot it out of mankind and raze it off the face of the Earth."[2] Despite his longstanding status as a radical

---

1. In May 1857, soldiers in the Indian army rebelled violently against the British authorities and marched on Delhi. Though the rebellion was multifarious in origin, the immediate cause of the uprising was attributed to the perceived assault on Hindu and Muslim culture with the introduction of the new Enfield rifle. To load the rifle, the sepoys ("soldiers") of native regiments had to bite off the ends of the paper cartridges, which had been reportedly greased with beef tallow (regarded as sacred to Hindus) and pig fat (regarded as unclean by the Muslims). When 85 sepoys in Meerut refused to use the new cartridges, they were imprisoned and sentenced to ten years' hard labor. In retaliation, Indian troops opened the jail and unleashed their fury on the British. The Mutiny spread rapidly through the Bengal Army as the ensuing bloodshed—the widespread killing by the British army of both Indian soldiers and civilians—sent shockwaves throughout colonial Britain. The most horrific of the many atrocities committed during the Mutiny was the Well of Cawnpore incident when, on June 15, Indian rebels massacred captured Europeans, including women and children. See Christopher Herbert, *War of No Pity: The Indian Mutiny and Victoria Trauma* (Princeton, NJ: Princeton University Press, 2009), Gautam Chakravarty, *The Indian Mutiny and the British Imagination* (Cambridge: Cambridge University Press, 2005), Bisvamoy Pati, *The Indian Rebellion* (New York: Oxford University Press, 2007).

2. Charles Dickens, *The Letters of Charles Dickens,* vols. I–XII (Oxford: Clarendon Press, 1965–2002), VIII, 459. Hereafter cited as *Letters.*

social reformer, Dickens's vengeful call to obliterate the sepoys from the face of the earth (an eerie precursor to Mr. Kurtz's call in Conrad's *Heart of Darkness* "to exterminate all the brutes") is hardly an anomaly in Dickens's more public representations of race and empire. Four years earlier, Dickens declared in his weekly journal *Household Words* that he did not "have the least belief in the Noble Savage": "I call him a savage, and I call a savage something highly desirable to be civilised off the face of the earth . . . he is a savage— cruel, false, thievish, murderous; addicted more or less to grease, entrails, and beastly customs; a wild animal."[3] Dickens was not alone in his demand for justice. As Grace Moore points out, the massacre at Cawnpore "unleashed an excess of emotion on a scale that had never been seen before . . . [t]he accusations of rape at Cawnpore, combined with evidence that defenceless women had been hacked to death in cold blood, outraged Victorian Britain and resulted in widespread calls for vengeance."[4] These highly-charged emotions ran rampant as the British reading public was deluged daily with lurid and grisly stories of the alleged atrocities committed by Indian insurgents and reports of British martyrs in the popular press.[5] Articles that were particularly inflammatory included so-called "eyewitness" accounts of rape and cannibalism.[6] Though British investigators dismissed these as either gross exaggerations or complete fabrications,[7] the savagery of the "laughing [Indian] fiends" had become fixed in England's cultural psyche, thus lending credence to Martha Nussbaum's argument that emotions and narrative are mutually constitutive: "Emotions . . . have a narrative structure. The understanding

---

3. "The Noble Savage," *Household Words*, 7 June 1853: 337.

4. Grace Moore, *Dickens and Empire: Discourses of Class, Race, and Colonialism in the Works of Charles Dickens* (Burlington, VT: Ashgate Press, 2004), 119.

5. Graham Dawson, *Soldier Heroes: British Adventure, Empire and the Imagining of Masculinities* (London and New York: Routledge, 1994), 94. Dawson demonstrates how numerous periodicals, including the *Times, Morning Post,* and *Lloyd's Weekly* repeatedly invoked the terms "vengeance" and "extermination" in their accounts of the news from India.

6. For example, in a letter printed in *The Times,* an eyewitness account described "the way in which poor, helpless men, women, and children were slaughtered without a moment's notice," "Escape from Delhi," *The Times,* 17 July 1857, 12. In another letter, a clergyman detailed the ongoing atrocities so that the English people would be "in possession of facts, lest there be any squeamishness about the punishment in store for the brutal and diabolical mutineers. The cruelties, committed by the wretches exceed all belief. They took 48 females, most of them girls of from 10 to 14, many delicately nurtured ladies,—violated them, and kept them for the base purposes of the heads of the insurrection for a whole week. At the end of that time they made them strip themselves, and gave them up to the lowest of the people, to abuse in broad daylight in the streets of Delhi," "The Indian Mutinies," *The Times,* 25 August 1857, 6. In September, *The Times* reported that "[c]hildren have been compelled to eat the quivering flesh of their murdered parents, after which they were literally torn asunder by the laughing fiends who surrounded them." "The Mutinies in India," *The Times,* 17 September 1857, 9.

7. See Jenny Sharpe, *Allegories of Empire: The Figure of the Woman in the Colonial Text* (Minneapolis: University of Minneapolis Press, 1993), 2, 64–66.

of a single emotion is incomplete unless its narrative history is grasped and studied for the light it sheds on the present response."[8] Rather than unleashing actual violence against the Hindu and Muslim sepoys who had rebelled against and murdered English officers, women, and children, Dickens used the extra Christmas number of *Household Words* as a vehicle to publicly vent his fury and to provoke further national hysteria. In a letter to Mrs. Richard Watson, Dickens made clear his intentions for *The Perils of Certain English Prisoners, and Their Treasure in Women, Children, Silver, and Jewels,* a fictive response to the uprising that Dickens collaborated on with his good friend and *Household Words* staff writer, Wilkie Collins:[9]

> I have been very busy with the Xmas number of Household Words, in which
> I have endeavoured to commemorate the foremost of the great English quali-
> ties shewn in Indian, without laying the scene there, or making any vulgar
> association with real events or calamities. I believe it is a rather remarkable
> production, and will make a great noise.[10]

That Dickens intended *The Perils* to "make a great noise" speaks to his own influence as a public figure to encourage and even fix among the mass reading public a cultural psychosis of panic and fear. As Sally Ledger notes, "*Household Words* was unusual amongst high-circulation family weeklies in the extent to which it sought to shape its readers' political opinions."[11] In fact, in the inaugural issue of *Household Words* in 1850, Dickens set forth his

---

8. Martha Nussbaum, *Upheavals of Thought: The Intelligence of Emotions* (Cambridge and New York: Cambridge University Press, 2001), 236. Similarly, in *Understanding Nationalism: On Narrative, Cognitive Science, and Identity,* Patrick Colm Hogan explains how "our emotion systems lead us to select, segment, and structure the world in the form of stories . . . all defined and organized by feeling" (Columbus: The Ohio State University Press, 2009), 187.

9. In the 1850s, Charles Dickens, who was at the height of his popularity, and Wilkie Collins, who was still a relatively unknown writer, collaborated on a number of short stories for the Extra Christmas numbers of *Household Words.*

10. Dickens to Mrs. Richard Watson, 7 December 1857 (*Letters,* VIII, 487). Similarly, in a letter to his *Household Words* colleague Henry Morley, Dickens explained that he "wish[ed] to avoid India itself" but wanted a setting "in which a few English people—gentleman, ladies, and children—a few English soldiers, would find themselves alone in a strange wild place and liable to hostile attack" (*Letters,* VII, 469).

11. Sally Ledger, *Dickens and the Popular Radical Imagination* (Cambridge: Cambridge University Press, 2007), 188. According to Harry Stone, Dickens aimed for and engaged a wide audience in *Household Words:* "Though [the journal] was directed primarily to members of the middle class, it was designed to appeal to many others. It was cheap enough and popular enough to be read by the literate lower classes, and it was interesting and diversified enough to attract the leisured as well." Moreover, *Household Words* very quickly became a "force to be reckon[ed] with," boasting an impressively large circulation with weekly sales averaging between 36,000 and 40,000 (the daily average for the *London Times*). In *The Uncollected Writings of Charles Dickens, Household Words 1850–1859,* Vol. I (Bloomington: Indiana University Press, 1968), 21.

purpose for the journal in a manifesto of sorts titled, "A Preliminary Word": "We aspire to live in the Household affections, and to be numbered among the Household thoughts, of our readers . . . [I]n this summer-dawn of time," the reader will be introduced to "the stirring world around us, the knowledge of many social wonders, good and evil."[12] While the journal would employ a variety of writers, its object was to achieve its cohesiveness through a distinct single voice, the ethnocentric Dickensian vision of life.[13] Dickens, and by extension, *Household Words,* imagined a community of English readers who would be bound together through a common discourse known as "Household affections." As Sara Ahmed notes, "a community of shared witnessing does not require subjects to be co-present, nor does is require that the speech act be mediation."[14] More specifically, Dickens's journal would bring together a community of shared witnessing to "the stirring world around us" and, in doing so, create a kind of cultural nationalism. This resonates with Benedict Anderson's concept of the nation as an imagined community that was fortified through print media.[15] The nation, Anderson writes, is imagined because "members . . . will never know most of their fellow members . . . yet in the minds of each lives the image of their communion."[16]

In transposing narrative events from India in 1857 to a British mining colony off the coast of Central America in 1744, Dickens claimed that he

---

12. "A Preliminary Word," *Household Words,* 30 March 1850, 1.

13. Stone, 14. Indeed, as the editor and publisher of *Household Words,* Dickens exercised considerable control over contributors, not only negotiating contracts, but also influencing and revising their work with regard to content, structure, and length. "The featuring of Dickens's name on the masthead and on the running heads, the suppression of all other by-lines and signatures, the accommodation of all views (whether on politics, funerals, education, or prisoners) to those Dickens held . . . [were all intended] to create a coherent identity" (Stone, *Uncollected Writings,* 14). As Lillian Nayder has pointed out, "Dickens allowed for a range of opinion . . . but he carefully monitored that range, defining and defending its boundaries." In *Unequal Partners: Charles Dickens, Wilkie Collins, and Victorian Authorship* (Ithaca, NY and London: Cornell University Press, 2002), 19.

14. Ahmed reminds us that "the speech act is always spoken to others, whose shared witnessing of the disgusting thing is required for the affect to have an effect." In *The Cultural Politics of Emotion* (New York: Routledge, 2004), 94.

15. The nation is a community, according to Anderson, that is "always conceived as a deep, horizontal comradeship." In *Imagining the Nation: Reflections on the Origin and Spread of Nationalism* (New York and London: Verso), 6–7. Following from Anderson, Homi Bhabha writes in *Nation and Narration,* "the very act of narrative performance interpellates a growing circle of national subjects" (New York: Routledge, 1990), 297. Bhabha extends his argument for understanding nations and cultures as "narrative" constructions in *The Location of Culture* (New York: Routledge, 1994),

16. As historian Bradley Thayer similarly notes, "When people identify with their nation, they are identifying with a wider kinship or with a fictive 'super-family.'" Thayer goes on to define the nation as a social group that "shares a sense of homogeneity, even if that homogeneity is illusory, based on ethnic as well as linguistic and cultural factors, such as a common language, territory, culture, and customs. This homogeneity delineates them from other nations . . . and nationalism implies fealty to one's nation." In *Darwin and International Relations: On the Evolutionary Origins of War and Ethnic Conflict* (Lexington: The University Press of Kentucky, 2004), 225–226.

wanted to avoid direct reference to Cawnpore and to instead describe fictively the heroism demonstrated by the British civilians captured during the Indian Mutiny. Given that Dickens's "influence could be exerted immediately and widely" as Stone notes,[17] clearly the propaganda function of this fictive analogue had a much broader and far-reaching purpose. Through such a geographic and historical displacement, Dickens could "stoke the fires of empire"[18] by extending a fear and distrust of the other[19] while also amplifying an already festering nationalism. As Thayer argues, people have "strong primordial attachments to their nation, and when appeals or exhortations are made by the leaders on this basis, for purposes of unity, defense, or aggression, they will respond vigorously."[20] Certainly if there was any doubt as to whether Dickens could be identified as "a leader," consider the following remark by the London *Times:* "The writer who would touch a national theme at all must have some claim to be national himself—national in his fame or national in his sympathies; and we question if any one of his harshest critics will deny that this qualification is possessed by Mr. Charles Dickens."[21] A reviewer for the London *Times* similarly noted the obligation of the novelist to assume a "patriotic interest in political crises": though "there is no mention of India or the Crimea in [*The Perils's*] pages . . . the moral elements are the same, in either the historical events and in the ideal narrative, and there is so far an identity in both *series of transactions* that the novelist may be charged with a public function and convicted of a patriotic interest in political crises."[22] Strategically published as the extra Christmas number of *Household Words* in 1857, *The Perils* functions as such a "patriotic" transaction—an affective economy that circulates, both literally and figuratively,

---

17. Stone, 21.

18. See Laura Peters, "'Double-dyed Traitors and Infernal Villains': *Illustrated London News, Household Words,* Charles Dickens and the Indian Rebellion," in *Negotiating India in the Nineteenth-Century Media.* Similarly, Patrick Brantlinger points out that relocating *The Perils* to South America rather than East India "does not provide [Dickens] the distance needed for considering the Mutiny dispassionately. Rather, it extends his view of the Mutiny to other parts of the Empire." In *Rule of Darkness: British Literature and Imperialism,* 1830–1914 (Ithaca, NY and London: Cornell University Press, 1990), 207.

19. For Dickens, the atrocities committed at Cawnpore were not unique to the Hindus and Muslims but to *all* nonwhite races.

20. Thayer, *Darwin and International Relations,* 228.

21. [Anon.], "Charles Dickens's Christmas Story," *The Times,* 24 December 1857, 4.

22. [Anon.], "Charles Dickens's Christmas Story," 4 (my emphasis). Indeed, both contemporary and modern critics have noted *The Perils's* clear parallels to the Indian Mutiny. In "Dickens and the Indian Mutiny," William Oddie points out that the character of the "sambo" Christian King George in *The Perils* is based on the real-life Indian leader, Nana Sahib, who ordered the English massacres, and the incompetent and ineffectual Commissioner Pordage is based on the lieutenant governor of India during 1857 who has been nicknamed "Clemency Canning." In *The Dickensian* 69 (1972): 3–15.

the horror of the events at Cawnpore and the fears of subsequent assaults on England by barbaric adversaries.[23] As Thayer points out, "Good propaganda requires not just the leaders or the elites to advance the message . . . they must also transmit a message that resonates with the masses. Messages based on 'us' versus 'them,' and those that inflate one nation at the expense of others or of minorities all too often resonate very well."[24] Thus, we can begin to see how xenophobia, the fear and distrust of all that is foreign, is bodied forth from ethnocentric thinking.[25]

In *The Cultural Politics of Emotion,* Sara Ahmed theorizes provocatively on how emotions, particularly hate and fear, work to shape the "surfaces" of individual and collective bodies. Following Ahmed, I am interested in those cognitive and affective processes that drive xenophobia, and in the ways that a text such as *The Perils* delineates such patterns of understanding and inference. Specifically, I explore how fear and loathing of foreigners are produced in the text and beyond as "effects of circulation." As Thayer explains, "Nations are likely to have a strong sense of xenophobia where the state either encourages it explicitly, through the speeches and actions of its politicians *and other elites,* or implicitly, by not opposing xenophobic arguments."[26] First however, a brief note: Employing the term *xenophobia* to describe the antipathy the English felt towards foreigners in the nineteenth century is certainly anachronistic—according to the *Oxford English Dictionary,* "xenophobia" does not enter the English language until 1909.[27] This is not to say, however, that fear of direct contact with strangers was non-existent in Victorian England; on the contrary, not only were xenophobic sentiments easily provoked at mid-century, but xenophobic discourses, practices, and ideologies were widespread and part and parcel of the English imaginary.

As a collaborative endeavor, *The Perils* highlights the curious mix of internationalism and xenophobia that defined Britain's expanding empire. *The Perils* consists of three chapters—Dickens wrote the first and third, describing the daily life of the English colonists on the island of Silver-Store prior to the pirate attack ("The Island of Silver-Store") and their eventual escape

---

23. According to Paul Schlicke, the circulation of the Extra Christmas Numbers—over 80,000—more than doubled that of *Household Word*'s weekly circulation. In *Oxford Reader's Companion to Dickens* (Oxford and New York: Oxford University Press, 1999).

24. Thayer, *Darwin and International Relations,* 252.

25. See Vernon Reynolds, Vincent Falger and Ian Vine, *The Sociobiology of Ethnocentrism* (London: Croom Helm, 1987). According to Reynolds et al., ethnocentrism is the conscious or unconscious belief that one's own culture/community/race is superior to all others and the tendency to be unaware of the biases involved.

26. Thayer, *Darwin and International Relations,* 258 (my emphasis).

27. According to the *Oxford English Dictionary,* "xenophobia" can mean a fear of, or aversion to, not only persons from other countries but also persons of other cultures, subcultures, and subsets of belief systems.

("The Rafts on the River"), while Collins's second chapter ("The Prison in the Woods") functions as a captivity narrative of sorts, chronicling the trials and tribulations of the colonists after they are attacked and imprisoned in the jungle by a band of so-called ruthless buccaneers. Dickens's sections of the tale fit into what Patrick Colm Hogan would describe as the "heroic narrative prototype," a universal narrative that is fundamental to "the organization of nationalist thought, feeling, and action in highly consequential ways." It lays the groundwork, in other words, for certain cognitive dispositions. The heroic prototype, specifically, "sets out a malevolent attack by an out-group— usually an invasion by a foreign power—as the absolute and singular origin of the narrative conflict." Moreover, this prototype "celebrates certain martial virtues, such as courage and loyalty . . . [and] is based on . . . an ethics of defense, an ethics of supporting one's in-group in times of conflict."[28]

Dickens's depiction of the "Sambo"[29] Christian King George, a mixed-race figure—an African and American Indian, who turns out to be a "double-dyed traitor, and a most infernal villain"[30]—and the other "savages" is clearly an attempt to amplify the fear and loathing towards non-English others that erupted in the aftermath of Cawnpore. Consider the opening pages of the narrative where Dickens's narrator Gill Davis (an illiterate private in the British Royal Marines) describes most unapologetically his violent antipathy towards this "barbarous" racial hybrid:

> Now, I confess, for myself, that on that first day, if I had been captain of the Christopher Columbus . . . I should have kicked Christian George King— who was no more a Christian than he was a King or a George—over the side, without exactly knowing why, except that it was the right thing to do. (2)

Davis's inexplicable loathing of Christian King George (he goes so far as to call him "a cannibal") extends more generally to the natives: "I have stated myself to be a man of no learning, and, if I entertain prejudices, I hope allowance may be made. I will confess to one. It may be a right one or it may be a wrong one; but, I never did like Natives, except in the form of oysters" (4). By virtue of his common origins (he is an English "founding child" who has "had a hard life"), Gill Davis's sentiments would likely have been received sympathetically, if not unquestioningly, by the middle- and working-

---

28. Patrick Colm Hogan, *Understanding Nationalism: On Narrative, Cognitive Science, and Identity* (Columbus: The Ohio State University Press, 2009), 169, 183, 195.

29. The British in India referred disparagingly to the natives there as "Sambos."

30. Charles Dickens, "The Perils of Certain English Prisoners and Their Treasure in Women, Children, Silver, and Jewels," *Household Words* (Extra Christmas Number), 7 December 1857, 9. Subsequent references to this text will be cited parenthetically.

class readers of *Household Words*—witnesses, so to speak, who are united in their shared aversion to foreign others: "it was the right thing to do." As Ahmed explains, hate works to form and secure collectives: it "works to stick or to bind the imagined subjects and the white nation together."[31] Indeed, the London *Times* corroborates Davis's wrath by referring to Christian King George as "an obsequious rascal." Similarly, Gill Davis's repeated derogatory references to the pirates as "savages," "devils," "demons," and "serpents" are examples of the generative effects of words, words which are formative of "Household affections" and which thus contribute to the narrative's discourse of xenophobia. Such words, according to Ahmed "create impressions of others as those who have invaded the space of the nation, threatening its existence."[32] *The Perils*—at least in the two chapters Dickens contributes—constructs the bodies of these foreign others as non-human, as fearful and threatening, precisely because they have gotten too close.

Focused primarily on the pirate attack and the so-called valor of the English colonists' efforts to ward off the "swarms of devils," the narrative energy of Dickens's first chapter is realized through a discourse of fear, a rhetorical strategy that is meant to provoke in his readers the sense that danger, dread, and fear are all-pervasive and lurking around every corner. As Hogan explains, "a crucial aspect of emotional response and causal attribution is [the] assumption that agents have a dispositional attitude toward us."[33] After the guards of Silver Store have been lured away to the mainland "to rid the world"[34] of those "pillaging and murdering pirates," the unsuspecting Davis and the other officers who have been charged with protecting the silver, women, and children of the settlement are attacked and quickly overpowered by their deceptive assailants.

---

31. Sara Ahmed, *The Cultural Politics of Emotion*, 46.

32. Moreover, in *Making the Social World: The Structure of Human Civilization* (New York: Oxford University Press, 2009), philosopher John Searle explains how a single, linguistic operation, repeated over and over, works to create and maintain the complex structures of social institutions. These institutions serve to create and distribute power relations that are pervasive and often invisible.

33. Hogan, *Understanding Nationalism*, 179.

34. This phrase, of course, is a clear echo of Dickens's desire to "exterminate the Race upon whom the stain of the late cruelties rested" (See Dickens to Angela Burdett-Coutts, note 2) and unequivocally resonates with the striking inflammatory rhetoric of "Our Indian Empire" published in *Bentley's Miscellany* 42 (September 1857): 258–265.

> We consider that the mutiny or insurrection, or whatever it may be, must be coped with, and the most exemplary severity displayed against the ruffians who have so ruthlessly shed English blood. For them there is no excuse, no palliation; and while yielding to the lust of power, they have degraded themselves below the level of brutes. Every wretch who has been engaged in these fearful excesses must be exterminated, trodden under foot like noxious vermin. (264)

> At that terrible word "Pirates!"—for, those villains had done such deeds in
> those seas as never can be told in writing, and can scarcely be so much as
> thought of—cries and screams rose up from every part of the place. (10)

Aided by the "treacherous mulatto" Christian George King—a betrayal
that serves to validate Davis's immediate antipathy towards him[35]—the
"whole crowd of Pirates" who lay siege to the English garrison include
"Malays, . . . Dutch, Maltese, Greeks, Sambos, Negroes, and Convict Englishmen from the West India Islands . . . some Portuguese, too, and a few
Spaniards" (12). The barbaric adversary is no longer just the Indian sepoys,
but rather a frighteningly diverse group of bloodthirsty others—"the scum
of all nations" (33)—who are all too capable of unspeakable atrocities. "The
worst men in the world picked out from the worst, to do the cruelest and most
atrocious deeds that ever stained it" (33).[36] As Ahmed notes, "fear responds
to what is approaching rather than what is already here."[37] The level of terror
is raised even further in this section of the narrative as the colonists are not
only completely taken by surprise, but they are also completely outnumbered
as well: "The cry arose again, and there was a terrible cry and confusing rush
of the women into the midst of the struggle. In another moment, something
came tumbling down upon me that I thought was the wall. It was a heap of
Sambos who had come over the wall; and four men who clung to my legs
like serpents" (13). During the siege, Miss Maryon, the female embodiment
of an imperiled England, exacts a promise from Davis: "[I]f we are defeated,
and you are absolutely sure of my being taken, you will kill me. . . . And if
you cannot save me from the Pirates living, you will save me dead" (10). The
implication here of course is that rape and other unnamable violations are
among the numerous atrocities the vicious pirates are all too willing to commit. More significantly, this narrative detail provokes a kind of ruminative
anger that strategically repeats the horror of interracial rape at Cawnpore.[38]

---

35. Christian King George's betrayal was just as surprising to the English colonists as the sepoy
insurgency was to the British in 1857.

36. This resonates with the ongoing incendiary reports in the popular press of the horrific
crimes that "barbarous" others were committing against the English people in India. In one letter
to *The Times*, for example, a military officer reported: "Give full stretch to your imagination—think
of everything that is cruel, inhuman, infernal, and you cannot then conceive anything so diabolical
as these demons in human form have perpetrated." "The Indian Mutinies: The Latest from Delhi,"
3 August 1857, 5.

37. Ahmed, *The Cultural Politics of Emotion*, 65. Ahmed further explains, the "language of fear
involves the intensification of 'threats,' which works to create a distinction between those who are
'under threat' and those who threaten. . . . Through the generation of 'the threat,' fear works to align
bodies with and against others" (72).

38. Davis soberly replies, "I shall not be alive to do so, Miss, I shall have died in your defence
before it comes to *that*" (my emphasis, 10).

Such an emotional recollection is what fuels xenophobia. As Hogan notes, "the crucial factor in sustaining and intensifying anger is the repeated recollection the anger-provoking incident."[39]

In Chapter II of *The Perils*—"The Prison in the Woods"—we see Collins's mutinous attempt to disrupt and destabilize Dickens's narrative vengeance particularly, and a xenophobic ideology more generally.[40] While Dickens attempts to bring his narrative to fever pitch by describing how the "the howling, murdering, black-flag waving, mad and drunken crowd of devils" (33) had treacherously overcome the unsuspecting English colonists and threatened to commit "the cruellest and most atrocious deeds," Collins diffuses that chaotic and fearful scene by revealing Dickens's "barbarous Pirates, scum of all nations" (33) as a band of cosmopolites, a wholly civil and unified regiment who are interested primarily in booty rather than bloodshed. They hold the colonists hostage as security for the retention of the stores of silver. Ironically, they are simply plundering what the English have already plundered: the natural resources of the land, treasure that rightfully belongs to neither group.

Moreover, the supposed imprisonment and subjugation of the English colonists is depicted by Collins as being anything but perilous. The sense of unfathomable terror that marks Davis's description of the English captives as they are torturously marched inland "to unknown sufferings and unknown fate" (18) is quickly diffused in "The Prison in the Woods" by the comically idyllic reality of their journey into a pre-Industrial pastoral landscape:

---

39. Hogan continues, "once the process of recollection and intensified frustration has begun, it tends to be self-perpetuating . . . as priming effects accumulate the anger circuit pervades our thought more fully, it comes to affect the way we interpret current conditions and imagine future possibilities, even outside the original context of the incident" (*Understanding Nationalism,* 111).

40. "The Prison in the Woods" appears as Chapter II in *The Perils of Certain English Prisoners, Household Words,* 7 December 1857, 14–30. Collins's unattributed contribution to *The Perils* anticipates his more complex explorations of imperial culture in his *Household Words* essay, "A Sermon for Sepoys" (27 February 1858, 244–247) and his novel, *The Moonstone* (1870). While he describes the sepoys in "A Sermon" as members of a treacherous race, he nevertheless calls into question widespread assumptions of English (and by extension, Christian) superiority by arguing for a kind of cultural relativism:

> While we are still fighting for the possession of India, benevolent men of various religious denominations are making their arrangements for taming the human tigers in that country by Christian means . . . [I]t might, perhaps, not be amiss to preach to the people of India. . . . to begin the attempt to purify their minds by referring them to the excellent moral lessons which they may learn from their own Oriental literature (Collins, 244).

And in *The Moonstone* Collins calls into question the prevailing ideology of Anglo-Saxon superiority that the English are more civilized than their colonial subjects See for instance, Tim Carens, "Outlandish English Subjects in *The Moonstone*" in *Reality's Dark Light: The Sensational Wilkie Collins* (Knoxville: University of Tennessee Press, 2003).

> The land that lay before us was wild and open, without fences or habitations. Here and there, cattle wandered about over it, and a few stray Indians. Beyond, in the distance, as far as we could see, rose a prospect of mountains and forests. Above us, was the pitiless sun, in a sky that was too brightly blue to look at. Behind us, was the calm murmuring ocean. . . . (18)

The sense of imminent peril for the captives fades further as they are described as being "not half so much broken in spirit by troubles . . . as some persons might be apt to imagine" (17). Moreover, the captured sailors are depicted as bearing a striking resemblance to Odysseus' men in the land of the Lotus-Eaters: "[t]hey sat together, chewing their quids and looking out good humouredly at the sea, like a gang of liberty-men resting themselves on shore. 'Take it easy, soldier,' says one of the six . . . 'And, if you can't do that, take it as easy as you can'" (17). In addition to the "torture" of their daily hike through lush tropical forests, "the gentlefolks [of] England" are compelled to sit, eat, and sleep on lush flowerbeds, "natural carpet[s] of beauty, of the sort that [are] painted in pictures with pretty fairies dancing on it" (17). Meanwhile, as the "prisoners" travel deeper into the dense forest, the sense of foreboding upon which Davis is so insistent somehow rings false: "We entered the forest, leaving behind us the last chance of escape, and the last hope of ever getting back to the regions of humanity and civilization" (20).

While Dickens had intended to showcase in *The Perils* "the best qualities of English character . . . shewn in India,"[41] Collins explicitly challenges that editorial imperative (as well as presumptions about British superiority) in his depiction of the English captives as being weak, incompetent, and completely lacking in self-confidence. In addition to the Pirate Captain (Pedro Mendez)'s repeated references to the prisoners as "English fools," Davis is all too aware of his countrymen's shortcoming as he reflects doubtfully on their fitness for "encountering bodily hardship and fatigue[,] . . . mental suspense and terror" (16). Davis reports that Mr. Pordage, the English commissioner, "is the most helpless individual in our unfortunate company" and a most ineffectual leader: his "unfortunate brains seemed to be completely discomposed as his Diplomatic coat" (16). Indeed, Pordage's position as Commissioner is dubious at best. He assumed "lawful" possession of the Island after "some Sambo chief or other had got drunk" (5) and was compelled to sign a document that transferred power. Unlike the Pirate Captain, Pordage has no plan of escape because, he tells his fellow prisoners, "I cannot take cognizance of our situation. No memorandum of it has been drawn up; no report in connexion with it has been presented to me" (16). Moreover, he defends his

---

41. Dickens to Mrs. Richard Watson, 7 December 1857 (*Letters,* VIII, 487).

inability to take charge as follows: "I cannot possibly recognise it until the necessary minutes and memorandums and reports have reached me through the proper channels. When our miserable situation presents itself to me, on paper, I shall bring it under the notice of Government" (16). And, in addition to Pordage's incompetence and "wanderings of mind," Sergeant Drooce is described as bordering on "stark mad[ness]" after sustaining a cut on his head in the attack and being unable to acclimate to the "heat of the climate" (16).

Though Collins does not retreat from casting the Pirate Captain and the native laborers as "other,"[42] his depiction is far from complicit with the xenophobic rhetoric that frames Dickens's two chapters. Despite Miss Maryon's plea to Gill Davis to "Dread the Pirate Captain . . . for the slightest caprice of his may ruin all our hopes" (27), Collins completely undercuts Dickens's depiction of the villainous pirate. No longer are associations of treachery with foreignness located in this "wild Portuguese demon." Instead, this diminutive "weazen, monkey-faced man"—who has a predilection for brightly colored fabrics embroidered with beads and feathers, three-cornered hats, gold and diamond jewelry, and scented handkerchiefs—bears a much closer resemblance to those "dandies in the Mall in London" than he does to the sadistic villain Dickens makes him out to be.[43] As Jared Diamond notes, "xenophobia comes especially naturally to our species" and "because so much of our behavior is culturally rather than genetically specified, and because cultural differences among human populations are so marked. . . . those features make it easy for us, unlike wolves and chimps, to recognize members of other groups at a glance by their clothes or hair style."[44] Following Diamond, we can see how Collins's depiction of the Pirate Captain and his band of buccaneers functions instead to ameliorate such xenophobic impulses by reducing in-group/out-group distinctions.

Davis notes that "judging by appearances," Mendez is the "very last man [he] would have picked as likely to fill a place of power among any body of men" (14). And Tom Packer, one of the captured British Marines, is incredulous that he is being held prisoner by someone as unthreatening as Mendez: "'I can stand a good deal,' whisper[ed] Tom Packer to me, looking hard at his guitar; 'but confound me, Davis, if it's not a trifle too much to be taken

---

42. As Davis recounts, "We sat on flowers, eat on flowers, slept on flowers . . . [i]t was a sight not easily described, to see niggers, savages, and Pirates, hideous, filthy, and ferocious in the last degree to look at, squatting about grimly on a natural carpet of beauty" (18–19).

43. Bhabha suggests that "colonial mimicry is the desire for a reformed recognizable Other, *as a subject of difference that is almost the same, but not quite* . . . the discourse of mimicry is constructed around an ambivalence. *The Location of Culture*, 122.

44. Jared Diamond, *The Third Chimpanzee: The Evolution and Future of the Human Animal* (New York: HarperCollins, 2006), 220.

prisoner by such a fellow as that!" (28). Despite the picture Collins gives us of the "murderous thief" Mendez, "languishing . . . with a nosegay in the bosom of his waistcoat" and strumming tunes on his skull-and-crossbones emblazoned guitar, "The Don" (as he is known to his men) is not to be underestimated. According to Bhabha, "the paranoid threat from the hybrid is finally uncontainable because it breaks down the symmetry and duality of self/other, inside/outside."[45] And, as Anne McClintock points out in *Imperial Leather,* "while cross-dressing, drag, passing, camp and voguing are all, generally speaking, forms of mimicry, they also tend to enact very different cultural possibilities."[46] Davis, in fact, finds it astonishing that "there was not one of his crew, from his mate ("a big hulking fellow") to his cabin-boy, who did not obey him as if he had been the greatest monarch in the world" (14). Moreover, Mendez possesses a cultural sophistication that is completely lacking among the English: he is a polyglot who is able to speak eloquently "in any tongue he liked;" he plays music;[47] and most important, he possesses exemplary leadership and diplomatic skills. He commands his multinational, multiethnic band of pirates with absolute authority and devises a masterful plan to hold the English colonists hostage so that the British Royal Navy cannot attack them or reclaim possession of their treasure:

> Hearing the clearness with which he gave his orders; knowing what the devil-
> ish scheme was that he had invented for preventing the recovery of the Trea-
> sure, even if our ships happened to meet and capture the pirates at sea. . . . I
> began to understand how it was that this little, weak, weazen, wicked spider
> had got the first place and kept it among the villains above him. (16)

Collins further attempts to complicate in-group/out-group distinctions in the scene where the prisoners and their "barbarous" captors share a meal together. At first glance, this cross-cultural encounter, because it takes place over food and is "bound up in 'what is eaten,'" fits Ahmed's paradigm of the "disgust encounter": "Disgust operates as a contact zone; it is about how things come into contact with other things."[48] And while food preferences may be one of the most familiar aspects of ethnocentrism—indeed, most cultures have distinct dietary habits and preferences that are a significant part of their group identity—Collins suggests that xenophobic sentiments

45. Bhabha, *The Location of Culture,* 165.

46. Anne McClintock, *Imperial Leather Race, Gender, and Sexuality in the Colonial Contest* (London: Routledge, 1995), 68.

47. Gil Davis is more incensed than astonished by the pirate captain's musical inclinations: "To think of the murderous thief having a turn for strumming tunes, and wanting to cultivate it on such an expedition as ours!" (18)

48. Ahmed, *The Cultural Politics of Emotion,* 85–87.

need *not* inevitably follow from ethnocentrism. During the march through the jungle, Davis recounts how they had to "share the miserable starvation diet of the country"—black beans and "flat cakes made of Indian corn" (tortillas)—with the Indians and the Sambos. Though he is disgusted initially at the "dirty manner in which the Indians prepared" the food (19), the English prisoners, after a bit of "grumbling among [the] men" and "some little fretfulness among the children," willingly partake of this "poor supper" (19). Even though the sharing of food across ethnic boundaries is necessitated by practical concerns—the prisoners are hungry—this brief moment in the narrative, a moment that is both intercorporeal and intercultural, is significant for the way it serves as a threshold for cultural tolerance and perhaps even cooperation. As Ahmed notes, "Survival makes us vulnerable in that it requires we let what is 'not us' in; to survive we open ourselves up, and we *keep the orifices of the body open.*"[49] While Collins ultimately stops short of positing the reconciliatory potential of food, he uses the ingestion of the disgusting as both a diminution of strangeness and as a reappropriation of power.

Later, Miss Maryon devises a plan to drug the pirates by mixing the dough of the tortilla cakes with the juice of a poisonous berry. Having eaten the tainted cakes, the pirates are left "absolutely insensible" as the prisoners escape in the dark of night on their makeshift rafts. *Household Words* readers would have likely noted the striking parallels between these "flat cakes made of Indian corn" and the "circulating chapattis" that puzzled the British in the weeks leading up to the events at Cawnpore in 1857. Apparently, Indian runners would relay the chapatti (a flat, pancake-like unleavened bread) from village to village throughout Northern India as a way of alerting the populace of an impending event of great, though undisclosed significance. This failure to understand the meaning of the circulating chapattis had the effect of creating much suspicion, anxiety, and fear among the British populace. For instance, an article entitled "Circulating Cakes" in the *Illustrated London News* reported:

> A strange and to some observers a very disagreeable incident has occurred in the north-west. A few days since a chowkeydar, or village policeman, of Cawnpore, ran up to another in Futteghur, and gave him two chupatties. These are indigestible little unleavened cakes, the common food of the poorer classes. He ordered him to make ten more, and give two to each of the five nearest chowkyars, with the same order. He was obeyed, and in a few hours, the whole country was in commotion with chowkeydars running about about with these cakes. . . . *Nobody has the least idea what it all means.*[50]

---

49. Ahmed, *The Cultural Politics of Emotion*, 83.
50. "Circulating Cakes," *Illustrated London News*, 18 April 1857, 369 (my emphasis).

While the English prisoners are able to use the tainted tortillas to stage their own rebellion against their oppressors, it would be somewhat off the mark to see their success simply as a fictive payback for the circulating chapattis. Rather, Collins implies here a more general strategy by which the English can reassert control and assure their survival: they must "open themselves up" (to use Ahmed's phrase) to what is different and strange and make the unfamiliar (as represented by the "disgusting" and "insipid" tortilla cakes) familiar.

Collins continues his narrative mutiny in "The Prison in the Woods" in his challenge to the ongoing public celebration of English superiority that had emanated from the Great Exhibition of 1851 and the ideology of empire that Dickens championed in *Household Words*.[51] From the opening sentence of his chapter, Collins turns the tables on imperial conquest as Davis describes his fellow English hostages as the most "helpless" and "forlorn company" that was ever "gathered together out of any nation in the world." For readers in 1857 that seemingly innocuous phrase—"any nation in the world"—would have called to mind immediately and particularly the Great Exhibition in which "all the nations of the world" were invited to display their finest technological products and artistic achievements in the grand emporium known as the Crystal Palace.[52] As the world's acknowledged leader in technology and commerce, the extravaganza in 1851 and beyond was for England (which featured the largest number of possessions) an implicit celebration of empire as it fueled the public desire for even more possessions, both material and colonial. While it has not gone unnoted that there are stark differences in both characterization and tone in Dickens's and Collins's sections,[53] what has not been accounted for is how this collaborative endeavor was itself a narrative battleground of power and prejudices, piracy and possession.[54] Lest we

---

51. See Grace Moore, *Dickens and Empire.*

52. There were over 13,000 exhibits featuring achievements from across the globe

53. In his biography of Collins, Nuel Pharr Davis argues that "The Prison in the Woods" makes a "burlesque out of Dickens's philippic against the sepoys." *The Life of Wilkie Collins* (Urbana: University of Illinois Press, 1956), 207–208. That Collins clearly defuses the sense of peril and urgency that Dickens attempts to build is echoed by Nicholas Rance as well: "The cold and sardonic tone of . . . Collins is not conducive to identifying with the prisoners in their plight." *Wilkie Collins and Other Sensation Novelists: Walking the Moral Hospital* (Rutherford, NJ: Fairleigh Dickinson University Press, 1991), 131. Nayder notes "Collins approaches the mutiny and the imprisonment of the English as a comic rather than a tragic subject" (121).

54. Dickens was already well-established as a major novelist and the editor of *Household Words* in 1851 when he met Collins, who was himself just embarking on his career as a serious writer. Collins soon became a good friend and traveling companion, and he worked as a staff writer for Dickens's *Household Worlds* and *All the Year Round* between 1856 and 1861. Despite their close personal friendship, Dickens and Collins had a complicated and vexed professional relationship. As a professional writer earning a respectable salary of five guineas a week at *Household Words* in 1856, Collins objected to the constraints that were put upon him. He was required to write only short essays or stories in four weekly parts, and he resented the fact that he was not credited with

forget that the full title of this Dickens–Collins collaboration was *The Perils of Certain English Prisoners, and Their Treasure in Women, Children, Silver, and Jewels* this narrative offers far more than a simple analogue to the Indian Mutiny. It embodies, rather, an ideological tug-of-war over rightful ownership of and control over nation and narrative.

Indeed, when Christian King George switches allegiances and facilitates the pirate "raid" on the British colonists, this is not an unprovoked attack by savage others who Dickens would like us to believe simply thrill in killing and plundering. Rather, power and possessions, as we see in the demands of the Portuguese Pirate Captain to the British Royal Navy, are what motivate the attack: "To the Captains of English men-of-war, and to the commanders of vessels of other nations," Mendez writes, "The precious metal and the jewels laid up in the English Island of Silver-Store, are in the possession of the Buccaniers, at sea. The women and children of the Island of Silver-Store . . . are in possession of the Buccaniers, on land" (15). It is this competition for valuable resources that fuels xenophobia. As Diamond reminds us, "Humans compete with each other for territory, as do members of most animal species. Because we live in groups, much of our competition has taken the form of war between adjacent groups . . . and the relations between adjacent groups has traditionally been marked by xenophobic hostility."[55] Moreover, the fact that the band of supposed outlaws do not represent any single nationality— the "buccaniers" are composed of both Europeans and colonized "others"—is an ironic reminder of both the Exhibition's and England's broken promises of universal harmony and cooperation.[56] Rather than feeding the fears of foreign invasion and "reverse colonization" that reverberated through all levels of English society during the 1850s, Collins's heterogeneous buccaneers embody a countervailing message. They embody social harmony and inter-ethnic cooperation; they represent the triumph of internationalism. Their power is located not in the figure of any one individual or nationality, but in

---

authorship. Collins, like the other writers, was required to publish only anonymously and submit to the editorial authority of Dickens, which included stipulations about the content of his fiction and essays. Adding to Collins's dissatisfaction was the fact that Dickens already had a history of censoring his work. As a writer who was coming up in the literary world and who yearned to throw off the shackles of professional subjugation, "The Prison in the Woods" is the perilous site of Collins's own narrative mutiny. That Dickens exercised considerable authority over Collins's portion of the manuscript is undeniable; interestingly, however, most collected editions of Dickens's work have omitted Collins's chapter presumably as inferior to the work of the "Inimitable."

55. Diamond, *The Third Chimpanzee*, 220.

56. The Exhibition was intended to foster universal harmony across national and cultural boundaries; in actuality it provoked hostile nationalism by arranging and classifying the products of each country separately. See James Buzard, "Conflicting Cartographies: Globalism, Nationalism, and the Crystal Palace Floor Plan," in *Victorian Prism: Refractions of the Crystal Palace.*

the "spirit of mutual reliance, . . . reciprocal service and sacrifice, which they have exhibited."[57]

After their "arduous" four-day walking tour through Shangri-La, the English captives led by Mendez's "fearsome regiment" finally reach a "mysterious ruined city." Here Collins again underscores the irrationality of English fears of anything unfamiliar as the prisoners encounter a gargantuan statue built of "a lost race of people." According to Davis, "altogether it was as horrible and ghastly an object to come upon suddenly, in the unknown depths of a great forest, as the mind . . . can conceive" (21). This scene well illustrates what neuroscientist Antonio Damasio has described as the "somatic marker mechanism"—the way in which cognitive representations of the external world interact with cognitive representations of the internal world: where perceptions interact with emotions.[58] In typical hyperbolic fashion, Davis describes the "terror" that is evoked by the presence of the unknown "Thing":

> I looked in that direction, and there, as if it had started up out of the ground to dispute our passage through the forest, was a hideous monster carved in stone, twice my height at least . . . Spots of rank moss stuck about over its great flaring stone-face; its stumpy hands were tucked up into its breast; its legs and feet were four times the size of any human limbs; its body and the flat space of spare stone which rose above its head, were all covered with mysterious devices—little grinning men's faces, heads of crocodiles and apes, twisting knots and twirling knobs, strangely shaped leaves, winding lattice work, legs, arms, fingers toes, skulls, bones, and such like . . . When I saw that the first meeting with the statue struck me speechless, nobody can wonder that the children actually screamed with terror at the site of it. (21)

In a moment that calls to mind (albeit anachronistically) the climactic scene in *Planet of the Apes* when Charleton Heston stumbles upon the ruins of the Statue of Liberty and is confronted with the horrific realization of humanity's demise, Davis describes "a sight which [he] shall never forget . . . to his dying day":

> A wilderness of ruins spread out before me . . . in every direction, look where I would, a frightful confusion of idols, pillars, blocks of stone, heaving walls, and flights of steps, met my eye; some, whole and upright; others broken and

---

57. A reviewer from *The Times* (25 August 1857) actually ascribed to these words to Dickens's fictive English colonists.

58. Antonio Damasio, *The Feeling of What Happens: Body, Emotion and the Making of Consciousness* (London: Heinemann, 1999).

scattered on the ground . . . High in the midst of this desolation, towered a broad platform of rocky earth, scarped away on three sides, so as to make it unapproachable except by scaling ladders. On the fourth side the flat of the platform was reached by a flight of stone steps of such mighty size and strength that they might have been made for the use of a race of giants. They led to a huge building girded all round with a row of thick pillars . . . This was the dismal ruin which was called the Palace; and this was the Prison in the Woods which was to be the place of our captivity. (22)

While Nayder has noted that Collins may have modeled this locale on descriptions of the ancient Mayan ruins at Copan that had been discovered in 1839,[59] I would argue that Collins's implicit allusions to the Crystal Palace (the original at Hyde Park and its successor at Sydenham) *and* to England's imperial designs would have been immediately recognizable and more relevant to readers in 1857. Though there has been considerable historical interest in the original Crystal Palace of 1851, there has been relative inattention to the subsequent relocation, reconstruction, and relevance of its successor, which was built on an even larger scale outside of London in Sydenham so "that England, in the midst of her material greatness, [would not] become a byword and a reproach amongst nations."[60] Throughout the 1850s however, readers of *Household Words* would have been well familiar with the ongoing reports and editorials in the popular press of the Palace at Sydenham's many problems, setbacks, and unlucky circumstances. Even though the Palace was enormously popular and counted over 15 million visitors during its first decade, its legitimacy as a symbol of England's continued "greatness" was severely compromised by ongoing engineering problems, financial crises, poor management, erratic attendance rates, as well as the outbreak of the Crimean War.

When it was re-erected in 1854, the Palace (conceived on a colossal scale that is unimaginable even today) represented the Promethean ambitions of its designer Joseph Paxton as well as the overreaching ambitions of England.[61] The building—1,848 feet long and 408 feet wide including two huge towers and countless fountains with over 11,000 jets rising into the air[62]—was

---

59. Lillian Nayder, *Unequal Partners,* 123.

60. See J. R. Piggott, *Palace of the People: The Crystal Palace at Sydenham* (Madison: University of Wisconsin Press, 2004), 29.

61. Indeed, in his intention to "vanquish" Chatsworth and Versailles in the complex and daring design of the Park and waterworks at Sydenham, Sir Joseph Paxton's ambitions and creative passions became synonymous with English superiority. It was, however, Paxton's megalomania for creating something that was completely unrivalled, that contributed to its demise (see Piggott, *Palace of the People,* 138–139).

62. Piggott, *Palace of the People,* 156. The towers, which were each 282 feet high, were considered in 1856 to be an engineering marvel. The first attempt, however, to erect them proved a

situated on the crown of a hill offering breathtaking panoramas of Surrey and Kent on one side and London on the other.[63] Moreover, according to the *Illustrated Crystal Palace Gazette,* the Palace at Sydenham went beyond the objectives of its predecessor in not just showing "the world as it is" with its exhibits of technological and artistic achievements, but also showing "the world as it has been" with its courts featuring the art and architecture of past civilizations.[64] The intention, according to Piggot, was to "help visitors to understand evolution and civilisation in relation to their own times [with] examples of the grandeur of the palace, temples and villas of proud or decadent civilisations," while throughout the expansive park, "intellectual profit was to accrue through enjoyment of the unfamiliar."[65] While *enjoyment of the unfamiliar* may have been possible at a safe remove—when the exotic is literally behind glass—Collins suggests that English spectators might be less enthralled if they were themselves foreign *others* on display. As Davis himself confesses, "nothing tried our courage and endurance like that interval of speechless waiting in the Palace, with the hush of the ruined city" (22).

It is within Collins's "dismal ruins" where the Pirate Captain intends to make his headquarters and hold his English captives in a massive, pillared building called by the Indians "El Palacio," the architectural details of which bear striking, if not ironic emblematic similarities to the Palace and Park at Sydenham—from the huge stone sphinxes that flanked the entrance to the Park to the massive flight of granite steps that were 96 feet wide by 12 feet long. That everything in Collins's "wilderness of ruins" is grossly "overgrown and clasped about by roots, branches, and curling vines" (22) contributes to his critique of the Palace and Park at Sydenham and of England as heirs to an imperial authority over "uncivilized" peoples and "uncivilized" nature. That is, while the 200-acre park was designed for recreation, the extensive botanical gardens and ambitious waterworks were intended to showcase the history and future of English garden design. Collins draws an implicit analogy here between the garden and that state; rather than man vanquishing nature, instead we see how nature has vanquished all that is *man-made.*

> Out of every ugly crevice crack in the great stairs, there sprouted up flowers, long grasses, and beautiful large-leaved plants and bushes. . . . surrounded

structural failure and an ongoing financial burden. Even when they were almost completed, they were still found to be structurally unsound—(they could not support the weight intended for them nor sustain the vibrations of the water spouts)—and had to be pulled down again.

63. The lower end of the expansive and intricately mapped out park included a primeval swamp with the first ever exhibition of dinosaurs. (The existence of dinosaurs had only been discovered some thirty years earlier.)

64. Piggott, *Palace of the People,* 37.

65. Piggott, *Palace of the People,* v, 138.

by broken stones and with a carved human head, five times the size of life, leaning against it: rose the straight, naked trunk of a beautiful tree, that shot up high above the ruins, and dropped its enormous branches from the very top of it, bending down towards us, in curves like plumes of immense green feathers. (22)

More generally, Collins implicitly calls into question the teleological evolutionary theories that depicted England as the most advanced of the world's nations and in doing so, exposes the shortcomings of the prevailing ethnocentric mindset. Indeed, the ruins of "El Palacio" seem to have been "made for the use of a race of giants" (22).

When the Pirate-Captain reveals to his captives that he has been keeping them alive because he "want[s] the use of [their] arms to work for [him]," Collins not only undercuts the savage intentions that Dickens assigned to Mendez, but he calls into question another primary objective of the Exhibition—"to bring together specimens of industry and ingenuity of all nations." Industry, in terms of sustained hard work and an institution (or institutions) for production or trade, was not only one of the central themes of the Exhibition but was at the very center of the Victorian middle-class value system. If the survival of the English captives is dependent upon the fruits of their labor and ingenuity then Collins finds the glorification of English industry and ingenuity and the presumption of English superiority to be dubious at best. Ultimately, the English prisoners do escape—indeed, Dickens would have insisted that they do so—though they are hardly stalwart survivors nor is their flight a glorious overthrow of the oppressor. Rather, the crude and rather bumbling plan that they devise—to drug the pirates' food and sneak away in the middle of the night while Mendez is sleeping is *not* the brainchild of the British Government as represented by the mentally incapacitated Mr. Pordage and Mr. Kitten, but rather the work of the uneducated and those who do not possess authority: Short, the sailor, and the English gentlewoman, Miss Maryon.

Though Collins's contribution to *The Perils of Certain English Prisoners* attempts to mitigate Dickens's xenophobic rhetoric and offer a counterdiscourse to the "logic" of empire, ultimately, Dickens has the last word. In the third and final chapter, "The Rafts on the River," the "animal," otherwise known as the traitorous Christian George King, is shot through the heart by the proper English authority—Captain Carton—and left hanging from a tree as a presumed symbol of English victory and valor.

Some of the people ran round to the spot, and drew him out with the slime and wet trickling down his face; but, his face itself would never stir anymore to the end of time . . . In the evening we went away, and he was left hanging to the tree, all alone, with the red sun making a kind of dead sunset on his black face. (35)

This "shared witnessing" of the "slimy" body of the traitor Christian King George acquires a fetishistic quality that iterates its own disgusting *affects*.[66] According to Ahmed, "the sticking of disgust to some bodies [is] a sticking which never finishes" because there is always the possibility that *other* bodies could be dangerous adversaries.[67] That is, the sharing of disgust becomes a shared rage or ruminative anger.[68] Moreover, disgust carries with it an imperative to expel.[69] As a one-time member of the "in-group," it is the betrayer Christian King George, rather than the pirate captain Pedro Mendez, who must be "exterminated." Such an expulsion however, according to Ahmed, "will never be over given the possibility that other others 'could be' the cause of our disgust; the unfinished nature of expulsion allows its perpetual rejustification."[70] In other words, Dickens's scene of retributive justice is not intended to provide a satisfying, albeit fictive, resolution to the horrors endured at Cawnpore. Rather, the spectacle of the disgusting and slimy body of Christian King George serves as a "priming effect" (to use Hogan's term) to recall and intensify in the minds of *Household Words* readers "household affections"—the disgust, rage, and hatred engendered by the Sepoy Rebellion. It is in the accumulation of such "priming effects" found in news, fiction, and history that fear and loathing, as cognitive dispositions, are normalized and become part of a "continuous attitude."[71] And it is thus within the formation of such "continuous attitudes" that we can begin to locate the roots of xenophobia.

---

66. Hogan explains that the obvious technique for producing disgust is to link the out-group with "well-established disgust triggers such as excrement, insects, . . . rodents" and in this case, "slime" (*Understanding Nationalism,* 114).

67. Ahmed, *The Cultural Politics of Emotion,* 99.

68. In *Upheavals of Thought,* Martha Nussbaum discusses the connection between disgust and various forms of discrimination.

69. Ahmed, *The Cultural Politics of Emotion,* 99. See also Julia Kristeva, *Powers of Horror: An Essay on Abjection* (Ithaca, NY: Cornell University Press, 1982).

70. Ahmed, *The Cultural Politics of Emotion,* 98.

71. *Understanding Nationalism,* 111. As Diamond suggests, "xenophobic murder has innumerable animal precursors, but only [humans] have developed it to the point of threatening to bring about our fall as a species" (*The Third Chimpanzee,* 221).

Works Cited

Ahmed, Sara. *The Cultural Politics of Emotion*. New York: Routledge, 2004.

Anderson, Benedict. *Imagining the Nation: Reflections on the Origin and Spread of Nationalism*. Rev. ed. New York and London: Verso, 1991.

Bhabha, Homi. *The Location of Culture*. New York: Routledge, 1994.

———. *Nation and Narration*. New York: Routledge, 1990.

Brantlinger, Patrick. *Rule of Darkness: British Literature and Imperialism, 1830–1914*. Ithaca, NY, and London: Cornell University Press, 1990.

Buzard, James. "Conflicting Cartographies: Globalism, Nationalism, and the Crystal Palace Floor Plan." In *Victorian Prism: Refractions of the Crystal Palace*, edited by James Buzard, Joseph W. Childers, and Eileen Gillooly. 40–54. Charlottesville and London: University of Virginia Press, 2007.

[Collins, Wilkie.] "The Prison in the Woods" in "The Perils of Certain English Prisoners and Their Treasure in Women, Children, Silver, and Jewels." *Household Words* (Extra Christmas Number), 7 December 1857.

Damasio, Antonio. *The Feeling of What Happens: Body, Emotion and the Making of Consciousness*. London: Heinemann, 1999.

Davis, Nuel Pharr. *The Life of Wilkie Collins*. Urbana: University of Illinois Press, 1956.

Dawson, Graham. *Soldier Heroes: British Adventure, Empire and the Imagining of Masculinities*. London and New York: Routledge, 1994.

Diamond, Jared. *The Third Chimpanzee: The Evolution and Future of the Human Animal*. New York: HarperCollins, 2006.

Dickens, Charles. *The Letters of Charles Dickens*. Edited by Graham Storey and Kathleen Tillotson, Vols. I–XII. Oxford: Clarendon Press, 1965–2002.

———. "The Perils of Certain English Prisoners and Their Treasure in Women, Children, Silver, and Jewels." *Household Words* (Extra Christmas Number), 7 December 1857.

Herbert, Christopher. *War of No Pity: The Indian Mutiny and Victorian Trauma*. Princeton, NJ: Princeton University Press, 2009.

Hogan, Patrick Colm. *Understanding Nationalism: On Narrative, Cognitive Science, and Identity*. Columbus: The Ohio State University Press, 2009.

Household Words: A Weekly Journal, 1850, 1853, 1857.

Ledger, Sally. *Dickens and the Popular Radical Imagination*. Cambridge: Cambridge University Press, 2007.

McClintock, Anne. *Imperial Leather: Race, Gender, and Sexuality in the Colonial Contest*. London: Routledge, 1995.

Moore, Grace. *Dickens and Empire: Discourses of Class, Race, and Colonialism in the Works of Charles Dickens*. Burlington, VT: Ashgate Press, 2004.

Nayder, Lillian. *Unequal Partners: Charles Dickens, Wilkie Collins, and Victorian Authorship*. Ithaca, NY and London: Cornell University Press, 2002.

Nussbaum, Martha. *Upheavals of Thought: The Intelligence of Emotions*. Cambridge and New York: Cambridge University Press, 2001.

Oddie, William. "Dickens and the Indian Mutiny." *The Dickensian* 69 (1972): 3–15.

Pah, Biswamoy, ed. *The 1857 Rebellion*. New York: Oxford University Press, 2007.

Peters, Laura. "Double-dyed Traitors and Infernal Villains': *Illustrated London News, Household Words*, Charles Dickens and the Indian Rebellion." In *Negotiating India in the Nineteenth-Century Media*, edited by David Finkelstein and Douglas M. Peers. 110–134. New York: St. Martin's Press, 2000.

Piggott, J. R. *Palace of the People: The Crystal Palace at Sydenham.* Madison: University of Wisconsin Press, 2004.

Rance, Nicholas. *Wilkie Collins and Other Sensation Novelists: Walking the Moral Hospital.* Rutherford, NJ: Fairleigh Dickinson University Press, 1991.

Reynolds, Vernon, Vincent Falger, and Ian Vine. *The Sociobiology of Ethnocentrism.* London: Croom Helm, 1987.

Schlicke, Paul. *Oxford Reader's Companion to Dickens.* Oxford and New York: Oxford University Press, 1999.

Searle, John. *Making the Social World: The Structure of Human Civilization.* New York: Oxford University Press, 2009.

Sharpe, Jenny. *Allegories of Empire: The Figure of the Woman in the Colonial Text.* Minneapolis: University of Minnesota Press, 1993.

Stone, Harry. *The Uncollected Writings of Charles Dickens: Household Words, 1850–1859,* Vol. I. Bloomington: Indiana University Press, 1968.

Thayer, Bradley. *Darwin and International Relations: On the Evolutionary Origins of War and Ethnic Conflict.* Lexington: The University Press of Kentucky, 2004.

5

Maudlin Profanity and Midnight Debauchery

Infanticide and the *Angelito*

❧

JENNIFER HAYWARD

In *The Araucanians; or Notes of a Tour among the Indian Tribes of Southern Chili* (1855), a young North American traveler, Edmond Reuel Smith, recounts how he witnessed a mysterious tableau while returning from a party in Valparaíso that was, at once, intriguing and repellant. Passing an open doorway, he pauses and is invited to enter. "'*Estamos velando un angelito de Dios*' ('We are watching an angel of God')," his hosts tell him. "Such an unintelligible answer only excited greater curiosity," says Smith,

> and I entered. The room was filled with a collection of men and women of the lower class, engaged in drinking and clapping their hands to the music. . . .
>
> But the most prominent object was a kind of altar, set round with lighted candles, and ornamented with tinsel flowers. In the midst of these sat the figure of an infant, of the size of life, profusely painted with red and white, dressed in tawdry finery, and adorned with gauze wings.
>
> 'It is only the image of some saint,' I thought, and was turning away; but a second glance convinced me that there was something unusual about the figure. The hair looked very natural; those eyes were strangely vacant and filmy; even the finger-nails were perfectly formed. There seemed to be 'too much of art for nature, yet too much of nature for art;' and I approached to scrutinize it closely. It was *a corpse!*
>
> 'What is that?' I asked of a by-stander.

> *'An angel, Sir,'* he replied.
> 'A what?'
> *'A dead child.'*
> I hurried away in disgust.
> A refined sentiment may induce the bereaved mother to strew the bier of her infant with fresh-blown flowers—emblems of youth, beauty, and innocence; but this display of tinsel and paint, this maudlin profanity, this midnight debauchery in the presence of the dead, is revolting.[1]

In *The Araucanians* Smith becomes one of many Anglo-Americans to describe the Chilean custom of holding a wake for dead children. Their accounts generally emphasize not the religious ritual itself, but the emotional, moral, and aesthetic reactions of a reluctant observer. Coded descriptions of *angelitos* and of infanticide—another hot-button topic for colonial writers—rehearse and thereby help to enact Anglo-American beliefs about the nature of maternal love, the implications of public versus private mourning rituals, and ultimately the superiority of British and North American moral and aesthetic sensibilities.

The body of a child: brutally murdered, abandoned in a gutter, or deposited in a basket by the church door. Or—still worse?—the body of a child: beautifully dressed, painted with cosmetics, and hung on display while adults drink and dance about its feet. Since the Victorian age, sentimental discourse has shaped the way British and North American readers will respond to these spectacles. Then as now, stories about dead babies virtually demand specific emotional reactions. These accounts therefore test moral and aesthetic values and activate the cultural imaginary. Shared condemnation of the reprehensible treatment of children by presumed "others" works to build an imagined community and so, ultimately, produces a stronger sense of national identity. Still today, news reports sensationalize stories of threatened children—alone, abducted, abused, abandoned in car seats by careless or overwhelmed parents—to make a public spectacle of adults who have violated a community's values.

In her essay tracing literary representations of women of African descent in England, Cora Kaplan notes that powerful discursive figures—in her case, the African woman on Anglo shores—crystallize in cultural representation "at particular historical moments, giving narrative shape and virtual embodi-

---

1. Edmond Reuel Smith, *The Araucanians, or Notes of a Tour Among Indian Tribes of Southern Chile* (New York: Harper & Brothers, 1855), 51–52. Anglo-American travelers in nineteenth-century Chili often wrote "Chili" and "Chilian"; since such errors were characteristics of colonial relations, this essay will preserve them in their original form, without inserting a cumbersome "[sic]" after each such error.

ment to temporarily specific constellations of hopes, fears and anxieties. The activity of condensation and projection that go[es] in to their articulation turns the question back to history as to why such associations should take place: why these, and not others?"[2] Why, to return to the case at hand, did the bodies of children infiltrate the texts produced by nineteenth-century Anglo-Americans in Chile?

Without entering into the debate, active since Philippe Ariès published his groundbreaking *Centuries of Childhood* in 1973, as to whether attitudes towards children shifted dramatically in the eighteenth century, it is clear that in the nineteenth century the child became a crucial counter in a cultural currency focusing on the family and the domestic, set over against the industrial capitalist world of work and commerce as well as the new world of empire. As a result, images of children served as touchstones to test coded values. From Swift's "A Modest Proposal" (1729) to Bram Stoker's *Dracula* (1897), imperiled children condemn a culture's lack of civilization or its evil; from Wordsworth through Dickens, adored children embody a culture's moral strength or essential goodness.

In the Anglo-American colony in Chile from the middle of the nineteenth century onwards, newspapers, travel literature, and other texts invoked the iconic figure of the injured child to communicate anxieties about the values, beliefs, habits—even humanity—of their Chilean hosts. But colonists had not always been so concerned to distinguish Anglo from Chilean values. Early in the nineteenth century, British colonists worked, lived near, and even intermarried with their Chilean hosts. By contrast, at the century's end, colonists considered Chileans profoundly "Not English," to echo the presciently xenophobic phrase that serves as Podsnap's touchstone in Charles Dickens's *Our Mutual Friend* (1864–1865). What factors account for this change of perspective from assimilation to a fear we would now label xenophobic?

This essay will explore the figure of the dead child as it circulates through the Anglo-Chilean imaginary. First, I survey the English-language newspapers published by the community during the nineteenth century; their virtual obsession with the practice of infanticide in Chile inscribes the fear generated by perceived differences between Anglo-American and Chilean values. With these news stories as a foundation, I read Anglo-American travel narratives' accounts of Chilean *angelitos* as part of a double-edged investigation of Victorian constructions of mourning and shifting views of national identity. Most—but not all—of the English-speaking colonists in Chile in the early nineteenth century were British (with a high percentage of Scots

---

2. Cora Kaplan, "Imagining Empire: History, Fantasy and Literature," in *At Home with the Empire: Metropolitan Culture and the Imperial World*, 208.

amongst them), drawn there either for economic opportunities or as mercenaries joining the Chilean navy to help win independence from Spain. As the century progressed, more North Americans joined the colony. Since the total number of English speakers in Chile was never large, British and Americans intermixed considerably, especially in cultural institutions such as churches, schools, and newspapers. Therefore, I will use "British" or "American" when the nationality of the individual in question is clear, "Anglo-American" when the nationality is not clear (as is the case for newspaper articles, since reporters were generally anonymous). I also discuss the fused Anglo-American or "English speaking" (often explicitly Protestant) identity that colonists increasingly claimed towards the end of the nineteenth century as a means of distinguishing themselves from Latin and Catholic values. En route, I compare Chilean ethnographic explanations for the rituals surrounding the *angelito* to Victorian iconicization of the child to highlight the ways these small bodies crystallized a wide range of national and imperial anxieties.

First, a brief overview of the small, isolated Anglo-American colony in Chile in the nineteenth century. While in 1854 only 1,934 British citizens lived in Chile (almost half of them in Valparaíso), by 1885 the number had increased to 5,184.[3] These were the decades of rapid expansion and formal consolidation of Empire worldwide; Victoria would not proclaim herself Empress of India until 1877, but the Indian Rebellion of 1857 had already recast British views of what Kipling would dub the "white man's burden." Meanwhile, the United States had begun its own imperial expansion, annexing Texas after the Mexican-US war of 1846–1848. When first permitted to settle in the country after it declared independence from Spain, early English and American settlers assimilated quickly into the host culture. As the century progressed, however, the colony's early integration shifted towards self-conscious isolation and increased nationalism.

Meanwhile, back "home" in England, citizens' lives were shaped by the existence of Empire in ways that were not necessarily overt or consciously acknowledged. As Catherine Hall and Sonya Rose explain in *At Home with the Empire,* "Empire was omnipresent in the everyday lives of 'ordinary people'—it was there as part of the mundane. . . . part of what Michael Billig has termed, 'banal nationalism.'"[4] Average citizens were often unconscious of the extent to which their lives intertwined with Britain's overseas territories, but colonial goods and peoples as well as imperial imperatives nevertheless shaped their everyday existence as well as their national identity.

---

3. John Mayo, *British Merchants and Chilean Development, 1851–1886* (Boulder, CO: Westview Press, 1987), 13.

4. Catherine Hall and Sonya O. Rose, *At Home with the Empire: Metropolitan Culture and the Imperial World* (Cambridge: Cambridge University Press, 2006), 22.

In countries such as Chile, where Britain did not establish a formal imperial presence but where political and economic influence was considerable from Independence onward, British citizens did not initially consider themselves part of "Empire." In the early stages of colonization, their subject positions shifted depending on context. When considered in relation to specific British national interests, for example when competing for a larger share of Chile's foreign trade, differences between the British and other European or English-speaking colonists loomed large. When considered over against Chilean interests, for example in debates as to whether Protestants should be allowed to practice their religion in a Catholic country, differences among British, American, and German colonists in particular diminished in importance. As the increased pace of global trade and travel enforced ever-increasing contact with others, however, the fear of foreigners we now label xenophobic—a term that did not exist for the Victorians—began to shape interactions with strangers in the contact zones. According to the *Oxford English Dictionary*, the roots of the word add a peculiarly ironic edge in the context of informal empire: the Greek root *xeno* means guest, stranger, person who looks different or foreign, and the Anglo-American colonists were of course the actual guests and strangers in Chile. Their xenophobic fear of their hosts thus reverses the typical direction of this phobia, generally used to describe natives' fear of immigrant others.

Like all colonies, the one in Valparaíso, Chile, eventually produced a written record that worked to unify the community despite individual members' sometimes conflicting affiliations and values. One primary means of forging unity came through the articulation of this new type of fear: we can trace an incipient xenophobia through texts that "expose" practices that British or North American observers found reprehensible. The stories told in these texts worked to shape the ways the settlers interacted not only with each other but with Chileans of all classes. At the same time, in a process predicted by Benedict Anderson's account of the ways that national identities were consolidated in tandem with the rise of print culture across Europe,[5] the production and distribution of English-language print media—especially newspapers—in Chile from the 1860s onward marks the establishment of a formal colony: a self-consciously united group settled in a foreign country but preserving the culture of "home" and a strong sense of national identity. The Anglo community's preferred narrative after mid-century becomes one of imperialists struggling to civilize a young, heretical nation against great odds of ingratitude, improvidence, and incomprehensibly Catholic "rituals" and "superstitions." In the process, these colonists, as well as travelers to the

---

5. Benedict Anderson, *Imagined Communities: Reflections on the Origin and Spread of Nationalism* (New York: Verso, 1991).

colony, contributed to new constructions of British and US national identity through the discourses they produced—including representations of child death. The figure of the damaged or desecrated child was perceived by Anglo observers as embodying Chilean national values and character, while the observers' own horror and disgust at the spectacle of these small, displayed bodies publicly performs, and thus confirms, an Anglo sensibility.

Over the course of the nineteenth century, colonists in Chile founded at least eleven English-language newspapers. These were not directed at a specifically British or American readership but emphasized their service to the "English speaking" community, thus helping to forge a shared Anglo-American identity developed over against the Chilean host culture. Despite frequent claims of neutrality (a political necessity, particularly in the early years of independence) these papers were sometimes sharply critical of Chilean politics, economic policies, and values. Journalists therefore both reflected and helped to shape the colony's attitudes towards their host country. The "provincial" columns of the papers provide a particularly sharp reading of Chilean culture, emphasizing sensational goings-on in the outposts of Empire and feeding readers' taste for the shocking and exotic through lurid accounts of Chilean religious "orgies," violent domestic squabbles, suicides, drunks, and so on. To give just one typical example, the *Chilean Times*'s correspondent from the province of Pabellon de Pico, describing the annual Dos de Mayo celebration as a locus of crime and violence, adds casually, "Of course all this dissipation could not well pass without a little shooting, robbing and so forth, but really these small diversions are such a matter of course here, that no one minds them much."[6] The reporter's ironic commentary underscores an implicit contrast between Chilean and Anglo-American codes of public behavior.

In 1853, two different groups of editors set out to establish the first general-interest publications for the Anglo-American community. The colony's extant paper, the *Mercantile Reporter,* focused quite narrowly on news of interest to the shipping and merchant communities up and down the coast of Chile. (The fact that editors chose to invest in general-interest papers indicates that the colony had expanded beyond its mercantile roots.) These two new papers were, first, the *Valparaíso Echo,* which announced itself as the "Organ of the Foreign Population in Chile," and, second, the *Valparaíso Herald.* The latter's first issue appeared on September 7, 1853; the editors announced their intention to publish local and international news, scientific and geographic discoveries, manufacturing and mercantile information of the Pacific Coast, and literary and sporting pages. The editors added,

---

6. *Mercantile Reporter,* 20 May 1876, 2.

It would be unpardonable in us not to give a sprinkling of gossip, horrible murders, shocking accidents, etc., and as it is probable that crime and carelessness will continue for some time longer notwithstanding all the efforts of Clergy, Police, Moral Reform, Temperance and Missionary Societies, we fear that matter for this department will not be wanting, though, with all good Christians, we pray for their speedy termination.[7]

Having boasted of their intention to emphasize the sensational news of the colony and its surrounds, albeit with an ironic disclaimer that may imply a distinction between Anglo "Christians," with their activist Societies bent on moral reform, and Chilean Catholics, the editors proceed to do so with gusto. In addition to murders, suicides, domestic disputes, and similar (most, though not all, concerning Chileans rather than Anglo-Americans) from about midcentury these papers begin to report on a supposed epidemic of infanticide in Chile. The *Valparaiso Echo* covered one sensational case extensively:

A young girl, aged 15, residing near Melipilla, was delivered of a child and had the cool barbarity of immediately cutting its throat with a pair of scizzors [*sic*] which was the only instrument she found at hand for her frightful purpose. Neither her delicate situation nor the want of strength usual on such occasions were sufficient to deter her from committing an act so repugnant to the noblest sentiment of a woman's heart. She was condemned in first instance to five year's [*sic*] imprisonment. A very mild sentence for such an unnatural crime.[8]

The emphasis on this girl's persistence in the crime *despite* her "delicate situation," and the absence of the (feminine) weakness "usual on such occasions," communicates this journalist's conclusion: that the Chilean girl was unfeminine, not governed by the "noblest sentiment of a woman's heart" and thus able to violate human decency in a way that—we are to presume—no Anglo woman could do. This journalist implicitly contrasts an idealized delicate, weakened Anglo mother with a dehumanized coarse, hardened Chilean woman, paralleling Smith's 1855 contrast between the "refined sentiment" of the (again implicitly Anglo) "bereaved mother" and the "maudlin profanity" of the Chilean parent. The contrast implies a class dynamic as well, with the Anglo mother described in terms reserved for the middle or upper classes, while the Chilean mother is coded as lower class.

Also in the *Echo,* an account titled "Another Infanticide" tells of a father

---

7. Lead editorial, *Valparaiso Herald* [Valparaíso, Chile], 7 September 1853, 1.

8. *Valparaiso Echo,* 14 November 1853, 3.

who was "charged with murdering two of his Children, both under 6 years. The criminal is well known by many people as a good and inoffensive man. No doubt exists that the recent death of his wife alienated his mind and led him to commit this double assassination."[9] Interestingly, the father is not condemned on moral grounds; rather, the fault seems to lie with his wife, whose death simultaneously drives her husband mad and leaves her children to his tender mercies. In both these accounts, the bodies of young children bear mute witness to their parents' insanity, improvidence, or otherwise "unnatural" behaviors.

The *Valparaiso Herald* sensationalized the death of young children in similar ways, for example publishing an article titled "Child Eater,"[10] running public notices of infanticides, and emphasizing child death as an issue of concern to the Anglo community. Eventually, the *Herald* urged a remedy for what it depicts as a surge in the killing of babies: "It is strongly recommended that a Foundling Asylum be established in Valparaíso, as it is said that the want of it causes a large amount of infanticide."[11]

The *Valparaiso Herald* ended its run after just a year, in 1854, presumably because the English-speaking community was still too small to support two general-interest papers. Over the next two decades, though, the colony's population increased markedly. Perhaps in response to worldwide events, or perhaps simply as a result of the rapid growth and consequent increasing isolation of the English-speaking community in Chile, Anglo national superiority became an increasingly prevalent theme throughout the colony's writings. In 1867, a new general-interest English-language newspaper proved more successful than its predecessors. *The Valparaiso and West Coast Mail,* like the *Echo* and the *Herald,* included local news, and it too published frequent accounts of infanticide, presenting the crime as an epidemic. Infanticides were listed in the "Local News" section. In October 1867, an anonymous reporter noted, "The body of a child was found on the 6th inst. at one of the doors of the church of La Merced." The next week, in a column labeled "Offenses," a reporter claimed, "Abandoning children appears to be have become quite a fashion here lately; on the 14th the body of a newborn infant was found on the Cerro de los Cardos, and another, but alive, was discovered in one of the cars of the street railway on the same date." Summarizing another incident of infant abandonment a few months later, a reporter noted that "no traces have been discovered of the unnatural mother."[12]

---

9. "Another Infanticide," *Valparaiso Echo,* 14 November 1853, 3.

10. "Child Eater," *Valparaiso Herald,* 1 November 1853, 4.

11. *Valparaiso Herald,* 1 January 1854, 2.

12. *The Valparaiso and West Coast Mail,* 10 October 1867, 1; 17 October 1867, 2; 10 February 1868.

Right from the first report of infanticide in the *Valparaiso Echo*, phrases like "unnatural mother" recur with startling frequency. One account describes "an unnatural mother" who abandoned her child; another condemns not only the mother, but the "unnatural parents" for the same act involving a three-day-old infant.[13] Why this obsession with infanticide and emphasis on natural versus unnatural parenting?

The answer might lie in historical fact: perhaps child murder occurred too frequently to be ignored. But infanticide became an increasingly urgent subject of reporting in Britain by the 1860s as well, and in that context, evidence indicates that there was no parallel increase in the actual number of children murdered. As Josephine McDonagh notes in the introduction to *Child Murder and British Culture*, accounts of child death "take on a life of their own. . . . child murder is invested with a bewildering excess of meanings, and it is this that contributes to its particularly potent and unstable character. . . . and connotes instead a host of other meanings, all of them suspended beyond the boundaries of positive knowledge, in the much more shadowy domain of the cultural imaginary."[14] In Britain in the 1850s and 1860s, McDonagh demonstrates that "Britain was stricken by an apparent epidemic of child murder," with doctors, coroners, legal professionals and editors combining forces to imagine an English landscape haunted by Gothic secrets: the mangled bodies of infants cast away like ghosts of a primitive past in collision with an industrial, "modern" present.[15] McDonagh argues that this panic was, however, a "mirage" conspired with the goal of "whipping up moral panic on an unprecedented scale . . . The new modern professionals seemed to have conjured the very barbaric practices that their success was predicated upon eliminating."[16] In Britain, then, child murder came to encapsulate anxieties surrounding the rapid transition to an urban metropolis, while providing those who harped on it with opportunity to demonstrate their own professional efficiency by eradicating the (manufactured) epidemic. Their accounts brought nostalgically imagined pastoral ideals into conflict with modern realities and focused these anxieties on the imagined threat of a new working-class and ethnic (specifically Irish) "other," whose barbarous practices threatened Britain's imagined national identity.

Meanwhile, in Chile, Anglo colonists may have imagined a parallel epidemic of child murder. They certainly wove their response to child death into a larger critique of Chilean parenting practices, a construction of enormous

---

13. *Valparaiso Echo*, June 3, 1868, 2; August 3, 1868, 2.

14. Josephine McDonagh, *Child Murder and British Culture, 1720–1900* (Cambridge: Cambridge University Press, 2003), 8, 13.

15. McDonagh, *Child Murder and British Culture*, 123–124.

16. McDonagh, *Child Murder and British Culture*, 126.

force in this era when the child had become an icon of purity and moral goodness and treatment of children functioned as a test of moral character. Their critique ironically echoes Matthew Arnold's excoriation of newspaper reportage that concludes, famously, "Wragg is in custody." In his essay "The Function of Criticism at the Present Time" (1865), Matthew Arnold includes a brief (and apparently misquoted) excerpt from a newspaper account of a girl, identified only as Wragg, accused of strangling her infant. For Arnold, this grim record of infanticide serves as a necessary counterweight to polemical criticism that insists on "our old Anglo-Saxon breed, the best in the whole world!" In Arnold's perspective—which is, in characteristic fashion, simultaneously a critique of upper class idealization of British working class realities and a profoundly nostalgic mourning for an era before the working classes existed—the glory days of England have been lost in "the workhouse, the dismal Mapperly Hills . . . the gloom, the smoke, the cold, the strangled illegitimate child." For Arnold, these are equally unfortunate by-products of Britain's industrial age; the dismal litany concludes with what Arnold terms "the final touch,—short, bleak, and inhuman: *Wragg is in custody.*"[17]

After the "epidemic" of reports of infanticide was well underway, an account of an *angelito* appeared in the *Chilian Times,* a newspaper that began in 1876 and ran through 1909, enjoying probably the largest circulation and longest run of the colony's papers. Appearing in its often sensational "Provincial" column, this article merges implications of infanticide with a conventional description of an *angelito*. "A short time ago," we are told,

> a child of tender age, a son of one of the laboring class, was taken ill, and after suffering for a few days it was pronounced by the doctor to be dead. In conformity with the custom still in use among the lower classes, the child was dressed up and friends were invited to the wake. Singing, dancing and drinking to the health of the *anjelito* was carried on throughout the night, and towards morning they proceeded to transfer the child to a coffin, when to the great astonishment of all present, the child opened its eyes and stretching forth its arms gave ocular evidence to the minds of those assembled that life was not yet extinct. Great was the confusion of all concerned, and all kinds of *remedios* were applied, but without effect, and on the morning following the child died in reality. And no wonder, after having been exposed all night to the cold air in an almost naked state. After this, some one will no doubt have the assurance to tell us that Chile is a civilized country![18]

---

17. All citations in this paragraph are from Matthew Arnold, "The Function of Criticism at the Present Time," in *Essays* (Oxford: Oxford University Press, 1914), 24.

18. *Chilian Times,* 22 July 1876, 3.

The terror of being buried alive influenced British coffin design during this period, so one might think that the practice of the wake would be appreciated as insurance against that fate. Instead, this reporter illogically reverses cause and effect, blaming the child's death on the wake itself rather than on the illness that most likely occasioned the *velorio* in the first place. Even more directly and impatiently than Edmund Reuel Smith's, this account reshapes events into allegory: underlying the mourning ritual we have the hidden morality tale of an infant essentially murdered by its unnatural parents. The resulting narrative works to reinforce an implicit class critique while justifying the Anglo-American colony's belief in its own superior state of civilization. References to the dead boy's "tender" age and outstretched arms associate him with Victorian depictions of childhood as a state of purity and innocence. But the emphasis in this passage is on the adults. Clearly labeled as lower class, they are associated with the kinds of behavior thought to be endemic to that class: singing, dancing, drinking, experiencing "astonishment" and "confusion" when the child proved to be living, relying on ineffectual folk remedies, and cruelly "expos[ing]" their own child to insalubrious conditions. These images combine to paint the Chilean adults as at best careless and ignorant, at worst savage, as the journalist emphasizes in the last line of the piece.

The casual use of untranslated Spanish words implies that the papers' readers were expected to be longtime residents of Chile, familiar with the language and mourning customs of the country. The reporter therefore does not bother to describe the *angelito* itself or explain the *velorio*. Moreover, the reporter's outrage does not derive from his or her inability to interpret the spectacle. Rather, these news pieces on infanticide and *angelitos* seem implicitly intended to reinforce what Anglo readers already assume about Chileans, especially those of the lower classes. In the process, journalists harness free-floating anxieties about geographical and cultural distance from an idealized English-speaking Home, transforming them into a performative rejection of "debauched" Latino mourning and childrearing practices and explicitly contrasting them with Anglo traditions. The popularity of descriptions of dead children in the colony's stories indicates the discursive means that English speakers in Chile adopted to define a national identity over against that of Chilean others. At about this time, the largely Protestant British began to depict themselves as a moral minority set over against a licentious Catholicism that threatened to swamp them.[19] Taken together, these discursive strat-

---

19. This increasingly nationalist and imperial attitude becomes particularly evident in the colony's active lobbying for and public debates over legalizing Protestant churches and Protestant marriage in the country (recorded in Chilean as well as Anglo newspapers). The first government-sanctioned Protestant church opened in 1858, but Protestant marriages were not permitted in the country, and marriages between Protestants and Catholics were not recognized, until much later.

egies rehearsed anxieties we would now term xenophobic: generalized and irrational fear of others.

In addition to the newspapers generated within the colony, Anglo-Chileans had another prolific source of stories that helped them to navigate their relationship with their host country: travel literature produced by visitors to the New World. In the first years of independence, this literature tended to focus on producing scientific (especially mineralogical, botanical, and zoological) and cultural knowledge for consumption by a nation of armchair scientists and travelers, and more importantly for potential emigrants back home. As the century progressed, travel literature about Chile became at once more practical and more general, emphasizing detailed information about mercantile, industrial, and other conditions for Anglo-Americans looking for new investment or work opportunities abroad, but also attempting to convey Chile's "mores and manners" as well as practical information on food, lodging and transportation to readers who might consider visiting the country. In the process of developing a "canon" of travel texts, writers increasingly relied on "set pieces" that recurred in many narratives. The *angelito* took its place among the experiences that writers frequently described.

In the typical account of an *angelito,* initially the author is mystified and, like Smith, has to puzzle out the meaning of the spectacle. Often, writers frame their descriptions of dead infants using Gothic tropes to heighten the emotional and moral impact of the scenes, and the infants themselves may be depicted as helpless, desecrated victims of Catholic self-indulgence and idolatry. Interestingly, several accounts code the practice using British racial distinctions, labeling it as "Celtic" rather than "Saxon" and comparing it to Irish wakes.[20] Not surprisingly, as the travel narrative becomes a popular genre, narratives begin to appropriate—openly or silently—images and descriptions from earlier writers. So these accounts confirm each other in a process that reinforced the Anglo-American colony's belief in its own moral superiority, as well as its construction of Chileans as others to be feared.

Smith's description of an *angelito,* given above, is one of the first published accounts. As a result, closer examination of the ways he represents the experience will help us to identify conventional tropes for describing the *angelito* as these hardened into convention. In shaping the raw material of his confrontation with a Chilean wake, Smith draws on conventions of Gothic, sensation, and sentimental literature to guide his readers' responses to Chilean mourning practices. Smith describes a morally tainted and excessive

20. See Loretta L. Merwin, *Three Years in Chile* (New York: Follett, Foster, 1863); May Crommelin, *Over the Andes from the Argentine to Chili and Peru* (London: Richard Bentley and Son, 1896); Francis J. G. Maitland, *Chile: Its Land and People* (London: Francis Griffiths, 1914); and C. J. Lambert, *Sweet Waters: A Chilean Farm* (London: Chatto and Windus, 1952).

ritual, using hyperbolic phrases like "maudlin profanity," "midnight debauchery," and so on to depict Chileans as exotic in both behavior and moral code. For Anglo-American travelers in the Victorian era, then, Chile parallels the construction of Italy by Ann Radcliffe and other early Gothic authors: it is depicted as Catholic, passionate, and primitive. The wake itself raises the specter of Gothic tropes like dark secrets, questions of paternity, problematic relationships between parents and children, and mistaken identity. Smith performs the Gothic uncanny for our titillation: the infant is simultaneously familiar and strange, sentimentalized and exoticized, with hair that "looked very natural" but eyes "strangely vacant and filmy," perfect fingernails, and so on. In this small body, there is "'too much of art for nature, yet too much of nature for art.'"[21] Here Smith anticipates Freud's theory of the uncanny, which builds on Ernst Jentsch's assertion "that a particularly favourable condition for awakening uncanny feelings is created when there is intellectual uncertainty whether an object is alive or not, and when an inanimate object becomes too much like an animate one."[22] And indeed, Freud ultimately connects uncanny sensations to childhood omnipotence of thought: the belief that our dolls, for example, could conceivably come to life if we wish hard enough. The relevance of this belief is clear for parents grieving the loss of young children in a country where child death was all too common for parents of all nationalities.[23]

While drawing on Gothic narrative codes, Smith heightens the allure of his account by using suspenseful elements familiar from both the Gothic and sensation literature, notably mistaken identity, false assumptions, and partial vision and understanding. Odd turns of phrase dramatize Smith's confusion; for example, before realizing that the child is dead, he tells himself, "It is only the image of some saint." The gratuitous "only" implies either his need to dismiss this graven image, or his desire to heighten suspense: it is *only* a saint, not something more shocking. In either case, the statement assumes that a saint—implicitly Catholic and thus itself a marker of excess, tawdriness, and often of lower class status as well when seen through Anglo eyes—can and should be dismissed. Smith reinforces the gap between his false assumptions and the shocking reality by structuring his depiction of the *angelito* through binary oppositions that reinforce the class distinctions we saw in accounts of infanticide; for example, he describes the customs of (presumably Anglo) "bereaved mothers" as "refined" while those of Chilean

21. Smith, *The Araucanians*, 51–52.

22. Sigmund Freud, *On Creativity and the Unconscious* (New York: Harper Books, 1958), 139.

23. Indeed, English and American colonists themselves imagined that their dead children had returned to life. See Henry Edward Swinglehurst, *Valparaíso Songs* (London: Dargan Ltd., n.d.), and John Trumbull, *Andean Melodies* (privately printed, n.d.).

parents become "revolting." He reinforces these patterns of opposition with literal or conceptual oxymorons: "tawdry finery," "tinsel flowers," a child "profusely painted." The dichotomy between "refined" and sentimentalized Anglo-European mourning practices and exotic and morally tainted Chilean ones becomes standard to later travelers' descriptions of *angelitos*.

To strengthen the contrast, Smith inserts a hypothetical, anguished North American mother into this scene, where she contrasts with the absent parents of this dead Chilean child (their invisibility within the crowd of carousing men and women implies them to be uncaring, or at least careless). The deliberate invocation of the sentimental image of an idealized Anglo-American woman speaks to the increasing feminization of the Anglo-Chilean colony. As more women traveled to South America, and as male and female colonists alike began to emphasize the creation of an English-speaking cultural space isolated within the larger geographic space of Chile, travel narratives moved away from exploratory surveys of the capitalist vanguard, and towards an insular domesticity emphasizing women's role in providing a safe, moral, and uplifting family life as a refuge from the Latin and Catholic chaos of world outside the home. Thus, such accounts reveal much about the colony's increased national self-consciousness, which resulted in its gradual isolation from Chileans and other "foreign" colonists alike.

As we have seen, in the decades after Smith visited Chile, the colony exploded in numbers and became increasingly self-sufficient. An increasingly strong reaction against Chilean customs became simultaneously a cause and a result of this pulling-away. In the accounts of infanticide examined earlier, images of dead children provided a particularly powerful means of distinguishing between Anglo and Chilean values, thus furthering xenophobic reactions against the colony's hosts. Just as stories about infanticide enforced distinctions between Anglo and Chilean mothers, so narratives of *angelitos* sharply contrast the iconic Anglo-American child with the grotesque figure of the Chilean child as spectacle.

In 1881, British traveler R. Nelson Boyd published *Chili: Sketches of Chili and the Chilians During the War 1879–1880* (his other titles include the still less riveting *Coal Mines Inspection: Its History and Results*). Boyd prepares his ground by announcing that "the [Chilean] wife and mother is not a favourable specimen of womankind," and then adds,

> superstition is rife among them, and few have any clear idea of the meaning of the religion they profess. One curious habit, which, though still common, is gradually dying out, came under my notice, namely, the manner of holding a wake over the body of a dead child. The little thing is decked out in finery it never had a chance of wearing while alive; its head is circled with a wreath

of flowers, its neck adorned with strings of beads, the hair neatly plaited, and the face painted in rose colour; and in this condition it is fixed up on a table in the corner of the hut, and left for weeks before burial, the object of the curiosity and admiration of the neighbours. During this time, such festivities as the parents can afford are freely indulged in.[24]

Here again we see imagery associated with Gothic excess: the Chileans are confused and superstitious; their religious rituals are reduced to "curious habit[s]" and the child itself becomes an iconographic "little thing" that is incongruously painted like a doll (or is it a harlot?) and then stood in a corner for weeks (weeks!) while its parents indulge their intemperate behavior.

By the end of the century, conventions for describing *angelitos* seem so well established that accounts are sometimes condensed to a few central assumptions. For example, the Irish war correspondent William Howard Russell tells us in 1890 that "the Chilians—so I heard again and again—are quite content when their children die, and celebrate the decease by liberal entertainment and carousal."[25] The practice of the *velorio* has become so much a part of British folklore about Chileans that Russell does not feel the need to state his authority. He makes no attempt to understand either the ritual itself or the functions it might serve for its practitioners; instead, Russell insists that Chilean parents are "quite content" when their children die—a reaction that seems unlikely, at best. Moreover, as we saw earlier in the *Chilian Times* account, the practice itself seems to have become unworthy of description; only the assumptions projected onto it by outside observers remain noteworthy, chief among these that the parents lack affect and that their baby's death serves as an excuse for celebration.

Russell's failure to investigate the truth or context of the stories he has been told indicates the shift in British attitudes towards their host country by the end of the nineteenth century. In contrast to the high rates of marriage and assimilation into Chilean families in the colony's early years, young clerks after the 1850s were actively discouraged (or even prevented) from marrying Chilean women, families stopped giving Spanish names to their children, and a nexus of specifically Anglo cultural institutions developed to further the split. Notably too, by this late stage of the colony's development, distinctions between British and American colonists have been elided. They merge into one "English speaking" community, united by a common fear of contagion

---

24. Nelson R. Boyd, *Chili: Sketches of Chili and the Chilians During the War, 1879–1880* (London: W. H. Allen, 1881), 41–42.

25. William Howard Russell, *A Visit to Chile and the Nitrate fields of Tarapacá, etc.* (London: J. S. Virtue, 1890), 80.

by Chilean habits, values, and morals. The Reverend Aitken, a Presbyterian minister who settled in the colony in the 1890s, wrote, "You may live in Valparaiso for many years and scarcely get as far towards acquaintance with Chileans as to learn to speak their language. . . . the English community people decline to mix with the natives in social life; native manners do not attract them and so little sympathy have they with Chilean ways of looking at things—the Chilean standard of morals for instance—that intercourse on a friendly footing is impossible."[26] So shifts in representation of the *angelito* reflect larger changes in prevailing Anglo attitude of the times: earlier in the century, such accounts may have helped colonists and visitors to understand their hosts, but later in the century they seem to unite Anglo and American readers in their opposition to threatening Chilean values.

BUT THE preceding accounts are all written by male travelers. Might female travel writers be expected to be more attentive to Chilean mourning practices? For reasons both practical and cultural, women travelers tended to have greater access to the domestic life of their host countries. Furthermore, generic expectations dictated that women writers should focus on "mores and manners" whilst male writers emphasized trade opportunities, political stability, and/or scientific exploration, particularly when travelling to potential sites of economic investment like South America. Although over a dozen women had published travel narratives about Chile by the end of the century, only a few—and just two well-known writers, the Austrian Ida Pfeiffer and the British May Crommelin—include extended descriptions of *angelitos*.

A number of factors account for this initially surprising silence. First and most obviously, after Maria Graham's *Journal of a Residence in Chile* (1824) we have no travel narratives written by women about Chile until the 1850s, for the simple reason that very few women traveled there. After midcentury, more foreign women visited and resided in the country, but by that point in the colony's history, Anglo-Americans had begun to establish their own churches, clubs, and sports facilities to emphasize an English-speaking cultural identity over against Chilean national identity. Women were not encouraged to leave the enclave on Cerro Alegre; in fact, some present-day Anglo-Chileans told me that their grandmothers never managed to learn Spanish at all, reports that confirm Reverend Aitken's claim (see note 26). So while male travelers stumbled across rural or working class traditions as they wandered through the countryside or explored the city's poorer regions,

---

26. Reverend Aitken, *The Record* (August 1898). Quoted in G. E. David Pytches, *Foreigners and Religious Liberty in Chile, 1810–1925* (Santiago, Chile: Anglican Church, 1979), 75.

women were too closely confined within the colony to have many opportunities to explore.[27]

Among the Anglo-American women writers who did describe the practice of mourning an *angelito* was a North American, Mrs. George B. Merwin (née Loretta Wood). Daughter of Ohio Governor Reuben Wood, Merwin followed her father and husband to Chile in 1853 after her father was appointed American Consul and her husband became his secretary. Merwin published her *Three Years in Chile* in 1861. Visiting Concepción, she tells us,

> One day while there, the sound of music attracted me to my door, when I witnessed a most singular pageant. A peon was carrying on his extended hands a board about five feet long, upon which lay the body of an infant, dressed in pink. The eyes stood wide open, and the cheeks were painted to simulate the flush of health. The man was followed first by two women, then by two men—one playing a fiddle and the other a guitar—while a halfscore of both sexes, brought up the rear, gaily laughing and chatting together. They were going to bury the angelita, over whom they had danced and frolicked for three days—perhaps *lending* it, in the mean time, once or twice to some family that was not so fortunate as to have a corpse of their own; and so furnishing an excuse for orgies quite as wild and ridiculous as those of an Irish wake. This custom is generally observed among the more degraded classes, who often keep a corpse for festive purposes until it becomes offensive to all who approach the house.[28]

Since this is quite an early account, Merwin describes the scene in detail. Like most observers, she emphasizes the uncanny artificiality of the child: the festive clothing, open eyes, and painted cheeks. As strongly as male writers, too, she implicitly condemns the tone of the "pageant": the music, gay laughter, dancing, and frolicking. Merwin goes beyond some other observers, though, in driving home her critique with an apparently invented extra bit of grotesquerie: the idea that the parents might be so heartless as to *lend* their child's body to others, a violation of notions of moral decency that she emphasizes with italics, the word "corpse," and the heavy irony conveyed by the idea of a family "not so fortunate as to have a corpse of their own." Finally, Merwin seems to have been the first overtly to compare Chilean to Irish mourning

27. Comparison of the narratives written by women in Chile with those written by men reinforces Sara Mills's point that female-authored texts are constrained by multiple factors—including gender, class, purpose of journey, textual conventions, and reception by critics and readers—so we should not be surprised to find that these texts do not cover the same material as those written by men.

28. Merwin, *Three Years in Chile*, 92–93.

practices—a parallel that others soon seized on, as we will see. Class and ethnic identities are conflated here and jointly condemned as "degraded."

The difficulty of gaining access to the world outside the increasingly isolated English-speaking colony is addressed by a later Anglo-American woman who described the *angelito:* May Crommelin, who in 1896 published a detailed portrait of the everyday lives of the British in Argentina and Chile in the last years of the century. Interestingly, Crommelin follows Merwin in emphasizing the Irish character of the *velorio.* But Merwin puts a distinctly disapproving spin on the influence: Chilean wakes are "orgies quite as wild and ridiculous as those of an Irish wake." Merwin's early xenophobia may have been shaped by ethnic tensions in her hometown of Cleveland, which by 1850 had experienced a sudden influx of immigrants as a result of Irish fleeing the Great Famine of 1845–1849.

By contrast, Crommelin herself was Irish and her account emphasizes her curiosity about the motivations underlying a tradition she too initially considers shocking. Introducing the *angelito,* Crommelin first alerts us to the difficulties foreigners faced when seeking to understand Chilean culture, saying,

> Among other sights, that of a child's wake is most interesting; but, of course, difficult for a foreigner to see, if not impossible. When riding with friends one day, I was surprised to see a man trudging towards a cemetery gate, carrying a small bright-blue coffin unconcernedly over his shoulder. Two women, shrouded in the usual black *mantos,* trotted behind without much semblance of grief. 'That is a very poor funeral,' said my companions. 'Generally a *huaso* gallops off after the wake with the coffin under his arm; he is half tipsy from drinking *chicha* in the house, so he and his comrades race along the roads, and maybe drop the coffin!' On inquiring further, full particulars were given me of this custom, which again reminded me of old Ireland, my native land.[29]

So Crommelin begins by reinforcing several conventions of Anglo portrayals of the *angelito:* first and most importantly, lack of affect on the part of the bereaved parents, which implies that they are unnatural; second, references to drunkenness and generally "inappropriate" behavior, again reinforcing a sense of the Chilean as lacking in decency; and third, associations with "Celtic" character traits—and, by implication, with Catholicism. Note also that Crommelin's companions seem rather disappointed with this "poor funeral," and describe the galloping *huaso* and dropped coffin as a comic spectacle, while Crommelin herself seems to view the funeral of a child as little more than a unique tourist attraction.

---

29. Crommelin, *Over the Andes from the Argentine to Chili and Peru,* 267.

On the other hand, the tone of Crommelin's comparison with Irish wakes is unexpected. Whereas Merwin dismisses Irish wakes as "wild and ridiculous," Crommelin embraces them as nostalgic reminder of "old Ireland" and avows a sense of connection. Merwin coded both Chilean and Irish ethnicities as lower class, while Crommelin implicitly separates class and ethnicity in asserting her own Irish identity. From her subject position, already on the margins of Empire, she is able to see the *angelito* differently.

As a result of this shift from distance to identification, Crommelin goes on to subvert some of the stereotypical representations of the *angelito*. She actively inquires into the custom and elicits "full particulars" of the practice—an unprecedented move that demonstrates genuine curiosity rather than projection of coded assumptions. In reporting what she learned from her research, Crommelin explains,

> Wakes for persons of all ages are not uncommon in Chili; but especially the *velono* [*sic*][30] of a child is made an occasion for feasting, as the sinless babe is supposed to become straightway a little angel, or *angelito*, without passing through the cares and sorrows of life. So this happy event is celebrated by much eating, more drinking, and the neighbours rejoice around the corpse, which is propped up like a small saint, surrounded by lights and flowers. My friend Mrs. C.[31] was one day passing the house of her washerwoman, when she saw a crowd within, singing and carousing. 'Look in, señorita; it is an *angelito's* wake,' said her maid . . . Peeping through the open door, she saw the corpse of a child of three hung up against the wall above the bed; it was dressed in white, and wreathed round with flowers. The poor mother hovered near, weeping, although partly consoled by her friends' joyful assurances that the *niño* was now become a 'little lamp of light,' which, when she herself died, would show her the way to heaven. The general merriment and singing are also supposed to cheer the infant soul itself on its flight from earth.[32]

What fascinates in this account is that while Crommelin is by no means sympathetic towards Chilean culture—her book includes many of the standard references to filth and squalor and echoes conventional views of the "Chilean peasants'" incurable habits of lying, drinking, and lazing about—she is by far the most informed reader of the practice of the *angelito*. Unlike other writers of her time, she explains the context and function of the ceremony by means of quite accurate summaries of Chilean folklore. Although she was

---

30. The misspelling *velono* was probably a common typesetter's missetting of the "ri" in *velorio* as "n" rather than a mistake on Crommelin's part.

31. Mrs. C was possibly one of the Coopers of Valparaíso.

32. Crommelin, *Over the Andes from the Argentine to Chili and Peru*, 268.

not a firsthand witness, she actively sought information about the practice and took the time to learn about the beliefs underlying it, apparently through women's domestic networks (her friend, and that friend's presumably Chilean washerwoman and maid). And these networks here function, interestingly enough, through a scene of surveillance as the Anglo mistress "peeps" covertly through an open door.

As we assess the degree to which different types of Anglo travelers informed themselves about the roots and functions of these children's wakes, the evidence of Chilean folklorists can inform our comparison. Briefly, the custom seems to have arisen as Catholic parents in South and Central American countries, struggling to find ways of reconciling themselves to the all too frequent death of young children, appropriated the Catholic belief that children who die before the age of seven bypass purgatory to go directly to heaven. Mourners combined this belief with indigenous burial customs and ceremonies. Folklorists have uncovered a complex array of determinants underlying the practice, including stipulations that "we must not cry for children who die, because while we mourn for them we prevent them from seeing the face of God"; that "the *angelito* in heaven is wounded when its mother cries too much"; and that "the mother who wants her child, dead at a young age, to go to heaven, must dance on the day following the burial."[33] The wakes incorporate traditional songs such as the following:

> don't cry, good mothers,
> although you loved your child:
> it saddens the *angelito*,
> and it angers Our Lord.[34]

This warning that too-sorrowful parents hinder their children's transition to heaven is reinforced repeatedly, for example in tales that too many parental tears wet the *angelito*'s wings so that it cannot fly, or descriptions of Jesus holding the *angelito* as the two look down from heaven to ensure the parents are suitably joyful. What is more, mothers receive spiritual benefits in return for her suffering: a mother who has given seven (or in some accounts nine) *angelitos* to Jesus assures herself a place for herself in heaven, where her dead children will be waiting to greet her.

---

33. Julio Vicuña Cifuentes, *Mitos y Supersticiones: estudios del folklore chileno recogidos de la tradicion oral,* 3rd ed. (Santiago: Editorial Nascimento, 1947), 185; rough translation mine.

34. Cifuentes, *Mitos y Supersticiones,* 185. Original text as follows; rough translation mine:

> No lloréis, madres amables,
> aunque les tengais amor:
> se entristece el angelito,
> se enoja Nuestro Señor.

If we revisit Smith's and others' accounts with the insights of Chilean anthropologists informing our perspective, ironically we see that Anglo-Americans' sensationalized tales reveal them as incompetent readers. In its cultural context, the custom of celebrating *angelitos* can be seen as a coping mechanism that developed in response to the high rate of child death. *Angelitos* were assured both continued life in Heaven and continued connection to their parents, bringing the parents nearer to salvation and greeting them when they ultimately arrived. So the mourning process becomes a marker, not of Gothic excess and the uncanny, not of drunken and callous parents, but of a structure, explanation, and meaning that may have helped parents to survive the deaths of their young children.

The fact that Crommelin's account, above, accords well with the evidence of Chilean folklorists indicates the effectiveness of female networks as a means of imparting cultural practices. Some—though clearly not all—women managed to learn more than might be expected about their host culture. Contrasting Crommelin's exploration with Russell's dismissive, Smith's horrified, or Merwin's ironic description, we can see that Crommelin not only took a different approach to researching a ritual she had first casually observed in the streets, but uses her text to perform cultural work quite different from that performed by other travel writers. What factors facilitated her closer research and, ultimately, her more nuanced representation of this cultural practice?

Crommelin was not only a woman but also Irish and of an old Huguenot family and thus doubly marginalized: by gender and by nationality. Scholars have recently begun to emphasize the fact that the identities of British women abroad could be remarkably complex in their relationship to the project of Empire. Crommelin, from her position on the margins of the power structure, represented the colonized world through very different eyes from those of either male or more securely English or North American travel writers. After noting Crommelin's empathy with grieving Chilean mothers and curiosity about the "truth" of the *velorio,* then, we might be tempted to conclude that her account of Chile is more objective than the others. But that would be too simple. Even Crommelin's narrative is full of contradictions. For example, her *huaso* with the blue coffin tossed carelessly over his shoulder echoes conventional descriptions of the *angelito,* while her summary of the beliefs governing the practice and the reference to the weeping mother subverts these conventions.

Taken together, these contradictory perspectives expose the multiple and often conflicting subject positions of nineteenth-century women travel writers. As Sara Mills points out in a different context, to regard women as somehow removed from the assumptions of colonialism, able to "see" the Other with untainted eyes, falls into the trap of "accepting the discursive stereotypes of women's superior moral position over men."[35] Mills's claims are reinforced by Merwin's stereotypical account, which enforces the impossibility of claiming that women travelers automatically possessed greater empathy for or insight into the domestic.

There is, then, no unmediated "truth" that we can access about the *velorios* and use to weigh the comparative merits of male versus female or English versus Irish accounts. Moreover, the available sample of accounts is far too small to allow claims about differing treatment by narrators from different subject positions. Instead, we can use all these accounts to map shifting anxieties of empire. As the British Empire slipped into decline, British travel writers began increasingly to stress the exotic, "Not English" character of Chilean mourning. For example, travelers' comparisons between Chilean national character and the Irish became more frequent after the Home Rule movement in Ireland gathered force in the late nineteenth and early twentieth centuries. Merwin seems to have initiated the explicit comparison between Chilean and Irish customs, but other authors continued it right through the early twentieth century. Crommelin's account proves that there are always exceptions to the rule. Even after her more sympathetic reading of the Celtic/Chilean connection, however, two later writers seem to explicitly echo her while ignoring her identification with, rather than rejection of, Chilean mourning: C. J. Lambert, publishing a book about his life in Chile just after World War II, tells us that "Like the Irish, the Chilean peons drown the grief of a death in an orgy of drinking and dancing, and this is especially the case if a baby dies."[36] And Francis Maitland, in his emigrants' guide *Chile: Its Land and People* (1914), gives Crommelin's account of an *angelito*'s wake almost word for word, but concludes quite differently: "One is tempted to wonder whether this custom—a tenacious one among the people—can have any effect upon the rate of infant mortality, which is appallingly high in Chile."[37] So in place of Crommelin's sympathetic glimpse of a weeping mother consoled by thoughts of the child as angel, Maitland returns to the Gothic roots of earlier accounts, with a difference: he combines earlier fascination with infanticide with his critique of the *angelito,* and concludes with barely veiled speculation that the *angelito* may have been murdered to secure its *parents'* place in heaven.

---

35. Sara Mills, *Discourses of Difference: An Analysis of Women's Travel Writing and Colonialism* (New York and London: Routledge, 1991), 20–30.

36. Lambert, *Sweet Waters: A Chilean Farm* (London: Chatto & Windus, 1952), 118.

37. Maitland, *Chile: Its Land and People* (London: Francis Griffiths, 1914), 186.

These conflations of Irish and Chilean "superstition" and licentious behavior demonstrate more than just the intertextuality building across travel narratives. The fear of "strangers" who are not necessarily racially or even ethnically distinct from ourselves that is now known as xenophobia develops over the course of the nineteenth century in tandem with historical events. With the rise in importance of the Irish conflict, qualities once dismissed as simply indicative of Spanish or Catholic or Indian cruelty or savagery or primitivism become attached to a new locus of anxiety: the Celtic threat.

The fact that observers were so strongly compelled to reject the practice of mourning the *angelito,* to define English culture over against a concept of childhood that Dickens's Podsnap would term "Not English!," underscores the instability of Victorian culture itself as well as the increasingly self-conscious domesticity of the colony in Chile. Thus *angelito* narratives tell us more about Victorian anxieties than about Chilean views of childhood. Because Chilean mourning practices clashed so markedly with English and North American burial rituals, Anglo observers seemed unable to gain any distance on the wake of an infant and thus depicted *angelitos,* as Smith does, as helpless, desecrated victims of Catholic excess, particularly self-indulgence in drink and dancing.

But while actual mourning practices in Britain and America may have been quite different from these wakes, there is also strong irony in Anglo-American outrage over the *angelito,* because in some ways *angelitos* closely resemble iconicized Victorian children. Paul Dombey, Little Nell, Eva, and the many other dying children of Anglo-American texts worked as savior-figures, blessing and exhorting adults from deathbeds draped with all the signifying conventions Victorian sentimentality could muster: the iconicized child is adored as purer than the rest of us and as sanctifying those lucky enough to be in its presence. Like *angelitos,* they are too pure for this world, so that we should not mourn their death but rather rejoice their passage into a better world. Also like *angelitos,* they leave the promise of our own salvation behind them. So the *angelito* terrifyingly literalizes Victorian worship of dying child-saints.

Of course Victorian adoration of the dead or dying child was not confined to novels. The cultural valence attached to the figure of the *angelito* invites comparison not only with the iconicized Child of literature, but with postmortem photographs of Victorian children. We have visual records of this practice in, for example, Stanley Burns's collection of pre- and postmortem photographs, *Sleeping Beauty.* The collection contains some images of adults, but most are hand-tinted portraits of dead children, arranged stiffly on their mothers' knees or in chairs, shaped by an iconography that strikingly parallels that of the *angelitos*—though the pretense of life and vitality in these images may now appear even more literally morbid than the transformation of the body of a dead child into a religious icon in the *velorio*.[38]

The Victorian fascination with the figure of the dead child has led to the assumption that nineteenth-century children died in staggering numbers. But as Ann Douglas points out, more recent research indicates that the infant mortality rate was not as high as had been thought—certainly no higher than in the eighteenth century.[39] This evidence parallels the lack of support for a fact-based explanation for the "epidemic" of infanticide in the mid nineteenth century. Something else was going on: a cultural shift that saw the dead child as a beacon of salvation. In his study of Victorian sentimentality, *Sacred Tears,* Fred Kaplan shows that Dickens and other authors "believed that the fictional presentations of the deaths of children had extraordinary corrective potential. . . . Intensely aware of children dead and dying, Dickens and many of his contemporaries thought it impossible to be excessively feeling or 'sentimental' in any pejorative way about such losses."[40]

To recapitulate the patterns observed in this essay: newspaper accounts of infanticide helped to build towards a xenophobic reaction against the host culture by using the icon of the dead child to cast suspicion on Chilean parenting practices—and thus on Chilean morality and even humanity. Smith's 1855 account reaffirmed colonists' solidarity with the values of the "Home Country" by explicitly contrasting the "revolting" "maudlin profanity [and] midnight debauchery" of the Chilean with the "refined sentiment" of the Anglo mother. Merwin, writing at roughly the same time, calls Chilean mourning as "wild and ridiculous" as an Irish wake; she is less interested in the child itself, describing it as open-eyed and painted but lacking Smith's *frisson* of the uncanny. By contrast with these early accounts, the *Chilian Times* in 1876 and William Russell in 1890 hardly bother to describe the *angelito* itself, merely using an assumed response to the practice to telegraph a message about Chile's lack of civilization and her citizens' lack of human feeling.

By the 1870s and after, as the "epidemic" of Chilean child murder reached its hypothetical height, the figure of the *angelito* seems frozen in

---

38. The difference can be seen by comparing Anglo postmortem photographs with a Chilean painting, "Velorio del angelito," by Arturo Gordon (Chile, early twentieth century). This painting belies Anglo accounts of the debauchery of these wakes by depicting a sombre, mournful crowd; it also subverts Anglo accounts of the *angelito* as a gaudy, tinsel-draped, brightly painted spectacle by depicting an infant as a small, still figure so white and blank that it virtually becomes the absent center of the painting.

39. Ann Douglas, "Heaven our Home: Consolation Literature in the Northern United States, 1830–1880," in *Death in America.*

40. Fred Kaplan, *Sacred Tears: Sentimentality in Victorian Literature* (Princeton, NJ: Princeton University Press, 1987), 50–51.

place, a pathetic victim of Catholic and Latino debauchery that serves to highlight the superior sensibility of the English-speaking community. The unquestioned perception that the Anglo-American cult of the dying child and Anglo-American mourning rituals are "refined" while the practice of the *angelito* is revolting and maudlin, that Chileans are involved in an epidemic of child-murder while the much-discussed "epidemic" at home in Britain can be ignored, reveals a curious blind spot in the colonists' perceptions of self and other. Only May Crommelin seems able to lift the xenophobic veil as she seeks understanding of the beliefs and emotions driving the ritual of the *angelito.*

What cultural work was performed by the colony's fascination with dead babies, and how does the circulation of these stories help Anglo-Americans— both at home and abroad—to consolidate a national identity? By interpreting the range of Anglo-American accounts of infanticide and *angelitos* published in Chile in the nineteenth and the early twentieth century, we cannot learn much about Chilean attitudes towards children or child death. We can, however, read these accounts for the information they provide about Britons and North Americans in Chile. By contrasting Loretta Merwin and May Crommelin's perspectives, for example, we learn that women were not, as has been implied in standard accounts, either entirely removed from the culture or centrally responsible for the domestication and isolation of the British in Chile.[41] Although *angelitos* become set pieces in travelers' descriptions of Chile, they are inflected by a range of factors: gender, regional, ethnic, and national affiliation; the larger context of the relation between the colony and its host country; more broadly still, the state of empire worldwide. Thus these stories enact very different agendas.

The discursive presence of the figure of the dead child in Chile is therefore doubly revealing of the ways that national identity is created and sustained. In their writings of all kinds, Britons and Americans implicitly or explicitly accused parents—especially mothers—of carelessness or worse in relation to their children; they ostentatiously regretted the public display of mourning that should, to Anglo eyes, be kept private; they compared supposed neglect of or even violence towards children in Chile to an idealized view of the careful nurturing of children in Britain and the United States. By the end of the century, then, developing xenophobic sentiments focused anxiety specifically

---

41. The few scholars who have written on the colony—mostly economists and political scientists—tend to attribute its change in attitude towards Chileans at least partly to the increasing numbers of women who arrived from Britain and the domesticity that resulted. This reading can be found implicitly in the work of John Mayo and explicitly in a privately printed study by the Reverend G. E. David Pytches, *Foreigners and Religious Liberty in Chile, 1810–1925* (Santiago, Chile: Anglican Church, 1979).

on the child's body, which became a site for claims about the immorality and lack of civilization of a culture that could (mis)treat young children so.

As Edward Said has pointed out, "stories are at the heart of what explorers and novelists say about strange regions of the world,"[42] and narratives describing *angelitos* trace the gradual development of an imperial Anglo national identity as the colony established itself in relation to its host country. In defining themselves over against the "debauched," "ridiculous," or uncivilized practices of Chilean others, Britons and North Americans used the corpses of children as sites onto which they could project shifting anxieties of empire. Xenophobia is fear of the guest, stranger, person that looks different, foreigner. But the English-speaking colonists themselves uncomfortably inhabited all these subject positions. While in the early years of their settlement in the New World, these English-speaking guests in Chile assimilated rapidly, learning Spanish and marrying into the host culture, by the end of the century colonists had reversed the expected order, treating Chileans no longer as hosts, but ironically as foreigners. In the process, colonists contributed to a developing culture of xenophobic rejection of the stranger within: an uncanny double who was not racially distinct and not always visibly distinguishable by ethnicity or class. As they seek to concretize a difference that threatens to elude ocular proof, the colonists' stories of infanticide and *angelitos* echo, refract and inflect one other. Together, they embroider a portrait of the lost child who becomes the uncanny, absent center of this tale: at once innocent and tawdry, savior and sorrow, relic and relinquished.

Works Cited

Arnold, Matthew. "The Function of Criticism at the Present Time." In *Essays*. 9–36. Oxford: Oxford University Press, 1914.

Boyd, R. Nelson. *Chili: Sketches of Chili and the Chilians During the War, 1879–1880*. London: W. H. Allen, 1881.

Burns, Stanley B. *Sleeping Beauty: Memorial Photography in America*. Altadena, CA: Twelvetrees Press, 1990.

Crommelin, May. *Over the Andes from the Argentine to Chili and Peru*. London: Richard Bentley and Son, 1896.

Douglas, Ann. "Heaven our Home: Consolation Literature in the Northern United States, 1830–1880." In *Death in America*, edited by David E. Stannard. 49–68. Philadelphia: University of Pennsylvania Press, 1975.

Freud, Sigmund. *On Creativity and the Unconscious*. Edited by Benjamin Nelson. Translated by Joan Riviere. New York: Harper Books, 1958.

Graham, María. *Journal of Residence in Chile during the year 1822. And a voyage from Chile*

---

42. Edward Said, *Culture and Imperialism* (New York: Random House, 1993), xii.

to Brazil in 1823. Edited by Jennifer Hayward. Charlottesville: University Press of Virginia, 2003.

Haigh, Samuel. *Sketches of Buenos Ayres and Chile*. London: J. Carpenter and Son, 1829.

Hall, Catherine, and Sonya O. Rose, eds. *At Home with the Empire: Metropolitan Culture and the Imperial World*. Cambridge: Cambridge University Press, 2006.

Kaplan, Cora. "Imagining Empire: History, Fantasy and Literature." In *At Home with the Empire: Metropolitan Culture and the Imperial World*, edited by Catherine Hall and Sonya O. Rose. 191–211. Cambridge: Cambridge University Press, 2006.

Kaplan, Fred. *Sacred Tears: Sentimentality in Victorian Literature*. Princeton, NJ: Princeton University Press, 1987.

Lambert, C. J. *Sweet Waters: A Chilean Farm*. London: Chatto & Windus, 1952.

Maitland, Francis J. G. *Chile: Its Land and People*. London: Francis Griffiths, 1914.

Mayo, John. *British Merchants and Chilean Development, 1851–1886*. Boulder, CO: Westview Press, 1987.

McDonagh, Josephine. *Child Murder and British Culture, 1720–1900*. Cambridge: Cambridge University Press, 2003.

Mercantile Reporter (Valparaíso).

Merwin, Loretta L. *Three Years in Chile*. New York: Follett, Foster, 1863.

Mills, Sara. *Discourses of Difference: An Analysis of Women's Travel Writing and Colonialism*. New York and London: Routledge, 1991.

Pfeiffer, Ida. *A Lady's Travels Round the World*. Translated by William Hazlitt. London: Routledge, 1852.

Pratt, Mary Louise. *Imperial Eyes: Travel Writing and Transculturation*. New York: Routledge, 1992.

Pytches, G. E. David. *Foreigners and Religious Liberty in Chile, 1810–1925*. Pamphlet. Santiago, Chile: Anglican Church, 1979.

Russell, William Howard. *A Visit to Chile and the Nitrate fields of Tarapacá, etc.* London: J. S. Virtue, 1890.

Said, Edward. *Culture and Imperialism*. New York: Random House, 1993.

Schor, Esther. *Bearing the Dead: The British Culture of Mourning from the Enlightenment to Victoria*. Princeton, NJ: Princeton University Press, 1994.

Smith, Edmond Reuel. *The Araucanians, or Notes of a Tour among Indian Tribes of Southern Chile*. New York: Harper & Brothers, 1855.

Valparaiso and West Coast Mail, The (Valparaíso).

Valparaiso Echo (Valparaíso).

Valparaiso Herald (Valparaíso).

Vincent, Lady Howard (Ethel Gwendoline) Moffatt. *China to Peru Over the Andes: A Journey Through South America*. London: S. Low, Marston, 1894.

PART II

Xenophobic Panic

❦

Panic is a social and affective product of xenophobia that typically has a visible, public dimension. Evident in both individual impulses and broader social practices, this feeling is traceable in the policies, politics, news, and events of the nineteenth century. Deeply intertwined with the fears and anxieties discussed in Part I of this volume, the textual and physical reactions this section seeks to explore are those often-vexed responses evinced by a culture in the grips of xenophobia. The essays here investigate the power of loathing and panic to define Englishness through the perceived characteristics of the foreigner, tracing the ways in which both the most tragic and the most celebratory historical moments and landscapes were articulated through Victorian xenophobia.

Charlotte Boyce's discussion, "Food, Famine, and the Abjection of Irish Identity in Early Victorian Representation," takes the diseased potato as a signifier of a flawed foreign Irishness that produced deep revulsion for the foreign, rather than compassion for the suffering the famine produced. Joy Sperling's "'Wot is to Be': The Visual Construction of Empire at the Crystal Palace Exhibition, London, 1851" speaks to the way that the layout of the Crystal Palace evinced xenophobic disgust, even while it offered to articulate the wonders of world advances. Patrick Brantlinger takes this thread across European history to explore England's conflicted relationship with Turkey in "Terrible Turks: Victorian Xenophobia and the Ottoman Empire." Finally, Thomas Prasch's "Ethnicity as Marker in Henry Mayhew's *London Labour and the London Poor* asks how foreignness and reactionary xenophobia have been underexplored in the reading of this important nineteenth-century text. All of these essays investigate how xenophobia is produced by and produces loathing and panic.

This section gestures towards the final part of this volume, "The Foreign Invasion," with which it overlaps as well. While one could certainly shift the placement of these essays because the themes are deeply interrelated, we hoped to signal some of the leitmotifs that emerged in our study of xenophobia with this structure. We have sought to signal the interdependency of these themes by opening Part III with Heidi Kaufman's essay on xenophobic panic, which bridges Parts II and III.

6

Food, Famine, and the Abjection of Irish Identity in Early Victorian Representation

❧

CHARLOTTE BOYCE

On May 27, 1848, with Ireland in the grip of a catastrophic famine, the result of the blight *phytophthora infestans* in the potato crop, the *Illustrated London News* (*ILN*) published a leader responding to the ongoing crisis:

> As usual, the affairs of Ireland continue to trouble and perplex the people of this country [England]. . . . So much has been said and written about Ireland—so many and so conflicting have been the statements put forth, that the people of this country begin to loathe the very name of Irish misery. They would relieve it if they knew how; but the task seems to be too great for their accomplishment or for their comprehension. . . . Potatoes are all [the Irish peasant's] diet. He has no other resource, unless grass or sea-weeds may be considered as aids to his dinners. He lives in a wigwam, and shares it with a pig. He speaks a barbarous language, and is in arrear with the intelligence of the world. . . . The masses of the people cannot be called civilized by any stretch of flattery. . . . The condition of the Esquimaux or Kaffirs is preferable to theirs. The weak Irish peasant may starve, but the strong Kaffir contrives to live. The Laplander can get rein-deer flesh or blubber to supply his need; but there is nothing but the potato, and not enough of that, for the Celt in

I am grateful to Dr Julia Thomas for her assistance in providing illustrations and to Dr Gavin Schaffer for his valuable comments on this essay.

Ireland. . . . We can, in fact, see no hope for Ireland until the people are raised
into the condition of bread-eaters.[1]

This article is remarkable for a number of reasons. First, it represents a discernible departure from the broadly sympathetic attitude that had characterized
previous *ILN* accounts of the Famine. In 1847, the newspaper had sent artist
James Mahony to report on the situation in some of the worst affected parts
of western Ireland. His illustrations, supplemented by harrowing descriptions of suffering and starvation, were designed to elicit the compassion of
the *ILN*'s substantial middle-class readership.[2] In the article above, however,
empathy has mutated into antipathy; what is accentuated here is the profound otherness of the Irish peasantry. As Leslie Williams notes, "the editorial viewpoint regarding the Irish is comparable to the proto-anthropological
view of the imperial or colonial reportage in the paper. The Irish experience
is seen by the *ILN* as foreign and is reported in that context."[3] Furthermore,
it is implied that Irish distress is determined by Irish alterity. Equated with
(and even subordinated to) "uncivilised" tribes from far-flung locations in
terms of habitation, diet, and intellect, the intractable and improvident Irish
are held implicitly responsible for their own wretchedness, owing to their reliance on a potato-based agricultural system. It appears that the article's open
acknowledgment of English "loathing" for recurrent tales of "Irish misery"
is paralleled by a tacit, insidious hostility towards Irish people themselves.[4]

Yet to read the *ILN*'s commentary simply in terms of hostility would be
reductive. Concomitant with the anti-Irish sentiment located in the text, and
most evident in the "proto-anthropological" tone identified by Williams, is a

---

1. "Irish Agitation and Irish Misery," *Illustrated London News* 12 (27 May 1848): 335–336.

2. Peter W. Sinnema suggests that "between 1842 and 1852, the *ILN*'s weekly circulation
expanded dramatically, from approximately 20,000 copies in its first few months of publication
to well over 100,000 a decade later." *Dynamics of the Pictured Page: Representing the Nation in the
Illustrated London News*, 207.

3. Leslie Williams, "Irish Identity and the *Illustrated London News*, 1846–1851," in *Representing Ireland: Gender, Class, Nationality*, 91.

4. While recognizing the existence of a consolidating British national identity in the nineteenth century, I will tend to use the terms "England" and "English," rather than "Britain" and
"British," throughout my analysis of attitudes towards the Irish in the early Victorian period, for a
number of reasons. First, this pattern of referencing echoes that used in much of the primary material on which this study draws. Second, during the nineteenth century, there was no consistently
"British" approach to Ireland; as Roy Foster argues, "Scotland's or Wales's relationship to Ireland is
on many levels a different entity from that of 'England.'" *Paddy and Mr Punch: Connections in Irish
and English History*, xii. For instance, an 1843 cartoon, "Rebecca and her Daughters," directly aligned
Daniel O'Connell's Irish Repealers with the Welsh Rebecca Rioters. *Punch* 5 (1843): 5, while, in a
footnote to his *Letters on the Condition of the People of Ireland*, Thomas Campbell Foster explicitly
linked the Irish to the Welsh, Scottish, and French by highlighting their shared Celtic origins (*Letters on the Condition of the People of Ireland*, 46). Later Victorian ethnological studies, such as John
Beddoe's *The Races of Britain*, emphasized these Celtic connections.

lingering sense of fascination. In spite of its professed aversion to the subject, the *ILN* leader appears compelled to add to the weight of material published on Ireland, precisely because Ireland remains fractious, intransigent, contradictory. The impenetrable "Irish problem" constantly confounds English attempts at comprehension and resolution and, therefore, requires endless analysis.

The *ILN*'s article, then, like much of the textual and visual material representing the Irish during the early Victorian period, vacillates anxiously between intense interest in and barely concealed repugnance for its subject matter. According to Cecilia Sjöholm, this "fascination and rejection of the other . . . belongs to the symptom of xenophobia," a cultural response more commonly understood as a simple hatred of foreigners.[5] However, it is worth noting that the Greek word "xenos," from which xenophobia derives, signifies not only the threatening outsider but also the welcomed guest. Thus, as Rajani Sudan argues, xenophobia is caught up in a rather more elaborate set of relations than straightforward aversion. Beginning with the idea that xenophobia "operates as a crucial ideological force in the task of organizing a space, of making and remaking the territories that . . . demarcate what is and what is not 'home,'" Sudan proceeds to argue that this process is not self-sufficient: "xenophobia also depends on an economy with another less familiar term, xenodochy."[6] Defined as the "entertainment of strangers" or "hospitality" (*OED*), xenodochy

> may take shape either as an expression of a mutual intertwining or as a form of maintenance. In either expression, foreign entertainment implies that the apparently radical differences between familiar and foreign are in fact contingent on each other . . . Xenophobia and xenodochy work as an economy because they are mutually constitutive, and it is through this economy that national and cultural identity is manifested.[7]

This economy of relations helps to explain interactions between England and Ireland in the early Victorian period. Since the 1800 Act of Union, Ireland had been politically bound to the British mainland and thus "intertwined" with the home nation in a complex relationship that was at least partially xenodochial. The Irish were welcomed (albeit sporadically and unevenly) into a variety of facets of English life. Roy Foster highlights the prominence of Irish figures, such as William Maginn, in the Victorian press, while

---

5. Cecilia Sjöholm, *Kristeva and the Political* (London and New York: Routledge, 2005), 66.

6. Rajani Sudan, *Fair Exotics: Xenophobic Subjects in English Literature, 1720–1850* (Philadelphia: University of Pennsylvania Press, 2002), 17.

7. Sudan, *Fair Exotics* 6–7.

Linda Colley points out that "Irishmen were . . . an important component
of Britain's armed forces" during the Napoleonic Wars and beyond.[8] Even
the traditionally Anglo-centric *Times* was forced to admit in 1848 the vital
role played by Irish industry in the English economy, conceding, "It is from
Ireland that we draw our rough labour. The Celt—and we are bound to give
him credit for it—is the hewer of wood and drawer of water to the Saxon."[9]

Yet, as the imperious tone employed by the *Times* here indicates, a troubling sense of the "foreignness" of the Irish remained. This manifested itself
clearly in the succession of parliamentary commissions and select committees
set up during the first half of the nineteenth century to investigate persistent
Irish poverty.[10] The almost obsessive determination to scrutinize Ireland and
its inhabitants betrayed a conviction that the Irish were essentially different
from (and implicitly inferior to) their fellow Britons. Melissa Fegan argues
that the massive body of literature on the Irish produced was motivated
less by humanitarian concerns than by "fear"—specifically, the English fear
"of retrograding to the Irish level."[11] The liberal middle classes in England
emphasized the universal human capacity for self-improvement, yet it seems
that the potential for Irish subjects to achieve equality with their English
counterparts was kept in continual ideological abeyance. Edward G. Lengel
argues that union with Ireland posed problems for the English psyche that
relations with colonial territories such as India did not: unlike the latter,
"[Ireland's] people would, it was hoped, ultimately 'amalgamate' with those
of England," but, importantly, "they would also always remain the 'other'"—
almost English, but not quite.[12]

It is this problem of the proximity of sameness and difference in the other
that elicits a phobic response. In *Strangers to Ourselves,* Julia Kristeva describes
the profoundly unsettling nature of exchanges with the foreigner in precisely
these terms:

> Strange indeed is the encounter with the other. . . . Confronting the foreigner
> whom I reject and with whom at the same time I identify, I lose my boundar-

8. Foster, *Paddy and Mr Punch,* 290; Linda Colley, *Britons: Forging the Nation, 1707–1837* (London: Vintage, 1996), 8.

9. *Times* (26 December 1848): 4.

10. Redcliffe N. Salaman suggests that "in the first thirty-one years of the century, parliament . . . appointed no less than one hundred and fourteen commissions and sixty-one committees
to report on Irish affairs" (*The History and Social Influence of the Potato* [1949; Cambridge: Cambridge University Press, 1985], 288).

11. Melissa Fegan, *Literature and the Irish Famine, 1845–1919* (Oxford: Oxford University
Press, 2002), 75.

12. Edward G. Lengel, *The Irish through British Eyes: Perceptions of Ireland in the Famine Era* (Westport, CT: Praeger, 2002), 20.

ies . . . I lose my composure. I feel "lost," "indistinct," "hazy." The uncanny
strangeness allows for many variations: they all repeat the difficulty I have in
situating myself with respect to the other.[13]

The language of confusion and disturbance here echoes the opening lines
of the *ILN* leader quoted at the beginning of this essay. Despite the availability of a vast body of knowledge on the subject ("so much has been said
and written"), Ireland remains an uncertain entity ("so conflicting have been
the statements put forth") that exceeds the limits of English comprehension
("they would relieve it if they knew how"), resulting in a temporary loss of
national composure and self-belief ("the task seems too great for their accom-
plishment"). Somewhat ironically, in confronting the "foreignness" of the
Irish, the *ILN*'s article instigates a disruptive process of self-questioning that
threatens to destabilize English national identity.

The loss of conceptual boundaries described by Kristeva in her analysis
of the encounter with the foreign is also reminiscent of, though less intense
than, the experience of abjection set out in her work *Powers of Horror.* Con-
ventionally defined as something "cast off" or "rejected" (*OED*), the abject,
for Kristeva, is that which must be "radically excluded" by the subject owing
to its ambiguity, its compositeness, its disruption of borders.[14] The abject
"disturbs identity, system, order," collapses the distinction between self and
other, and, in doing so, serves to remind the subject of both the trauma of
the initial process of ego-formation and the fragility of the ego now constituted (*PH*, 4). The subject's sense of autonomous self-hood is threatened by
the abject—but is also strangely attracted to the possibility of non-identity.
Kristeva writes of the "vortex of summons and repulsion" that overwhelms
those beset by abjection (*PH*, 1). Significantly, this dynamic mirrors the vac-
illation between fascination and loathing inherent in the xenophobic drive.
Indeed, Sjöholm argues that "modern pathologies such as racism and xenophobia . . . are in one way or another functions of abjection," which is therefore "not just an affair of the subject" but rather "co-extensive with the social
and symbolic dimension of society."[15]

How might abjection help to explain xenophobic responses to the Irish
in early Victorian representation? Since the publication of L. Perry Curtis
Jr.'s highly influential *Anglo-Saxons and Celts* and *Apes and Angels,* race has
been privileged as a key marker of Irish otherness in the nineteenth century,

---

13. Julia Kristeva, *Strangers to Ourselves,* trans. Leon S. Roudiez (London and New York: Harvester Wheatsheaf, 1991), 187.

14. Julia Kristeva, *Powers of Horror: An Essay on Abjection,* trans. Leon S. Roudiez (New York:
Columbia University Press, 1982), 2 (hereafter cited in text as *PH*).

15. Sjöholm, *Kristeva and the Political,* 98.

although a number of critics suggest that his accounts overdetermine the role of racial prejudice in representation.[16] As Roberto Romani points out, the term "race" was used rather loosely by early Victorian commentators; signifying anything from ethnicity to nationality, language to religion, "its range of application was mobile and indistinct."[17] A concern with race, in its modern sense, would therefore seem to offer too narrow a basis for interpreting the complex relations between Ireland and England in the 1830s and 1840s. A more productive strategy might be to examine the broader habits, characteristics, and cultural practices that served to distinguish the two nations in print culture. As Fintan Cullen points out, such differences were not necessarily conceived of negatively; xenodochial relations resulted in the construction of benevolent stereotypes, which co-existed with those of a less flattering nature.[18] Following the emergence of the potato blight in 1845, however, antipathetic representations of the Irish predominated. The very proximity of the ensuing Famine sparked fears in the press that a similar disaster could strike England; it was therefore ideologically imperative to explain the calamity in terms of Irish otherness.

One important marker of this cultural difference was food. Notably, the 1848 *ILN* leader, cited earlier, appears to attribute Ireland's distress to its over-dependence on the potato, a crop with which the country had long been linked in the English popular imagination. According to the *ILN,* the potato situates the Irish below even the "Kaffirs" and "Laplanders" (who, in spite of their supposed primitivity, exist on a protein diet), and in implicit opposition to the English, the "bread-eaters" whose dietary preferences and agricultural practices must be mimicked if the material conditions of Irish existence are to improve. Throughout history, food has been used in this way to demarcate cultural differences and codify xenophobic impulses. As Allison James suggests, "simple equations such as 'we eat meat, they don't,' 'we eat horse, they don't,' 'they eat insects, we don't,' affirm, in shared patterns of consumption and shared notions of edibility, our difference from others."[19] The food of the other can incite feelings of disgust and repulsion; its ingestion threatens to unsettle the safe boundaries of the self. Consequently, food can precipitate abjection and this, I argue, is crucial to understanding English representa-

---

16. See, for instance, Sheridan Gilley, "English Attitudes to the Irish in England, 1780–1900," in *Immigrants and Minorities in British Society;* Thomas Campbell Foster, *Paddy and Mr Punch,* 171–194; and Edward G. Lengel, *The Irish through British Eyes,* 4–6.

17. Roberto Romani, *National Character and Public Spirit in Britain and France, 1750–1914* (Cambridge: Cambridge University Press, 2002), 214.

18. Fintan Cullen, *Visual Politics: The Representation of Ireland, 1750–1930* (Cork: Cork University Press, 1997), 83.

19. Allison James, "How British is British Food?" in *Food, Health and Identity,* 72.

tions of the Irish during the Great Famine.[20] As the following sections of this essay will show, in a range of early Victorian texts and images, potatoes are conflated with Irish identity to the extent that the margins between the two collapse. A representational paradigm is formed in which the boundaries between subject and object, human and animal, consumer and consumed are broken down, and the Irish positioned as abject in an attempt to safeguard English identity at a moment of profound historical crisis.

Food

The link between potatoes and Ireland has a long history. First introduced to the country towards the end of the sixteenth century, the potato quickly became its major food crop. Redcliffe N. Salaman suggests that this preponderance relates to the agricultural system in place: Irish laborers found the potato "easier to raise, and safer and cheaper to store" than the cereal crops that tended to prevail in England.[21]

Potatoes, then, became an integral part of the Irish diet. According to Salaman, "at the time of the Union, about nine-tenths of the Irish population was subsisting almost entirely" on this single source of food.[22] Recent scholarship has debated these findings, but early Victorian travel literature provides anecdotal support for Salaman's account of the potato's dominance in Ireland.[23] Texts such as Emily Taylor's *The Irish Tourist,* Mr and Mrs S. C. Hall's *Ireland: Its Scenery, Character, Etc.* and Thackeray's *Irish Sketch-Book* made much of the quantity of potatoes consumed in Ireland and the manner of their consumption. Apparently oblivious to the political implications of poverty, Lady Chatterton, English wife of an Irish landowner and author of the popular *Rambles in the South of Ireland during the Year 1838,* noted that

---

20. Significantly, Kristeva claims that "food loathing is perhaps the most elementary and most archaic form of abjection" (*Powers of Horror,* 2).

21. Salaman, *The Influence of the Potato on the Course of Irish History* (Dublin: Browne and Nolan, 1943), 12. Notably, some of Salaman's claims about the Irish adoption of the potato reproduce the rhetoric located in the works of nineteenth-century commentator William Cobbett, discussed later in this essay. See, for instance, Salaman's assertion that "as soon as the potato was established [in Ireland], the standard of living automatically became fixed at a level commensurate with the energy its production demanded. The more the potato fulfilled the requirements of the household, the sooner endeavour damped down, and sloth and slovenliness exalted" (*The History and Social Influence of the Potato,* 343).

22. Salaman, *The History and Social Influence of the Potato,* 274.

23. Cormac Ó Gráda, for instance, argues that "contrary to common belief, the potato never became virtually the sole means of nourishment of the vast majority of the people of Ireland." *Black '47 and Beyond: The Great Irish Famine in History, Economy, and Memory* (Princeton, NJ: Princeton University Press, 2000), 17.

"a miserable-looking, tattered Irish boy, munching a potatoe . . . appears a dull reality to another ragged boy in the same predicament; but to a looker-on in a higher rank of life, he is a picturesque and interesting object."[24] In her 1852 *Letters from Ireland,* the rather more politically conscious Harriet Martineau showed a similar preoccupation with the sight of children in the west of Ireland "munching raw potato as English children munch apples."[25] In another acknowledgment of the cultural contrast between the two nations, travel writers often expressed bemusement that Irish paupers begged for alms in the form of potatoes rather than money.[26] It seems that while the authors of Victorian travel narratives were invariably sympathetic towards Ireland, often having connections to the country through birth or marriage, they nevertheless served to reinforce the "foreignness" of the Irish in their writings, notably through references to food.

Irish eating habits were also subject to commentary in socio-political analyses of the condition of early Victorian England. During the months that intervened between the potato-planting season and the time for harvest, an annual migration took place as Irish laborers crossed to the British mainland in search of temporary employment. Here, they were scrutinized by a number of cultural commentators, including Thomas Carlyle, who described the immigrants as a pestilential influx, willing to undercut their English counterparts in the labor market "for wages that will purchase . . . potatoes."[27] Other, less belligerent accounts also characterized Irish immigrants in terms of their dietary preferences. Friedrich Engels's *The Condition of the Working Class in England* and Henry Mayhew's *London Labour and the London Poor,* for instance, both drew attention to Irish workers' prodigious appetite for potatoes.[28]

Even Victorian cookery books, such as Eliza Acton's *Modern Cookery for Private Families,* implicitly correlated Ireland with the potato. Under the

---

24. Lady Chatterton, *Rambles in the South of Ireland during the Year 1838* (London: Saunders and Otley, 1839), 114.
25. Harriet Martineau, *Letters from Ireland,* ed. Glen Hooper (Dublin and Portland: Irish Academic Press, 2001), 110. In a footnote, Martineau added, "An Irish friend protests . . . that nobody in the world ever ate raw potato. He declares it must have been Swedish turnip. All we can say is that we did not judge by the eye alone. We asked the children what raw root they were eating, and they said 'potato.' They might however be only gnawing it." After allowing the validity of her observations to be called temporarily into question, Martineau quickly reasserts a sense of Irish alterity through her use of the word "gnawing," with its bestial connotations (185n1).
26. See Chatterton, *Rambles in the South of Ireland,* 131 and Emily Taylor, *The Irish Tourist; or, The People and Provinces of Ireland* (London: Darton and Harvey, 1837), 129.
27. Thomas Carlyle, *Chartism* (London: James Fraser, 1840), 28–29.
28. See Friedrich Engels, *The Condition of the Working Class in England,* ed. David McLellan (1845; Oxford: Oxford University Press, 1993), 102; and Henry Mayhew, *London Labor and the London Poor,* vol. 1 (1851; London: Frank Cass, 1967), 113.

sub-heading, "Potatoes: Remarks on their properties and importance," Acton asserted that these "nutritious" items sustained "the strength of thousands of people whose almost sole food [they constituted]," before cautioning against over-dependence on a crop "so frequently in these days destroyed or greatly injured by disease."[29] This passage makes no direct reference to Ireland, but its allusions to the prevalence of potato-eating among an "entire people" and the devastating impact of disease in the potato crop would have automatically signaled "Irishness" to contemporary middle-class readers, already inundated with accounts of the Famine in the English press. There is, however, some residual ambiguity in Acton's text. Potatoes represented a staple item in the diet of the majority of British laborers in the nineteenth century, finding particular favor among urban workers when the price of grain (and therefore bread) was high. As Acton points out, potatoes were "cheap, wholesome and satisfying"; the reference to the "thousands of people" who consumed them could, therefore, pertain to the working classes in general, as opposed to the Irish in particular.[30] Interestingly, an article published in *Punch* in 1844, a year before the emergence of the blight, suggested that the potato was popular with *all* Britons: "from the time that Raleigh first landed at the Custom-house with a sack of the nutritious vegetable, the potato has been a welcome guest at the British dinner-table," it announced.[31] Engels, too, acknowledged the ubiquity of the potato in English working-class households, especially those where money was limited, but then re-affiliated this item with the immigrant Irish population: "on the lowest round of the ladder," he affirmed, "among the Irish, potatoes form the sole food."[32]

The very persistence with which references to the Irish and potatoes occurred in Victorian culture suggests that the two enjoyed a special relationship in the popular consciousness that exceeded the simple association of producer with produce, consumer with consumable. As Roland Barthes points out, food is freighted with ideological meaning. Its relationship to the consuming subject is discursive as well as material; food "sums up and transmits a situation; it constitutes an information; *it signifies*."[33] This process of signification can be identified in a range of Victorian literature, where "potatoes" work as efficacious, metonymic indicators of "Irishness." When the egotistical George Osborne is disinherited by his father in Thackeray's *Vanity*

---

29. Eliza Acton, *Modern Cookery for Private Families* (Lewes: Southover Press, 1993), 267.

30. Acton, *Modern Cookery for Private Families,* 267.

31. "The Potato Panic," *Punch* 6 (1844): 186. Interestingly, this article responded to claims of a scarcity of potatoes in Scotland, reassuring readers that "the cry has proved to be false." No mention is made of Ireland.

32. Engels, *Condition of the Working Class,* 84.

33. Roland Barthes, "Toward a Psychosociology of Contemporary Food Consumption," 21 (my emphasis).

Fair, he tells his friend Dobbin that he is unsuited to a life of penury, quali-
fying his claim with the declaration: "*I* wasn't brought up on . . . potatoes,
like old O'Dowd," the Irish major of his regiment.[34] In Charlotte Brontë's
Shirley, meanwhile, Mr Malone, the curate of Briarfield, is said to speak "in
a tone which . . . proclaims him at once a native of the land of shamrocks
and potatoes."[35] In each of these cases, the Irishness of the character under
discussion is not cited explicitly, nor need it be: casual references to potatoes
would have signified clearly to contemporary readers the Celtic cultural origins of both O'Dowd and Malone.

"Potatoes" could also operate metaphorically; in certain instances, they
described as well as designated Irish national identity, as we shall see. If
food functions like a language, then within its manifold textures, aromas and
tastes, its various modes of production and rituals of consumption, a nexus of
culturally coded meanings is inscribed. Crucially, these meanings tend to be
neither neutral nor benign. As Mary Douglas argues, food transmits messages
about the "different degrees of hierarchy, inclusion and exclusion, boundaries
and transactions across . . . boundaries" within a given culture.[36] In the early
years of the Union, therefore, the potato functioned not only as a signifier of
Irish identity but also as a phobic marker of distinction between the English
and Irish peasantry.

One of the main figures to deploy such politicized culinary rhetoric in
the 1820s was the radical journalist William Cobbett. In his *Cottage Economy*
and *Rural Rides,* Cobbett conflated the supposed qualities of the potato with
the presumed attributes of the Irish national character in order to assert and
justify his antipathy to both. Labeling the potato "Ireland's *lazy* root," Cobbett urged English agricultural laborers (and Parliament) to abandon this
crop in favor of a grain-based economy.[37] "The *misery* and *degradation* of the
Irish [are] chiefly owing to the *use of the potatoe as the almost sole food of the
people,*" he proclaimed, noting elsewhere, "its cultivation has increased in
England with the increase of the paupers" (*CE,* 81, 62). If Cobbett's dislike
of potatoes stemmed from their association with Irish poverty, his aversion to
the Irish, by a process of circular reasoning, emanated from their preference
for potatoes. "Ireland's lazy root," he suggested, "is the root, also, of slovenliness, filth, misery, and slavery" (*CE,* 62). The adjective "lazy" is conjoined
with the potato throughout Cobbett's work because, in his opinion, such

---

34. William Makepeace Thackeray, *Vanity Fair,* ed. J. I. M. Stewart (1848; London: Penguin,
1968), 290.

35. Charlotte Brontë, *Shirley* (1849; London: Penguin, 1974), 41.

36. Mary Douglas, *Implicit Meanings: Selected Essays in Anthropology* (London and New York:
Routledge, 1999), 231.

37. William Cobbett, *Cottage Economy* (1823; Bromyard: Landsman, 1974), 79 (hereafter cited
in text as *CE*). Italics in original.

items were not only exceptionally easy to cultivate, but also very easy to cook, requiring no particular "skill in their preparation" (*CE*, 59).[38] A self-fulfilling logic is at work here: the potato is a "lazy root" because, requiring little effort to produce or prepare, it is the chosen crop of the "lazy" Irish, and the Irish are a "lazy" people because of their preference for the sloth-promoting potato.

Dietary stereotypes also explain the strength and vigor of the English peasantry in Cobbett's work. A turnip-hoer in Sussex, seen breakfasting on a "good lump of household *bread* and not a very small piece of *bacon*," incited him to exclaim: "What sort of *breakfast* would this man have had in a mess of *cold potatoes*? Could he have *worked*, and worked in the wet, too, with such food? Monstrous! No society ought to exist, where the laborers live in a hog-like sort of way."[39] The reference to "hogs" here is significant because, for Cobbett, the potato-diet of the Irish "is but one remove from that of the pig" and engenders pig-like habits (*CE*, 58). In *Cottage Economy*, he describes with disgust the "Irish style" of consumption: after "[scratching] them out of the earth with their paws," the Irish "toss" their potatoes "into a pot without washing, and when boiled . . . peel the skin and dirt from one at a time and eat the inside" (*CE*, 60). The suggestion of foraging and substitution of the word "paws" for "hands" here is noteworthy; by introducing this bestial imagery into his account, Cobbett effectively intimates not only the "slovenly and beastly" culinary habits of the Irish but also the transformative effect of the potato (*CE*, 59). This "hog-like" food transmutes the Irish consumer into the animal with which it is culturally aligned: in representational terms, the Irish *become* pigs, debased and dehumanized beasts, directly opposed to the civilized English.

Examples of this transmutation go on to pervade early Victorian texts, including those which are predominantly xenodochial in character. For instance, American Asenath Nicholson's account of her journey through Ireland in 1844 and 1845, intended to establish the true sufferings of the people and arouse the compassion of her countrymen, nonetheless positioned humans and animals in unsettling proximity in Irish households. Having lost her way in County Waterford, Nicholson was invited into the cabin of a local woman where she perceived

---

38. Significantly, the Irish method of planting potatoes was known in the nineteenth century as the "lazybed system," an appellation that, Salaman notes, "unfairly prejudices any issue as to its merits" (*The Influence of the Potato on the Course of Irish History*, 9). Austin Bourke suggests that "it may have been from the French '*laisser*'—as in *laissez faire*—that the term 'lazy bed' was derived. Whatever its origin, the name provided an added weapon to those who ridiculed the ridges. The irony of the situation was that the lazy beds represented, in fact, a 'laborious system of culture.'" *"The Visitation of God?": The Potato and the Great Irish Famine* (Dublin: The Lilliput Press, 1993), 66.

39. Cobbett, *Rural Rides*, vol. 1 (1830; London: Peter Davies, 1930), 167.

in the centre of the room . . . the dinner table, with the remains of the potatoes on which the family had been dining. A tub of potato-skins and water
stood near the table, from which two huge matronly swine, and eleven young
sucklings, were eating their dinner, and I, in return for the civility shown me,
could do no less than extol the beauty of the little *bonnels,* and the fine bulk
of the mother. The mistress took a wooden bowl, mashed a few fine potatoes
into it with her hands, and, adding milk, called a couple of more favored
ones, and fed them from it.[40]

The proximity of pigs to people in this narrative operates on a number of
levels. Most obviously, the pigs share a living space with the humans; interestingly, however, they appear also to share their habits. The animals' dinner-
time is virtually contemporary with their owners'; both meals take place in
the environs of the dinner-table and consist of the same type of food. Furthermore, Nicholson's language anthropomorphizes the animals, attaching
quasi-human familial relations to the "matronly swine" and piglets. A close
kinship seems also to exist with the Irishwoman; feeding the young by hand,
she too takes on a "matronly" role, suggesting that the pigs are an incorporated part of the family unit.[41] Nicholson does not criticize this arrangement
(indeed, she has nothing but praise for the hospitality she receives from her
hosts); however, the anecdote serves to emphasize Irish otherness, creating a
critical distance between the subject of the text and its target: the implied,
middle-class, Christian reader.

This critical distance is even more perceptible in accounts calculated to
stimulate readers' disgust. Irish immigrants to Victorian England were often
affiliated with pigs in a xenophobic discourse deployed to classify and stratify
the working classes. Engels compared the "Englishman's level of civilization"
with the feral habits of "the Irishman who goes in rags, eats potatoes, and
sleeps in a pigsty."[42] Later, he declared, with evident repugnance, "the Irishman loves his pig. . . . he eats and sleeps with it, his children play with it,
ride upon it, roll in the dirt with it, as anyone may see a thousand times

---

40. Asenath Nicholson, *Ireland's Welcome to the Stranger, or an Excursion through Ireland in 1844
& 1845, for the Purpose of Personally Investigating the Condition of the Poor* (New York: Baker and
Scribner, 1847), 125.

41. Pigs were commonly kept, fattened, and then sold by Irish tenants to pay the landlord his
rent. Many English writers expressed incredulity at the care and attention lavished on these animals,
particularly during times of scarcity. Thomas Campbell Foster, for instance, wrote that "the pig which
[the Irish peasant] rears, and which occupies the most comfortable portion of the cabin, is invariably
disposed of for the landlord; and the peasant would as soon think of eating the landlord himself as
of eating the pig." *Letters on the Condition of the People of Ireland,* 44.

42. Engels, *Condition of the Working Class,* 88–89.

repeated in all the great towns of England."[43] The closeness of human and beast, here again, effectively conflates the one with the other. A flawed, yet pervasive syllogism suffused Victorian socio-political and popular discourse: the Irish peasantry eat potatoes; the pigs with which they live eat potatoes; therefore, the Irish peasantry are akin to pigs. A superficially innocuous alignment of consumer and foodstuff in fact worked to expedite an insidious xenophobia—with devastating consequences during the years of the Famine, when prejudices regarding the potato, Irish habits, and Irish character directly affected English responses to the disaster.

Famine

When the potato blight struck in 1845, the economy of xenodochial and xenophobic relations between England and Ireland took on a new urgency and relevance. These relations were mediated to English audiences largely through the print press. Williams points out that "the Irish Famine occurred at a time when the British press was experiencing great expansion and innovation"; unsurprisingly, then, it was primarily within the pages of newspapers and journals that the events of the Famine took shape for the English middle classes. These periodicals played a "pivotal role" in determining public and political opinion, standing "at the apex of a triangular relationship that linked politicians and the public, government and citizens, to each other."[44] Yet there seems to have been no consistent editorial line on the catastrophe in Ireland. As Williams notes, "reversals were common," not only between but also within publications.[45]

Nowhere are these fluctuating attitudes more evident than within the pages of the popular satirical weekly, *Punch*. At times, during the period 1845–1852, a sense of sympathy prevailed. The starving Irish required maintenance from the hospitable English, as an 1846 cartoon, "Union Is Strength," made clear (see figure 6.1). Here, a portly, patrician John Bull is depicted handing over a basket of bread and a shovel to the head of an impoverished Irish family, with the charitable words, "Here are a few things to go on with, brother, and I'll soon put you in a way to earn your own living." Responses modified, however, as the Famine continued and the Irish came to be represented as an unwelcome drain on English resources. As Foster suggests, by 1848, support for the Young Ireland movement was perceived by

---

43. Engels, *Conditions of the Working Class,* 103.

44. Leslie A. Williams, *Daniel O'Connell, the British Press and the Irish Famine: Killing Remarks* (Aldershot: Ashgate, 2003), 8, 3, 5.

45. Leslie A. Williams, "Irish Identity and the *Illustrated London News,*" 87.

UNION IS STRENGTH.

John Bull. "HERE ARE A FEW THINGS TO GO ON WITH, BROTHER, AND I'LL SOON PUT YOU IN A
WAY TO EARN YOUR OWN LIVING."

Figure 6.1 "Union Is Strength." *Punch* 11 (1846): 166

Punch as evidence of Irish ingratitude, while "liberal policies like a £50,000 grant-in-aid for relieving Famine distress were attacked as subsidizing lazy Irish peasants rather than deserving English agricultural laborers."[46] In *Punch*, as in other publications from the family-friendly *ILN* to the weightier *Times*, a tentative xenodochy was gradually supplanted by a more persistent xenophobia, as the Irish problem was explained increasingly in terms of Irish inadequacy.

What is most notable, though, in this shifting economy of relations is that, whether Ireland was positioned as deserving dependent or ungrateful antagonist, the structural superiority of England (as benefactor or moral enforcer) remained unchanged. Thus, the instability inherent in representations of the Irish ultimately reinforced rather than undermined English dominance; as Homi Bhabha argues, the very flexibility of ambivalent stereotypes renders them "a productive source of discriminatory power."[47] England remained anxious about Ireland, nevertheless. Metaphors of disease and contagion figured prominently in responses to the Famine, and to the consequent influx of Irish paupers into English industrial towns. An 1848 article in the traditionally Tory *Blackwood's Edinburgh Magazine* asserted that "the starvation and anarchy of that kingdom [Ireland] is a leprosy, which will soon spread."[48] Fears that Irish improvidence might infect the English working classes necessitated a strategy of conceptual partition.

In this light, it is interesting to note that, in figure 6.1, John Bull hands the family of Famine victims a basket of *bread.* Williams argues that

> grain bias was deeply embedded within British concepts of social and individual morality. Grain cultivation was seen as the basis for the "proper" economic and social order of rural Britain . . . demand[ing] a very visible cycle of production that, to the Victorian mind, seemed to point to a proper moral order. It took planning and continual work, involving agricultural laborers working under the watchful gaze of the "master."[49]

The hint given in *Punch*'s ostensibly sympathetic cartoon, then, is that the Irish need to replace their current agricultural system with an English, cereal-based model, founded on proper, capitalist relations of production, if they are

---

46. Foster, *Paddy and Mr Punch,* 180.

47. Homi K. Bhabha, *The Location of Culture* (London and New York: Routledge, 2004), 95.

48. "Continental Revolutions—Irish Rebellion—English Distress," *Blackwood's Edinburgh Magazine* 64 (1848): 480. The quotation is taken from an earlier assessment of the Irish problem in *Blackwood's*; the editors suggest they have reprinted it because its comments are so precisely "applicable to the present time, that were we to write anew on the subject, we should certainly reproduce the same ideas, and probably, in a great degree, make use of the same words" (485).

49. Williams, *Daniel O'Connell, the British Press and the Irish Famine,* 354.

to improve their physical and moral condition. Subtly here, but more openly in other Victorian representation, William Cobbett's rhetoric is revivified; the language of food is once more used to differentiate the industrious English from the indolent Irish peasantry, as blame for the Famine begins to load onto "Ireland's lazy root."

Symptomatic of this, an 1846 edition of *Punch* imagined a comic exchange between Cobbett and Sir Walter Raleigh, in which the former accuses the latter of introducing into Ireland "that vile, watery, rotgut *thing*, the potato," which "[makes] pigs of the poor people who use it."[50] By 1849, the periodical seems to have adopted Cobbett's line. "The Irish peasant [must] . . . no longer kneel to the potato," *Punch* advised; "straightaway he must learn a better faith: we must convert him to wheat. With wheat may come better field habits. The potato . . . infects with idleness."[51] The Quaker Sandham Elly utilized similar language, though in less satirical vein, in his 1848 pamphlet, *Potatoes, Pigs, and Politics: The Curse of Ireland and the Cause of England's Embarrassments.* Priced at one shilling, and recommending itself "to the serious reflection of every Irish landlord, and every member of parliament," Elly's tract proclaimed, in a denouncement worthy of Cobbett himself, "The grand cause [of the Irish crisis] lies in the potato;—sloth and idleness are its attendants; man and swine feed alike on it; both meet on equal terms—not that the pig is elevated to the rank of man,—but that man has been sunk to the level of the brute."[52]

Perhaps the most important exponent of this kind of "dietary determinism" (to adopt Terry Eagleton's useful phrase) was Charles Trevelyan, Assistant Secretary to the Treasury and chief administrator of Famine relief for Lord John Russell's Whig government.[53] Trevelyan's account of *The Irish Crisis* was first published in January 1848 in the *Edinburgh Review,* a leading Whig-leaning periodical. It appeared in book form later that year, positioning itself, rather prematurely, as a denouement to the disaster; in *The Irish Crisis,* the Famine is already a historical event, one clearly attributable to Irish dependence on the potato. The usual suspects of "Absenteeism," "Roman Catholic bigotry," and "Ribbandism" are curable evils, the author suggests, "but what hope is there for a nation which lives on potatoes?"[54] None, the reader is

---

50. "Punch's Imaginary Conversations. William Cobbett and Sir Walter Raleigh," *Punch* 11 (1846): 237.

51. "Half a Word about a Bit of Ireland," *Punch* 17 (1849): 26.

52. Sandham Elly, *Potatoes, Pigs, and Politics: The Curse of Ireland and the Cause of England's Embarrassments* (London: Kent and Richards, 1848), 7.

53. Terry Eagleton, *Heathcliff and the Great Hunger: Studies in Irish Culture* (London: Verso, 1995), 16.

54. C. E. Trevelyan, *The Irish Crisis* (London: Longman, Brown, Green and Longmans, 1848), 2.

invited to reply as, over several pages, Trevelyan appeals to the customary potato prejudices: the cultivation of "Lumpers" encourages "slovenly" and "negligent" agricultural practices; it supports a rapidly expanding peasantry; and it results in a household routine barely comprehensible to middle-class England.[55] "The domestic habits arising out of this mode of subsistence [are] of the lowest and most degrading kind," Trevelyan argues, before adding, with perceptible disgust, "the pigs and poultry, which share the food of the peasant's family [become], in course, inmates of the cabin also."[56]

The familiar litany of potatoes, pigs, and Irish culpability is of particular consequence in this case because, as Williams points out, Trevelyan wielded massive administrative power, carefully controlling public funds destined for Ireland.[57] His ideas, and those of the political class to which he belonged, had material effects; English aid efforts in the late 1840s were tempered by the conviction that, at some level, Ireland was to blame for its own dire situation and needed reform as much as charity. Victorian print culture reflected but also shaped and stimulated these values. The persistent, syllogistic association of Irish idleness, potatoes, and pigs can be read as an "identifiable discursive formation" through which the Famine was mediated and understood—one that, significantly, helped to deflect awkward questions about English accountability for the suffering experienced in Ireland.[58]

In pictorial representation, this tripartite discursive formation manifested itself in a succession of grotesque images that blurred the boundaries among human, animal, and eatable. For example, a William Newman cartoon in *Punch,* entitled "The Real Potato Blight of Ireland," depicted Daniel O'Connell as a hideously misshapen, giant tuber (see figure 6.2). One of a series of outlandish caricatures of O'Connell, Newman's image worked primarily to critique the leader of the repeal movement's alleged rapaciousness (a plate of coins, collected from the starving Irish peasantry, lies before him).

---

55. Trevelyan, *The Irish Crisis,* 4–7.

56. Trevelyan, *The Irish Crisis,* 7.

57. Williams, *Daniel O'Connell, the British Press and the Irish Famine,* 259.

58. Christopher Morash, *Writing the Irish Famine* (Oxford: Clarendon Press, 1995), 5. Much debate has surrounded the issue of English culpability for the Famine. Nineteenth-century Irish nationalists such as John Mitchel suggested that English policy was directly responsible. In *The Last Conquest of Ireland (Perhaps),* Mitchel points out that the potato crop failed throughout Europe in the 1840s, "yet there was no famine save in Ireland. . . . The Almighty, indeed, sent the potato blight, but the English created the famine." *The Last Conquest of Ireland (Perhaps)* (Glasgow: R. & T. Washbourne, n.d.), 219. He further describes "the Famine-policy of the Government" as "a machinery, deliberately devised and skilfully worked, for the entire subjugation of the island—, the slaughter of a portion of its people, and the pauperization of the rest" (157). More recently, Terry Eagleton has argued that "there was no question of a calculated genocide" in Ireland, although he does suggest that Government "measures, half-measures and non-measures . . . despatched hundreds of thousands to their needless deaths." *Heathcliff and the Great Hunger,* 24. For further perspectives on English Famine policy, see Bourke and Ó Gráda.

THE REAL POTATO BLIGHT OF IRELAND.

(FROM A SKETCH TAKEN IN CONCILIATION HALL.)

Figure 6.2 "The Real Potato Blight of Ireland." *Punch* 9 (1845): 255

Yet, on another level, the cartoon makes a more general point about Irishness by underscoring the correlation between potatoes and laziness; significantly, the grotesque O'Connell is shown reposing languorously on a couch. This emphasis on lethargy is also a feature of textual portraits of O'Connell from the 1840s: a *Times* leader from 1845 contrasted the supposed torpor of "the King of Tara" in the wake of the potato blight with the activity of his English counterparts, arguing that "the only men who have grappled with this great disaster—who have attacked it with the hope of retarding or destroying it—have been English gentlemen."[59] (In fact, O'Connell was, at this point, busy setting up the Mansion House Committee in Dublin and preparing to lobby the Lord Lieutenant of Ireland on a range of emergency measures, including the facilitation of food imports and immediate stoppage of food exports from Ireland.[60])

Attacks on English political figures could, similarly, include latent commentary on Irish identity. John Leech's cartoon, "Justice to Ireland," is ostensibly concerned with Sir Robert Peel's Coercion Bill, portraying the Prime Minister as "the old woman who lived in a shoe," hounding her children (the troublesome Irish) to bed with the aid of a broom.[61] Yet the depiction of the Irish, here, is itself worthy of note. While a number of the older male figures have the simianized features that Curtis analyses in *Apes and Angels,* and the women are mostly frail and beautiful, there are also dispersed among the crowd faces whose globular, lumpy quality recalls the tuber-esque representation of O'Connell.[62] One such face belongs to a figure in the center of the image, who cradles a piglet in his arms; the strange, quasi-maternal proximity of human and beast here re-emphasizes to English readers the otherness of Irish domestic habits.

Of course, *Punch* was in the business of caricature, as Foster points out; grotesquerie and exaggeration were its stock in trade.[63] Yet alienating images of Irish Famine victims could also be found in more sober, subtle publications. "It seems to have become more and more difficult for the *ILN* to represent the famine-struck Irish peasant as human," Williams argues, suggesting that, by 1849, the newspaper often reverted to illustrations of the "unshaven, dirty, lumpy . . . Paddy type."[64] It is illuminating to consider the differences between images accompanying reports of English and Irish poverty in

59. *Times* (30 October 1845): 4.

60. See Angus MacIntyre, *The Liberator: Daniel O'Connell and the Irish Party, 1830–1847* (London: Hamish Hamilton, 1965), 284–285.

61. John Leech, "Justice to Ireland," *Punch* 10 (1846): 171.

62. Significantly, the potatoes favored by the Irish peasantry were known as "lumpers."

63. Foster, *Paddy and Mr Punch,* 192.

64. Williams, "Irish Identity and the *Illustrated London News,*" 86.

the *ILN*. An 1846 feature on "The Peasantry of Dorsetshire," responding to letters in the *Times* about the "privation and suffering" of the locale's laboring population, was attended by an illustration of neatly dressed agricultural workers with clearly-defined facial features.[65] By contrast, a report on the Famine in Ireland, published just over four months later, was supplemented by a sketch of a funeral at Skibbereen in which two onlookers, dressed in rags, are represented with lumpen, featureless faces.[66] The English peasants are poor but cognizably human; the impoverished Irish are shapeless creatures, indistinct and dehumanized.

In December 1849, the *ILN* carried another special report on conditions in Ireland, which, again, aimed at sympathy but actually accentuated Irish alterity. The text associated with an illustration of two youngsters "Searching for Potatoes in a Stubble Field" (one of them on his knees, turning the earth desperately with his hands) used bestial language to describe the scene: "The people were digging and hunting . . . like dogs after truffles."[67] The animal imagery deployed here effectively highlights the difference and distance between the Famine victims and the *ILN*'s readership. As Williams notes,

> Images, verbal or visual, of intense distress and suffering, might excite human empathy. They may, however, simultaneously raise barriers against it. Accounts of half-naked, starving people may generate pity and alms but also revulsion. For many people, there is a point at which the sufferer moves from the category of a human being to that of a grotesque.[68]

That point appears to have been reached by the *ILN*'s correspondent, who wrote that "the once frolicsome people—even the saucy beggars—have disappeared, and given place to wan and haggard objects, who are . . . resigned to their doom."[69] The rather mournful tone here implies that Ireland's inhabitants' transition from "people" to "objects" is something to be lamented; however, the objectification of the Irish also provided English readers with a conceptual buffer, substantiating Peter W. Sinnema's point that the *ILN* was extremely adept "in accommodating readers to potentially traumatizing narratives."[70]

---

65. "The Peasantry of Dorsetshire," *Illustrated London News* 9 (5 September 1846): 156–158.

66. "The Famine in Ireland—Funeral at Skibbereen—From a Sketch by Mr. H. Smith, Cork," *Illustrated London News* 10 (January 30, 1847): 65.

67. "Condition of Ireland: Illustrations of the New Poor-Law," *Illustrated London News* 15 (22 December 1849): 406.

68. Williams, *Daniel O'Connell, the British Press and the Irish Famine,* 349.

69. "Condition of Ireland: Illustrations of the New Poor-Law," *Illustrated London News* 15 (22 December 1849): 404.

70. Sinnema, *Dynamics of the Pictured Page,* 208.

Does "objectification," though, properly describe the strategies of estrangement through which the English press "othered" the Famine and its victims? Objects are definable entities with discrete boundaries; according to the *OED*, they are things that can be "perceived, thought of, known." As the examples above demonstrate, representations of the Irish during the Famine elude easy categorization, troubling binaries and "undermining basic categories of perception."[71] The *OED* also states that objects are things "external to or distinct from the apprehending mind, subject, or self," a definition to which the Irish, again, fail satisfactorily to conform. England and Ireland were inexorably bound by the Union, a fact recognized by the majority of Victorian publications. As a *Times* leader from 1848 conceded, "Ireland is part and parcel of ourselves."[72] It appears, then, that the complex relationship between England and Ireland during the Famine ultimately confounded the reassuring distinction between subject and object. In this way, I suggest, early Victorian efforts to *ob*jectify Irish identity (through the kinds of representations examined above) resulted, instead, in *ab*jection, a profound ambiguity that threatened to dissolve all difference, annihilating the protective limits between self and other.

Abjection

"Abject and abjection are my safeguards," writes Kristeva, "the primers of my culture" (*PH*, 2). Fear, loathing and disgust—the sensations attending the encounter with the abject—function as phobic markers, helping to delineate that which must be excluded in order for the subject to maintain its physical and psychical integrity. The ability to discriminate, separate, and segregate is an essential part of subjectivity; for Kristeva, it is what distinguishes the fully-constituted human subject from the proto-subject that exists prior to ego-formation and the subject's accession into the symbolic order (the system of language which is itself predicated on differentiation). Yet, the process of exclusion associated with abjection does not align itself comfortably with the familiar defense strategies employed by the unconscious. Abjection is unlike repression or denial, Kristeva argues, because it does not involve outright repudiation or rejection; it allows "a defensive *position* to be established" but it does not permit "a secure differentiation between subject and object" (*PH*, 7). This is because the abject is not an object, not an absolute "otherness," which, through its opposition to the subject, enables a coherent self-identity

---

71. Morash, *Writing the Irish Famine*, 17.
72. *Times* (11 July 1848): 5.

to take shape. Rather, it is a (paradoxically inassimilable) component of the subject, "something rejected from which one does not part," the residual threat of non-differentiation to which one is troublingly attracted (*PH,* 4). The abject, then, both deflects and perpetuates crises of identity.

Phobia is closely linked with abjection. Indeed, Kristeva maintains that "the phobic has no other object than the abject" (*PH,* 6). Both phobia and abjection underline the fragility of the subject's signifying system; they testify to the tenuous and illusory nature of the subject's understanding of itself as a distinct and integral entity. The anxious fascination constituting xenophobia, therefore, may be explained in terms of a fear of the foreign resident *within* the subject, as much as a fear of that which menaces from without. Importantly, this process is not limited to the individual; it also takes place at the level of the social. Kristeva draws attention to the corresponding structures that shape the subject and the wider symbolic order (*PH,* 67). The abjection that haunts one's struggle for a discrete identity also troubles the coherence of articulations of national or cultural identity.

The unsettling ambivalence of abjection, comprising both intimacy and repulsion, can be detected in press accounts of relations between England and Ireland during the late 1840s. As Melissa Fegan notes, "the familial metaphors commonly used at the time make it clear that the Famine was closer than English journalists might have liked."[73] She quotes from an 1848 article in the *Times,* which juxtaposed assertions of Irish alterity with a reluctant admission of Anglo-Irish identification:

> It will be difficult to most of our readers to feel near akin with a class which at
> the best wallows in pigsties, and hugs the most brutish degradation. But when
> we take the sum of the British people, the "ill-fed, ill-clothed, ill-housed"
> children of the Celt count with VICTORIA's own children.[74]

A year later, the *ILN* imagined an even closer kinship between the two nations, though its analogy, like that of the *Times,* is tinged with disgust: "England and Ireland are like the Siamese twins. The gangrene of the one must extend to the other; and the social pestilence that attacks the life of Ireland must of necessity make some inroad upon that of England."[75] The allusion to necrosis here indicates abjection. According to Kristeva, blood, pus, and decay are unwelcome reminders of the provisionality and permeability of the (indi-

---

73. Fegan, *Literature and the Irish Famine,* 50.

74. Fegan, *Literature and the Irish Famine,* 51. Original reference from the *Times* (3 January 1848): 4.

75. "Ireland and its Ministerial Treatment," *Illustrated London News* 14 (10 February 1849): 82.

vidual or social) body and thus must be "thrust aside" in order to sustain the fiction of intactness, inviolability (*PH*, 3). The conjointness imagined by the *ILN* article, however, renders such absolute rejection impossible. English identity is endangered here by the mortification of its Irish twin.

The confrontation with "death infecting life" represents the "utmost of abjection" for Kristeva, and pervaded Victorian commentary on the crisis in Ireland (*PH*, 4). Many accounts dwelt obsessively on the proximity of living and dead bodies in famine-ridden areas. A fourteen-page article on the "Famine in the South of Ireland" in *Fraser's Magazine* relayed story after story of unburied cadavers co-existing with skeletal survivors: wives, unable to purchase a funeral, sleeping next to their dead husbands, children clinging to the corpses of their dead mothers, animals mutilating the rotting remains of those who had perished.[76] These stories, filtered first through the Irish press, were endlessly recounted in the English media, to the extent that "Ireland" in 1847 became virtually synonymous with "death." This, in turn, proved a source of concern for England. Contemplating the state of relations within the Union, the *Times* observed,

> Ireland and England have resembled nothing else so much as the dead and the living body bound together by the fetters of a cruel caprice. The dead body has been convulsed with painful imitation of its breathing neighbour; the living has drunk in inevitable corruption from the contagious mortality of its companion.[77]

Less than two months later, the newspaper returned to this language of abjection, quoting from its continental contemporary, the *Journal des Débats:* "England . . . resembles the tortured of former times, who was attached to a dead body." Significantly, in the light of Kristeva's ideas, the French newspaper also referred to the ubiquity and inevitability of death as a spur to English compassion. "Hear the voice of a starving people," it urged; "remember that you are but dust."[78] Metaphorically conjoined in a series of texts with the dead or decomposing body of Ireland, English identity was repeatedly beleaguered by abjection and threatened with the prospect of dissolution, negation, nonentity.

At such moments of cultural crisis, Sjöholm proposes, societies typically turn to secular or religious rituals of purification and sacrifice. These help to maintain the social order by "exorcis[ing] the abject, that which threatens the

---

76. "Famine in the South of Ireland," *Fraser's Magazine for Town and Country* 35 (1847): 491–504.

77. *Times* (25 January 1847): 4.

78. *Times* (1 March 1847): 4.

distinct borders of the community."[79] The language of sacrifice is prominent in a number of Victorian responses to the Famine. In *The Irish Crisis,* for instance, Trevelyan confidently predicted that the Famine would mark "the commencement of a salutary revolution in the habits of a nation long singularly unfortunate . . . on this, as on many other occasions, Supreme Wisdom has educed permanent good out of transient evil."[80] The Famine (still ongoing at the time Trevelyan was writing) is positioned here as a distressing but necessary social purge, administered by a divine source. Peter Gray argues that such "Christian providentialism" (the idea that the potato blight could be interpreted as "an instrument of divine mercy, not displeasure") pervaded successive governments' policy and practice on Ireland during the 1840s.[81]

It also proved a compelling explanatory tool in retrospective analyses of the Famine. In her *Letters from Ireland,* first published in the liberal-leaning *Daily News,* Martineau told readers that she consoled herself, when travelling through uninhabited villages in the West of the country, with the recognition that

> this visitation . . . will bring in a better time than Ireland has ever known yet. It will compel a vast emigration, and thus clear the land for improved management; it will bring over British settlers to "plant" the lands which will be deserted. . . . [it will bring] freedom, in short, to begin afresh, with the advantage of modern knowledge and manageable numbers.[82]

A committed advocate of political economy, Martineau interpreted the destructive force of the Famine as a prelude to the panacea of modernization. Anthony Trollope's 1860 novel, *Castle Richmond,* meanwhile, adopted a Biblical tone in its portrayal of the Famine as a divinely ordained, and ultimately beneficial, process of purification. "The destruction of the potato was the work of God," we are told in a lengthy authorial digression:

> Such having been the state of the country, such its wretchedness, a merciful God sent the remedy which might avail to arrest it. . . . If this beneficent agency did not from time to time disencumber our crowded places, we should ever be living in narrow alleys with stinking gutters, and supply of water at the minimum.[83]

---

79. Sjöholm, *Kristeva and the Political,* 85.
80. Trevelyan, *The Irish Crisis,* 1.
81. Peter Gray, "'Potatoes and Providence': British Government Responses to the Great Famine," *Bullán* 1, no. 1 (1994): 79.
82. Martineau, *Letters from Ireland,* 111.
83. Anthony Trollope, *Castle Richmond* (1860; London: The Trollope Society, 1994), 64, 67.

In Trollope's Malthusian discourse, sacrifice is essential to progress: here, the horror of the Famine is sublimated into a language of social sanitization.

Yet the concept of sacrifice failed to afford a comprehensive sense of closure to the events of the 1840s. The specter of the Famine continued to haunt Victorian culture, coming sharply into focus in 1879, when *phytophthora infestans* re-emerged in Ireland, destroying up to 75 percent of the potato crop and instigating a period of distress that continued intermittently through the 1880s. Once again, during a moment of historical crisis, a complex economy of xenodochial and xenophobic cultural exchange materialized. Salaman reports that £250,000 was collected for relief in 1880, and in a *Punch* cartoon from that year Ireland was represented as a beautiful, distraught maiden receiving solace from her redoubtable sister, Britannia.[84] Concurrent with such sympathetic concern for Irish hunger, though, was an overwhelming anxiety regarding Irish anger. In response to the increasing threat of violent agitation regarding the land question, the English press once more introjected ideas of difference as a strategy of national self-defense. This time, however, the focus fell less on potatoes and indolence than on pigs and belligerence. In a series of images, confrontational Irishmen were represented as anthropomorphized swine. In *Punch,* Foster notes, "the favorite cliché of the Irish pig as 'The Gintleman that Pays the Rent' was converted into a murderous wild boar, armed with a blunderbuss: 'the gentleman that *won't* pay the rent.'"[85] Michael de Nie detects a similar representational fusion in an 1881 edition of the comic newspaper *Funny Folks,* which appropriated and transformed the story of "The Dragon and St. George" by depicting William Forster, Chief Secretary for Ireland, in the guise of England's patron saint, lying prostrate beneath rebellious Ireland, figured as "a completely dehumanised" creature with "a snarling pig's head [and] the body of a dragon."[86] Double, heterogeneous, animal, metamorphosed—these images fit Kristeva's description of the abject. Although, as this essay has indicated, Victorian representations of Ireland and the Irish were fluid, contradictory, and contingent, immersed in vacillating economies of xenodochy and xenophobia, fascination and fear, it seems that, at moments of extreme crisis, abjection repeatedly emerged, besetting discursive attempts to exclude alterity from an anxious English cultural identity.

---

84. See Salaman, *The History and Social Influence of the Potato,* 607; "Justice to Ireland!" *Punch* 78 (1880): 19.

85. Foster, *Paddy and Mr Punch,* 186. For the original cartoon, see "The Pig that *Won't* 'Pay the Rint!'" *Punch* 80 (1881): 115.

86. Michael de Nie, "Britannia's Sick Sister: Irish Identity and the British Press, 1798–1882," in *Writing Irishness in Nineteenth-Century British Culture,* 188. For the original image, see "The Dragon and St. George," *Funny Folks* 7 (11 June 1881): 177.

Works Cited

Acton, Eliza. *Modern Cookery for Private Families*. 1855. Reprint, Lewes: Southover Press, 1993.

Barthes, Roland. "Toward a Psychosociology of Contemporary Food Consumption." In *Food and Culture: A Reader*, edited by Carole Counihan and Penny Van Esterik. 20–27. London and New York: Routledge, 1997.

Beddoe, J. *The Races of Britain: A Contribution to the Anthropology of Western Europe*. Bristol: J. W. Arrowsmith, 1885.

Bhabha, Homi K. *The Location of Culture*. 2nd ed. London and New York: Routledge, 2004.

Brontë, Charlotte. *Shirley*. Edited by Andrew and Judith Hook. London: Penguin, 1974.

Bourke, Austin. "*The Visitation of God?*": *The Potato and the Great Irish Famine*. Edited by Jacqueline Hill and Cormac Ó Gráda. Dublin: The Lilliput Press, 1993: 11–25.

Carlyle, Thomas. *Chartism*. 2nd ed. London: James Fraser, 1840.

Chatterton, Lady. *Rambles in the South of Ireland during the Year 1838*. London: Saunders and Otley, 1839.

Cobbett, William. *Cottage Economy*. 1823. Bromyard: Landsman, 1974.

———. *Rural Rides*. Vol. 1. 1830. Reprint, London: Peter Davies, 1930.

Colley, Linda. *Britons: Forging the Nation, 1707–1837*. London: Vintage, 1996.

"Condition of Ireland: Illustrations of the New Poor-Law." *Illustrated London News* 15 (22 December 1849): 404–406.

"Continental Revolutions—Irish Rebellion—English Distress." *Blackwood's Edinburgh Magazine* 64 (1848): 475–498.

Cullen, Fintan. *Visual Politics: The Representation of Ireland, 1750–1930*. Cork: Cork University Press, 1997.

Curtis, L. Perry, Jr. *Anglo-Saxons and Celts: A Study of Anti-Irish Prejudice in Victorian England*. Bridgeport, CT: Conference on British Studies at the University of Bridgeport, 1968.

———. *Apes and Angels: The Irishman in Victorian Caricature*. Rev. ed. Washington and London: Smithsonian Institution, 1997.

"The Dragon and St. George." *Funny Folks* 7, 11 June 1881, 177.

Douglas, Mary. *Implicit Meanings: Selected Essays in Anthropology*. 2nd ed. London and New York: Routledge, 1999.

Eagleton, Terry. *Heathcliff and the Great Hunger: Studies in Irish Culture*. London: Verso, 1995.

Elly, Sandham. *Potatoes, Pigs, and Politics: The Curse of Ireland and the Cause of England's Embarrassments*. London: Kent and Richards, 1848.

Engels, Friedrich. *The Condition of the Working Class in England*. Edited by David McLellan. Oxford: Oxford University Press, 1993.

"The Famine in Ireland—Funeral at Skibbereen—From a Sketch by Mr. H. Smith, Cork." *Illustrated London News* 10 (30 January 1847): 65.

"Famine in the South of Ireland." *Fraser's Magazine for Town and Country* 35 (1847): 491–504.

Fegan, Melissa. *Literature and the Irish Famine, 1845–1919*. Oxford: Oxford University Press, 2002.

Foster, Roy. *Paddy and Mr Punch: Connections in Irish and English History*. London: Allen Lane, 1993.

Foster, Thomas Campbell. *Letters on the Condition of the People of Ireland.* London: Chapman and Hall, 1846.

Gilley, Sheridan. "English Attitudes to the Irish in England, 1780–1900." In *Immigrants and Minorities in British Society,* edited by Colin Holmes. 81–210. London: George Allen & Unwin, 1978.

Gray, Peter. "'Potatoes and Providence': British Government Responses to the Great Famine." *Bullán* 1.1 (1994): 75–90.

"Half a Word about a Bit of Ireland." *Punch* 17 (1849): 26.

Hall, Mr and Mrs S. C. *Ireland: Its Scenery, Character, Etc.* London: How and Parsons, 1842.

"Ireland and its Ministerial Treatment." *Illustrated London News* 14 (10 February 1849): 81–82.

"Irish Agitation and Irish Misery." *Illustrated London News* 12 (27 May 1848): 335–336.

James, Allison. "How British Is British Food?" In *Food, Health and Identity,* edited by Pat Caplan. 71–86. London and New York: Routledge, 1997.

"Justice to Ireland!" *Punch* 78 (1880): 19.

Kristeva, Julia. *Powers of Horror: An Essay on Abjection.* Translated by Leon S. Roudiez. New York: Columbia University Press, 1982.

———. *Strangers to Ourselves.* Translated by Leon S. Roudiez. London and New York: Harvester Wheatsheaf, 1991.

Leech, John. "Justice to Ireland." *Punch* 10 (1846): 171.

Lengel, Edward G. *The Irish through British Eyes: Perceptions of Ireland in the Famine Era.* Westport, CT: Praeger, 2002.

MacIntyre, Angus. *The Liberator: Daniel O'Connell and the Irish Party, 1830–1847.* London: Hamish Hamilton, 1965.

Martineau, Harriet. *Letters from Ireland.* Edited by Glen Hooper. Dublin and Portland: Irish Academic Press, 2001.

Mayhew, Henry. *London Labour and the London Poor.* Vol. 1. 1851. Reprint, London: Frank Cass, 1967.

Mitchel, John. *The Last Conquest of Ireland (Perhaps).* Glasgow: R. & T. Washbourne, n.d.

Morash, Christopher. *Writing the Irish Famine.* Oxford: Clarendon Press, 1995.

Nicholson, Asenath. *Ireland's Welcome to the Stranger, or an Excursion through Ireland in 1844 & 1845, for the Purpose of Personally Investigating the Condition of the Poor.* New York: Baker and Scribner, 1847.

Nie, Michael de. "Britannia's Sick Sister: Irish Identity and the British Press, 1798–1882." In *Writing Irishness in Nineteenth-Century British Culture,* edited by Neil McCaw. 173–193. Aldershot: Ashgate, 2004.

Ó Gráda, Cormac. *Black '47 and Beyond: The Great Irish Famine in History, Economy, and Memory.* Princeton, NJ: Princeton University Press, 2000.

"The Peasantry of Dorsetshire." *Illustrated London News* 9 (5 September 1846): 156–158.

"The Pig that *Won't* 'Pay the Rint!'" *Punch* 80 (1881): 115.

"The Potato Panic." *Punch* 6 (1844): 186.

"Punch's Imaginary Conversations. William Cobbett and Sir Walter Raleigh." *Punch* 11 (1846): 237.

"Rebecca and her Daughters." *Punch* 5 (1843): 5.

Romani, Roberto. *National Character and Public Spirit in Britain and France, 1750–1914.* Cambridge: Cambridge University Press, 2002.

Salaman, Redcliffe N. *The History and Social Influence of the Potato.* 1949. Reprint, with a new introduction by J. G. Hawkes. Cambridge: Cambridge University Press, 1985.

——. *The Influence of the Potato on the Course of Irish History.* Dublin: Browne and Nolan, 1943.

Sinnema, Peter W. *Dynamics of the Pictured Page: Representing the Nation in the* Illustrated London News. Aldershot: Ashgate, 1998.

Sjöholm, Cecilia. *Kristeva and the Political.* London and New York: Routledge, 2005.

Sudan, Rajani. *Fair Exotics: Xenophobic Subjects in English Literature, 1720–1850.* Philadelphia: University of Pennsylvania Press, 2002.

Taylor, Emily. *The Irish Tourist; Or, The People and Provinces of Ireland.* London: Darton and Harvey, 1837.

Thackeray, William Makepeace. *The Irish Sketch-Book.* 2nd ed. London: Chapman and Hall, 1845.

——. *Vanity Fair.* Edited by J. I. M. Stewart. London: Penguin, 1968.

Times, 30 October 1845, 4.

Times, 25 January 1847, 4.

Times, 1 March 1847, 4.

Times, 3 January 1848, 4.

Times, 11 July 1848, 5.

Times, 26 December 1848, 4.

Trevelyan, C. E. *The Irish Crisis.* London: Longman, Brown, Green and Longmans, 1848.

Trollope, Anthony. *Castle Richmond.* London: The Trollope Society, 1994.

Williams, Leslie A. *Daniel O'Connell, the British Press and the Irish Famine: Killing Remarks.* Edited by William H. A. Williams. Aldershot: Ashgate, 2003.

——. "Irish Identity and the *Illustrated London News,* 1846–1851." In *Representing Ireland: Gender, Class, Nationality,* edited by Susan Shaw Sailer. 57–93. Gainesville: University Press of Florida, 1997.

7

"Wot is to Be"

The Visual Construction of Empire at the
Crystal Palace Exhibition, London, 1851

❧

JOY SPERLING

On 1 May 1851, Queen Victoria opened the Great Exhibition of the Industry of All Nations in Hyde Park, London. Thousands of onlookers and dozens of foreign dignitaries attended the grand inaugural celebration.[1] The
exhibition was housed in a vast prefabricated glasshouse designed by Joseph
Paxton and placed on nineteen acres of parkland in Hyde Park. It was immediately dubbed the "Crystal Palace." Not surprisingly, the exhibition's organizing principals privileged the British displays. The pieces of the visual
hierarchies created by the geography of the exhibition spaces fit together so
neatly that they seemed to produce a naturally occurring and inevitable visuality. Indeed, its visual taxonomy served as a palimpsest for dozens of later
international exhibitions.[2] Yet, even as the narrative of the Great Exhibition,
as Eric Hobsbawm suggests, formed a "kind of planetary system circulat-

---

1. Representatives of the following nations attended the opening of the Great Exhibition:
Austria, Bavaria, Belgium, Brunswick, Denmark, the Duchy of Nassau, Egypt, the Electorate of
Hesse and Cassel, the Duchy of Hesse, France, Greece, Hamburg, Hanover, Netherlands, Portugal,
Prussia, Rome, Russia, Sardinia, Saxony, Spain, Sweden and Norway, Switzerland, Tunis, Turkey,
the United States, Wurtemburg, and the Zollverein.

2. On world's fairs see Paul Greenlaugh, *Ephemeral Vistas: A History of the Expositions Universelles, the Great Exhibitions and World's Fairs, 1851–1939* (Manchester, Manchester University
Press, 1988), and Robert W. Rydell and Nancy E. Gwinn, *Fair Representations: World's Fairs and the
Modern World* (Amsterdam: VU University Press, 1994). On the concept of dominant visualities,
see Nicholas Mirzoeff, *An Introduction to Visual Culture* (London: Routledge, 2009), 7, 89–93.

ing around the economic sun of Britain,"[3] its taxonomic system was less than universally accepted. Indeed, the visual geography of the Great Exhibition was cobbled together so quickly and extemporaneously that, like British society at the time, it was subject to cracks and fissures that revealed barely suppressed apprehensions about the veracity of its claims. The superficial logic of the exhibition's organizing principals were designed to establish and formalize an imaginary set of stable Anglo-centric global, national, cultural, social, gendered, and racial hierarchies, but ironically it revealed the inverse.

The Great Exhibition took place when an inwardly-looking British nationalism was on the cusp of an outwardly-looking imperialism and Britain's ever-expanding middle classes claimed the center of British culture. By mid-century two imagined communities—the British middle classes and the British nation—jointly established a set of standards that constituted the British norm. The British regions of Scotland, Ireland, and Wales were regarded with some suspicion by the English center, while Europe and beyond were viewed as dangerous, polluting forces. As the incipient British Empire greedily eyed the natural resources, raw materials, and inexpensive labor forces of the rest of the world, it was forced to confront the fact that contact with the foreign not only consolidated empire, but also threatened Britain's still unfixed identity. The Great Exhibition's widely advertised claim that it brought together the "Industry of All Nations" in friendly competition was disingenuous given the nation's palpable anxiety about foreigners and foreign competition.[4] In fact, the real mandate of the exhibition was to advance British industrial prowess vis-à-vis that of its major competitors, to legitimize Britain's right to imperial rule, and to consolidate a British identity towards mitigating internal social, economic, and political conflicts. This narrative played out visually in the cartography of the exhibition. Crudely stated, the British exhibits expanded in a leisurely and rational way to encompass the entire western half of the Crystal Palace, while the rest of the world was clustered awkwardly in the eastern half; the British exhibits focused primarily on Britain's industrial, economic, and social progress with the rest of the world presented as an emporium from whose natural and industrial resources Britain could literally pick and choose.[5]

---

3. Eric Hobsbawm, *Industry and Empire* (Harmondsworth: Penguin, 1994) 114, as quoted by Paul Young, *Globalization and the Great Exhibition: The Victorian New World Order* (Basingstoke: Palgrave, Macmillan, 2009) 10. See also *The Crystal Palace: Report of the Meeting at Mr. Oliviera's, March 29th, 1852* (London: James Ridgway, 1852): "This structure is the very thing required to keep this country at the head of civilization" (30).

4. See John Tallis, Beard, Mayall, etc., *Tallis's History and Description of the Crystal Palace, and the Exhibition of the World's Industry in 1851, Illustrated by Beautiful Steel Engravings, from Original Drawings and Daguerreotypes,* ed. J. G. Strutt, Esq., 3 volumes (London: Tallis, 1851), volume 1, 7, 15, 27, 57, 147.

5. Tallis I: 37, 43; II: 116.

There is substantial scholarship on the national, imperial, and racial imperatives of the Great Exhibition, but the investigation of the xenophobic narrative embedded in it is as yet underdeveloped.[6] Although xenophobia only entered the English lexicon in the early twentieth century, its essential component—a deep-rooted antipathy or fear of the foreign—was already on full view at the Great Exhibition. This particular manifestation of xenophobia was located in the internal insecurities of a not-fully-formed British identity jeopardized by the internal consequences of the industrial revolution (particularly class conflicts) and the external consequences of increasing trade, commerce, and contact with the outside world. The latter development, particularly, generated a fear that a closer proximity with the foreign would dilute (or pollute) British national identity; threat to the British identity was both ideational (what it meant to be foreign as opposed to British) and material (the emergence of other industrial competitors in Europe and North America). This line of argumentation also assumes that the reification of an imaginary national "us" was reliant on its inverse, the presence of a foreign "them." National identity is constituted by a varying admixture of two components, the internal (the various elements constituting the national collective identity) and the external (those elements differentiating the nation from other countries). The weaker the internal foundation of nationalism, the greater is the likelihood that the external foundation of nationalism will take on xenophobic characteristics. The wellspring of xenophobia is manifestly different than that of a more corporeal and precisely targeted racism; it is instead an essential component in the construction of national identity, which shapes the ways in which nationalism is expressed or manifested both internally and externally. This essay explores the institutionalized xenophobic narrative of the Great Exhibition and demonstrates the ways in which Britain's abstracted fear of the foreign was on display in the ostensibly neutral spaces of the Great Exhibition and specifically was drawn on the print and photographic record of it.

---

6. Secondary scholarship on the Great Exhibition includes: Jeffrey A. Auerbach and Peter H. Hollenberg, eds., *Britain and Empire, and the World at the Exhibition of 1851;* James Buzard, Joseph Childers, and Eileen Gillooly, eds., *Victorian Prism: Refractions of the Crystal Palace;* Tom Corfe, *The Great Exhibition* (Cambridge: Cambridge University Press, 1979); John Davis, *The Great Exhibition* (Gloucester: Sutton, 1999); Ronald S. Ely, *Crystal Palaces: Visions of Splendor: An Anthology;* Yvonne French, *The Great Exhibition: 1851* (London, Harvill, 1950); Christopher Hobhouse, *1851 and the Crystal Palace: Being an Account of the Great Exhibition and its Contents; of Sir Joseph Paxton; and of the Erection, the Subsequent History and the Subsequent Destruction of His Masterpiece* (London: Murray, 1937); Hermione Hobhouse, *The Crystal Palace and the Great Exhibition* (London: Athlone, 2002); John Mackenzie, *The Victorian Vision: Inventing New Britain* (London: V&A, 2001); Nickolaus Pevsner, *High Victorian Design: A Study of the Exhibits of 1851* (London: Architectural, 1951); *The Great Exhibition of 1851: New Interdisciplinary Essays* (Manchester: Manchester University Press, 2001); Paul Young, *Globalization and the Great Exhibition: The Victorian New World Order* (Basingstoke: Palgrave Macmillan, 2009).

Britain, Xenophobia, and the Great Exhibition

The Great Exhibition was organized in the late 1840s, when the internal structure of British society and the negotiation of its place in the world were neither fixed nor inevitable. Plans for the exhibition emerged in the late-1840s under the direction of Prince Albert and a Royal Commission,[7] who were tasked with organizing an extravagant display of British might to both intimidate the rest of the world and to tamp down the multitude of social, economic, and political instabilities that racked Britain, including the sometimes difficult political and social accommodation of a rising industrial ruling class, a deep economic depression, working-class unrest, and the threat of revolution spreading from Europe. The plan of the Great Exhibition collapsed space and time, and in doing so served as a visual surrogate for Britain's aspirations of political, economic, and industrial global dominance. The major refrain and minor variations of the Great Exhibition served as a visual super- and sub-structure constructing and buttressing an unstable national identity that was defined in opposition to a foreign other and revealed a newly imagined xenophobic British "self."

Core dimensions of British xenophobia were grafted onto the Great Exhibition. While the xenophobic impulse is frequently and erroneously conflated with racism, xenophobia is indirect and takes aim at much less specific, less conceptually realized targets; it requires no direct material contact with the other. Xenophobia oftentimes takes on the character of a formless fear of the instability triggered by an undifferentiated foreign or unknown; it can be either local or global. Xenophobia also manifests as an aversion to, or an identified or acknowledged fear of, several kinds and degrees of the foreign. A middle-class London resident in 1851 might harbor one kind of xenophobic resentment toward the Irish other, another toward the European foreigner, and quite another toward the non-European foreigner. The key point, however, is that the xenophobic impulse is less obviously antipathetic than racism. Xenophobia can masquerade as an exoticizing or patronizing impulse that finds humor in or startled amazement at the curious habits of the other, even in the absence of actual contact. Indeed, xenophobia sometimes presented

---

7. Members of the Royal Commission included HRH Prince Albert, I. K. Brunel, Charles Cockerell, Professor Donaldson, Mr. Alderman Thompson, R. Stephenson, William Hopkins, T. F. Gibson, Richard Cobden, Charles Barry, John Shepherd, Philip Pusey, John Gottard, Wm. Cubitt, Thomas Baring, Charles Lyell, R. Westmacott, Rt. Hon. H. Labouchere, Lord Overstone, Earl Granville, Earl of Reese, Sir C. L. Eastlake, Rt. Hon. W. E. Gladstone, Lord John Russell, Lord Stanley, Earl of Ellsemere, Duke of Buccleuch. Special Commissioners included Dr. Lyon Playfair, Lieut. Colonel Lloyd. The Executive Commission included George Drew Francis Fuller, Charles Wentworth Dilke, Henry Cole, Lieut. William Read. The architect was Joseph Paxton; Contractor: Mr. Fox; and the Superintendents of the Works were C. H. Wild, Owen Jones.

itself at the Great Exhibition as a barely conscious skein of anxious insecurity that ran almost invisibly through Britain's display of national hubris.

In the months leading up to the opening of the Great Exhibition, the press and people of London seemed to anticipate eagerly and simultaneously fear the expected influx of "millions" of visitors from the regions and abroad.[8] Foreigners were described in the press with a frisson of fear, anxiety, and curiosity, were hailed variously as entertaining diversions from the ordinary, as destabilizing forces that might breach British social mores, and as diseased polluters of English culture. The fact that many fewer foreigners came to London than expected caused economic disappointment and cultural relief; those who did come were subjects of suspicion, fear, and deprecating humor.[9]

The finer points of English xenophobia in 1851 were most visibly realized in the visual geography of the Great Exhibition as a sharp visual contrast between the powerful English body, signified by the clear, strong skeletal structure of the building, and the orderly exhibition of British industry and technology in the west nave, and the disorderly jumble of foreign raw materials and products of the enervated, exoticized, Orientalized, trivialized, feminized, infantilized and generalized foreign body clustered around the transept and in the east nave. The placement of the new Shepherd Electric Clock, which dominated the public entrance to the central transept even seemed to impose English time as well as space.[10]

By the time the Great Exhibition closed on 15 October 1851, more than six million visitors had paid to see it and even more had read about it in extensively documented catalogues, pamphlets, magazines, and newspapers. A prodigious number of objects and images were sold as souvenirs of the exhibition.[11] The Great Exhibition was the first international exposition in Europe to be so extensively promoted, recorded, and evaluated for posterity in inexpensive publications, images, and souvenirs. The visuality produced by the exhibition and related ephemera reveals much about the ways in which a wide swathe of the British public wanted to be viewed, as well as the ways they viewed the foreign. Two visual objects from the exhibition that par-

---

8. Tallis I: 27; "There is Much Speculation Afloat," *Times* (3 January 1851): 18. Qtd. in Young, 176; "Business and Bayonet," *Punch* 19 (1850): 234. Qtd. in Young, 176.

9. See, for example, Henry Mayhew and George Cruikshank, *1851: Or the Adventures of Mr. and Mrs. Sandboys and family, Who Came Up to London to 'Enjoy Themselves,' and to See the Great Exhibition* (London: Bogue, 1851) 66, 71, 85, 102, 106, 108, 113, 114, 118, 139, 141, 145, 149, 172, etc.; and Richard D. Altick, *Punch: The Lively Youth of a British Institution* (Columbus: The Ohio State University Press, 1997), 613–634.

10. Greenwich Mean Time, formerly named Mean Solar Time, was subject to debate in England in the 1840s, because railway systems and manufacturing needed a standardized national time. GMT was established formally in 1884 at the International Meridian Conference, Washington, D.C.

11. *The Crystal Palace*, 39–40.

ticularly reveal differing shades of British xenophobia are a cotton souvenir handkerchief entitled "The Great Exhibition 'Wot is to Be'" (see figure 7.1) and a photographic wet-plate print from a salt-print calotype negative of the interior of the Crystal Palace by Benjamin Brecknell Turner (see figure 7.2), one of the first commercial calotype photographers in London (1815–1894).

The images on the handkerchief were based on George Augustus Sala's well-known panoramic pamphlet, "Wot is to Be," which caricatured the blowhard pomp of the fair's opening and the suspicious reception of foreign dignitaries. Sala's caricature was sub-titled, "Vates Secundus for the Committee of the Society for Keeping Things in their Places."[12] The handkerchief is illustrated by four rows of figures parading to the exhibition. The parade begins at the bottom right: the Royal Commissioner arrives with a "Strong Detachment of Police" (to quell the rowdiness of the masses), followed by a pompous Prince Albert on horseback, Joseph Paxton, and the contractor Mr. Fox with a model of the Palace accompanied by yet another policeman. Above them, the Lord Mayor of London perches on an elephant, the Corporation of London are outfitted in a hodge-podge of foreign costumes, while James Wyld (1812–1887) carries his famous globe.[13] A band leads a clutch of pensioners and government ministers, who are followed by "A Party of Very Distinguished Foreigners Indeed" in flamboyant costumes who look bewildered and agape. In the next row, several British politicians are followed by the Dey of Algiers (an astonished "oriental gentleman"), a Russian gentleman in furs with a bludgeon, and a monarchical dancing rat. Above them, the Italian delegation genuflects to the church, an American whips an African-American slave, three Germans literally inhale Professor Sauerkraut's tomes on smoke, a heavily bearded French "Red Republican" is dressed as a peasant, and an effete French dancing master with the famous French chef in London Monsieur Soyer (1810–1858) follow.[14] On the top row, John Hobhouse, Baron Broughton (1798–1869) is shown as a Janus-faced French sympathizer, a group of slovenly Irish follow in rags, Benjamin

---

12. George Augustus Sala as Vates Secundus, *The Great Exhibition: 'Wot is to Be,' or Probable Results of the Industry of All Nations in the Year '51; Showing What's to Be Exhibited, Who is to Exhibit . . . In Short, How Its [sic] All Going to Be Done* (London: Publisher unknown, 1850).

13. Wyld's Great Globe, or Wyld's Monster Globe, was constructed by James Wyld (1812–1887) to coincide with the Great Exhibition. He had originally wanted to include it in the Great Exhibition, but it was too large (at more than 60 feet in diameter) and too commercial for the exhibition. It was finally located in the gardens of Leicester Square, where it became one of London's most popular attractions between 1851 and 1862. See Richard D. Altick, *The Shows of London* (Cambridge: Belknap and Harvard University Press, 1978), 464.

14. See Paul Young, "The Cooking Animal: Economic Man at the Great Exhibition," *Victorian Literature and Culture* 36 (2008): 569–586; and "Refreshments at the Crystal Palace," *Punch* (25 January 1851).

Figure 7.1 Anon., *The Great Exhibition 'Wot is to Be,'* 1851 (printed handkerchief). Oxford: Bodleian Library, John Johnson Collection. JJ Printed Fabrics 1

Figure 7.2 Benjamin Brecknell Turner, *The Nave at the Crystal Palace, Hyde Park, March 1852* (albumen print form waxed-paper calotype negative, 42.4 cm. × 56 cm.). © Victoria and Albert Museum, London. PH1–1982

Disraeli (1804–1881) is represented as a "Hebrew Gent," and a solid and portly John Bull brings up the rear.

The handkerchief caricatures British and foreign exhibition organizers, exhibitors, and visitors. The caricatures are crude and blunt, but they are also differentiated; the English characters are individualized specific named people, while the foreigners are generalized types. The English characters include Prince Albert, Paxton, Disraeli, and Hobhouse; and the foreigners include Irish peasants, German pseudo-intellects, and rabble-rousing or effete French. The inexpensive souvenir handkerchief was probably sold in the environs of the Exhibition, and would have been affordable to most middle-class fair-goers who appreciated (even ironically) the human and material spectacle of the fair.

The large, salt-print calotype by Benjamin Brecknell Turner by contrast was a more expensive image, probably sold with others in folio form. It shows the interior of the vacant Crystal Palace after the exhibitions had been removed and the structure returned to its original open, cleanly delineated structural state. There are almost no extant photographs (Daguerreotypes, calotypes, or wet-plate stereographs) of the interior of the Crystal Palace with the exhibitions installed; there are a few, such as Turner's, of the expansive interior structure, and there are many more of the exterior. But photographs of the Crystal Palace are relatively rare compared to the thousands of extant images (steel- and wood-engravings, lithographs and chromolithographs) of the same subject. This can be partly explained by the technical limitations of photography in 1851, which operated only in daylight, but it was also because large-scale salt-print calotypes such as Turner's were not easily reproducible, still quite costly, and beyond the means of many exhibition visitors. These photographs would have been purchased by a small segment of the upper-middle class who were more concerned with England's political profile abroad and the resiliency of its industry and manufactures at home. In Turner's photograph the Crystal Palace is shown as standing tall, strong, and unassailable, as if asserting that it, like England, had survived the exhibition intact and "unpolluted." The contrast between the Turner's photograph and the souvenir handkerchief is dramatic: the handkerchief illustrates the presence of the foreign in England, while the photograph renders the foreign invisible. I would argue that both are xenophobic, but that Turner's photograph is more subtle and purposeful precisely because it is a photograph. Photography as a visual medium poses as a transparent (or objective) object to be looked through, but its meaning is in fact just as fictional as that on the handkerchief: both are densely obscure, deeply encoded, socially constructed (or subjective) vessels of meaning. The photograph may attempt to mask its agency, in this case an unacknowledged antipathy for the foreign, but the editorial process has left its mark, signifying through what has been erased. To comprehend this dynamic more thoroughly it is necessary to examine the visual geography of the Great Exhibition, the facets of xenophobia on display, and the several ways in which Crystal Palace prints and photography, and Turner's photograph specifically, communicated meaning in 1851.

The Visual Geography of the Great Exhibition

The Great Exhibition of the Industry of All Nations functioned as a diplomatic offensive in 1851, signaling Britain's assertion of its global rank as a great power, if not *the* great power. Its overt purpose was to demonstrate that Britain was capable of commanding the world's resources through the innate superiority of its people, to champion the still-disputed virtues of free trade, and to marry Britain's foreign policy to claims that Britain was uniquely positioned to forge international cooperation, to universalize commercial liberalism, and to maintain peace and prosperity for all.[15]

The installation of objects in the Great Exhibition was heir to two major aspects of nineteenth-century exhibitionary culture: the obsessive encyclopedic collecting and cluttered display of the Cabinet of Curiosities tradition; and the visceral visual thrill generated by London's popular entertainments, such as the panorama, diorama, or Phantasmagoria, clustered around Leicester Square.[16] The frisson between cool rationality and the erotics of looking at the Great Exhibition was a result of a practical compromise by the Royal Commission.[17] Originally, the Commission rejected a proposition to orga-

---

15. Prince Albert's involvement in the nonpartisan Royal Commission was critical: he rallied the support not only of British Prime Minister John Russell (1792–1878), the Parliamentary opposition, and the aristocracy but also of virtually every segment of British society (with the notable exception of the radical working class) in addition to numerous foreign governments. Parliament was increasingly polarized after the repeal of the Corn Laws, and free trade became the central plank of British foreign economic policy. Many in Parliament wished for the continuation of protection of British products in the national and international markets.

16. These included phantasmagoria, panoramas, dioramas, and waxworks, a number of which were advertised in *The Official Catalogue's Advertiser: Catlin's American Indian Gallery,* The Gallery of Illustration, The Diorama of the Overland Mail to India, The Diorama of "Our Native Land," Madame Tussaud and Sons' Historical Gallery, The Great Exhibition of Paintings at 236, High Holborn, Dissolving Views (Phantsamagoria, Chromatropes and Dissolving Views). See also *A Description of the Series of Tableaux of the Crystal Palace Exhibition in the Royal Cyclorama, Albany Street, Regent's Park* (London: E. Carrall, 1852). For exhibitions in London see Richard D. Altick, *The Shows of London* (Cambridge, MA: Belknap-Harvard University Press, 1978); Tony Bennett, *The Birth of the Museum, History, Theory, Politics* (London: Routledge, 1995) 59–88; Barbara J. Black, *On Exhibit: Victorians and their Museums* (Charlottesville: University of Virginia Press, 2000); *Palaces of Art: Art Galleries in Britain, 1790–1990* (London: Dulwich Picture Gallery and the National Gallery of Scotland, 1991).

17. Laura Mulvey, "Visual Pleasure and Narrative Cinema," in *The Feminism and Visual Culture Reader.*

nize the exhibition by nation in favor of a more dramatic grouping of like objects together in four general categories: Manufacturing, Machinery, Raw Materials, and Fine Arts. This taxonomy was intended to enable direct visual comparisons to be made among national products, and to privilege Britain, which would dominate both in quantity of objects displayed and, it was expected, in quality in the Manufacturing and Machinery categories. Britain's colonies, in turn, would dominate the Raw Materials category. And, by restricting Fine Arts submissions to sculpture, the French, who led Europe in painting, would be disadvantaged significantly, just as the British, who had made significant investments in new sculptural processes, would be advantaged.[18] By December 1850, however, the planning committee was forced to confront the logistical impossibility of keeping track and storing thousands of exhibition objects arriving in London from dozens of nations, revisited the earlier plan, and finally decided to combine both plans so that exhibits would be catalogued by nation and sub-divided by category. Not only did the new organization enhance the commission's imperial narrative, but it also cultivated and legitimized Britain's xenophobic tendencies by drawing visual comparisons of civilization according to a scale devised by the commission to favor Britain.

The revised taxonomy also necessitated a revision of space; the British exhibits were granted the entire western nave and the rest of the world was clustered into the eastern nave in a mess of befuddling and conflicting cartographies. The clear, cool organization of the British nave described an orderly, civilized, peaceful, and dominant Britain. Its large, open, northern galleries featured heavy machinery, including a large section dedicated to railroad innovations, which far outstripped those found in Europe.[19] Its equally large southern galleries featured British consumer goods with a special emphasis on textiles, over which Britain was currently locked in a battle for commercial supremacy with France. The smaller, upper northern galleries displayed smaller machines, philosophical, medical, and musical instruments, photography, and the Fine Arts. The upper southern galleries included displays of timepieces, jewelry, plate, silks, and shawls. The finest British pottery was displayed in a group of intimate galleries framing the transept. As visitors entered the central transept they were treated to a magnificent display of British monumental sculpture of the royal couple and a

---

18. Tallis I: 38–40; Joy Sperling, "Multiples and Reproductions: Prints and Photographs in Nineteenth-Century England—Visual Communities and Class" in *A History of Visual Culture: Western Civilization from the 18th to the 21st Century*; and Geoffrey A. Godden, "The Victorian Art Union Movement," *Apollo* (September 1961): 69.

19. Tallis I: 5, 56, 143; II: 116, 119. See also Henry Mayhew, *London Labor and London Poor* (London: David Bogue, 1852), 23: "Never was there anything so puerile as the classification of the works of industry in our exhibition."

fabulously large crystal fountain. The exhibits of Britain's colonial possessions, featuring mostly exotic luxury goods and raw materials, were tucked
in a jumble of small galleries around the entrance with India, Jersey, Ceylon,
and Malta to the north and Africa, Australia, Canada, and the West Indies
to the south.

The rest of the world was packed into the eastern nave where location
was assigned according to the seemingly irrational precept of relative distance from the equator. This cleverly removed Britain's keenest economic
and industrial competitors (France and America) as far away as possible from
the British exhibits.[20] And Britain's most proximate exhibits were a group of
visibly less competitive, less-industrially developed countries such as Persia,
Egypt, Turkey, Spain, Portugal, Greece, Italy, and Sardinia to the north; and
China, Tunis and Switzerland to the south. The French exhibits were allo-
cated a large bank of spaces immediately to the east of Switzerland and both
south and north of the nave. The effect created a doubly disjointed exhibition
by space and taxonomy. The other European exhibitors, Austria, Russia, the
major German states, Denmark, Greece, Italy, the German Zollverein, and
Belgium were clustered around the French spaces and were also divided by
the nave. The U.S. exhibit was exiled to a large bank of spaces at the very end
of the eastern nave; fewer objects than expected were sent and the exhibit was
divided by the nave, sub-divided by state, and then by category so that the
entire exhibit appeared weak, thin, and sparse.

The grandeur of the multi-story transept functioned as a space of British
equanimity and power; it asserted British global dominance and established a
dividing line between east and west, north and south, British order and foreign disorder. In sum, the visual geography of the Crystal Palace represented
an extravagant demonstration of imperial hubris in which Britain claimed the
global center and relegated the rest of the world to the margins.

Xenophobia:
Class, Gender, and Foreignness at the Great Exhibition

The Great Exhibition also cultivated xenophobia through its secondary narratives of class, gender, and foreignness. Indeed, although the exhibition was
described as the people's palace and open to almost everyone, the Royal Com-

---

20. *Official Descriptive and Illustrated Catalogue of the Great Exhibition of the Works of Industry
of All Nations, 1851,* 16 volumes, 16, 17; and *Punch* 20 (January to July 1851): 247. See also James
Buzard, "Conflicting Cartographies: Globalism, Nationalism and the Crystal Palace Floor Plan," in
Victorian Prism: Refractions of the Crystal Palace; and Elizabeth Bonyham and Anthony Burton, *The
Great Exhibitor: The Life and Work of Henry Cole.*

mission segregated the classes by instituting a sliding scale of admission fees.[21] Saturdays were the most exclusive and expensive day, intentionally reserved for the elite, but they proved more popular than expected because status-conscious, upwardly aspiring, middle-class visitors tried to attend them in order to see and be seen with the elite. The working classes were admitted on the Monday-to-Friday shilling days (also working days) and were assiduously avoided by the middle classes.

The civilized, rational British gaze at the Crystal Palace was also male. It was expected that men would embrace the opportunity to flex the power of their scrutinizing gaze at the fair, to study it vigilantly, and to comprehend its logical order, rational design, and grand themes. It was expected that women, on the other hand, would respond naturally and empathetically to the exhibition, to be overcome emotionally by its vastness, its dizzying heights, fractured vistas, and mass of visual stimuli, and to be capable of apprehending only its most superficial details, and appreciating only its consumable goods. Queen Victoria confessed in her journal that the exhibition exhausted her emotionally, although she visited it several times.[22] And many other women thrilled over its bazaar-like tangle of visually tempting objects displayed as if in a department store awaiting consumption.[23] The concept of foreignness at the exhibition was frequently feminized in opposition to the white male norm. Foreign people were characterized, like women, as closer to nature, less intellectually developed, more primitive, and incapable of making sufficient rational progress towards civilization without the assistance of British men. The threat of the disorderly, destabilizing imaginary foreign was a palpable presence in Victorian society that generated a deeper, unacknowledged anxiety about the unassailability of the orderly middle-class male British self.

Britain's colonies fared very poorly in presentation; they were usually and uniformly caricatured as remote, exotic lands that were frequently domi-

---

21. See Tallis I: 102, 147, 148. The total gate at the Great Exhibition was £469,115 and on opening day, £4, 25,000 was paid for seats inside the palace. Between May 2 and May 24 the charge for admittance was five shillings; between May 25 and August 2, the charge was one shilling Monday through Thursday, two shillings and sixpence on Friday, and five shillings on Saturday. Attendance was double Friday or Saturday on shilling days.

22. Barbara Harlow and Mia Carter, *Imperialism and Orientalism: A Documentary Sourcebook* (London: Blackwell, 1999), 334, 336; Tallis I: 146; Frederika Bremer, *England in 1851: or Sketches of a Tour in England* (Boulogne: Merridrew, 1853); Karen L. Kilcup, *From Beacon Hill to the Crystal Palace: The 1851 Travel Diary of a Working Class Woman by Lorenza Stevens Berbineau* (Ames: University of Iowa Press, 2002).

23. The objects displayed at the Great Exhibition were not offered for direct sale but there was a thriving business in "knock-off" objects (and photographs) just outside the park. See Erika Rappaport, "A New Era in Shopping," in *The Nineteenth Century Visual Culture Reader*. See also Tallis I: 43.

nated by "oriental" despots prior to British intervention. Their people were described as impoverished peasants living in primitive squalor, capable only of making the elaborate hand-crafted luxury items on display at the exhibition, but incapable of developing industry by themselves. The nature and extent of each colony's raw materials, critical to British industry, were extensively catalogued for readers.[24] The colonial possessions fell into two categories: those that had once been civilized but stalled at some point in the past and were thus incapable of developing further unassisted; and those that had never developed beyond the "primitive" and incapable of development at all without British intervention.[25] Indeed, a commonly expressed conceit was that British rule was kindly and beneficent, and that British culture was a great gift bestowed upon the colonized that more than compensated them for their economic exploitation and cultural subjugation.[26]

In the months leading up to the Great Exhibition, the British braced themselves for direct contact with the foreign. The press was peppered with descriptions of foreigners as primitive beings with laughably strange social skills and stupidly confounded by Britain's complex social, political, and economic systems.[27] Foreignness clearly threatened the British body politic; foreigners were described in the lexicology of disease as contagions threatening to infect or breach British social defenses.[28] Henry Mayhew, in his novel about the exhibition (illustrated by George Cruikshank),[29] described foreign

---

24. See Tallis I: 37. See also Timothy Mitchell, "Orientalism and the Exhibitionary Order," in *Colonialism and Culture*; Linda Nochlin, "The Imaginary Orient," in *The Nineteenth Century Visual Culture Reader*; Edward Said, *Orientalism* (1978; Harmondsworth: Penguin, 1995); Carol A. Breckenridge, "The Aesthetics and Politics of Colonial Collecting: India at World Fairs," *Contemporary Studies in Society and History* 31 (spring 1989): 195–216; and Paul Young, "'Carbon, Mere Carbon': The Kohinoor, The Crystal Palace and the Mission to Make Sense of British India," *Nineteenth Century Contexts*, 29.4 (December 2007): 343–358.

25. See Tallis I: 13, 14, 36, 227; II: 68. See also J. M. Blaut, *The Colonizer's Model of the World: Geographical Diffusionism and Eurocentric History* (New York, Guildford,1993); Homi K. Bhabha, *The Location of Culture* (London: Routledge, 2004); Felix Driver and David Gilbert, *Imperial Cities: Landscape, Display and Identity* (Manchester: University of Manchester Press, 1999); *Colonialism and Culture* (Ann Arbor: University of Michigan Press, 1992); Niall Ferguson, *Empire: How Britain Made the Modern World* (London: Penguin, 2004); and Eric Hobsbawm, *Industry and Empire: From 1750 to the Present Day,* rev. ed. (London: Penguin, 1999).

26. Tallis I: 5, 13, 17, 36; II: 128. See also Peter Mandler, "Race and Nation in Mid-Victorian Thought," in *British Intellectual History 1750–1900,* 230, 242, 243.

27. See Tallis I: 18, 20; Mayhew, 118.

28. See "The Exhibition Plague," *Punch* 19 (1850): 191, which includes the following: "The Black Jaundice, From America; / Palsy, from Russia; / Convulsion fits, from France; / The Mumps, from Greece; / The King's Evil, from Naples; / Rickets, from Spain; / St. Anthony's Fire, from Portugal; / Dropsy, from Holland; and/The Scarlet Fever, from Rome." And "Rules for the Prevention of Plague Next Year." *Punch* 19 (1850): 191. Qtd. in Young, "Carbon," 150. See also "Meditations on the Exhibition by Mr. Doldrums." *Punch* 21 (1851), 9.

29. Henry Mayhew and George Cruikshank, *1851, or the Adventures of Mr. and Mrs. Sandboys and Family, Who Came Up to London to "Enjoy Themselves," and to See the Great Exhibition* (London: George Newbold, 1851).

boarders in London as socially disruptive, speaking in incomprehensible tongues, singing and shouting at inappropriate times, as dishonest, cheating social pariahs who didn't pay their bills, or as distastefully dirty or bizarrely dressed; and as cooking and eating badly smelling or disgusting foods. But their greatest threat was the possibility of foreign predators taking sexual advantage of British women or girls. Mayhew describes a sly, ingratiating, and duplicitous Frenchman's dishonorable treatment of an innocent Indian girl in London, unable even to imagine his pathogenic impact on an English girl.[30]

When foreign visitors actually arrived in London in 1851, previous abstract xenophobic strategies of containment proved insufficient. As foreigners took on human form they generated palpable fear by unexpectedly disrupting several fragile markers of British superiority. Many foreign visitors turned out to be unexpectedly civilized, educated, and as comfortably middle class as their British counterparts, and some even looked down upon the British and their pretensions of grandeur. As xenophobia turned to racism, the negotiation of status at the Great Exhibition took on an increasingly serious, material, and fearful aspect.

Prints and Photography at the Great Exhibition

Arguably the most widely disseminated ephemera of the Great Exhibition were printed visual imagery. Images of the animated spectacle and rich decorative displays of the exhibition translated from drawings, watercolor paintings, or on occasion photographs into steel or wood engravings and lithographs or chromolithographs (chromos) were easily and cheaply accessible (see figure 7.3). Other prints featured personages or types of peoples satirized and caricatured and sometimes printed on various kinds of souvenir objects such as the handkerchief with images taken from Sala's pamphlet, "Wot is to Be." By mid-century, access to visual materials was so broad and deep that it reached almost every social stratum in Britain, including the semi- and illiterate, thereby forging a larger and more inclusive visually imagined national community than Benedict Anderson imagined for the written text.[31] Printed images of all kinds primed an imagined national community to view the Great Exhibition as a national rallying point.[32]

---

30. Mayhew, *1851*, 106, 107, 140, 145, 172.

31. See Benedict Anderson, *Imagined Communities: Reflections on the Origin and Spread of Nationalism* (London: Verso, 1991), 5–7, 83–111 and *The Invention of Tradition* (Cambridge: Cambridge University Press, 1993), 1–14, 43–100. See also *Proserpina, Ariadne Florentina, The Opening of the Crystal Palace* (Boston: Dana Estes, 1851), 33.

32. *The Crystal Palace*, 26; and Barbara Harlow and Mia Carter, *Imperialism and Orientalism: A Documentary Sourcebook* (Malden: Blackwell, 1999), 332, 333.

THE TRANSEPT FROM   THE GRAND ENTRANCE.

Figure 7.3 Owen Jones, *Decoration of the Transept of the Great Exhibition*, 1851 (watercolor 85 cm. × 63.5 cm.). © Victoria and Albert Museum, London. AL.8270

The role of photography in constructing national identity and as a conduit for xenophobia is particularly interesting. The expensive and weighty six-volume *Official Report of the Great Exhibition of the Works of Industry of all Nations, 1851* (1852) described the history and origins of the exhibition and listed its entire contents. It was not illustrated by the cheaper lithographs originally planned, but at the last moment by 150 exquisite, individually hand-tipped, salted-paper photographic prints (versions of calotypes).[33] The choice of photography specifically and of the purposefully direct and clinical photographic image for these volumes signified Britain's desire to impress and to assert its might and right to empire.[34] Several less-expensive privately printed ancillary catalogues were illustrated with the more usual steel- or wood-engravings, and some even included prints redrawn from photographic images.[35] The most widely read and purchased catalogue was John Tallis's

---

33. *Official Descriptive and Illustrated Catalogue of the Great Exhibition of the Works of Industry of All Nations, 1851*, 16 volumes (London: Spicer Brothers, stationers; W. Clowes and Sons, printers, 1851) was commissioned by the Royal Commission and was printed in six volumes for 20 guineas (Imperial quarto edition). It included the *Official Description and Illustrated Catalogue, Reports by the Juries,* and *Reports by the Royal Commission.*

34. See William Foster, *The Closing of the Great Exhibition or England's Mission to All Nations: A Discourse* (London: Cassell, 1851); Prior, Shepherd, Delamotte, Gilks, Bissagar, and Other Eminent Artists, *London as it is Today: Where to Go, and What to See, During the Great Exhibition: Illustrated with a Map of London, and Upwards of Two Hundred Engravings on Wood* (London: H. G. Clarke, 1851); Thomas Binney, *The Royal Exchange and the Palace of Industry; or The Possible Future of Europe and the World* (London: Jones, 1851); *Lectures on the Results of the Great Exhibition: Delivered before the Society of Arts, Manufactures and Commerce,* 2 volumes (London: Bogue, 1852–1853); Ian Leith, *Delamotte's Crystal Palace: A Victorian Pleasure Dome Revealed* (Swindon: English Heritage, 2005); and Peter H. Hoffenberg, *An Empire on Display: English, Indian and Australian Exhibitions from the Crystal Palace to the Great War* (Berkeley: University of California Press, 2001). In 1852, when the New Crystal Palace was reconstructed at Sydenham, seven miles south of London, Philip Delamotte was commissioned to document its rebuilding, its opening, and its exhibitions in photograph form. These photographs were published in print form as *The Crystal Palace, A Guide to the Palace and Park, by Samuel Phillips, illustrated by Philip H. Delamotte (1854), The Opening Ceremony By Queen Victoria of the Rebuilt Crystal Palace, Sydenham, 10 June 1854* (1854). See also Joseph Cundall, *Photographic Views of the Progress of the Crystal Palace, Sydenham* (1855). Publications on the rebuilt Crystal Palace at Sydenham, which operated the Crystal Palace Library, include Mrs. Jameson, *A Handbook of the Courts of Modern Sculpture, Crystal Palace Library* (1854); R. G. Latham and Edward Forbes, *The Natural History Department of the Palace Described and Ethnology* (1854); Richard Owens, *Geology and Inhabitants of the Ancient World* (1854); Owen Jones, *An Apology for the Coloring of the Greek Court at the Crystal Palace* (1854); M. Digby Wyatt and J. B. Waring, *The Italian Court in the Crystal Palace* (1854); M. Digby Wyatt and J. B. Waring, *The Medieval Court in the Crystal Palace* (1854); M. Digby Wyatt and J. B. Waring, *The Renaissance Court in the Crystal Palace* (1854); Austen Henry Layard, *The Ninevah Court in the Crystal Palace* (1854); Joseph Cundall, *Examples of Ornament, Selected Chiefly from Works of Art in the British Museum, the Museum of Economic Geography, the Museum of Ornamental Art, and the New Crystal Palace* (London: Bell and Daly, 1855); Sir J. Gardner Wilkinson, *The Egyptians in the Tome of the Pharaohs, Being a Companion to the Crystal Palace Egyptian Collections and An Introduction to the Study of the Egyptian Hieroglyphics by Samuel Birch* (London: Published for the Crystal Palace Company, 1857).

35. The Royal Commission published an *Official Descriptive and Illustrated Catalogue of the*

History and Description of the Crystal Palace and the Exhibition of the World's Industry in 1851, which he published in one-, two-, or three-volume editions, illustrated by wood- and steel-engravings, some of which, he boasted, were drawn from Daguerreotypes by Jazeb Edwin Mayall (1813–1901) and Richard Beard (1801–1885). A number of illustrated magazines also published illustrated catalogues: *The Art Journal's Illustrated Catalogue: The Industry of All Nations* (1851), for instance, was published in several monthly issues, while *The Crystal Palace and its Contents, being An Illustrated Cyclopedia of the Great Exhibition of the Industry of All Nations (1851)* was published every two weeks between October 1851 and March 1852. (Both publications were illustrated by engravings.)

The Great Exhibition was the first international exhibition to include displays of photographs and photographic technology, although they were mostly exhibited in *Class X* among other philosophical, musical, and scientific instruments. The English, Americans, and French exhibited the most photographs (roughly a dozen batches each) and the Scots, Italians, and Germans each exhibited two batches. The English photographers included the successful London Daguerreotypists Jazeb Edwin Mayall, Richard Beard, and Antoine Claudet (1797–1867). Mayall exhibited photographs *and* made

---

Great Exhibition of the Works of Industry of All Nations, 1851 (London: Spicer and Clowes, 1851) with an introduction by Henry Cole (volume 1, 1–35). The most widely read catalogue was by John Tallis, Beard, Mayall etc., *Tallis's History and Description of the Crystal Palace, and the Exhibition of the World's Industry in 1851, Illustrated by Beautiful Steel Engravings, from Original Drawings and Daguerreotypes*, 3 volumes (London: Tallis, 1851). Other illustrated catalogues included *The Art-Journal Illustrated Catalogue: The Industry of All Nations, 1851* (London: Virtue, 1851); Peter Berlyn and Charles Fowler, *The Crystal Palace: Its Architectural History and Constructive Marvels* (London: Gilbert, 1851); Peter Berlyn, *Popular Narrative of the Origins, History, Progress, and Prospects of the Great Industrial Exhibition, 1851; with a Guide to the Future Roles and Arrangement* (London: Gilbert, 1851); *The Crystal Palace and its Contents: Being an Illustrated Cyclopedia of the Great Exhibition of the Industry of All Nations, 1851, Embellished with Upwards of 500 Engravings* (London: Clark, 1852); *Dickinson's Comprehensive Pictures of the Great Exhibition of 1851: From the Originals painted for H.R.H Prince Albert by Messrs. Nash, Haghe, and Roberts, R.A. Published Under the Express Sanction of His Royal Highness Prince Albert, President of the Royal Commission, To Whom The Work is, by Permission, Dedicated*, 2 volumes (London: Dickinson Brothers, Her Majesty's Printers, 1852). Published in eighteen parts, each costing one guinea, and with fifty plates of folio chromolithographs; Charles Downes, *The Building Erected in Hyde Park for the Great Exhibition of All Nations, 1851* (1852); *The Guide-Book to the Industrial Exhibition: With Facts, Figures, and Observations on the Manufactures and Produce Exhibited* (London: Partridge, 1851); *Hunt's Handbook to the Official Catalogues: An Explanatory Note to the National Products and Manufactures of the Great Exhibition of the Industry of All Nations, 1851*, 2 volumes (London: Spicer Brothers, 1851); *The Illustrated Exhibitor: A Tribute to the World's Industrial Jubilee; Comprising Sketches, by Pen and Pencil, of the Principal Objects in the Great Exhibition of the Industry of All Nations, 1851* (London: Cassell, 1852); *The Palace of Glass and the Gathering of People: A Book for the Exhibition* (London: Jones, 1851); *The Palace of Industry: A Brief History of its Origins and Progress* (London: Oliver, 1851); and Roberts Stephenson, *The Great Exhibition: Its Palace, and its Principal Contents with Notices of the Public Buildings of the Metropolis, Places of Amusement, etc.* (London: Routledge, 1851).

views of the exhibition for Tallis's catalogue.[36] Beard and Claudet even posted advertisements at the back of the official catalogue *Advertiser,* and Claudet presented a set of stereographic views of the exhibition to the Tsar of Russia.[37] The rest of the English photographs were divided almost equally between Daguerreotypes and calotypes.[38] Artistically conceived calotypes of Newhaven "types" by the Edinburgh-based photographers David Octavius Hill (1802–1870) and Robert Adamson (1821–1848) were expected to take the highest photographic prizes.[39] The French exhibited some Daguerreotypes, but the landscape calotypes of Gustave Le Gray 1820–1884) and Henri LeSecq (1818–1882) won the calotype awards, much to the shock of the English.[40] The Americans submitted Daguerreotypes by Matthew

---

36. Tallis I: 134–138.

37. Tallis I: 136, 138. See also *Official Catalogue Advertiser, 1851,* 9, 23, for advertisements by Beard and Claudet.

38. The English exhibitors included (from the *Official Catalogue,* 66, 67, 153, 154, 162): #220—Horne, Thornthwaite and Wood, 123 Newgate St.—Dissolving views. Transparency of the moon . . . Daguerreotype and calotype apparatus and chemicals. #250—Field & Son, 113 New St. Birmingham, Mann.—compound achromatic lenses for photographic purposes. Calotype pictures. #291—Mayall, J. E. 433 West Strand, Prod.—Daguerreotype panorama. #292—Beard, R. 85 King Wm. St. City, Pat.—Photographic pictures by a new process, whereby daguerreotypes are enamelled. #294—Kilburn, W. E. 234 Regent St. Prod.—Photographic miniatures. #295—Paine, W. 5 Trinity Row, Islington, Prod.—Photographic pictures, showing the progress of the art. #296—Claudet, A. F. J. 18 King Wm. St. Charing Cross, Inv.—Photographic plates and pictures, and apparatus for photographic purposes. #297—Henneman & Malone, 122 Regent St. Westminster, Des.—Talbotype apparatus of improved design, made by J. Newmen. Talbotype pictures. Talbotypes tinted by means of caustic potash and a lead salt. Specimens of Sir J. Herschel's cyanotype and chrysotype, and of Mr. Robert Hunt's chromatype pictures. #299—Tyree Brothers, 44 Regent's Circus, Piccadilly, Inv.—Daguerreotypes. #302—Bingham, R. J.—Talbotype pictures. #303—Colls, R. & L. 168 New Bond St. Prod.—Sun pictures, on paper. #252—Laroche, M. 65 Oxford St. Des. and Prod.—The Bath. The Evening Star. Daguerreotype. #254—Voigtlander, Evans, & Co. 3 Lowndes Ter. Knightsbridge, Pro.—Daguerreotype portraits, by an improved instantaneous process. Artist. E. T. Pickering. #301—Buckle, S. Peterborough, Prod.—A series of pictures from nature, taken by Talbot's photographic process, called calotype, and printed from paper negatives. #22—Collie, W. Belmont House.—Specimens of calotypes, done from life (from the *Official Catalogue of the Great Exhibition of the Works of Industry of All Nations, 1851).*

39. The Scottish entries included (from the *Official Catalogue,* 67): #300—Hill, D. O. Calton Hill Stairs, Edinburgh, Prod. and Des.—Calotypes of the fishermen and women of Newhaven, near Edinburgh; groups, portraits, and studies from nature: produced by the Exhibitor and the late R. Adamson; and #299—Ross & Thomson, Edinburgh, Prod.—Frames containing Talbotype pictures from negatives or albumenized glass.

40. The French exhibits included (from *The Official Catalogue,* 232, 233, 241): #585—Le Gray, G. Chemin de Ronde de la Barrière de Clichy, Paris.—Specimens of photography. #592—Lesecq, H. Designer, 35 Quai Bourbon, Paris.—Two frames, with specimens of photography. #610—Marteus, F. 6 Rue du Pot-de-Fer, Paris.—Three frames with daguerreotypes. #620—Maucomble,—. 26 Rue de Grammont, Paris.—Five coloured daguerreotype portraits. #690—Saugrin,—. 11 Boulevard Montmartre, Paris.—Daguerreotype miniatures. #1038—Thierry, J. Manufacturer, Rue Bat d' Argent, Hotel des Négociants, Lyones (Rhône).—A frame, containing nine photographic proofs. #1102—Bouasse, V. Legel, & Co. Rue du Petit Bourbon, Paris.—Samples of gelatin pictures. Page 247 #1467—Sabatier, H. 65 Palais National, Paris.—Daguerreotype portrait. See also Tallis I : 135.

Brady (ca. 1823–1896), Marcus A. Root (n.d.) and John Adams Whipple (1822–1891) among others. Brady's "plain style" of portraiture and Whipple's extraordinary photographs of the moon taken with Harvard University's refractor telescope took the prizes in Daguerreotype photography, this time shocking the French.[41] The German states submitted few actual photographs but exhibited more equipment and materials than any other nation.[42]

Many more photographs were taken *of* the exhibition than were exhibited *in* it. Mayall, Claudet, and Turner did both. Turner produced an expensive limited edition set of large views of the Crystal Palace using a modified calotype process (see figure 7.2), as did the lesser-known Robert Howlett (1831–1858), but relatively few large-scale photographs were made of the Crystal Palace. Smaller scaled, less expensive stereographs, launched internationally at the fair and sold singly or in sets, were much more common. One of its early English promoters of the stereoscope (viewing device) and stereograph (photograph) was David Brewster (1781–1868), who produced a high-quality stereoscope in Paris in collaboration with Louis Jules Dubosq (1817–1886) that they exhibited at the Great Exhibition. Dubosq, a successful special effects and magic lantern slide designer, presented a stereoscope and cards to Queen Victoria, who had admired them in the Exhibition. This prompted Victoria and Albert to become photographers and stereograph collectors themselves and started a wildfire craze for stereoscopes that swept the world and made the stereoscope one of the century's most popular parlor entertainments. Enrico Negretti (1817–1879) and Joseph Zambra (d. 1877), the Great Exhibition's official photographers, published an extensively

41. The American exhibits included (from the *Official Catalogue,* 184, 186, 188, 190, 191): #42—Root, M. A. Philadelphia.—Daguerreotypes. #105—Evans, O. B. Buffalo, New York.—Specimens of daguerreotyping. #109—Mead & Brothers, New York.—Daguerreotypes. #125—Gavit, D. E. New York.—Daguerreotypes. #137—Brady, M. B. New York—Daguerreotypes; likenesses of illustrious Americans. #151—Lawrence, M. M. New York.—Daguerreotypes. #223—Harrison, C. C. New York.—Camera obscura, and daguerreotypes. #264—Pratt, W. A. & Co. Richmond, Virginia.—Daguerreotypes. #377—Whitehurst, J. H. Baltimore, Massachusetts.—Daguerreotypes: Falls of Niagara. #451—Whipple, J. A. Boston.—Daguerreotypes. See also Tallis, 136; and Berlyn, 9. For a full list of medals see *Art Journal* (1852): 62.

42. The German Photographic exhibits included (from the *Official Catalogue,* 282, 287, 256, 258, 259, 269, 271, 287, 206): #33—Strauch, F. Prod.—Photography; and coloured photography. #103—Kohnke, F. J.—A daguerreotype painting, coloured. Equipment included: #89—Busch, E. Rathenow, Manu.—&c. Daguerreotype portraits. #203—Schneider, F. Berlin, Inv.—Daguerreotype plates, plated by galvanic process, and flattened without hammering. #243—Kersten, A. Berlin, Manu.—Papier-maché frames for daguerreotype pictures. Sundry articles, as pocketbooks, cigarcases, &c. used as frames for daguerreotype pictures. #661—Biefang, C. Dusseldorf, Manu.—Various frames for daguerreotypes and pictures, in velvet, bronze, and marble. #763—Fleischmann, A. Sonneberg, Saxe Meiningen, Manu. (Agent in London, J. Kendall, 8 Harp Lane, Gt. Tower St.)—Daguerreotype frames. #53—Korlan, G.—Frames for daguerreotype. The Italian exhibits included: #739—Vogel, C. F. Milan.—Photographs. #740—Pucher, J. Veldes, Upper Carniola. Inven.—Photographs on glass, a new discovery.

Figure 7.4 J. McNeven (artist), William Simpson (lithographer), Ackerman and Company (publisher), *The Transept of the Grand Entrance, Souvenir of the Great Exhibition,* 1851 (chromolithograph, 31.5 cm. × 46.9 cm.). © Victoria and Albert Museum, London. # 19627

consumed set of stereographs of the Crystal Palace.[43] And Thomas R. Williams (n.d.) produced a more modest set. Several of Negretti and Zambra's photographs were engraved by William Simpson (n.d) and chromolithographs by artists such as J. Mc Neven (n.d) were distributed by publishers such as Ackerman and Company (see figure 7.4) or David Bogue (1807–ca. 1856).

Conclusion: Photography, Benjamin Brecknell Turner, and the Crystal Palace

The photographic image functions in an ambivalent manner. It is a magical and mysterious thing; it has the ability to represent the directly observed visual world, seemingly unmediated by subjective perception. Photograph, derived from the Greek φῶς (*phos*) "light" and γραφή (*graphê*) "drawing," suggests an object that signifies more indexically than symbolically. But the photographic image is in fact a symbolic image and subject to manipulation and deception. Its seductive power lies in an exquisite anxiety at its core; it is neither fact nor fiction, real nor unreal. The photograph's ghostly trace of visual reality seems to promise immortality for the photographed because of the image's spatial proximity to the viewer, but it actually delivers mortality through its insistent temporal distance from the original. Photographs of the Crystal Palace seemed to record its palpable presence, but they also fixed its existence in the historical mind.

Victorian society was a mass of contradictions in 1851. Its xenophobic chauvinism belied a fraught internal social anxiety. As Victorian society's imperial gaze turned outward, its domestic gaze turned inward; the home became the family castle, a bastion of the British realm that rebuffed the foreign. The visual entertainments of Leicester Square earlier in the century had become tarnished by 1850 so that the area was no longer deemed either appropriate or safe for the middle-class family. The Great Exhibition's restricted access and bordered parkland offered safe, contained family entertainment. So too did a number of home-oriented popular entertainments promoted at the exhibition, such as stereoscopes, magic lantern slides and projectors, and picture books with prints or photographic images. Many of

---

43. Other photographers included Nicholas Henneman (1813–1894) and Hugh Owens (n.d.). Nicolaas Hennemann, one of Talbot's former assistants, produced a number of salt-paper prints and also printed several of Hugh Owen's negatives on paper. Friedrich von Martens (n.d.) also made at least one gelatin silver print of the east end of the exterior in 1852 (now in the Eastman House collection). In 1854 Philip Henry Delamotte (1820–1889) produced thousands of photographs of the rebuilt Crystal Palace at Sydenham.

the images produced by and for these technologies represented the foreign to be consumed in the privacy of the home. They included images of exotic locales, foreign peoples, or even comparative physiognomic and phrenological studies, photographs of the insane, the criminal, the degenerate, the poor, and the foreign; indeed any images that might help determine a visual set of "scientific" diagnostic characteristics to determine rank in society and ranking of societies.[44]

Pornographic photography in particular, already widely collected by 1851, fed the Victorian xenophobic impulse; in it the disorderly and socially destabilizing feminized other was not just exotic and foreign but also explicitly sexual.[45] Such photographs were consumed vicariously in private and represented the irrational underside of social order; they revealed dark, irrational, chaotic, exaggerated, and highly charged emotional aspects of the dangerous, distrusted, and disliked in society—the foreign in race, class, gender, and morality who operated in the unstable interstices of Victorian society—and within the heart of the consumer.

In contrast to these, Turner's photograph of the interior of the Crystal Palace (see figure 7.2) is a cool, tightly controlled image for public consumption and domestic display. Indeed, it actively tries to communicate that it is objective, analytical, and neutral. But like the more charged and openly xenophobic images discussed, this image masks a mass of barely sublimated contradictions, anxieties, and ambivalences. Its xenophobia is simply constructed more subtly. Turner's choices of viewpoint, composition, framing, subject, and style were exactly that: choices to determine the narrative content of his photograph. Turner looked through his camera lens with both physical and cultural eyes. He chose what he wanted to see and how he wanted to record it. Turner's photograph shows us a long sweeping perspectival funnel drafted by the Crystal Palace's structurally circumscribed space, repeating iron girders, and transparent panes of glass. The carefully restricted point of view emphasizes rational order and a well-regulated architectural (and intellectual) space. But the space in the photograph feels hermetic, compressed, flat, and dead. The image emphasizes fixity and containment over visual interest or obvious content. In fact, he consciously eliminates the spectacular, emo-

---

44. See also Sander L. Gilman, ed., *The Face of Madness: Hugh W. Diamond and the Origin of Psychiatric Photography* (New York: Brunner Mazel, 1976) and Jonathan Mathew Finn, *Capturing the Criminal Image: From Mug Shot to Surveillance Society* (Minneapolis: University of Minnesota, 2009); James R. Ryan, *Picturing Empire: Photography and the Visualization of the British Empire* (Chicago: University of Chicago Press, 2001); and Molly Rogers, *Delia's Tears: Race, Science and Photography in Nineteenth Century Photography* (New Haven, CT: Yale University Press, 2010).

45. See Inderpal Grewal, *Home and Harem: Nation, Gender, Empire and the Cultures of Travel* (Durham, NC: Duke University Press, 1996) and Ruth Bernard Yeazell, *Harems of the Mind: Passages of Western Art and Literature* (New Haven, CT: Yale University Press, 2000).

tional, and exotic; this photograph is a taut statement paralleling the Victorian mind because Turner, like the mid-Victorian middle-class man, has tried to keep order by attempting to erase the foreign from the visible world and the conscious mind.

Turner's photograph renders the foreign invisible but not absent. His photograph constructs a visual reality that refracts rather than reflects observed reality. There is no direct visual evidence of xenophobia *in* Turner's photograph of the Crystal Palace. In fact, the photographer took extreme measures to reduce our perception of his human transaction with the photograph. There is no framing device, no central subject, no precise sense of scale in the photograph; it is neither picturesque nor sublime nor beautiful. It reveals no humanity; it is scientific, technological, and mathematical. Whereas "Wot is to be" bluntly parades an anxious xenophobic dread of foreigners, thinly veiled as satire, Turner bleeds all foreign disorder from his photograph. His image is tightly controlled, compactly ordered, compressed, and self-contained, avoiding even the smallest hint of the disorder and chaos that might exist beyond its edges. Turner's photograph is adamantly neutral, masculine, and rational. It does not invite casual observation. There is nothing relaxed, superficial, or carefree about this photograph; it leaves no door open to deviance of vision or thought. This photograph communicates the shades of British middle-class xenophobic anxiety more effectively than "Wot is to be" *because* in it the abstract fear of the foreign and the unknown hovers just beyond the edges of vision, consciousness, and apprehension. Like the upper middle-class audience that consumed this photograph, Turner's image is tightly wound, carefully controlled, and an obsessively appropriate portrait of Victorian xenophobia. It adamantly refuses to turn its gaze towards the actual foreign, but by doing so it reveals both the nationalistic bravura and xenophobic undercurrents at the heart of the Great Exhibition and in Victorian England. Turner's photograph provides a visual representation of British xenophobia in 1851 that is invisible, abstracted, and generalized, but palpably present.

Works Cited

Altick, Richard D. *Punch: The Lively Youth of a British Institution.* Columbus: The Ohio State University Press, 1997.
———. *The Shows of London.* Cambridge MA: Belknap-Harvard University Press, 1978.
Anderson, Benedict. *Imagined Communities: Reflections on the Origin and Spread of Nationalism.* London: Verso, 1991.
Archer, Frederick Scott. *The Collodion Process on Glass.* London: A. F., 1854.

Auerbach, Jeffrey A. and Peter H. Hollenberg, eds. *Britain, the Empire, and the World at the Great Exhibition of 1851.* Aldershot: Ashgate, 2008.

Bennett, Tony. *The Birth of the Museum: History, Theory, Politics.* London: Routledge: 1995.

Bhabha, Homi K. *The Location of Culture.* London: Routledge, 2004.

Black, Barbara J. *On Exhibit: Victorians and their Museums.* Charlottesville: University of Virginia Press, 2000.

Blaut, J. M. *The Colonizer's Model of the World: Geographical Diffusionism and Eurocentric History.* New York: Guildford, 1993.

Bonyham, Elizabeth and Anthony Burton. *The Great Exhibitor: The Life and Work of Henry Cole.* London: V & A, 2003.

Breckenridge, Carol A. "The Aesthetics and Politics of Colonial Collecting: India at World Fairs." *Contemporary Studies in Society and History* 31 (spring 1989): 195–216.

Bremer, Frederika. *England in 1851: or Sketches of a Tour in England.* Translated by L. A. H. Boulogne: Merridrew, 1853.

Buzard, James, Joseph Childers, and Eileen Gillooly, eds. *Victorian Prism: Refractions of the Crystal Palace.* Charlottesville: University of Virginia Press, 2007.

Corfe, Tom. *The Great Exhibition.* Cambridge: Cambridge University Press, 1979.

The Crystal Palace: Report of the Meeting at Mr. Oliviera's, March 29th, 1852. London: James Ridgway, 1852.

Davis, John. *The Great Exhibition.* Gloucestershire: Sutton, 1999.

Dirks, Nicholas B., ed. *Colonialism and Culture.* Ann Arbor: University of Michigan Press, 1992.

Driver, Felix, and David Gilbert. *Imperial Cities: Landscape, Display and Identity.* Manchester: University of Manchester Press, 1999.

Ely, Ronald S. *Crystal Palaces: Visions of Splendor: An Anthology.* Ripley: R. S. Ely, 2004.

Ferguson, Niall. *Empire: How Britain Made the Modern World.* London: Penguin, 2004.

Finn, Jonathan Mathew. *Capturing the Criminal Image: From Mug Shot to Surveillance Society.* Minneapolis: University of Minnesota Press, 2009.

Foster, William. *The Closing of the Great Exhibition or England's Mission to All Nations: A Discourse.* London: Cassell, 1851.

French, Yvonne. *The Great Exhibition: 1851.* London: Harvill, 1950.

Gilman, Sander L., ed. *The Face of Madness: Hugh W. Diamond and the Origin of Psychiatric Photography.* New York: Brunner Mazel, 1976.

Godden, Geoffrey A. "The Victorian Art Union Movement." *Apollo* (September 1961): 69.

Greenlaugh, Paul. *Ephemeral Vistas: A History of the Expositions Universelles, the Great Exhibitions and World's Fairs, 1851–1939.* Manchester: Manchester University Press, 1988.

Grewal, Inderpal. *Home and Harem: Nation, Gender, Empire and the Cultures of Travel.* Durham, NC: Duke University Press, 1996.

Harlow, Barbara and Mia Carter. *Imperialism and Orientalism: A Documentary Sourcebook.* London: Blackwell, 1999.

Hobhouse, Christopher. *1851 and the Crystal Palace: Being an Account of the Great Exhibition and its Contents; of Sir Joseph Paxton; and of the Erection, the Subsequent History and the Subsequent Destruction of His Masterpiece.* London: Murray, 1937.

Hobhouse, Hermione. *The Crystal Palace and the Great Exhibition.* London: Athlone, 2002.

Hobsbawm, Eric. *Industry and Empire.* Harmondsworth: Penguin, 1994.

———. *Industry and Empire: From 1750 to the Present Day.* London: Penguin, 1999.

Hobsbawm, Eric and Terence Ranger. *The Invention of Tradition.* Cambridge: Cambridge University Press, 1993.

Kilcup, Karen L. *From Beacon Hill to the Crystal Palace: The 1851 Travel Diary of a Working Class Woman by Lorenza Stevens Berbineau.* Ames: University of Iowa Press, 2002.

Mackenzie, John. *Victorian Vision: Inventing New Britain.* London: V&A Publications, 2001.

Mandler, Peter. "Race and Nation in Mid-Victorian Thought." In *British Intellectual History, 1750–1900,* edited by Stefan Collins, Richard Whatmore, and Brian Young. 224–244. Cambridge: Cambridge University Press, 2000.

Mayhew, Henry and George Cruikshank. *1851: Or the Adventures of Mr. and Mrs. Sandboys and family, Who Came Up to London to 'Enjoy Themselves,' and to See the Great Exhibition.* London: Bogue, 1851.

Mayhew, Henry. *London Labor and London Poor.* London: David Bogue, 1852.

Mirzoeff, Nicholas. *An Introduction to Visual Culture.* London: Routledge, 2009.

Mitchell, Timothy. "Orientalism and the Exhibitionary Order." In *Colonialism and Culture,* edited by Nicholas B. Dirks. 289–318. Ann Arbor: University of Michigan Press, 1992.

Mulvey, Laura. "Visual Pleasure and Narrative Cinema." In *The Feminism and Visual Culture Reader,* edited by Amelia Jones. 44–53. London: Routledge, 2003.

Nochlin, Linda. "The Imaginary Orient." In *The Nineteenth Century Visual Culture Reader,* edited by Vanessa Schwartz and Jeannene M. Przblyski. 289–298. London: Routledge, 2004.

Official Descriptive and Illustrated Catalogue of the Great Exhibition of the Works of Industry of All Nations, 1851, 16 volumes. London: Spicer Brothers, stationers; W. Clowes and Sons, printers, 1851.

Pevsner, Nickolaus. *High Victorian Design: A Study of the Exhibits of 1851.* London: Architectural, 1951.

Pubrick, Louise, Editor. *The Great Exhibition of 1851: New Interdisciplinary Essays.* Manchester: Manchester University Press: 2001.

Rappaport, Erika. "A New Era in Shopping." In *The Nineteenth Century Visual Culture Reader,* edited by Vanessa R. Schwartz and Jeannene M. Przblyski. 151–164. London: Routledge, 2004.

Rogers, Molly. *Delia's Tears: Race, Science and Photography in Nineteenth Century America.* New Haven, CT: Yale University Press, 2010.

Ruskin, John. *Proserpina, Ariadne Florentina, The Opening of the Crystal Palace.* Boston: Dana Estes, 1851.

Ryan, James R. *Picturing Empire: Photography and the Visualization of the British Empire.* Chicago: University of Chicago Press, 2001.

Rydell, Robert W. and Nancy E. Gwinn. *Fair Representations: World's Fairs and the Modern World.* Amsterdam: VU University Press, 1994.

Said, Edward. *Orientalism.* Harmondsworth: Penguin, 1995. Originally published in 1978.

Sala, George Augustus, as Vates Secundus. *The Great Exhibition: 'Wot is to Be,' or Probable Results of the Industry of All Nations in the Year '51; Showing What's to Be Exhibited, Who is to Exhibit . . . In Short, How Its [sic] All Going to Be Done.* London: Publisher unknown, 1850.

Sperling, Joy. "Multiples and Reproductions: Prints and Photographs in Nineteenth-Century England—Visual Communities and Class." In *A History of Visual Culture: West-*

ern Civilization from the 18th to the 21st Century, edited by Jane Kromm and Susan Bakewell. 296–308. Oxford and New York: Berg, 2010.

Tallis, John, Beard, Mayall et al. *Tallis's History and Description of the Crystal Palace, and the Exhibition of the World's Industry in 1851; Illustrated by Beautiful Steel Engravings, from Original Drawings and Daguerreotypes.* Edited by J. G. Strutt, Esq. 3 volumes. London: Tallis, 1851.

Waterford, Giles, ed. *Palaces of Art: Art Galleries in Britain, 1790–1990.* London: Dulwich Picture Gallery and the National Gallery of Scotland, 1991.

Yeazell, Ruth Bernard. *Harems of the Mind: Passages of Western Art and Literature.* New Haven, CT: Yale University Press, 2000.

Young, Paul. "'Carbon, Mere Carbon': The Kohinoor, The Crystal Palace and the Mission to Make Sense of British India." *Nineteenth Century Contexts* 29.4 (December 2007): 343–358.

———. "The Cooking Animal: Economic Man at the Great Exhibition." *Victorian Literature and Culture* 36 (2008): 569–586.

———. *Globalization and the Great Exhibition: The Victorian New World Order.* Basingstoke: Palgrave Macmillan, 2009.

8

Terrible Turks

Victorian Xenophobia and the Ottoman Empire

❧

PATRICK BRANTLINGER

By the start of Queen Victoria's reign, the Terrible Turk was an ancient stereotype, with roots in the anti-Islamism that inspired the crusades. The specifically Turkish element emerged with the conquest of Constantinople in 1453 by the Ottoman forces of Mehmed II. From then until the Enlightenment, the Ottoman Empire provided a counterimage, arousing "imperial envy," for the British Empire.[1] In the 1800s, as the Ottoman regime disintegrated, the British Empire progressed apparently from triumph to triumph. But for centuries, "the multiple attitudes towards the Ottomans . . . [in] the British Isles," writes Gerald MacLean, "most commonly reiterated a long tradition of Islamophobic fears, rhetoric, and imagery in which the cruel figure of the 'terrible Turk' lusted and savaged his way across a menacingly large empire."[2]

Both the Ottoman Empire and its rulers were "terrible" in the twin senses of powerful and awe-inspiring. So were the feared janissaries of their armies. Ottoman sultans and pashas were deemed arbitrary and cruel despots, even though Ottoman rule was for many of its subjects peaceful, prosperous, and tolerant of various races, cultures, and religions. But in Renaissance literature, the Terrible Turk was a barbaric, often "raging" and also lascivious ruler whose methods included arbitrary judgment, treachery, torture, and assas-

---

1. Gerald MacLean, *Looking East: English Writing and the Ottoman Empire before 1800* (Houndsmills: Palgrave Macmillan, 2007), 20.

2. MacLean, *Looking East*, 8.

sination.[3] In *The Ottomans,* Andrew Wheatcroft claims that British writers expressed two anti-Turkish stereotypes, the "Lustful Turk" as well as the "Terrible Turk." He acknowledges, however, that these were really one, and that "The linkage between sex and brutality, the open 'floodgates of lust' and the dire 'refinements of cruelty,' was made explicit by Gladstone" during the Bulgarian crisis of the 1870s, and was especially evident in his widely circulated 1876 pamphlet *Bulgarian Horrors and the Question of the East.* The Terrible Turk formed a single sadomasochistic image that pervaded Romantic and Victorian discourse about the Ottoman Empire. Even when British foreign policy supported the Ottomans, which it usually did, the stereotype continued to circulate in the press, in novels, in the theater, and in British imaginations.

In Romantic and Victorian culture, the stereotype of the Terrible Turk was less racist in emphasis than xenophobic, a fear of one or more of the features commonly identified with the Ottoman Empire, its rulers, and its armies. In many versions of xenophobia, as also of racism, fear and attraction are interwoven in often hidden, complex patterns, and this is true of the Terrible Turk. By the early 1800s, "the East" and Constantinople exercised an allure for many Romantic writers, including Byron and Shelley, and it continued to do so for many Victorians. By the end of the Napoleonic wars in 1815, tourism to the Middle East and the "Holy Land" grew easier and more frequent. Byron's martyrdom at Missolonghi in 1824, where he hoped to fight for independence from Ottoman rule, rendered his highly popular "eastern tales," featuring Terrible Turks as villains, even more popular. The villains in earlier Oriental tales by British authors, such as William Beckford's *Vathek* (1786), are apt to be Arabian or Indian rather than Turkish, but they display the same blend of cruelty, lasciviousness, and despotism.

Despite the stereotype of the Terrible Turk, for most of the nineteenth century British foreign policy sought to prop up the increasingly feeble Ottoman Empire as a bulwark against Russian expansion. Early Victorian travelers to Constantinople and the East such as Alexander Kinglake also introduced a note of realism into depictions of Turks, from pashas to street vendors. But the Bulgarian crisis of 1876 brought the Terrible Turk again into the foreground and made it difficult if not impossible to defend the old, Palmerstonian policy of supporting "the Porte" or "the Sublime Porte," as the central Ottoman government was often called.[4] Although in the 1800s contacts

---

3. Linda McJannet, *The Sultan Speaks: Dialogue in English Plays and Histories about the Ottoman Turks* (Houndsmills: Palgrave Macmillan, 2006).

4. Because of the great expanse of the Ottoman Empire, "Turk" was often used to refer to any of its subjects who were not more specifically identifiable as, say, Arabs, Albanians, or Egyptians. Among its various meanings, "terrible" can mean sublime, as in "the Sublime Porte," a phrase that

between "Orientals" of all sorts and Britons increased, including a growing number of Turks and other Muslims who traveled to Britain and began to form small communities there (Ansari), these did little to counteract the stereotype, which lasted at least until the final collapse of the Ottoman Empire during World War I.

From the Renaissance to the 1830s

Starting in the Elizabethan period, as trade between Britain and the Ottoman Empire developed, so did cultural relations and understandings. The Levant Company was founded in 1581. In 1599, Queen Elizabeth sent Thomas Dallman to Constantinople with musical instruments for the Sultan.[5] Travelogues and histories began to appear in Britain in the second half of the 1500s. These include the English translation of Paulo Giovio's *Shorte Treatise upon the Turkes* (1546), Richard Knolles's *Generall Historie of the Turkes* (1603), and Sir Paul Rycaut's *History of the Present State of the Ottoman Empire* (1666).[6] While these texts increased British knowledge of the Turks and their empire, they did little to counteract the burgeoning stereotype of the terrible or the "raging" Turk that became a favorite character on the seventeenth-century stage (one play was even entitled *The Raging Turke*). "The most common pejorative western stereotype for the Ottomans was 'the raging Turk,'" writes Linda McJannet in *The Sultan Speaks*.[7] In short, side-by-side with increasing knowledge grew the stereotype; travel, trade, and diplomacy seem to have had little effect on rendering dramatic and literary representations of the Ottomans or more generally of "Musulman" characters something other than "terrible."

Renaissance writers including Shakespeare and Christopher Marlowe sometimes expressed admiration for the rulers of the Ottoman Empire. Nevertheless, for Protestant Britain, the Pope and "the Great Turk" were "the twin representatives of the antichrist." The cruelties of the Terrible Turk were seemingly matched by the cruelties of the Inquisition.[8] Dramatic and literary representations of Turkish or Ottoman rulers invariably suggested some sort of contrast to the supposedly more civilized, Christian behaviors of Western-

---

originally referred to the main gate at Topkapi Palace in Constantinople but that became synonymous with the Ottoman Empire.

5. McJannet, *The Sultan Speaks*, 5.

6. Filiz Turhan, *The Other Empire: British Romantic Writings about the Ottoman Empire* (New York and London: Routledge, 2003), 11–18.

7. McJannet, *The Sultan Speaks*, 17.

8. McJannet, *The Sultan Speaks*, 60.

ers, though of course the latter could also behave in cruel, barbaric fashion. Britons who lived and traveled in Ottoman domains, like Lady Mary Wortley Mongtagu in the 1700s, often depicted Turkish rulers, officials, and attendants as polite, pacific, and sophisticated. These depictions, however, were contradicted by news about political assassinations and about massacres of Christians and Jews and atrocities in wars in the Middle East and eastern Europe. Depictions of the Terrible Turk were seldom balanced by news of atrocities committed by Christian rulers and their armies.

By the Romantic period, authors frequently depicted Greece as a fair, white maiden caught in the toils of lustful Turks. "Even though the analogy of Greece-in-chains/woman-in-bondage had become a literary topos by 1813, the year *The Giaour* appeared," writes David Roessel, "the immense popularity of Byron's poem ensured that his version heavily influenced later writers."[9] While Byron's eastern tales portray sympathetic Turkish characters such as Selim in *The Bride of Abydos,* his villains, such as Hassam in *The Giaour* and Giaffir in *Bride,* are Terrible Turks. The pattern is evident in the portrayal of Pasha Ali, "Albania's chief," in canto 2 of *Childe Harold's Pilgrimage,* "whose dread command / Is lawless law; for with a bloody hand / He sways a nation, turbulent and bold."[10] In his harem, Ali is all "gentleness," but not in war or while ruling Albania.[11]

Shelley, too, in *Hellas* and *The Revolt of Islam,* supported the Greek struggle for independence, declaring in the preface to the former poem, "We are all Greeks." The chorus of Hellas is composed of captive Greek women in the Sultan's seraglio. When Daood informs his master, Sultan Mahmud, that the janissaries are "clamouring" for their pay, the Sultan's reply exemplifies the Terrible Turk:

Go! bid them pay themselves
With Christian blood! Are there no Grecian virgins
Whose shrieks and spasms and tears they may enjoy?
No infidel children to impale on spears?
. . . Go! bid them kill
Blood is the seed of gold.[12]

---

9. David Roessel, *In Byron's Shadow: Modern Greece in the English and American Imagination* (Oxford: Oxford University Press, 2002), 64.

10. George Gordon, Lord Byron, *Childe Harold, The Poetical Works of Lord Byron* (London: Oxford University Press, 1960), canto II, stanza 47.

11. Byron, *Childe Harold,* II.62.

12. Percy Bysshe Shelley, *The Major Works* (Oxford: Oxford University Press, 2003), 11.242–249.

Roessel points out that, although *The Revolt of Islam* makes little attempt to depict Muslim customs, one of its "Eastern" moments is "the harem rape of the heroine."[13]

The story of Safie in Mary Shelley's *Frankenstein* (1818) suggests that women's lives under the Ottomans, or more generally under Islam, amounted to slavery. Safie would far rather be married to a Christian and living in the Christian West than "immured within the walls of a haram."[14] Her Turkish father is a merchant rather than a pasha or a soldier, but he is nevertheless cruel and dishonest. Once Felix has liberated him from prison in Paris, "the treacherous Turk" (84) orders his daughter to follow him to Constantinople rather than marrying Felix. But "a residence in Turkey was abhorrent to her; her [Christian] religion and feelings were alike adverse to her" (85). So she rejoins Felix, Agatha, and DeLacey at their cottage in the Alps, where the monster observes them from his hiding place.

The motif of the Greek slave as a fair woman in the clutches of a Terrible Turk continued into the Victorian period. It was powerfully, albeit pornographically, rendered by American Hiram Powers's nude statue "The Greek Slave" for the Great Exhibition of 1851. His statue in turn inspired Elizabeth Barrett Browning's sonnet, "Hiram Powers' Greek Slave":

> They say Ideal beauty cannot enter
> The house of anguish. On the threshold stands
> An alien Image with enshackled hands,
> Called the Greek Slave! as if the artist meant her
> (That passionless perfection which he lent her,
> Shadowed not darkened where the sill expands)
> To so confront man's crimes in different lands
> With man's ideal sense. Pierce to the centre,
> Art's fiery finger! and break up ere long
> The serfdom of this world. Appeal, fair stone,
> From God's pure heights of beauty against man's wrong!
> Catch up in thy divine face, not alone
> East griefs but west, and strike and shame the strong,
> By thunders of white silence, overthrown.

Although the sonnet does not specifically identify the Terrible Turk as the villain, but instead denounces "man's crimes in distant lands," perhaps that

---

13. Roessel, *In Byron's Shadow*, 64.

14. Mary Shelley, *Frankenstein* (New York: W. W. Norton, 1996), 83. Subsequent references to this text will be cited parenthetically.

is because both Barrett Browning and Hiram Powers knew, as did their audiences, who were the enslavers of beautiful, naked Greek women.

Echoing Gayatri Spivak, Roessel notes that in the 1820s, "The picture of a chained Greek woman who, it is implied, is at the mercy of a Turkish man was one of the most effective and pervasive means of evoking sympathy for the Greek cause."[15] In these and many other instances from the 1700s on, "The romance of Greek liberation can succinctly be summed up as a white man saving a lapsed white woman from the Turk, a brown man."[16] Stories of Christians captured by Muslims emerged during the crusades, but the captives were usually men, like Sir Walter Scott's Richard the Lionhearted in *Ivanhoe.* As Linda Colley notes in *Captives,* before approximately 1750, narratives of captivity along the Barbary Coast did not portray the corsairs and their North African rulers as lustful in heterosexual terms. Because the great majority of British and European captives were male, the main sexual threat was sodomy. But with Elizabeth Marsh's *The Female Captive* (1769), the threat of heterosexual slavery to lustful Muslims becomes evident—increasingly so through Marsh's several revisions of her account. Colley writes:

> Only when Ottoman and North African power were broadly recognized as receding, did . . . accusations of sodomy become thoroughly drowned out by an emphasis instead on the supposed heterosexual lusts of Muslim men and on their harems of docile, scented females. Claiming that Turks, or Moroccans, or Algerians collected and domineered over sexually pliant women . . . was a way also of saying that these peoples were no longer in a position seriously to threaten European males.[17]

Now British and European men were called upon, even if only allegorically, to rescue white women from brown men.

Support for the Ottomans and Benjamin Disraeli

According to historian Richard Shannon, "Palmerston formulated in the eighteen-thirties a policy postulating an independent, vigorous Ottoman Empire as a barrier against Russian and French ambitions in the Near East."[18]

---

15. Roessel, *In Byron's Shadow,* 60.

16. Roessel, *In Byron's Shadow,* 61.

17. Linda Colley, *Captives: Britain, Empire and the World, 1600–1850* (New York: Anchor Books, 2004), 130.

18. Cited in Frank Edgar Bailey, *British Policy and the Turkish Reform Movement: A Study in Anglo-Turkish Relations, 1826–1853* (Cambridge, MA: Harvard University Press, 1942), 129.

This policy remained standard down to and even beyond the Bulgarian crisis of the 1870s. Despite the philhellenism of Byron, Shelley, and other Romantics, numerous travelers, diplomats, and politicians such as David Urquhart were Turkophiles.[19] Women travelers, too, such as Elizabeth Craven and Julia Pardoe, sometimes wrote mostly favorable accounts of conditions in the Ottoman Empire.[20]

In *The Spirit of the East* (1838) and his other writings, Urquhart vigorously advocated British support for Ottoman attempts to reform their empire. For Urquhart and other Turkophiles, the chief enemy that the British Empire had to fear was Russia. By supporting reforming Sultans such as Mahmud II and the Tanzimat or Ottoman reform movement that began in the 1830s, Britain could foil Russian designs on Persia, Afghanistan, and India. Russophobia was also fueled by stereotypic thinking. For Urquhart, "the cruelty of the Czar and the barbarism of the Russians" was much more terrible than the behaviors of Ottoman rulers.[21] "Ottoman tyranny," Urquhart believed, was little different from the "'tyranny of the law'" in Britain.[22] He recognized, according to Geoffrey Nash, that "the Ottoman empire had stood for as long as it had because of the principle of non-interference in the local administration of the countries it ruled."[23] Yet by the 1800s, that "principle" was due to the weakness of Ottoman rulers rather than to anything purposeful.

Urquhart held that Protestant Christianity and Islam were in agreement on all essential religious issues; the Koran was just "a repetition of the Gospels." Nash writes that, for Urquhart, "Only the Muslim declaration of faith, and the claim of finality for its Prophet . . . separated the two religions."[24] Although he did not convert to Islam, Urquhart was viewed by his critics, in part because of his advocacy of "the Porte," but also because he adopted Turkish dress and customs while residing in Constantinople, as "turning Turk." That aspersion could also have been cast on the young Disraeli as well. "The experiences of the roué and dandy of 1830–31" on his eastern tour, writes Robert Blake, "were to affect the attitude of the Prime Minister and statesman nearly half a century later at the Congress of Berlin."[25]

19. See Geoffrey P. Nash, *From Empire to Orient: Travellers to the Middle East, 1830–1926* (London: I. B. Tauris, 2005).

20. See Billie Melman, *Women's Orients: English Women and the Middle East, 1718–1918: Sexuality, Religion and Work* (Ann Arbor: The University of Michigan Press, 1992).

21. Richard Cobden, writing about Urquhart. Qtd. in Nash, *From Empire to Orient,* 45.

22. Nash, *From Empire to Orient,* 51.

23. Nash, *From Empire to Orient,* 56.

24. Nash, *From Empire to Orient,* 47.

25. Robert Blake, *Disraeli's Grand Tour: Benjamin Disraeli and the Holy Land, 1830–31* (London: Weidenfeld and Nicholson, 1982).

With Byron as one of his role models, Disraeli fancied himself a potential shaper of the political destinies of the places he visited in the early 1830s. However, his political views were decidedly different from Byron's. In his letters home during the tour, and in the fictional account of his travels in *Contarini Fleming* (1832), Disraeli expresses much sympathy for the Ottoman Empire versus Greek nationalism. Yet in *The Rise of Iskander* (1833), the hero-liberator is an Albanian who fought against Muslim domination, suggesting that Disraeli was more interested in heroism, rebellion, and liberation in general than in particular racial, cultural, or national identities. During his stay at Malta, however, Disraeli declared he wanted to join the Ottoman campaign against the rebel Albanians, expressing a desire to see military action at first hand that Contarini Fleming fulfills.[26] To side with the Turks against the Greeks was, for a young Byronian and radical (as Disraeli viewed himself in the 1830s) strangely un-radical and un-Byronic. "Disraeli, for whatever reason," writes Blake, "took the view that the polyglot empire of the Sultan was a barrier against anarchy and barbarism. He was [also], all his life, totally unsympathetic to the spirit of nationalism which was the dominating force in his time."[27]

Disraeli's attitudes toward nationalism were more complicated than Blake suggests for at least two reasons. First, the ideologies of nationalism and imperialism are not clearly antithetical: once they have broken free from older dominations and established independent nation-states, nationalist movements often become imperialistic. And second, Disraeli's pro-Semitism was also a proto-Zionism and idealistic nationalism in contrast to the narrow-minded nationalisms, racisms, and religious prejudices that plagued him throughout his career. In *Alroy* (1835), the hero's attempt to liberate the Jews from their Moslem overlords is couched in nationalistic terms that foreshadow Zionism:

> Empires and dynasties flourish and pass away; the proud metropolis becomes a solitude, the conquering kingdom even a desert; but Israel still remains, still a descendant of the most ancient kings breathed amid these royal ruins, and still the eternal sun could never rise without gilding the towers of living Jerusalem. A word, a deed, a single day, a single man, and we might be a nation.[28]

Nevertheless, in regard to Greek nationalism versus Ottoman imperialism, the young Disraeli took a position exactly opposite to that of his hero Byron

---

26. Benjamin Disraeli, *Letters,* vol. 1, ed. J. A. W. Gunn (Toronto: University of Toronto Press, 1982), 173; Blake, *Disraeli's Grand Tour,* 29.

27. Blake, *Disraeli's Grand Tour,* 30.

28. Benjamin Disraeli, *Alroy* (London: Longman, Green, 1881), 40.

(whose life he celebrated, along with Shelley's, in *Venetia*, 1837). Throughout his letters from Greece and Turkey, Disraeli expresses much sympathy for the Turks, little for the Greeks. "I confess . . . that my Turkish prejudices," he wrote to Bulwer-Lytton, "are very much confirmed by my residence in Turkey."[29]

That Disraeli interpreted much of what he encountered during his eastern travels in terms of literary, Orientalist preconceptions is evident throughout his letters and novels. "I longed to write an Eastern tale," Contarini Fleming declares in the midst of his own eastern tale.[30] Contarini travels through such colorfully exotic scenes that, despite the desolation of recent warfare, he is enchanted by "the now almost obsolete magnificence of Oriental life. . . . It seemed to me that my first day in a Turkish city [Yanina in Albania] brought before me all the popular characteristics of which I had read. . . . I gazed about me with a mingled feeling of delight and wonder."[31] It is a "delight and wonder" both in the "infinite novelty" (324) that Contarini discovers especially in Constantinople and in a thoroughly conventional, stereotypic sense of Oriental changelessness that fits neither the changing scenery nor the warfare in which Contarini participates.

Part of Disraeli's fascination related to costumes as much as customs. As a young dandy, Disraeli saw the world, pace Carlyle's Teufelsdröckh, very much in terms of clothes. That "the Turks indulge[d] in all combinations of costume" was not the least of their charms; "the meanest merchant in the Bazaar looks like a Sultan in an Eastern fairy tale."[32] Moreover, the effect of his own wardrobe on the Turks and their subjects was not lost upon Disraeli. About his experiences in Navarino in Greece, he wrote:

> I am quite a Turk, wear a turban, smoke a pipe six feet long, and squat on a Divan. . . . I find the habits of this calm and luxurious people [the Turks] entirely agree with my own preconceived opinions of propriety and enjoyment, and I detest the Greeks more than ever. I do not find mere Travelling on the whole very expensive, but I am ruined by my wardrobe. . . . When I was presented to the Grand Vizier I made up such a costume from my heterogenous wardrobe, that the Turks, who are mad on the subject of dress, were utterly astounded. . . . Nothing wo[ul]d persuade the Greeks that we were not come about the new King and I really believe that if I had 25,000£ to throw away I might increase my headache by wearing a crown.[33]

29. Disraeli, *Letters,* I: 179.
30. Benjamin Disraeli, *Contarini Fleming* (London: Longman, Green, 1881), 307.
31. Disraeli, *Contarini Fleming,* 307, my italics.
32. Disraeli, *Letters,* I: 183.
33. Disraeli, *Letters,* I: 174.

While this sartorial fantasy is playful, and while it invites the very critique of superficiality and inauthenticity that Carlyle, for one, would later make of Disraeli (Carlyle's Jewish "old clothes dealer"), it nevertheless expresses a modern, political pragmatism that recognizes the importance of image-making, symbolism, and belief in the forging of status and power, as well as in the always political process of self-fashioning.

"There is only one way to travel in the East with ease, and that is with an appearance of pomp," Contarini Fleming declares. "The Turks are much influenced by the exterior, and although they are not mercenary, a well-dressed and well-attended infidel will command respect."[34] Similar statements about the political importance of image-making are frequent in western travelogues and exploration journals throughout the nineteenth century, according to which keeping up appearances is at least as important for pacifying restless natives as gifts and gunboats. At the same time, Disraeli's letter about his wardrobe contains a considerable dose of ironic egocentrism. If only, Disraeli speculates, he had been able to complement his exotic but elegant dress with a crown, the Greeks might have taken him for their new King. But "Disraeli was no doubt joking."[35] Later writings by the future Prime Minister suggest that he was not entirely joking. Tancred, in the 1847 novel that bears his name, after his supposedly visionary encounter with the Angel of Arabia on Mt. Sinai, dreams with his Syrian friend Fakredeen of founding a global empire based on spiritual principles. When Prime Minister Disraeli in 1875 purchased 176,000 shares in the Suez Canal for Britain, he was not dreaming.

Victorian Literature and the Terrible Turk

In contrast to Disraeli's pro-Turkish stance, Byronic themes including the Greek struggle for independence from Ottoman rule became a staple on the nineteenth-century stage, expressed in melodramas such as William Hepworth Dixon's *Azamoglan, a Tragedy: An Incident in the Greek Revolution* (1845) and Edward Fitzball's *The Greek Slave* (1851). Yet from the 1830s through the Crimean War, many travelogues and other texts represented the Turks and the Ottoman Empire in complex, comparatively favorable terms. Julia Pardoe's *The Beauties of the Bosphorus* (1839) and *City of the Sultan* (1837) express one early Victorian woman's mostly positive impressions of "life in the East." Other women, too, including Lady Mary Wortley Montagu in the 1700s and Lady Hester Stanhope in the early 1800s, lived in

34. Disraeli, *Contarini Fleming,* 344.
35. Blake, *Disraeli's Grand Tour,* 47.

and wrote about the Ottoman Empire in fairly non-stereotypic ways. In Alexander Kinglake's highly popular *Eothen; or Traces of Travel Brought Home from the East* (1844), the Terrible Turk is mainly a matter of dress, as in Disraeli's tourist letters. Turkish troops "under the command of a Pasha," writes Kinglake, generally wear "the old Turkish costume," including "a whole bundle of weapons; no man bore less than one brace of immensely long pistols and a yataghan (or cutlass), with a dagger or two of various shapes and sizes."[36] However, Kinglake does not claim that he ever saw these weapons in use.

The most terrible aspect of travel in the East that Kinglake encountered was "the plague," which he did not catch. Perhaps more terrible were the various attempts to rob and perhaps kill him and his servants. But the would-be robbers aren't Turks, and they are generally poor, pathetic, and easily foiled. Ominous, too, is the "specimen of Oriental architecture" that Kinglake mentions early in his narrative, consisting of "thirty thousand skulls contributed by the rebellious Servians in the early part (I believe) of this century."[37] With the insouciance of a young Victorian gentleman, however, Kinglake brushes these potential terrors aside, just as he both emphasizes and plays down the threat of the plague. No one Kinglake meets during his journey fits the stereotype of the terrible Turk.

Eothen was addressed to another traveler, Eliot Warburton, whose equally popular *The Crescent and the Cross* appeared in 1845 (by 1858, it had gone through fourteen editions). Like Kinglake, though he is occasionally threatened by robbers, Warburton does not rely on the stereotype of the Terrible Turk. Early in his narrative, he mentions the treacherous massacre of the Mameluke Beys by Mehemet Ali in Egypt.[38] Later, however, Warburton presents this act as a necessary and beneficial reform, which he likens to the destruction of the janissaries by Mahmud II. According to Warburton, Mehemet Ali is a capable ruler and military commander who is "severe, but not cruel" (183). He "tolerated all religions, and discountenanced fanaticism," and he has made Egypt safe for travelers: "Cairo is now the crowded thoroughfare of England and India" (185).

While Mehemet Ali earns Warburton's respect, that cannot be said of Sultan Mahmud at Constantinople. His efforts to reform "a corrupt people" have been an utter failure (331). The reforms "destroyed" "the old," without leading to anything new: "there was no reproductive principle in the Turkish

---

36. Alexander Kinglake, *Eothen; or Traces of Travel Brought Home from the East* (Oxford: Oxford University Press, 1982), 10.

37. Kinglake, *Eothen,* 27.

38. Eliot Warburton, *The Crescent and the Cross; or, Romance and Realities of Eastern Travel 1845* (London: Hurst and Blackett, 1858), 34–35. Subsequent references to this text will be cited parenthetically.

character" (331). Feeble and corrupt, the modern Turks are no longer terrible. They used to have only "contempt" for Europeans and Christians; but now they respect and "fear" them—"such fear, at least, as a Turk can know, for they are a gallant people still, those Osmanlis . . ." (332). The weakness and decrepitude of the Ottoman Empire, Warburton suggests, is to be measured against Greece's "sublime story" of "freedom" (341).

Other early Victorian accounts of eastern travel, such as Thackeray's *Notes of a Journey from Cornhill to Grand Cairo* (1844) and Albert Smith's *A Month at Constantinople* (1850), represent the Terrible Turk as a creature of the past. For both Thackeray and Smith, British commerce and industry are the engines that will modernize and liberate "the East." Muslim swords will be turned into British ploughshares. As Warburton puts it, "England is expected in the East" (163). Nevertheless, Thackeray writes: "the much-maligned Orient, I am confident, has not been maligned near enough; for the good reason that none of us can tell the amount of horrible sensuality practised there."[39] Even as Turkish imperial and military power waned, the lustful aspect of the stereotype lingered, and was called up in virtually every Victorian commentary upon harems. Yet the women of the harems were not always depicted as unhappy slaves to their masters. Warburton, for example, writes: "Born and brought up in the hareem, women never seem to pine at its imprisonment: like cage-born birds, they sing among their bars . . ." (42). And Julia Pardoe and several other women travelers, in contrast to Mary Wollstonecraft, claimed that the harem provided its denizens with types of privacy and even freedom unknown to wives in the West.[40]

Stereotypes are usually overdetermined by many factors, and Pardoe, Kinglake, Warburton, Thackeray, Smith, and other Victorian travelers are well aware of at least some of those factors. All of these travelers criticize aspects of the Terrible Turk. Smith, for example, while emphasizing the trade and manufacturing carried on by Europeans in the Ottoman capital, suggests that Turkish guides and "dragomen" themselves exaggerate the "terribleness" of the Sultan and his minions.[41] Politically just as influential in the first several decades of Victoria's reign as the Terrible Turk were accounts of the corruption and weakness of the Ottoman government. Britain's alliance with the Ottomans during the Crimean War produced many reports of the ineptitude of Turkish forces, though British, French, and Russian forces were also inept. And the creeping bankruptcy of the Ottoman treasury worried its investors. Yet some Victorian writers revisited notions of terribleness

---

39. William Makepeace Thackeray, *Notes of a Journey from Cornhill to Grand Cairo, Oxford Illustrated Thackeray,* vol. 9 (Oxford: Humphrey Milford, n.d.), 235.

40. Melman, *Women's Orients,* 59–76; Turhan, *Other Empires,* 39.

41. Albert Smith, *A Month at Constantinople* (Boston: Bradbury and Guild, 1852), 55.

in regard to Turkish or Ottoman characters, recalling the list of traits of the "Turke" in Joshua Poole's *The English Parnassus* (1654), which included these items: "cruel, unpitying, mercilesse, unrelenting, inexorable, warlick [warlike] . . . bloody."[42] Victorian writers, moreover, often distinguished between Turks and Arabs by granting the latter the chivalric virtues of nomadic barbarians, while the Turks bore mainly negative characteristics. Arabian or Bedouin virtues were much admired by Sir Richard Burton, Wilfrid Scawen Blunt, and T. E. Lawrence, among others; things Ottoman or Turkish mainly represented gross sensuality and decadence.

In 1828, *The Lustful Turk; or, Lascivious Scenes from a Harum* appeared anonymously in Britain. In this pornographic novel, Emily Barlow and her traveling companion Eliza Gibbs are captured by a "barbarian" pirate ship, captained by a renegade Englishman, and turned into "white slaves" in the harem of the Dey of Algiers, an Ottoman potentate. As Steven Marcus notes in *The Other Victorians, The Lustful Turk* provided subterranean reading for many decades. Emily's "deflowering" by the Dey is described as though he were running her through and "cutting [her] to pieces" with his sword, "his terrible shaft."[43] In Emily's account of another rape, a Greek girl, about to be married to her Greek lover, "is snatched away from him at the very altar by the intervention of the Turkish local governor. Her lover and father are then slaughtered before her eyes." Marcus comments: "It is a story of Greek oppression and Turkish rule" (200). He goes on to note that there are traces of Byronism throughout *The Lustful Turk*. Even the wicked Dey of Algiers is something of a Byronic hero, except that, unlike Byron, "he is not cursed with a conscience, nor does he suffer from inward conflicts."[44]

Another novel in which the Terrible Turk makes a brief appearance is Charlotte Brontë's *Jane Eyre* (1847). Jane condemns Rochester's claim that "I would not exchange this one little English girl [Jane] for the grand Turk's whole seraglio; gazelle-eyes, houri forms and all!"[45] "If you have a fancy for anything in that line," Jane retorts, "away with you, sir, to the bazaars of Stamboul [Istanbul] without delay; and lay out in extensive slave-purchases some of that spare cash you seem at a loss to spend satisfactorily here" (302). When Rochester asks what she will do with herself while he is bargaining "for so many tons of flesh and such an assortment of black eyes" for his harem, Jane replies:

---

42. Qtd. in MacLean, *Looking East,* 7.

43. Qtd. in Steven Marcus, *The Other Victorians: A Study of Sexuality and Pornography in Mid-Nineteenth-Century England* (New York: Basic Books, 1964), 198.

44. Marcus, *The Other Victorians,* 209.

45. Charlotte Brontë, *Jane Eyre* (London: Penguin, 1996), 301. Subsequent references to this text will be cited parenthetically.

"I'll be preparing myself to go out as a missionary to preach liberty to them that are enslaved—your harem inmates amongst the rest. I'll get admitted there, and I'll stir up mutiny; and you, three-tailed bashaw as you are, sir, shall in a trice find yourself fettered amongst our hands: nor will I, for one, consent to cut your bonds till you have signed a charter, the most liberal that despot ever yet conferred." (302)

This liberal charter would, Jane implies, grant freedom to all of Rochester's fantasy slaves—the Oriental concubines he imagines locking up in his seraglio. Is Jane's feminist and abolitionist stance compromised by the sacrifice of Bertha or by Jane's marriage to Rochester? Some feminist and postcolonial critics think so. Joyce Zonana contends that Brontë's "sultan/slave simile displaces the source of patriarchal oppression onto an 'Oriental,' 'Mahometan' society, enabling British readers to contemplate local problems without questioning their own self-definition as Westerners and Christians."[46] Perhaps so, but Rochester is the "sultan" in question.

Brontë's deployment of "feminist Orientalism," Zonana notes, "is both embedded in and brings into focus a long tradition of Western feminist writing"[47] that often utilizes the discourse of slavery and abolition. Rhoda Broughton no doubt has *Jane Eyre* in mind when, in her 1867 novel *Not Wisely, But Too Well*, "good and docile" Kate "stands before" her would-be seducer "on approval, like a Circassian slave at the market of Constantinople."[48] "Feminist Orientalism" is an accurate phrase for later uses of Turkish or Ottoman slavery and seraglio metaphors in the struggle for women's rights. In discussing debates over women's suffrage at the time of the Second Reform Bill, Jane Rendall quotes the *Manchester Examiner* and *Times*, which declared that arguments against granting the vote to women were "not distinguishable in principle from those which have held rule for ages in the mountains of Circassia, in the slave markets of Constantinople, and in the plantations of the southern states of America."[49] And in 1867, concerning opposition to women's suffrage, Mrs. William Grey wrote, "Surely we are in England, not in Turkey. It is of Englishwomen we are speaking, not of the secluded inhabitants of an Oriental zenana."[50] As already noted, however, some observers claimed that women in harems had greater privacy and freedom than Western wives.

---

46. Joyce Zonana, "The Sultan and the Slave: Feminist Orientalism and the Structure of *Jane Eyre*," *Signs* 18:3 (spring 1993): 592–617, 593.

47. Zonana, 593.

48. Rhoda Broughton, *Not Wisely, But Too Well* (London: Richard Bentley, 1893), 105.

49. Jane Rendall, "The Citizenship of Women and the Reform Act of 1867," in *Defining the Victorian Nation: Class, Race, Gender, and the Reform Act of 1867*, 174.

50. Qtd. in Rendall, 176.

Still another Victorian novel in which the Terrible Turk appears is Dickens's *The Mystery of Edwin Drood* (1870). In its first paragraph, choirmaster John Jasper, waking from an opium dream, sees a "spike of rusty iron in the air."[51] He wonders who has put it there.

> Maybe it is set up by the Sultan's orders for the impaling of a horde of Turkish robbers, one by one. It is so, for cymbals clash, and the Sultan goes by to his palace in long procession. Ten thousand scimitars flash in the sunlight, and thrice ten thousand dancing girls strew flowers. . . . (1)

"The Sultan" perhaps refers to the ruler of the Ottoman Empire, but the mention of "white elephants caparisoned in countless gorgeous colours" suggests an Indian setting, although in that case "Mughal Emperor" would be more accurate than "Sultan." In any event, the "horde of Turkish robbers" are evidently barbarians who, according to the Sultan's barbaric judgment, merit impalement on the spike "one by one." An episode in Kinglake's *Eothen* may have prompted Dickens's imagery of impaled robbers, although Kinglake's point in mentioning it is that it evoked little or no terror. "We ought, at least, to have met with a few perils," writes Kinglake, "but the only robbers we saw anything of had been long since dead and gone; the poor fellows had been impaled on high poles [so that] their skeletons . . . still sat lolling in the sunshine, and listlessly stared without eyes."[52] Kinglake later mentions a number of attempts to rob him, but he thwarts these and no one gets impaled.

Jasper's Oriental hallucination, like numerous Romantic and Victorian depictions of eastern cultures and societies, jumbles various stereotypic ingredients together. The eastern imagery at the start of *Drood* serves as a contrast to the seemingly peaceful "ancient English Cathedral Town," the main setting of Dickens's last, unfinished novel. Because Jasper is probably the murderer of his nephew, both Turkish robbery and the Sultan's impaling the robbers seem portents of the choirmaster's own criminal behavior. Whatever Dickens's intentions, the association of both the Sultan and the Turkish robbers with cruelty and barbarism is inescapable.[53]

Although Dickens probably did not have Vlad the Impaler in mind, that

---

51. Charles Dickens, *The Mystery of Edwin Drood* (Oxford: Oxford University Press), 1. Subsequent references to this text are cited parenthetically.

52. Kinglake, *Eothen*, 27.

53. The general Orientalist stereotype in *Drood*, extending beyond Turkish robbers and the Ottoman Empire, emerges with Neville and Helena Landless, the "gipsy"-like twins who have grown up in Ceylon. Neville believes that he has "some affinity" with the "inferior race" among whom he spent his childhood: "'Sometimes, I don't know but that it may be a drop of what is tigerish in their blood'" (47) that makes him so quick to anger. But Jasper hallucinates specifically about "Turkish robbers" and their impaling "Sultan."

medieval butcher, warring against the Turks, was a model for Bram Stoker's famous vampire, Count Dracula. Starting with John Polidori's *The Vampyre* (1820), this favorite Gothic monster has typically been located in eastern Europe, in present or former Ottoman domains. Polidori's monster is a British nobleman, Lord Ruthven, but his victims only begin to pile up when he travels to Greece. A veteran of the Crimean War, George Melville-Whyte penned a short story entitled "A Vampire," which he published in his anthology *"Bones and I": or, The Skeleton at Home* (1868). Again, the vampire is British, this time a woman, but the narrator first travels to Greece and recollects bloody battle scenes before he encounters her. Sheridan Le Fanu's *Carmilla* (1872) also features a female vampire, and is set in Styria, a province of the Austro-Hungarian Empire, in the 1600s. Le Fanu understood that, after the Battle of Mohacs in 1526, Styria was devastated by the retreating Ottoman armies. Like Styria, moreover, Transylvania was a wild borderland between Christendom and Islam, Austro-Hungary, and the Ottomans, where—as Count Dracula boasts—bloodletting was everyday practice. At the start of Stoker's tale, when Jonathan Harker crosses the Danube he finds himself in "the East" and "among the traditions of Turkish rule,"[54] though Dracula himself is not Turkish. Dr. Van Helsing concludes that the Count "'must, indeed, have been that Voivode Dracula who won his name against the Turk'"—that is, Vlad the Impaler—by being even more terrible and a creature of the devil (212).

The stereotype of the sadistic (both "lustful" and "terrible") Turk appears also in the boys' adventure novel Jack Harkaway's *Boy Tinker among the Turks* by Bracebridge Hemyng, published in 1870, six years before the Bulgarian crisis. Jack avers that "Bluebeard was a pasha."[55] When the pasha he encounters offers another English character a wife from his seraglio, Jack advises him not to refuse the offer: "These Turks are cruel, vindictive, and revengeful. The last Englishman who refused [such an offer] was, by order of the pasha, skinned alive, placed on the sunny side of a wall, and blown to death by flies."[56]

Gladstone and the Bulgarian Crisis of 1876

According to E. J. Feuchtwanger, Disraeli's foreign policy involved the support of the Ottoman Empire that went back to the days of Palmerston and

---

54. Bram Stoker, *Dracula* (New York: W. W. Norton, 1997), 1. Subsequent references cited parenthetically.

55. Bracebridge Hemyng, *Jack Harkaway's Boy Tinker among the Turks* (Chicago: M. A. Donohue, 1870), 8.

56. Bracebridge, *Jack Haraway's Boy Tinker among the Turks,* 9.

Stratford Canning in the 1830s: "Disraeli's desire to play a more assertive role in Europe and his vision of eastern empire combined with the traditional national interest in the exclusion of Russia from Constantinople and the Straits of the Dardanelles. The generally accepted view was that the containment of Russia could be accomplished only by the maintenance of the Ottoman Empire and that it was worthwhile to face great difficulties in order to keep the sick man of Europe alive."[57] Disraeli's pro-Turkish policy met its match, however, with the widespread agitation against the massacres of Serbians and Bulgarians committed by Ottoman troops in the mid-1870s. For the protestors, whose most prominent leader was William Ewart Gladstone, the massacres proved the validity of the stereotype of the terrible Turk.

In his study of Gladstone and the Bulgarian crisis, Richard Shannon writes: "There was nothing new or unusual in the fact either of insurrection or of massacre. Both were endemic features of Ottoman administration. The massacres in Bulgaria were not unusually extensive, and there is no reason to assume that they were unusually atrocious."[58] Why, then, did they arouse such moral condemnation in Britain? Part of the answer is that they allowed Liberal dissenters to forge an anti-Islamic crusade that repudiated what was widely seen as the lack of moral principle in the Conservative party in general and in Disraeli in particular. The crusade both relied upon and reinvigorated the stereotype of the Terrible Turk as it sought to elevate British foreign policy from what it perceived as mere expediency to the moral high ground. Gladstone and his fellow crusaders did not stop to ask how many massacres and atrocities British forces had committed over the centuries in Ireland, India, and elsewhere. Against Ottoman corruption and evil, with the Terrible Turk as its incarnation, British imperial rectitude supposedly shone forth in brilliant contrast.

Adding fuel to the anti-Turkish fire, the bankruptcy of the Ottoman treasury by 1875 left British and French creditors in a lurch. "Thus after economic (1838) and military (1839) bankruptcy," writes Sina Akşin, "the Empire had become financially bankrupt and more dependent on European goodwill than ever before. The bond-holders' 50% loss of revenue led to furious protests from British and French creditors." The bankruptcy made the traditional support for the Ottoman Empire very difficult to sustain. "Until the Reduction of Interest Decision [in 1875], there had been sympathy for their plight and a belief that they were doing their best to make progress. This

---

57. E. J. Feuchtwanger, *Democracy and Empire: Britain, 1865–1914* (London: Edwin Arnold, 1985), 97.

58. R. T. Shannon, *Gladstone and the Bulgarian Agitation, 1876* (London: Thomas Nelson and Sons, 1963), 22.

was now reversed and the Ottoman state was viewed [once again] as sunk in barbarism."[59]

From June 1876, revelations of atrocities in Bulgaria, including rape and the slaughter of Christian women and children, led to the moral crusade that propelled Gladstone back into the political spotlight. His pamphlet, *Bulgarian Horrors and the Question of the East,* expresses his moral outrage that Britain should continue to support the Ottoman Empire, which was ruled by a "race" of Turkish "savages." "There is not a criminal in an European gaol, there is not a cannibal in the South Sea Islands," Gladstone declared, "whose indignation would not rise and overboil at the recital of that which has been done" in Bulgaria by Turkish forces, "but which remains unavenged."[60] The bloodthirsty Turks have perpetrated a "murderous harvest," tantamount to what today would be called "ethnic cleansing" or even "genocide."

Gladstone does not question the composition and command—or lack of command—of the irregular forces or "bashi-bazooks" in Bulgaria that committed these "outrages." They are Terrible Turks, plain and simple. Nor does he refer to atrocities committed by the anti-Ottoman rebels. Besides blaming "England" for its "moral complicity with the basest and blackest outrages upon record within the present century, if not within the memory of man" (9), Gladstone blames "the Turkish race." "They are not the mild Mahometans of India, nor the chivalrous Saladins of Syria, nor the cultured Moors of Spain. They [the Turks] were, upon the whole, from the black day when they first entered Europe, the one great anti-human specimen of humanity" whose "advancing curse menaced the whole of Europe" (12–13). According to Gladstone, the "Turkish race," whose rule "was for centuries the terror of the world," now threatens genocide to all Christians within Ottoman territory (43).

Gladstone does not hesitate to apply apocalyptic rhetoric to the "Bulgarian horrors": they are "fell Satanic orgies," expressions of Turkey's "unbounded savagery, her unbridled and bestial lust" (53). The "horrors" are, moreover, perhaps only the prelude to the devastation the Terrible Turk may wreak throughout the crumbling and thoroughly corrupt Ottoman Empire:

> What seems now to be certain . . . are the wholesale massacres . . . the elaborate and refined cruelty—the only refinement of which Turkey boasts!—the utter disregard of sex and age—the abominable and bestial lust—and the entire and violent lawlessness which stalks over the land. (32–33)

---

59. Sina Akşin, *Turkey: From Empire to Revolutionary Republic* (London: Hurst, 2007), 38.

60. William Gladstone, *Bulgarian Horrors and the Question of the East* (London: John Murray, 1876), 62. Subsequent references to this text will be cited parenthetically.

At the very least, Gladstone demands that the British government reverse its pro-Turkish policy and work to evict the Turks from Bulgaria and, indeed, from Europe. Gladstone's pamphlet, "designed for a working-class audience—sold 40,000 copies within three or four days of its publication," and "the Nonconformists, who were amongst the most active supporters of the anti-Turkish agitation, greeted him as 'a prophet of the most high God . . . called to the side of truth, righteousness & humanity.'"[61] Gladstone was inveighing not just against Turkish atrocities, but also against the Tory government's complicity in the "horrors." The "extraordinary enthusiasm" of the "Gladstonized" crowds that heard him speak about the "horrors" were, as one witness put it, "the inarticulate condemnation which Democracy was pronouncing upon the Ottomans" and also upon Disraeli's government.[62]

Gladstone's anti-Turkish crusade drew a huge following, including many writers, artists, and intellectuals. The "Eastern question" brought William Morris into his first role as a political activist; he became treasurer of the Eastern Association, whose leader was Gladstone. Most of the Pre-Raphaelite Brotherhood followed Morris in joining the Association. Figures as diverse as Anthony Trollope, Thomas Carlyle, and Charles Algernon Swinburne also supported the anti-Turkish cause. Far to the political right of Morris, Alfred Tennyson penned his sonnet "Montenegro" at Gladstone's behest, publishing it in *The Nineteenth-Century* as a preface to an essay by Gladstone. But, because of the old fear of Russia, Tennyson soon changed his mind. Two years after the Bulgarian crisis, Thomas Hardy published *The Return of the Native*. Although there is no reference to that crisis in the novel, with massacres by Turkish forces in the Victorian reader's mind, Eustacia Vye's acting in the mummers' play, in the role of the Turkish Knight who is beheaded by St. George, must have made her behavior seem particularly outlandish, perhaps even terrible.

In part because of his anti-Turkish campaigning, Gladstone was propelled back into the political spotlight, becoming Prime Minister again in 1880. The old foreign policy of propping up the Sultanate at Constantinople as a foil to Russian aggression continued, however. And Gladstone also found himself compelled to agree to the British takeover in Egypt in 1882, a move that led to further imperial expansion in East Africa (the Sudan, Uganda, Kenya). Both a decrepit Ottoman Empire and the British presence at Cairo seemed to insure the security of India until World War I, when Ottoman

61. Eugenio F. Biagini, *Liberty, Retrenchment and Reform: Popular Liberalism in the Age of Gladstone, 1860–1880* (Cambridge: Cambridge University Press, 1992), 388–389.

62. Qtd. in Biagini, 389; see also Paul Auchterlonie, "From the Eastern Question to the Death of General Gordon: Representations of the Middle East in the Victorian Periodical Press, 1876–1885," *British Journal of Middle Eastern Studies* 28.1 (2001): 5–24.

support of Germany and Austria ended the British government's pro-Turkish stance.

When news of the massacres of Armenians began appearing in the West in 1894, Gladstone, aged eighty-six, responded much as he had done to the "Bulgarian horrors." His speech denouncing the Sultan as an "assassin" was "the last great public speech of his life."[63] Gladstone "told his sons that he wished only that God would give him the strength to lead a new crusade, and to arouse the British nation against the unspeakable Turk."[64] Like the Bulgarian horrors before it, the Armenian genocide, still denied by the current government of Turkey (although not by all Turks), perhaps lends some credence to the stereotype of the "unspeakable" or the Terrible Turk. Sadly, over the course of the last two centuries, there have been many massacres and genocides around the world, many of them committed by supposedly civilized regimes. Some have even occurred within the British Empire—in Kenya, for example, as recently as the 1950s.[65]

The Terrible Turk was a staple of British literature, including pornographic literature, from the Elizabethan through the Victorian period. This xenophobic stereotype did not accord with British foreign policy between 1830 and World War I, which tried to prop up an increasingly feeble Ottoman Empire. It also did not accord with the general allure of "the East" and of Constantinople, or with Victorian interest in Turkish design and artifacts such as carpets and ottomans. Nor does it seem to have had much effect on the everyday behaviors of Britons toward the small number of Turkish merchants, diplomats, and immigrants in their midst. The stereotype surfaced with a vengeance, however, when Gladstone took up the cause of Bulgarian and Serbian rebels against the Ottomans. And it was one cause among many that helped to undermine British support of Constantinople from the 1890s through World War I.

In *The Lords of Humankind*, Victor Kiernan writes: "Shakespeare had talked of the cruelty of 'stubborn Turks and Tartars,' but both names were taking on the half-playful overtones they still have today. . . ." Kiernan notes that "the drums and cymbals of the janissaries, that once appalled Europe, were incorporated" into European orchestras, and that "Pasha Selim in Mozart's *Il Seraglio* was a true man of the Enlightenment, a devotee of reason, resisting more successfully than Count Almaviva the temptation to abuse his power over women."[66] But he adds that aspects of Ottoman rule in the

63. Philip Magnus, *Gladstone: A Biography* (New York: Dutton, 1964), 430.

64. Magnus, *Gladstone*, 431.

65. Caroline Elkins, *Imperial Reckoning: The Untold Story of Britain's Gulag in Kenya* (New York: Henry Holt, 2005).

66. Victor Kiernan, *The Lords of Humankind: European Attitudes towards the Outside World in*

1800s contributed to Western negative opinions about it. "Too confused and distracted to stick to any one line of policy," the Sultanate in Constantinople "alternated between fits of torpor and fits of violence. Massacre became, not in the European provinces only, part of the routine of administration. The struggle in Greece in the 1820s was peculiarly atrocious on both sides."[67] And so were later events:

> Massacres of Bulgars and Armenians revived half-forgotten memories of older Ottoman savagery, and the phrase 'Unspeakable Turk' was repeated. Gladstone talked fiercely in his Midlothian election campaign in 1880 about how the Turks ought to be cleared out of Europe altogether. . . . Abdul Hamid II, Sultan from 1876 to 1909, was . . . denounced in sermons as Abdul the Damned.[68]

The failures of successive Ottoman rulers to reform their government only exacerbated the Western stereotype of the Terrible Turk. Today, as Turkey's secular and modernizing government seeks admission to the European Union, the stereotype perhaps still lingers, in large measure because of its denial that, under Ottoman rule, Armenians were the victims of genocide.

Works Cited

Akşin, Sina. *Turkey: From Empire to Revolutionary Republic.* London: Hurst, 2007.

Ansari, Humayun. *"The Infidel Within": Muslims in Britain since 1800.* London: Hurst, 2004.

Auchterlonie, Paul. "From the Eastern Question to the Death of General Gordon: Representations of the Middle East in the Victorian Periodical Press, 1876–1885." *British Journal of Middle Eastern Studies* 28.1 (2001): 5–24.

Bailey, Frank Edgar. *British Policy and the Turkish Reform Movement: A Study in Anglo-Turkish Relations, 1826–1853.* Cambridge: Harvard University Press, 1942.

Biagini, Eugenio F. Liberty. *Retrenchment and Reform: Popular Liberalism in the Age of Gladstone, 1860–1880.* Cambridge, MA: Cambridge University Press, 1992.

Blake, Robert. *Disraeli.* Garden City, NY: Anchor Books, 1968.

———. *Disraeli's Grand Tour: Benjamin Disraeli and the Holy Land, 1830–31.* New York: Oxford University Press, 1982.

Brontë, Charlotte. *Jane Eyre.* London: Penguin, 1996.

Broughton, Rhoda. *Not Wisely, But Too Well.* 1867. London: Richard Bentley, 1893.

Byron, Lord George Gordon. *The Poetical Works of Lord Byron.* London: Oxford University Press, 1960.

---

the Imperial Age (London: Weidenfeld and Nicolson, 1969), 109.

    67. Kiernan, *The Lords of Humankind,* 111.

    68. Kiernan, *The Lords of Humankind,* 112.

Colley, Linda. *Captives: Britain, Empire and the World, 1600–1850*. New York: Anchor Books, 2004.

Dickens, Charles. *The Mystery of Edwin Drood*. Oxford: Oxford University Press, 1999.

Disraeli, Benjamin. *Alroy*. 1833. Hughenden Edition. London: Longman, Green, 1881.

———. *Contarini Fleming*. 1832. Hughenden Edition. London: Longman, Green, 1881.

———. *Letters*. Vol. 1. Edited by J. A. W. Gunn. Toronto: University of Toronto Press, 1982.

Elkins, Caroline. *Imperial Reckoning: The Untold Story of Britain's Gulag in Kenya*. New York: Henry Holt, 2005.

Feuchtwanger, E. J. *Democracy and Empire: Britain, 1865–1914*. London: Edwin Arnold, 1985.

Gladstone, William. *Bulgarian Horrors and the Question of the East*. London: John Murray, 1876.

Hemyng, Bracebridge. *Jack Harkaway's Boy Tinker among the Turks*. Chicago: M. A. Donohue, n.d.

Kiernan, Victor. *The Lords of Humankind: European Attitudes towards the Outside World in the Imperial Age*. London: Weidenfeld and Nicolson, 1969.

Kinglake, Alexander. *Eothen; or Traces of Travel Brought Home from the East*. Oxford: Oxford University Press, 1982.

Leask, Nigel. *British Romantic Writers and the East: Anxieties of Empire*. Cambridge: Cambridge University Press, 1992.

MacLean, Gerald. *Looking East: English Writing and the Ottoman Empire before 1800*. Houndsmills: Palgrave Macmillan, 2007.

Magnus, Philip. *Gladstone: A Biography*. New York: Dutton, 1964.

Marcus, Steven. *The Other Victorians: A Study of Sexuality and Pornography in Mid-Nineteenth-Century England*. New York: Basic Books, 1964.

McJannet, Linda. *The Sultan Speaks: Dialogue in English Plays and Histories about the Ottoman Turks*. Houndsmill: Palgrave Macmillan, 2006.

Melman, Billie. *Women's Orients: English Women and the Middle East, 1718–1918: Sexuality, Religion and Work*. Ann Arbor: The University of Michigan Press, 1992.

Melville-Whyte, George. *"Bones and I": or, The Skeleton at Home*. London: Chapman and Hall, 1868.

Nash, Geoffrey P. *From Empire to Orient: Travellers to the Middle East, 1830–1926*. London: I. B. Tauris, 2005.

Pardoe, Julia. *The Beauties of the Bosphorhus*. London: George Virlire, 1838.

———. *The City of the Sultan, and Domestic Manners of the Turks*. 2 vols. London: Henry Colburn, 1837.

Rendall, Jane. "The Citizenship of Women and the Reform Act of 1867." In *Defining the Victorian Nation: Class, Race, Gender and the Reform Act of 1867*, edited by Catherine Hall, Keith McClelland, and Jane Rendall. 119–178. Cambridge: Cambridge University Press, 2000.

Roessel, David. *In Byron's Shadow: Modern Greece in the English and American Imagination*. Oxford: Oxford University Press, 2002.

Shannon, R. T. *Gladstone and the Bulgarian Agitation 1876*. London: Thomas Nelson and Sons, 1963.

Shelley, Mary. *Frankenstein*. New York: W. W. Norton, 1996.

Shelley, Percy Bysshe. *The Major Works*. Oxford: Oxford University Press, 2003.

Smith, Albert. *A Month at Constantinople*. Boston: Bradbury and Guild, 1852.

Stoker, Bram. *Dracula.* New York: W. W. Norton, 1997.

Thackeray, William Makepeace. *Notes of a Journey from Cornhill to Grand Cairo.* Oxford Illustrated Thackeray. Vol. 9. Oxford: Humphrey Milford, n.d.

Turhan, Filiz. *The Other Empire: British Romantic Writings about the Ottoman Empire.* New York and London: Routledge, 2003.

Warburton, Eliot. *The Crescent and the Cross; or, Romance and Realities of Eastern Travel.* London: Hurst and Blackett, 1858.

Wheatcroft, Andrew. *The Ottomans.* London: Viking Penguin, 1993.

Zonana, Joyce. "The Sultan and the Slave: Feminist Orientalism and the Structure of *Jane Eyre.*" *Signs* 18.3 (spring 1993): 592–617.

9

Ethnicity as Marker in Henry Mayhew's *London Labour and the London Poor*

❧

THOMAS PRASCH

Consider the sheer, almost bewildering range of ethnic types that strut through the pages of Henry Mayhew's classic survey of the urban under-classes of mid-Victorian London, *London Labour and the London Poor* (1861–1862): turbaned Doctor Bokavy, the street herbalist vending his East Indian wares; the "anomalous body of men"—Malays, Hindoos, Negroes—selling Christian tracts in the streets of London, although many "are Mahometans, or worshippers of Bramah!"; the Arab Jews from Morocco who dominated the street trade in rhubarb and spices and tortoises; the "black" servant of an Indian whose bed housed vermin the exterminator pronounced "the fin-est and fattest bugs I ever saw"; the Arab boys (one compared to Othello, the other labeled a "rank nigger") following the example of street Indians by playing tom-toms; Ramo Samee, the Indian who brought juggling to the English streets; the black and Indian crossing-sweeps and beggars; gypsy horse thieves; the opium-smoking Indian who, like "Malays, Lascars, and Orientals generally," brought to a house of ill-repute "the most frightful form" of sexually transmitted disease; the Chinese sailor who kept an English prosti-tute; and the range of Asians, Indians, and Africans resident in English casual wards.[1] All of these street vendors figure—along with the even more pre-

---

1. Henry Mayhew, *London Labour and the London Poor* (New York: Dover, 1968): Dr. Bokavy at I: facing page 197 (Dr. Bokavy appears only in the illustrations, not in Mayhew's text); the tract sellers at I: 242 (they reappear at III: 185, and, reclassified as fraudulent beggars, at IV: 423–424,

dominant Irish and Jews,[2] both groups seen as racially and physiognomically distinct by the English[3]—as markers of racial otherness in Mayhew's portrait of the street culture of mid-Victorian England.[4] Indeed, racial diversity was so central to some aspects of London street culture that English street artists imitated otherness, as with the tattooed man who claimed to be a New Zealand aboriginal, the street juggler who dressed as an Indian, the acrobat who Italianized his name, the white beggars who blackened their faces to cash in on sympathy for freed slaves, or the blackfaced Ethiopian bands, English street versions of American minstrel shows (as one informant told Mayhew: "Some niggers are Irish. There's Scottish niggers, too. I don't know a Welsh one, but one of the street nigger-singers *is* a real black—an African").[5] Clearly ethnicity could be good for street trade.

Such diversity might be taken simply as an index of London's status as metropole to a growing, and increasingly mobilized, empire. After cataloging some of the range of immigrants, for example, Adam Hansen notes: "The exploited and dejected of the nineteenth century were coming to Britain along the routes of an empire otherwise impossible without mobility."[6] More generally, their presence can be taken to signal the centrality of London to an increasingly world-wide nexus of trade and interchange. In combination with the wide range of other foreigners that were a part of Mayhew's London street life—the Italians who dominated the street performance and music scene;[7] the German bands, clock-sellers, prostitutes, and pickpockets;[8] the

---

and IV: 440); rhubarb and spice merchants at I: 452–454 and tortoise traders at II: 80; the exterminator's story at III: 37; the tom-tom players at III: 185–189; Ramo Samee at III: 62, 104; crossing sweeps at II: 185, 490, III: 428 and beggars at IV: 423–426; gypsy horse thieves at IV: 369, 376 (although Mayhew handles the racial distinctiveness of gypsies ambivalently, sometimes insisting on their tribal difference and other times noting that down-and-out English could simply join them; see also II: 72, II: 369), the Indian in the low lodging house at IV: 231–232 (the race of his companion is not entirely clear); the Chinese sailor at IV: 232–233; the casual-ward residents at III: 384–385, 406, 408, 421, with a breakdown of one ward's population by nationality in a table (406). Further references to Mayhew's text, where brevity permits, will be presented parenthetically.

2. The Irish and Jews figure prominently throughout Mayhew's text and offer subcultures distinctive enough that Mayhew devotes chapters to each (the street-Irish in I: 104–120; the street-Jews in II: 115–135—and see also I: 86–88).

3. On this point see George Stocking, Jr., *Victorian Anthropology* (New York: Free Press, 1987), 20, 63, 213, 229–230; Mary Cowling, *The Artist as Anthropologist: The Representation of Type and Character in Victorian Art* (Cambridge University Press, 1989), 35, 125–129, 332–333.

4. The focus of this paper is the structure of racial and ethnic otherness in the final book form of Mayhew's work.

5. Quotation at Mayhew, III: 191. For the other examples see II: 90, III: 104, III: 95, IV: 425, III: 190–194.

6. Adam Hansen, "Exhibiting Vagrancy, 1851: Victorian London and the 'Vagabond Savage,'" in *A Mighty Mass of Brick and Smoke: Victorian and Edwardian Representations of London,* 74.

7. See Mayhew, vol. 3, practically passim, but specifically 45–49, 72–73, 77–78, 90, 139–140, 155, 171–182, 199. Also I: 457 (women street vendors), 197, 470 (musicians), IV: 269 (prostitutes), 344 (burglars).

8. Mayhew, III: 163–164, 189; II: 23; IV: 228, 230; IV: 308.

French musicians, prostitutes, and thieves;[9] the Polish tailors, Spanish refugees, Scottish bagpipers, and all the rest[10]—such a street presence reflected London's place as the central metropolis for the widening sphere of English direct empire and commercial hegemony. The ethnically diverse street life of London thus underlined the centrality of the city as the cosmopolitan center of an increasingly interconnected world economy, the human side of the trading empire that brought tea, coffee, and tobacco to the city.

But for Mayhew the ethnic diversity of the streets of London had no such neutral meaning. Rather, in the structure of *London Labour*, ethnic difference, read by Mayhew as racial otherness, was constructed as a threat to English labor, which itself was imaged in terms of race (as white but "nomadic").[11] Thus the construction of race within Mayhew's text can be read as part of the ideological work by which, as Paul Gilroy puts it, "blackness and Englishness appear as mutually exclusive attributes."[12] Mayhew fashions his image of Englishness against the image of a racial other in the midst (yet at the margins) of English life.[13] The racial/ethnic others whose presence increasingly impinged on the truly English, however marginal, street poor of London constitute for Mayhew a new sort of threat to the traditions and stability of lower-class life, a threat working from the most marginal edges of the social order. And this construction of otherness had as well an explicitly political meaning, drawing the boundaries of citizenship through an account that equated race with culture and culture with political awareness. However marginal their lives might be, the English poor retained a sense of their membership in the political order and of the rights and privileges entailed by that membership. The ethnic outsiders who increasingly impinged on the street trades of London entirely lacked this sense of membership and remained more permanently outsiders. Mayhew thus articulates a new xenophobia (even if the term itself was not yet coined). In responding to the changing ethnic and

---

9. Mayhew, III: 171–173; IV: 214–215, 269–272; IV: 308.

10. Mayhew II: 333; II: 262; III: 164, 167, 169–171; see also III: 406.

11. The image of the English working class as white, despite the presence of workers of other races among them at least back to the eighteenth century (especially in London and port cities), remains deeply entrenched. Note, for example, the all-white representation of twentieth-century Liverpool labor in Terence Davies's film *Distant Mirror, Still Lives* (1988). Blindness to racial and gender dimensions of working-class identity is a troubling characteristic of the major works of, for instance, E. P. Thompson and E. J. Hobsbawm.

12. Gilroy, "Cultural Studies and Ethnic Absolutism," in *Cultural Studies* 190. Gilroy develops the countercase more fully, of course, in *The Black Atlantic: Modernity and Double Consciousness* (Cambridge, MA: Harvard University Press, 1993). A parallel argument has regularly been made by Salman Rushdie; see, for example, "The New Empire within Britain," reprinted in *Imaginary Homelands* (New York: Viking, 1991), 129–138.

13. For a parallel reading of Mayhew, which employs "nomadism" rather than race as the central term of an otherness that must be controlled through the mechanisms of social science, see Patrick Brantlinger and Donald Ulin, "Policing Nomads: Discourse and Social Control in Early Victorian England," *Cultural Critique* 25 (1993): 33–63, especially 47–61.

racial character of the urban population, which was brought about by the growing place of London in the nexus of global commerce and exchange, Mayhew's work presents a fundamental challenge to English identity and security in the presence of foreigners on the streets of London. If this challenge was felt first among the city's least secure, its most marginal and already most imperiled members, Mayhew's *London Labour* implies that the consequences of their displacement would come in time to threaten the whole edifice of the English political and social structure.

Mayhew was as interested in insisting that class difference had a racial component as he was in arguing for the racial foundations of ethnic subcultures. This produces in *London Labour* an interestingly complex—and internally contradictory—argument about race and class.[14] On the one hand, Mayhew presented London's street culture as a racially distinctive and by implication homogenous class, typified by the costermonger, "by far the largest and certainly most broadly marked class" who "appear to be a distinct race" (I: 6). The racial argument Mayhew deploys here is one of association: the costermongers are like other "nomadic" or "wandering" tribes in their habits, physiognomy, and relation to the civilized world.[15] This assertion of resemblance is reinforced by common bonds of blood.

On the other hand, the unitary conception of a nomadic underclass is undercut in Mayhew's own text by the sheer diversity of his representative types. This has led some commentators to underline the internal contradictions and collapsing categories of Mayhew's racial epistemology. As Tim Barringer, playing Mayhew's text against representations of Africans in travel literature, notes, Mayhew posits a unitary racial divide between the "nomad" and the "civilized," but "this absolute formulation of difference collapses under the close interrogation made possible by the revelations of Mayhew's text. . . . The unity of the urban other . . . proves to be mythical; the racial characteristics which were presented as uniting them disappear amid the disparate nature of the evidence."[16] A. L. Beier, while specifically focusing on the language of the underclass in his treatment, identifies a similar breakdown of any unified category: "Although Mayhew asserted that there was a single language used among the underclass of the mid-nineteenth century, his

---

14. The internal contradictions between these arguments are quite distinct from the sorts of contradictions between Mayhew's voice and the voices of his "nomadic" informants that are the focus in Brantlinger and Ulin, "Policing Nomads." I am proposing here an incoherence within Mayhew's voice, an inconsistency about the relationship between race and class that leads, as will be seen, to a hierarchy of marginalization that in turn allows for multiple positions in relation to "Englishness" and the English polity.

15. Mayhew, I: 1–3, 213, III: 233–234, 317.

16. Tim Barringer, "Images of Otherness and the Visual Production of Difference: Race and Labour in Illustrated Texts, 1850–1865," in *The Victorians and Race,* 50.

own evidence shows that the situation was more complex than that. This is because in the course of his many interviews Mayhew recorded the speech of representatives of many groups—ethnicities (e.g., the French, Germans, the Irish, and Italians), a variety of trades, as well as the vagrant and criminal."[17] In both readings, an argument for the racial distinction of the nomadic falters because of distinctions among the varied peoples who are identified as nomads.

Part of the difficulty here, no doubt, lies in the simple contradictory inconsistency of different parts of Mayhew's text. Some of the inconsistencies arise from the work's highly complex publishing history, a convoluted story of a generation buried in the familiar four-volume final form typically referenced in recent scholarship.[18] Mayhew's initial engagement with the subject of the urban poor began in the series of reports he penned for the *Morning Chronicle* in 1849–1850,[19] and some of those original reports were recycled into *London Labour,* mostly in volume three. But the direction and argument of the book vary significantly from the original newspaper reports. As a book, conceptualized after Mayhew's break from the *Morning Chronicle* in 1850, *London Labour* began as a serial publication, collected into two volumes, in 1850–1851; the serial publications included an interesting feedback mechanism for his readers, printing "Answers to Correspondents" on the wrappers of each installment.[20] But then the work was abandoned until 1856. When work on the project resumes,[21] Mayhew's vision of it had broadened significantly: in 1856 he published the first (and, in the end, only) volume of *The Great World of London* (featuring a striking panoramic view of the city from a

17. A. L. Beier, "'Takin' It to the Streets,' Henry Mayhew and the Language of the Underclass in Mid-Nineteenth-Century London," in *Cast Out: Vagrancy and Homelessness in Global and Historical Perspective.*

18. On the genesis of the project, the different versions, and the rather complex publishing history, the fullest explication can be found in Anne Humpherys, on whose account the following, save where noted, depends. See *Travels into the Poor Man's Country: The Works of Henry Mayhew* (Athens: University of Georgia Press, 1977), chap. 3; *Henry Mayhew* (Boston: Twayne Publishers, 1984), chap. 3. See also Gertrude Himmelfarb, *The Idea of Poverty* (New York: Knopf, 1987), 322–323, 566n.35; E. P. Thompson, "The Political Education of Henry Mayhew," *Victorian Studies* 11.1 (1967): 41–62.

19. Some of these are reprinted in *The Unknown Mayhew: Selections from the Morning Chronicle, 1849–50;* some in Anne Humpherys, ed., *Voices of the Poor: Selections from the Morning Chronicle "Labour and the Poor"* (London: Routledge, 1971). There is also a six-volume complete edition: Henry Mayhew, *The Morning Chronicle Survey of Labour and the Poor: The Metropolitan Districts* (Firle, Eng.: Caliban Books, 1980–1982).

20. One of the editions of volume 2 available through Google Books—the copy with the Cruikshank-looking drawn frontispiece, held at University of Michigan's Parsons Library—includes the "Answers to Correspondents." Humpherys draws on them extensively for her discussion (see n.18).

21. Humpherys discusses serial publication of material that was later to become volume three, but in different order, in 1856; see *Henry Mayhew,* 135–138; see also *Travels,* 107–108. She also notes that plans to reprint vol. 2 in 1856 apparently bore no fruit; see *Travels,* 106.

balloon in its opening pages[22]), into which it was clearly Mayhew's intent to fold *London Labour*'s volumes, along with more broad-ranging perspectives. After introductory surveys, and short treatments of professional and legal London, however, the book focuses on a detailed account of the city's criminal prisons.[23] That work breaks off mid-sentence in a discussion of rules of the House of Detention at Wadsworth, with an added note on the final page: "A severe attack of illness rendered it necessary that he [Mayhew] should abstain from all mental exertion, and it is only very recently that he has been permitted by his physician to resume his literary labours."[24] The promised completion, however, would be delayed by the death of his publisher.

It is only with a new publisher, and after another gap of several years, that the familiar four-volume *London Labour* takes shape. Yet even at this final point, there are complications. As Humpherys makes clear, Mayhew was abroad when the book version of *London Labour* was assembled, and thus had little to do with the precise arrangement of contents in the four-volume form (or with the final form of *Criminal Prisons,* originally *Great World,* reprinted as something of a fifth volume in 1862). This long generation and complicated publishing history of the final work ensures above all else a systematic inconsistency in approach and argument, but to an extent that had been there all along. Mayhew's own shifting attention and focus derail anything like a sustained single argument in the final product. Categorization schemes multiply, later arguments contradict earlier assertions, and even the broad contours of the project seem both jumbled and incomplete.

The difficulties of publication are acerbated by problems of authorship. From the outset, Mayhew makes clear his reliance on other sources for his collection of data. In the "Preface" to the first volume, Mayhew notes: "I should make special mention of the assistance I have received in the compilation of the present volume from Mr. HENRY WOOD and Mr. Richard Knight (Late of the City Mission), gentlemen who have been engaged with me from nearly the commencement of my inquiries. . . . Mr. Wood, indeed, has contributed so large a proportion of the contents of the present volume that he may fairly be considered as one of its authors."[25] He also depended

22. Henry Mayhew, *Great World of London* (London: David Bogue, 1856), 7–10.

23. When, indeed, the work was republished as Henry Mayhew and John Binny, *The Criminal Prisons of London* (London: Griffin, Bohn and Company, 1862), to coincide with the completion of the four-volume final version of *London Labour,* it would be reprinted without a change, even though the new title made the preliminary panorama and the rest of the first eighty pages largely irrelevant. In the "Advertisement" opening the republication, however, it is noted: "The present volume completes the series of papers on the lower phases of London life, so ably commenced by Henry Mayhew."

24. Mayhew, *Great World,* unnumbered final page, dated 1 November 1856.

25. Mayhew, *London Labour,* I: xvi. The attribution appears in identical form in the 1851 edition of the volume.

heavily on work by his brother, Augustus Mayhew, in compiling material. Indeed, Augustus, who would recycle some of that material into his novel *Paved with Gold* (1858), notes in the preface to that work: "some portions of this book (such as the chapters on 'The Crossing-Sweepers' and 'The Rat Match' at the 'Jolly Trainer') were originally undertaken by me at the request of my brother, Mr. Henry Mayhew, and will, I believe, shortly appear . . . in the concluding volume of his invaluable work on 'London Labour and the Labouring Poor.'"[26] Mayhew may well have depended on other collectors of material as well.

Authorship becomes even more problematic for the later volumes of the final version, completed and published while Mayhew was abroad. Portions of it—including almost all of volume four—were explicitly authored by others: Rev. William Tuckniss (credited with the section on "Agencies at Present in Operation within the Metropolis, for the Suppression of Vice and Crime,"), Bracebridge Hemyng (listed as co-author of the general discussion of prostitutes and sole author of "Prostitution in London"), John Binny ("Thieves and Swindlers"), and Andrew Halliday ("Beggars"). Binny would also, around the same time, complete the work on *Criminal Prisons of London*. As the publishers explain in the opening "Advertisement": "The publishers think it right to state that, in consequence of Mr. Mayhew's absence from England, they placed the completion of the volume in the hands of Mr. Binny, who has supplied all after page 498."[27] Clearly, not all these varied voices quite shared the same views. A. L. Beier, for example, in his discussion of Mayhew's use of the "dangerous classes" trope, implies that it figures especially strongly in material contributed by Binny and Halliday.[28] If one trope might figure more strongly in the other authors, others might as well.

---

26. Augustus Mayhew, "Preface," *Paved with Gold: or, the Romance and Reality of the London Streets* (London: Chapman and Hall, 1858). The preface is dated 1 March 1858, between the faltering of the *Great Worlds* project and the 1861–1862 four-volume edition. Anne Humpherys notes that Henry Mayhew was co-author of the novel in its serial format but abandoned his work on it after the fifth number; see *Henry Mayhew*, 11. Humpherys also notes the routine collaboration of the two brothers. Henry Mayhew was not above recycling material as well, not only incorporating portions of his *Morning Chronicle* journalism into *London Labour*, as noted above, but also plugging *London Labour*–rooted material (and his journalistic work on the Great Exhibition) into his comic novel *1851*. For a good example, see "Mr. Sandboys's visit to the Old Clothes Marts" in Henry Mayhew and George Cruikshank, *1851: or, The Adventures of Mr. and Mrs. Sandboys, Their Son and Daughter, Who Came Up to London to Enjoy Themselves, and to See the Great Exhibition* (New York: Stringer and Townsend, 1851), 98–101. (Cruikshank, although credited as co-author, seems likely to have created nothing but the illustrations.)

27. "Advertisement," Mayhew and Binny, *Criminal Prisons of London*. As noted above, the published work retained the panoramic but now irrelevant frame from *Great World*.

28. See A. L. Beier, "'Takin' It to the Streets': Henry Mayhew and the Language of the Underclass in Mid-Nineteenth-Century London," in *Cast Out: Vagrancy and Homelessness in Global and Historical Perspective*, 94–95.

It follows that "Henry Mayhew," as author of *London Labour,* is something of an artificial construct, but one which, for present purposes, and for simple convenience, we will retain. Whatever the inconsistencies and erratic shifts in the final text, in its internal inconsistencies and contradictory classification systems, in terms of the broad issues of race and ethnicity, there remains in the whole a coherent dual argument.

The dual argument about race in *London Labour* distinguishes perspectives from outside (from the position of Mayhew himself as representative middle-class observer) and from within. Thus, in one respect, all the varied street types, insofar as they share nomadism as a defining trait (both culturally and racially), are of one race, while at the same time a range of ethnic types (read as racial and organized in hierarchies) figure within the populations of the street. And it is in that latter constellation of race as marking difference within street populations that the reactive xenophobic side of Mayhew's account can be traced.

Thus, in Mayhew's text, English costermongers—and English laborers generally[29]—are depicted as a class under threat, being undermined by competition from foreigners.[30] The foreign threat to English labor came, in Mayhew's view, at a point when English workers were especially vulnerable: when some established trades were in decline, forcing ever more workers into the nomadic "street" sphere of marginal economic activity. This side of Mayhew's argument is grounded in difference: accounts of the longstanding traditions of English street traders[31] (with a particular emphasis on the decline of their

---

29. It is undoubtedly the case that Mayhew's investigations highlight marginal laborers to the near exclusion of skilled, or even most unskilled, workers. Himmelfarb makes much of the distinction, largely in the interest of negating the claims of left historians inclined to see Mayhew as an objective observer of working-class culture; see *Idea of Poverty,* 346–355. In Mayhew's view, however, the marginal class included *both* those "bred" to it, in his language, and those forced into it by loss of more regular employment. These latter constitute, for example, an eighth of the costermongers proper (I: 7), the preponderance of traders involved in producing and selling food on the streets (I: 158), many vendors of needles to tailors (I: 340), some of the scavengers (II: 208), a portion of the city's cabdrivers (III: 351), and at least a few casual dock workers (III: 304). Pressure from foreigners operates especially to the disadvantage of those not "bred" to the business of the streets, as with the mechanic costermongers (I: 7).

30. Audrey Jaffe gets this partly right when arguing, of the foreign "false beggar" in Mayhew, that "this figure also aroused anxiety for his potential to take the place of the English or Irish laborers, thereby producing underemployment (and 'false beggars') in the native population." *Scenes of Sympathy: Identity and Representation in Victorian Fiction* (Ithaca, NY: Cornell University Press, 2000), 69. But Jaffe mistakes, as I will show, Mayhew's position on the Irish, who themselves threaten native street populations.

31. See, for instance, the heritage of costermongers' cries, I: 7–8; their traditional rights, I: 58–59; the old patterer's speeches, I: 216–217; the traditional ballads, I: 273–275; or the extended history of Punch and Judy shows, III: 43–60. For a discussion of some of these forms as expressions of linguistic distinctiveness, see Beier, "'Takin' It to the Streets.'"

trades in recent times[32]) is balanced against assertions about the different styles and cultures of the racially distinct others who threaten them. While the argument on difference makes use of the full range of racial others, it focuses principally on the two fully installed competing subcultures,[33] those of the street-Irish and the street-Jews. Taking the side of the native street traders against the outsiders, Mayhew simultaneously asserts the essential character of their labor (that they are, for instance, "the principal purveyors of food to the poor, and that consequently they are as important a body of people as they are numerous" (I: 101) and the competitive disadvantages they face compared to immigrant communities.

The English costermonger is figured both outside and within Mayhew's construction of Englishness: outside insofar as the group was a racially distinct vestige of nomadism; inside insofar as they are, at least, English nomads, their own venerable traditions linking them back to the Elizabethan age that seems central to Mayhew's conception of Englishness. The racial other against whom Mayhew shapes his Englishness is similarly both inside and outside the domestic underclass of street laborers. They are central to a range of street trades (and to Mayhew's imagistic menagerie of the street); at the same time, they remain outsiders, readily distinguishable from the "thoroughbred costers" (I: 7). These racially other outsiders become the focus of Mayhew's xenophobia, embodying both a racial threat to English nationhood and a more fundamental existential threat to established English subclasses.

Thus Mayhew establishes a hierarchy of relative membership in the English polity—the English costermonger marginally included; the Irish and Jews,[34] excluded but operating within their own alternative communities; the Indians, blacks, and others more marginalized still. These multiple positions of relation to Englishness end up being reflected in political attitudes as well. Mayhew's text is therefore not only about racial difference, measured in a strictly binary way (as white or other), but about racial hierarchies. This is perhaps most evident in the case of the two "Indian" (actually Arab) tom-tom players. The "Othello" of the two is a "handsome lad . . . as gracefully

---

32. Declining trade and worsening conditions are a recurrent theme in Mayhew, especially in the first three volumes. See I: 7, 22, 53, 55, 66, 90, 94, 100, 102, 126, 139, 158–160, 170, 180, 182, 194–196, 198–200, 205, 221, 234, 239–241, 268, 272, 305, 323, 326, 338, 354, 361, 376, 377, 379, 388, 391, 398, 427, 429, 444, 450, 453, 454; II: 5, 15, 33, 45, 81, 90, 104, 118–119, 120, 228–229, 235–236, 428; III: 29, 45, 120, 162, 163, 174, 180, 181, 226, 261, 274, 329.

33. Fully installed, that is, both within Mayhew's text, each group receiving separate attention, and in Mayhew's view of English society, both groups characterized by a range of support systems and networks of kinship so as to constitute an autonomous internal community.

34. And, to an extent, in vol. III, the Italians; although they are not granted the same status in Mayhew's text (no subsection of their very own), their internal community works in much the same way. See Mayhew II: 506, III: 173–180.

proportioned, as a bronze image"; the other, "what a Yankee would call 'a rank nigger,'" offered "a comical contrast," and a face "as black and elastic-looking as a printer's dabber." Not surprisingly, the blacker boy, "Beyond 'Yes' and 'No' . . . [was] perfectly unacquainted with the English language," while his lighter, more handsome companion "spoke English perfectly." The latter, knowing his place, tells Mayhew: "The Arabs are just equally as good as the Indians at playing the tom-tom, but they haven't got exactly the learning to manufacture them yet" (III: 185). The passage provides a racial hierarchy of civilization extending downward from the Indians, with preindustrial manu-facturing capabilities closest to the white race, through the Arabs, literate but unmechanical, to the African. By emplotting racial hierarchy within his account of the structure of English street culture, Mayhew could simultane-ously insist on the racial gap that separated the street vendor and the "civi-lized" English people and, in more xenophobic terms, the racial gulf that separated the English costermongers from their (irremediably) foreign rivals.

Between Mayhew's arguments for the nomadism of English street-folk and for their difference from other racial others, his account of nomadism is the more familiar, established in *London Labour*'s opening pages: "there are— socially, morally, and perhaps even physically considered—but two distinct and broadly marked races, viz., the wanderers and the settler—the vagabond and the citizen—the nomadic and the civilized tribes" (I: 1). Anchoring his account with ethnological comparisons (costermonger is to Englishman as Bushman is to Hottentot, Lapp to Finn, Bedouin to settled Arab) and cita-tions (most crucially of ethnologist James Prichard),[35] Mayhew established the ground for the social-scientific categorization of street labor.[36] The con-nections between English "nomads" and the uncivilized are reinforced by repetition.[37] The explicitly racial dynamic of this difference is underlined by a pattern of references to miscegenation.[38] Thus both culture and blood marked the English street-folk as racially distinct.[39]

---

35. For discussions of Prichard, the shift from his cultural anthropology to one more rooted in physical racial difference by midcentury, and Mayhew's own position within anthropological discourse, see Stocking, *Victorian Anthropology*, 48–53, 62–64, 213–219. Mayhew misspells this name as "Pritchard." The spelling has been silently corrected in this essay.

36. On Mayhew's categorization system as science, see Cowling, *The Artist as Anthropologist*, 125–126, 196, 295–296; Brantlinger and Ulin, "Policing Nomads," 48–49, 52–53.

37. For example, Mayhew, I: 213, 320; III: 233.

38. Most frequently with the Irish (I: 6, 289; II: 11, 506; III: 88), but also with Indians (III: 186; IV: 231–232, 424), American blacks (III: 384–385, 421), Chinese (IV: 232–233), and the full racial range of sailors (IV: 229).

39. A range of commentators have sought to minimize the racial argument in Mayhew. Thus Himmelfarb sees in Mayhew only the "typical, loose Victorian sense of the term" race (*Idea of Poverty*, 324); Eileen Yeo believes Mayhew's use of the term "race" merely reflected his inability to develop fully an argument about subcultures ("Mayhew as Social Investigator," in *Unknown Mayhew*, 86–87);

In Mayhew's account, race is at once physiognomic and cultural. Thus, on the one hand, the street vendor is physically distinct from other English people, characterized by differences in head shape (powerfully reinforced in his text by the selection of types used for illustration).[40] On the page, these differences, as Beier has made clear, are reinforced as well by linguistic practice.[41] At the same time, racial difference marked the distinct culture of the costermonger, characterized above all by its radical difference from middle-class English conventions (thus their improvidence, love of gambling, lack of education, irreligion, and preference for concubinage over marriage).[42] Assuming that such cultural practices are a function of race, it should be noted, also tends to make them ineradicable.

The moral culture of the street vendors both marks the distinction between them and "civilized" English and places them at a disadvantage in the competition on the street with the more markedly different races, especially the Irish and the Jews.[43] Both groups had made significant inroads in the street trades of England. The Irish had become dominant in the street vending of oranges and other fruit, onions and herbs, potatoes, belts, wash leathers, lucifers, and flypaper; most hansellers, linen packmen, shoe "translators" (i.e., remakers), apparel manufacturers, crossing sweeps, refuse and dung gatherers, cigar-end collectors, and rubbish-carters, as well as many of the lower level casual laborers at the docks and most of the presumably "Scottish" bagpipers, were Irish.[44] For their part, the Jews had major roles in the old-clothes trade, jewelry and trinket sales, the peddling of manufactured goods, the sponge market and the sale of items like spectacles and telescopes;

Humphreys insists that Mayhew "partly abjured" racial theory (*Travels,* 72). Such arguments do not hold up against the repeated emphasis on racial difference that continued not only throughout *London Labour* but also into his next project; see Henry Mayhew and John Binny, *The Criminal Prisons of London,* 381–383.

40. On illustrations in Mayhew, see Barringer, "Images of Otherness"; Thomas Prasch, "Photography and the Image of the London Poor," in *Victorian Urban Settings: Essays on the Nineteenth-Century City and Its Contexts,* 179–186; Thomas Prasch, "Fixed Positions: Working-Class Subjects and Photographic Hegemony in Victorian Britain," 219–229.

41. This is the central argument of Beier, "'Takin' It to the Streets.'"

42. Mayhew, I: 11–22. This set of cultural traits is what Himmelfarb terms the "moral physiognomy of the street-folk"; see *Idea of Poverty,* 323–331.

43. Missing the distinction (or not seeing the contradiction) between these two aspects of Mayhew's argument, Catherine Gallagher takes an Irish woman as representative of Mayhew's nomadism and thus insists on the indeterminacy of the "social body" in his account; see "The Body Versus the Social Body in Malthus and Mayhew," in *The Making of the Modern Body: Sexuality and Society in the Nineteenth Century,* 100–101. It is not the case that "As he details their lives, though, the charges [of promiscuity, etc.] evaporate" (100), but rather that those charges hold for English costermongers but *not* for Irish immigrants.

44. Mayhew, I: 79, 80, 82, 84, 94, 117–118, 171, 326–327, 377–378, 408, 433, 444; II: 26, 29–33, 34, 142–143, 145, 333, 337, 467, 481–484, 493–494; III: 162–164, 168, 278–280, 290, 299.

they had control over the wholesale provision of fruit and fish, pastry and cakes, as well as old clothes, and ran the "swag shops" that recirculated merchandise.[45] Jews controlled the street markets of Petticoat Lane (II: 36–39) and the wholesale venue of the Exchange (I: 368–369); Irish dominated the markets of Rosemary Lane (II: 39–40).[46] They also both contributed to the criminal culture of the street, the Jews primarily in accessory roles (as owners of houses of prostitution and receivers of stolen goods),[47] and the Irish as the predominant figures in prostitution and practically all the forms of sneaking and thievery outlined in the final volume of *London Labour,* on those who "will not work."[48]

The cultures and trading styles of the Irish and Jew were quite distinct from each other. Jews thrived by buying cheap and selling hard, and they also tended to develop control over wholesale supplies[49]; the Irish, in contrast, succeeded by underselling their competition and living on less.[50] Jews never accepted charity from others (depending, however, on the support of their own community); the Irish, unlike either Jews or the English poor, resorted without hesitancy to begging and parish charity.[51] In direct competition, the Irish tactic of underselling competition and living more marginally was effectively removing Jewish domination from some markets (as of oranges, I: 106–107). But against the two groups, the English trader was even more severely pinched. As one fish seller complained: "The Jews are my ruin," because they compete more cunningly on market prices; but the same tradesman also griped: "My trade has been impaired, too, by the great increase of Irish costermongers, for an Irishman will starve out an Englishman any day" (I: 68). In a wide range of other markets, as well, the English street sellers

---

45. Mayhew, I: 61, 79, 86–90, 107, 198, 304, 333, 346, 347, 376, 442, 443, 444, II: 13, 22, 24, 27, 103, 118, 124.

46. No other ethnic/racial group exercised such control over areas of the market, although the rhubarb and spice trade seemed to be dominated by Moroccan Jews (I: 452–455), who also had a monopoly on the tortoise trade (II: 80). Moroccan Jews are treated by Mayhew as quite distinct from other Jewish groups; he labels them Arabs.

47. Mayhew, II: 117, 124; III: 315; IV: 223, 241, 242. In these passages, Mayhew's recourse to the traditional lines of anti-Semitic argument is often quite clear. As Himmelfarb notes, this anti-Semitism in Mayhew's work can be traced back to the period of his split with the *Morning Chronicle;* see *Idea of Poverty,* 322, 344.

48. Mayhew, IV: 231–232, 238, 273, 283, 289, 297, 304, 308, 331, 344, 359, 365, 366, 373. It is worth recalling that Mayhew did not pen most of vol. 4, and this makes some difference in regard to racial type. John Binny, who handles "Thieves," for example, repeatedly refers to an "Irish cockney" class undefined elsewhere in *London Labour.*

49. Mayhew, I: 126–129, 204, 294, 336, 348; II: 29, 36.

50. Mayhew, I: 5, 68, 114, 257, 409, 460; II: 119.

51. On Jewish dependence on community support, see Mayhew, II: 126–127; III: 408. On the Irish use of charity systems, see Mayhew, I: 115, 116, 457, 462; II: 250; III: 372–375, 395–396, 400–404; see also the table at IV: 406.

were caught at a competitive disadvantage, neither as skillful at sales as the Jew nor as willing to live cheap as the Irish.[52]

But what put English costermongers at a particular disadvantage was precisely their nomadic culture, a culture shared by neither Irish nor Jew. Both the Irish and the Jewish immigrants were marked out by their autonomous cultural formations, morally distinct and economically different from those of the "native" trader. Morally, both Irish and Jew shared a religiosity, a respect for the institution of marriage, less love of drink (despite the stereotypes associated with the Irish), and a more provident attitude toward money than their English counterparts.[53] Economically, the communal ties of Irish and Jewish groups guaranteed support for members in desperate straits (I: 115; II: 127–130). In contrast, the very independence of the English costermongers, their existence outside the realm of English community, made them prey, for example, to usurious rates for rental of the wheelbarrows and carts they needed for their trade (I: 29–32).[54]

That same independence that put them at a competitive disadvantage in the markets of the streets, however, made English costermongers at least potential citizens. Politically, the native costermonger (in contrast even to lower elements within the English street crowd) had clearly defined views: "The politics of these people are detailed in a few words: they are nearly all Chartists" (I: 20). In contrast, Mayhew writes: "Of politics, I think, the street Irish understand nothing" (I: 109), and of the Jews he declares: "Perhaps there is no people in the world . . . who care so little for politics as the general body of the Jews" (II: 126).[55] As the costermongers show, poverty need not be apolitical; in the case of both Irish and Jewish communities, however, communal identity (at least in Mayhew's account) produced no political involvement.

From the perspective of a middle-class observer in the immediate wake of the major Chartist demonstrations, the Jewish/Irish indifference to the political realm might seem preferable to native costermongers' political commitment. But Mayhew makes it clear that he thinks otherwise. He develops a contrast between the "unskilled labourers"—"As yet they are as unpolitical as

---

52. The intermediaries in the labor market were guilty, in Mayhew's account, of magnifying the crisis by deliberately seeking the importation of foreign labor, the cheaper the better. See Mayhew, II: 316, 317; III: 294.

53. Mayhew, I: 104–105, 107–108, 110, 114; II: 124–126.

54. Given the stereotypical association of Jews with usury, Mayhew interestingly notes: "There is not among the Jewish street-traders, as among the costermongers . . . a class . . . living by usury and loan-mongering. . . . Whatever may be thought of Jews' usurious dealings as regards the general public, the poorer classes of their people are not subjected to the exaction of usury" (II: 129).

55. To an extent, at least in Mayhew's account, the Jewish community has, in the Board of Deputies, its own autonomous political body (II: 130).

footmen, and instead of entertaining violent political opinions, they appear to have no political opinions whatever"—with the more skilled labor of tailors' operatives. Among them, "there appeared to be a general bias towards the six points of the Charter"—precisely the position of the costermongers, that is—but they were also "extremely proud of their having turned out to a man . . . and become special constables for the maintenance of law and order on the day of the great Chartist demonstration." Mayhew continues, "As to which of these classes are the better members of the state, it is not for me to offer an opinion; I merely assert a social fact." But, of course, he does have an opinion, that "[t]he artisans of the metropolis are intelligent, and dissatisfied with their political position: the labourers of London appear to be the reverse." And the English costermongers, despite their position within Mayhew's scheme—marked as racially distinct and economically outmaneuvered by foreign competitors—share at least the dissatisfaction of their more skilled fellow workers. To that degree, they participate in the "political character and sentiments of the working classes," which Mayhew describes as "a distinctive feature of the age, and . . . a necessary consequence of the dawning intelligence of the mass" (III: 233). And to that degree at least, the culture of race could be overcome.

For neither costermonger nor, for that matter, skilled laborer does this dawning political intelligence constitute grounds for full citizenship. Chartism had, after all, failed, and the claim for universal manhood suffrage with it. Working-class political participation remained restricted by a property-based franchise. And insofar as full participatory citizenship remained linked to property qualifications, the vestiges of nomadism that thrived at the interstices of modern civilization were, even more fundamentally than the industrial laborers of the era, excluded from full membership. Their nomadism was a racial trait, and "those who have once adopted the savage and wandering mode of life, rarely abandon it" (I: 2). But because citizenship and political participation cannot be completely equated—because there is room for at least some claims of citizenship even for the disenfranchised—membership in the community can be construed as less monolithic in character. Like race in Mayhew's conception, it was not a simply binary relation, but a construction that allowed for degrees, for hierarchies of relatively complete or incomplete membership.

It is because, for Mayhew, the democratization of the age demanded the political participation of the worker that forms of combination, even among members of that class so different as to be seen as racially distinct, had such a central role in his agenda of reform.[56] It is because other even more

---

56. Himmelfarb, deriding Mayhew's suggestion for a Friendly Association as "hard to take seri-

distinct races had, in his xenophobic view, no such political instinct that they remained outside the pale, forever non-citizens, permanent foreigners. And it is from the ideological inscription of hierarchies of race and class in works such as Mayhew's text that we can trace both the rigidification of lines between (and even within) the English class system (in the language of race as class) and the even more solidly marked lines that kept Englishness white.

Works Cited

Barringer, Tim. "Images of Otherness and the Visual Production of Difference: Race and Labour in Illustrated Texts, 1850–1865." In *The Victorians and Race,* edited by Shearer West. 34–52. Brookfield, VT: Scolar Press, 1996.

Beier, A. L. "'Takin' It to the Street': Henry Mayhew and the Language of the Underclass in Mid-Nineteenth-Century London." In *Cast Out: Vagrancy and Homelessness in Global and Historical Perspective,* edited by A. L. Beier and Paul Ocobock. 88–116. Athens: Ohio University Press, 2008.

Brantlinger, Patrick, and Donald Ulin. "Policing Nomads: Discourse and Social Control in Early Victorian England." *Cultural Critique* 25 (1993): 33–63.

Cowling, Mary. *The Artist as Anthropologist: The Representation of Type and Character in Victorian Art.* Cambridge: Cambridge University Press, 1989.

Gallagher, Catherine. "The Body versus the Social Body in Malthus and Mayhew." In *The Making of the Modern Body: Sexuality and Society in the Nineteenth Century,* edited by Catherine Gallagher and Thomas Laqueur. 86–106. Berkeley: University of California, 1987.

Gilroy, Paul. *The Black Atlantic: Modernity and Double Consciousness.* Cambridge, MA: Harvard University Press, 1993.

Gilroy, Paul. "Cultural Studies and Ethnic Absolutism." In *Cultural Studies,* edited by Lawrence Grossberg, Cary Nelson, and Paula Treichler. 187–198. New York: Routledge, 1992.

Hansen, Adam. "Exhibiting Vagrancy, 1851: Victorian London and the 'Vagabond Savage.'" In *A Mighty Mass of Brick and Smoke: Victorian and Edwardian Representations of London,* edited by Lawrence Phillips. 61–84. Amsterdam and New York: Rodopi, 2007.

Himmelfarb, Gertrude. *The Idea of Poverty.* New York: Knopf, 1987.

Humpherys, Anne. *Travels into the Poor Man's Country: The Works of Henry Mayhew.* Athens: University of Georgia Press, 1977.

Jaffe, Audrey. *Scenes of Sympathy: Identity and Representation in Victorian Fiction.* Ithaca, NY: Cornell University Press, 2000.

Mayhew, Henry. *London Labour and the London Poor.* 4 vols. 1861–1862. Reprint, New York: Dover, 1968.

———. *The Morning Chronicle Survey of Labour and the Poor: The Metropolitan Districts.* 6 vols. Horsham, England: Caliban, 1980–1982.

———. *The Unknown Mayhew.* Edited by Eileen Yeo and E. P. Thompson. New York: Pantheon Books, 1971.

---

ously," misses the point the centrality of direct political participation in Mayhew's argument (see *Idea of Poverty,* 329).

————. *Voices of the Poor: Selections from the "Morning Chronicle" and "Labour and the Poor," 1849–1850.* Edited by Anne Humpherys. London: Routledge, 1971.

Mayhew, Henry, and John Binny. *Criminal Prisons of London.* London: Griffin, Bohn, 1862.

Prasch, Thomas. "Fixed Positions: Working-Class Subjects and Photographic Hegemony in Victorian Britain." PhD Dissertation, Indiana University, 1996.

————. "Photography and the Image of the London Poor." In *Victorian Urban Settings: Essays on the Nineteenth-Century City and Its Contexts,* edited by Debra N. Mancoff and D. J. Trela. 179–194. New York: Garland, 1996.

Rushdie, Salman. *Imaginary Homelands.* New York: Viking, 1991.

Stocking, George, Jr. *Victorian Anthropology.* New York: Free Press, 1987.

Thompson, E. P. "The Political Education of Henry Mayhew." *Victorian Studies* 11.1 (1967): 41–62.

Yeo, Eileen. "Mayhew as Social Investigator." In *Unknown Mayhew,* edited by Eileen Yeo and E. P. Thompson. 51–95. New York: Pantheon, 1971.

PART III

The Foreign Invasion

༄

To speak of a "foreign invasion" evokes the fearful consequences of outsiders breaking through the gate; invading against the will of those on the inside; corrupting the presumed purity of the protected center. No one welcomes the foreign invader. Indeed, the presence of the foreign is thought to exist at the peril of those deemed not foreign. The perception of an invasion, then, is more than a sign that the walls have been broken. It suggests that the body at the center will be overtaken or corrupted at the moment of contact. Depictions of these kinds of foreign invasions in Victorian culture frequently expressed fears—albeit irrational or subconscious—of cultural slaughter.

The essays in this section challenge and interrogate such xenophobic myths by focusing on the image of the invading foreigner. Imperialism, immigration, and a growing ease of travel altered the construction of English identity; in turn, writing throughout the century frequently pointed to cultural discomfort about the implications of the ways in which Englishness was reframed in light of these developments and ideologies. The following essays examine the kinds of xenophobic reactions triggered by the fear that if foreigners live in England, this must be a sign that an invasion has taken place or that English life is under siege. In some cases textual production sought to resolve the presumed problem of the other within. In other works authors or artists used the discourse of invasion to explore the sources or consequences of the fear itself or to suggest something about English insularity.

With these concerns in mind, this section begins with Heidi Kaufman's discussion of the challenge of defining the foreigner in George Eliot's *Daniel Deronda*. Delineating insiders from outsiders is a problem in this novel, Kaufman argues, and leads characters toward a form of xenophobic thinking that is distinct from other expressions of hatred in the novel, such as racism and anti-Semitism. Elizabeth Miller's essay follows with a discussion of the ways in which late-century literature about anarchism helped to bolster the image of the foreigner as a dangerous invader, capable of eroding Englishness as a racial-cultural category. Thus, the image of the invader-anarchist in literary culture became an outlet for the expression of xenophobic anxieties and anti-immigration sentiment. Yet, Victorian fears about the foreigner were not merely about the presence of the foreigner invading England; they were also, as Annemarie McAllister argues, "projections of insecurities and undeclared desires" of the English. In her essay McAllister examines the logic behind *Punch*'s campaign against Italian organ-grinders, and in the process shows what xenophobic expressions reveal about those who make them. Minna Vuohelainen argues that in addition to functioning as conduits for xenophobic expressions, the breakdown of language can achieve the same ends. In her discussion of Richard Marsh's *The Beetle* Vuohelainen demonstrates how silences or lost language work to expose the sense of chaos associated with the foreign invasion. In the final essay in this section, Thomas McLean shows that efforts in literary culture to affirm boundaries and ease English fears over immigration were often signs of deeper anxieties about mixed ancestry, or the illusion of racial and ethnic purity. Thus, McLean examines *Dracula* amidst the rise of immigration to London in the wake of the revolutions of 1848, at a moment when the difficulties of delineating peoples and races, or of knowing how to identify the so-called invading foreigner, took center stage in British literary culture.

Together, the following group of essays suggest that print culture was not just a showcase for the Victorian fascination with the foreigner; it was also a psychological outlet, or a forum in which to contest, question, or ease fears and phobias over invading foreigners. Yet, in the process of presenting the foreigner as a threat, popular narrative and visual texts frequently exposed the fact that pure English identity itself was a myth. Thus, this section recalls two central Victorian contexts in relation to the fear of the foreign invader—concern over a perceived demise of genuine Englishness, on the one hand, and the invasion of a pervasive strand of xenophobic rhetoric in print media, on the other.

10

Jewish Space and the English Foreigner in George Eliot's *Daniel Deronda*

⊙╬⊙

HEIDI KAUFMAN

In chapter 32 of George Eliot's *Daniel Deronda* (1876), the narrator describes the eponymous hero's wanderings through the Juden-gasse in Frankfurt—a space in which he is a foreigner.[1] Mesmerized by the "human types" he sees in the Jewish quarter and their connection with "past phases" of the Jewish "race,"[2] Deronda imagines Judaism as a two-sided creature, created from a beautiful, if idealized, religious heritage set against the ugliness of Jewish racial types. Upon entering a bookshop he notices "a deaf and grisly trades-man" who "apparently combining advantages of business with religion, and shoutingly proposed to him in Jew-dialect by a dingy man in a tall coat hanging from neck to heel, a bag in hand, and a broad low hat surmounting his chosen nose—who had no sooner disappeared than another dingy man of the same pattern issued from the backward glooms of the shop and also shouted in the same dialect" (366). Deronda's assumption is that all of the Jewish people in this bookstore are alike; and all are marked by their grisly nature, their tendency to shout, and their chosen noses. In contrast, when he arrives at the Synagogue a short while later Deronda observes

---

1. Eliot uses an antiquated spelling of the city, "Frankfort." In direct quotes I have used Eliot's spelling; in my discussion I use the modern spelling, Frankfurt.

2. George Eliot, *Daniel Deronda* (London: Penguin, 1995), 363. Subsequent references to this text will be cited parenthetically.

the chant of the *Chazan's* or Reader's grand wide-ranging voice with its passage
from monotony to sudden cries, the outburst of sweet boys' voices from the
little quire, the devotional swaying of men's bodies backwards and forwards,
the very commonness of the building and shabbiness of the scene where a
national faith, which had penetrated the thinking of half the world, and
moulded the splendid forms of that world's religion, was finding a remote,
obscure echo—all were blent for him as one expression of a binding history,
tragic and yet glorious. (367–368)

In this emotive haze Deronda perceives a glorious form of Judaism as having
capitulated tragically to the forces of vulgar modernity. Noteworthy in such
passages is Deronda's use of time and space to delineate Judaism's demise.
Thus, the common buildings of here and now are set against the echo of
a faith whose ancient beliefs and religious rituals have penetrated half the
world everywhere.

While observing the prayer rituals in the Synagogue, Deronda attempts to
avoid contact with a gazing stranger; the man, we learn later, is Joseph Kalonymos, the friend of Deronda's deceased grandfather. When the two finally
make awkward contact, the narrator explains, suddenly Deronda "felt a hand
on his arm, and turning with the rather unpleasant sensation which this
abrupt sort of claim is apt to bring, he saw close to him the white-bearded
face of that neighbour, who said to him in German, 'Excuse me, young
gentleman—allow me—what is your parentage—your mother's family—her
maiden name?'" (368). Rattled by the address, Deronda responds with "a
strongly resistant feeling: he was inclined to shake off hastily the touch on his
arm; but he managed to slip it away and said coldly, 'I am an Englishman'"
(368).

In this moment readers encounter the exposure and retreat of Deronda's
"resistant feeling." Yet, the context provides little clue as to what he resists. In
fact, even Deronda is unsure; for the narrator adds, "whether under a sense of
having made a mistake or of having been repulsed, Deronda was uncertain.
In his walk back to the hotel he tried to still any uneasiness on the subject
by reflecting that he could not have acted differently. How could he say that
he did not know the name of his mother's family to that total stranger?"
(368). Acting, it seems, offers Deronda a way of negotiating his space and
surroundings, and of keeping his distance from those he meets along the
way. Curiously, and ironically given the revelation of his Jewish ancestry
later in the novel, Deronda believes that his identity as an Englishman—a
foreigner and outsider in the Frankfurt Synagogue—will distance him from
associations with Kalonymos, the Jewish foreigner. Yet, in this moment read-

ers witness a host of intersecting anxieties about both the slipperiness of the designation "foreigner" and Deronda's fear of association with Jewish people. I suggest that in his rebuke and subsequent act Deronda expresses a form of xenophobic panic, born not just from the fear of contact with the Jew's body, but from anxiety about the Jew's ability to claim him, or to turn him into a foreign Jew.

I have paused on the details of Deronda's meanderings through the Judengasse to highlight one of the central problems raised by this text: how do we read Deronda's construction of Jewish foreignness in these scenes? Using a nostalgic lens, Deronda creates a glorious Jewish past; but he sets it against a discourse of Jewish racial decay and vulgarity. Jewish religious practices are thus emotionally stirring to Deronda, while Jewish bodies and behavior repulse him. Would we classify his fear and loathing of Jewish bodies as a sign of Victorian anti-Semitic discourse? Or does it fall within the scope of Victorian xenophobia? And from which fear or hatred does his version of an idealized, beautiful Jewish past derive?

Recent critical debates over this novel have been attentive to the ways in which its questions concerning Zionism, Jewish religious or racial particularity, and nation-building are mediated by discourses of modernity, realism, and imperialism. In many of these discussions configurations of national identity circle around Deronda's ultimate desire to secure a national and political existence to the Jewish people; or, alternately, on the parameters of Englishness, and the possibilities or limits of overwriting Jewish difference within the liberalizing discourse of the modern nation. Yet, most of these contexts identify "space" within a national, political, geographic, or domestic framework—such as England, empire, Palestine, or Offendene. Accordingly, home and homeland are thought to be coherent entities, or places on the map with boundary markers and bodies that share a sense of collective identity.

The following discussion examines space in a different light, by considering Jewish space as the location where foreigners like the Englishman Deronda make contact with those deemed foreign; or where the boundaries of insider and outsider are exposed as illusory. Deronda's response to the absence of boundaries is to divide Judaism into two time zones. Hence, he imagines a glorious Jewish past—a fantasy world—which he deems worthy of his love interest, Mirah Lapidoth; simultaneously, he locates his construction of ugly Jewish bodies in the present, as mostly detached from his construction of a glorious Jewish heritage. I do not read Deronda's nostalgic impulse as a form of philo-Semitism, nor do I see it as an expression of genuine interest in Jewish history; I suggest, rather, that his response is an outgrowth of xenophobic panic. If anti-Semitic discourse in this novel rests upon the belief that the terms, "Jew," "Christian," "foreigner," and "Englishman" are stable, distinct, separable categories, Deronda's xenophobia grows from his tacit sense that such rigid categorization is impossible.

The Difference That Different Hatred Makes

Deronda's travels into Jewish city spaces raise various problems in terms of defining the contours of racial, religious, and ethnic discourses in the novel. It is difficult to know where Deronda's anti-Semitism, anti-Judaism, philo-Semitism, and xenophobia begin and end. The following passage depicting Deronda's sojourn into East London helps to illustrate this complexity. Here Deronda's curiosity appears to be driven unreflectively by irrational assumptions about both Jewish people and foreigners:

> He was rather tired of the streets and had paused to hail a hansom cab which he saw coming, when his attention was caught by some fine old clasps in chased silver displayed in the window at his right hand. . . . [T]hen his eyes travelled over the other contents of the window, and he saw that the shop was that kind of pawnbroker's. . . . A placard in one corner announced—*Watches and Jewellery exchanged and repaired.* But his survey had been noticed from within, and a figure appeared at the door, looking round at him, and saying in a tone of cordial encouragement, 'Good day, sir.' The instant was enough for Deronda to see that the face, unmistakeably Jewish, belonged to a young man about thirty; and wincing from the shopkeeper's persuasiveness that would probably follow, he had no sooner returned the 'good day,' than he passed to the other side of the street and beckoned to the cabman to draw up there. From that station he saw the name over the shop-window—*Ezra Cohen.* (382)

Deronda's response to the shopkeeper—his wincing and scurrying across the street—recalls his earlier retreat from Kalonymos in the Frankfurt Synagogue. If this were a situation where Deronda feared physical contact with street Jews, he would refrain from traveling to the Juden-gasse or Whitechapel. Instead, he is drawn in and returns repeatedly, each time with curiosity and trepidation. And yet, it is not until Deronda has passed to the other side of the street, safe from the "threat" of the Jewish shop-keeper, that he reads the sign above the shop door. At this moment he learns that Mirah Lapidoth's history might be tied in some way to the man from whom he has just staged his escape.

Rajani Sudan has argued persuasively that in the Romantic era xenophobia operates as a "psychological hinge between imperialism and nationalism."[3] She adds, "The same insecurities defining the subaltern space for the British also delineate their own domestic space. Thus, from a British standpoint, what connects the 'home' country, the domestic habitat (in the sense of native) to its fantasy of the East . . . also subjects the domestic to a need for continual recontainment."[4] The need or desire for such recontainment appears in *Daniel Deronda* every time Deronda tries to distinguish himself from the foreigners he meets on the street. Moreover, his forays into East London are an occasion for delineating the parameters of his home or national space. Located in the heart of the metropolis, but containing a foreign element, Jewish Whitechapel is intrinsically dubious for Deronda; for it doubles as home and other, an extension of and separable from the rest of London. Robert Wistrich explains that "[v]irtually every culture exhibits some kind of desire to distinguish itself from others, to assert and maintain its identity, to draw boundaries between 'us' and 'them.' At what point" Wistrich wonders, "does 'normal' ethnocentrism turn into xenophobia, racism, or antisemitism?"[5] This is precisely the problem we face when we look at Deronda's strange behavior as a foreigner in a different nation (Frankfurt's Juden-gasse) and in a different part of his own nation (Whitechapel). It seems that his status as an outsider in Jewish city space is the very thing he holds in common with the foreigners he meets in those spaces.

According to the *OED,* when it first appeared in 1909 the term "xenophobia" meant "a deep antipathy to foreigners."[6] Yet the meaning is complicated in the Victorian period in part because of the difficulty of determining the foreigners from the insiders. Indeed, the term "foreigner" is almost meaningless in a novel such as *Daniel Deronda* where so many characters belong to one place, travel to others, or are seen to be interlopers in the social worlds they've penetrated. Like "xenophobia," the word "anti-Semitism" emerged just a few years after the publication of this novel. Gavin Langmuir explains that this word

> was invented about 1873 by Wilhelm Marr to describe the policy toward Jews based on 'racism' that he and others advocated. . . . It proclaimed that humans were divided into clearly distinguishable races and that the intellectual, moral, and social conduct and potential of the members of these races were biologi-

---

3. Rajani Sudan, *Fair Exotics: Xenophobic Subjects in English Literature, 1720–1850* (Philadelphia: University of Pennsylvania Press, 2002), 15.

4. Sudan, *Fair Exotics,* 17.

5. Robert S. Wistrich, "Introduction: The Devil, The Jews, and Hatred of the 'Other,'" in *Demonizing the Other: Antisemitism, Racism, and Xenophobia,* 2.

6. *OED* Online, s.v. "xenophobia," http://www.oed.com/view/Entry/230996?redirectedFrom =xenophobia. Accessed June 19, 2011.

254 ~~~~ *Part III · Chapter 10*

cally determined. As elaborated in the Aryan myth, it reasoned that Jews were a race and that, not only were they, like other races, inferior to the Aryan race, but also that Jews were the most dangerous of those inferior races.[7]

In Marr's view "anti-Semitism" was a concept rooted in the logic of distinguishable body types and biological makeup that determined human behavior. Yet, as scores of scholars have attested, forms of anti-Semitism flourished long before 1873. There is often a delay between belief systems and the invention of words to define them. In fact, even the word "racism" was slow to be coined despite its long history. David Theo Goldberg explains,

> Terminologically, the word 'racism' was first used in English by Ruth Benedict in the 1940s. Benedict, in turn, was influenced by the first use of 'racisme' in France in the title of a book published in 1938. The use and meanings of both terms were strongly influenced by the wartime experience of anti-Semitism. 'Racialism,' it is true, was used in the late nineteenth century. However, racist conditions clearly predate by a considerable time the emergence of a word in any language to refer to them: the creation of words often emerges more slowly than the expressions that inspire need for them.[8]

We may read Deronda's repulsion toward modern Jewish bodies as a sign of the very phenomena that came to be categorized by the words "racism" or "anti-Semitism." Yet, in Deronda's rebuke of Kalonymos, and the subsequent depictions of his failed efforts to achieve distance from Jewish foreigners, Eliot expresses concerns about the challenge of making such delineations; for clearly, when Deronda is in the Juden-gasse or in Whitechapel he is a foreigner among foreigners, not because he is a Jew, but because he is an Englishman.

Eliot's interlacing of two perspectives of the East End—Deronda's and Jewish East Enders's—exposes some of the ways in which perspective serves as a breeding ground for xenophobia. Certainly the discourse of the other has had a long history, and was intensified by the prominence of nationalist discourse in this period. However, the literature of London, and in particular depictions of places like the East End, helped to create both stringent turf boundaries and geographically demarcated hierarchies. As wealthy English

---

7. Gavin I. Langmuir, *Toward a Definition of Antisemitism* (Berkeley: University of California Press, 1990), 311. Langmuir adds, "the word 'antisemitism' has been given many meanings. Since there is in fact no such thing as 'Semitism,' save when referring to a language, the term is literally meaningless when applied to Jews, which is why I refuse to hyphenate 'antisemitism'." Gavin Langmuir, *Toward a Definition of Antisemitism*, 16.

8. David Theo Goldberg, *Racist Culture: Philosophy and the Politics of Meaning* (Malden, MA: Wiley-Blackwell, 1993), 98.

people, figures just like Deronda, recorded their travels to places like East London, they participated in a long history of peripatetic accounts depicting urban landscapes they deemed foreign, dangerous, and un-English. But they did so as outsiders, as foreigners themselves, who lurked and observed only to return later to the safe world of their homes, far from the threat of foreigners—or so they believed. Their narrative and visual accounts of this space, which grew in number and popularity over the course of the century, attempted to submerge or ignore the perspectives and prejudices of their so-called privileged positions as outsiders. Like the description of Deronda's wanderings, their reflections of the East End, created through the stark realism of photography, social journalism, and modernist sensibilities, had only the appearance of objectivity and authority.

Eliot's depictions of Jewish city space are unique in that they foreground the challenge of seeing, or of reading a culture as a foreigner or interloper. The social drama in *Daniel Deronda* thus emerges in part from Eliot's depictions not of a sensationalized East End or of a dirty Juden-gasse, but of the bumbling flaneur, Deronda—the foreign interloper who panics every time his identity becomes uncertain in the face of other foreign figures. Clearly, to be foreign holds a different meaning than simply that of coming from a different place; it carries the sting of outcast and interloper, of someone who has entered or penetrated the inner sphere and must be kept at some distance to preserve the interests or identities of genuine insiders. While Deronda expresses fear of the foreigner, we are faced with the ironic challenge of positioning Deronda—the character who turns out to be Jewish and whose family comes from Europe—as the English insider. And when he divides Judaism into a Janus-faced entity, created by his nostalgic and racializing gazes, we detect a host of resulting problems in need of clarification.

Strange(r) Wanderings

In his recent study of late-century East End discourse, Nils Roemer argues that outsiders like Deronda who ventured into and described the East End held "a privileged viewing position." He adds that "their portrayals inevitably sensationalized the practice of exploring these unknown territories" and in particular, the "immigrant subcultures" living there.[9] According to Judith Walkowitz, "[a]s early as the 1840s, these urban explorers adapted the language of imperialism to evoke features of their own cities. Imperialist rhetoric

---

9. Nils Roemer, "London and the East End as Spectacles of Urban Tourism," *Jewish Quarterly Review* 99.3 (2009): 419–420.

transformed the unexplored territory of the London poor into an alien place, both exciting and dangerous."[10] Yet, in *Daniel Deronda* Eliot's depiction of Jewish city spaces turns this so-called "privileged" lens on its head. Instead of presenting Jewish urban space unquestioningly, Eliot makes readers aware of how Deronda's vision and perspective shape what he sees and understands. Thus, the emphasis in these scenes is not on the space itself, but on Deronda's flawed, and at times comical, efforts to interpret that space. In the end, the territory Deronda perceives as "unknown" is exposed as one that is both very well known among its inhabitants, and foreign only to foreigners like Deronda.

Deronda's desire to venture into the Juden-gasse and East London is nothing unusual in Victorian England. Seth Koven's work on Victorian slumming points to the popularity of such travels, and of the important ways that knowledge of city spaces was produced by those who yearned to see how the other half lived, or to better represent current social problems.[11] Writers and artists popularized this trend by the early decades of the century. According to Deborah Epstein Nord, "[i]n the literature of the nineteenth-century city, the figure of the observer—the rambler, the stroller, the spectator, the flaneur—is a man. . . . He begins as a visible character in the urban sketch, a signature—like 'Boz' or 'Spec'—who is both authorial persona and fictional actor on the city streets, and ends as the invisible but all-seeing novelist, effacing all of himself but his voice in the evocation of an urban panorama."[12] Moving through urban space invisibly, interpreting and inventing along the way, the flaneur becomes part of the urban scene and is, in a sense, overtaken by the space he narrates and invents. According to Walter Benjamin, the "Dialectic of flanerie" is, "on the one side, the man who feels himself viewed by all and sundry as a true suspect and, on the other side, the man who is utterly undiscoverable, the hidden man."[13] Yet, Walkowitz adds that "the public landscape of the privileged urban flaneur of the period had become an unstable construct: threatened internally by contradictions and tensions and constantly challenged from without by social forces that pressed these dominant representations to be reworked, shorn up, reconstructed."[14]

Eliot's depiction of Deronda's strange wanderings might be read in light of this unstable shift in the figure of the flaneur. In this case we see both

---

10. Judith R. Walkowitz, *City of Dreadful Delight: Narratives of Sexual Danger in Late-Victorian London* (Chicago: University of Chicago Press, 1992), 18.

11. Seth Koven, *Slumming: Sexual and Social Politics in Victorian London* (Princeton, NJ: Princeton University Press, 2006).

12. Deborah Epstein Nord, *Walking the Victorian Streets: Women, Representation, and the City* (Ithaca, NY: Cornell University Press, 1995), 1.

13. Walter Benjamin, *The Arcades Project* (Cambridge, MA: Belknap Press, 1999), 420.

14. Walkowitz, *City of Dreadful Delight*, 17–18.

Deronda's struggle to record the city from a detached position as well as his interior mind working to distance himself from associations with Jewish people. In both areas he fails, yet it is in these moments where Eliot politicizes perception itself, and the presumed privilege and objectivity of the observer. Ultimately she dismantles the line delineating the insider from the outsider; for Deronda calls himself an Englishman, but he is clearly uncomfortable in an area of London, in the metropolitan center of his "own" nation. He is thus at once the foreigner and the Englishman, identities that are only further conflicted when he learns he is Jewish. In these plot twists Eliot presents belonging both as a profound challenge of defining oneself amidst shifting geographies and irrational fears, and as a struggle that emerges through the exchanges that take place on the city stage.

Although it is tempting to read Deronda's walks through Jewish city spaces as part of a longer tradition of the flaneur, I would suggest that something else is going on in these moments. Deronda, in fact, bungles every effort at remaining ubiquitous and invisible. He stands out, is caught, touched, questioned, and in response he is described as acting, wincing, retreating, and worrying that he has erred in his responses to the Jewish people he meets. His behavior seems to be governed by his neurotic fears of Jewish foreigners. As long as he keeps his distance or remains detached, he reasons, the East End cannot threaten to affect him. And as we shall see, he is completely wrong on this point. The Victorian interplay of desire for and distance from the other was driven by more than just a curious interest in the sensational. Amanda Anderson notes, for example, that the "distinctly modern practices of detachment, a preoccupation characterized by ambivalence and uncertainty about what the significance and consequences of such practices might be" was uniquely Victorian.[15] The moments where Deronda examines his own behavior, wondering why he acted in a particular way or observing his failure to gain distance from the shop-keeper, expose his desire for forms of distance and detachment that he never achieves. In the process we see him trapped between his longing for knowledge of Jewish culture and his repulsion for what he encounters along the way.

Just before meeting Kalonymos, the narrator describes Deronda sauntering through Frankfurt's Jewish quarter on a warm summer evening in search of a Synagogue. Innocently, Deronda stops in a book shop to ask "the exact time of service" at the Orthodox Synagogue (366). Evening Shabbat services begin at sunset—a fact Eliot would have known at the point when she wrote this novel.[16] Surely his accent or clothing mark him as a foreigner, but his

---

15. Amanda Anderson, *The Powers of Distance: Cosmopolitanism and the Cultivation of Detachment* (Princeton, NJ: Princeton University Press, 2001), 3.

16. In his biography Gordon S. Haight notes that in 1873, "Marian now began a closer study

need to ask the time of Synagogue services signals to his audience—the Jewish people in the bookshop—that he is not only a foreigner, but that he is unfamiliar with Jewish religious practices. In response, a "precocious Jewish youth" proceeds to overcharge Deronda for a book, and then leads him to the wrong Synagogue, suspecting that a non-Jew would never know the difference anyway.

As he moves through the streets Deronda weighs his impressions against his prejudices. For example, he is fully aware that he views the Jewish people in the Juden-gasse with "guile"; and he admits that he becomes "more conscious that he was falling into unfairness and ridiculous exaggeration" (367). Guiltily, he overpays the child who leads him to the Synagogue. Moving through the streets, in and out of buildings, Deronda very obviously fails to penetrate this foreign Jewish world. Even as Deronda observes foreign space and people, he begins to scrutinize the limits of his own vision and knowledge.

In the very next chapter Deronda bumbles his way into the East End, or "those parts of London which are most inhabited by common Jews" in his search for Mirah's family (380). The narrator adds, "he walked to the synagogues at times of service, he looked into shops, he observed faces:—a process not very promising of particular discovery. Why did he not address himself to an influential Rabbi or other member of a Jewish community, to consult on the chances of finding a mother named Cohen, with a son named Ezra, and a lost daughter named Mirah?" (380). The narrator raises a good question. After all, what are the odds of his finding a particular person named Cohen in a predominantly Jewish neighborhood? This futile search seems to

---

of Jewish matters. They were reading aloud Erckmann-Chatrian's *Le Juif polonaise* and Kompert's *Geschichte einer Gasse*. At Frankfurt on the way home Lewes 'bought books—books on *Jewish subjects* for Polly's novel—and made inquiries.' They stayed till Friday so that she could go to the synagogue at sunset" (just like Deronda in Chapter 32, where the narrator details his interactions in the bookshop). Gordon S. Haight, *George Eliot: A Biography* (Oxford: Oxford University Press, 1968), 472. According to Gerlinde Röder-Bolton, "Marian and Lewes passed through Frankfurt again in 1858 and probably in 1867, but there is no evidence that they went to the *Judengasse* on these occasions. During the early 1870s, they again visited Frankfurt while staying in nearby Bad Homburg. In October 1872, they came to Frankfurt to buy books. . . . They stayed in Frankfurt for five days in August 1873 to attend services at the synagogue." Gerlinde Röder-Bolton, *George Eliot in Germany, 1854–55* (Burlington, VT: Ashgate, 2006), 36, note 30. Röder-Bolton adds, "Jews had been known to live in Frankfurt since at least the middle of the twelfth century. When the *Code Napoléon* gave them equal rights in 1811, some Jews took on citizenship and wealthier Jews left the *Judengasse* and moved to the better residential areas north of the *Zeil* or outside the former city walls. A census of 1858 shows that only some 15 percent of Frankfurt Jews still lived in the old ghetto. By the time of Marian and Lewes's visit, the *Judengasse* was occupied mainly by poorer Jews and Jewish immigrants from Eastern Europe. The old synagogue was pulled down that year and replaced by a large new synagogue which was designed to accommodate the requirements of the Jewish Reform Movement." Gerlinde Röder-Bolton, *George Eliot in Germany, 1854–55*, 28.

be governed by his fear of success. He keeps his distance, and obfuscates, as the narrator tells us, because of a "suppressed consciousness that a not unlike possibility of collision might lie hidden in his own lot" (381). In short, self-discovery will be the unwanted consequence of finding Mirah's family.

Throughout this search Deronda returns to his fantasy of construing modern Judaism as a sad reminder of its former glory. Although sympathetic, the narrator's tone pokes light fun at Deronda's absurd, overwrought nostalgia:

> Lying dreamily in a boat, imagining one's self in quest of a beautiful maiden's relatives in Cordova elbowed by Jews in the time of Ibn-Gebirol, all the physical incidents can be borne without shock. Or if the scenery of St Mary Axe and Whitechapel were imaginatively transported to the borders of the Rhine at the end of the eleventh century, when in the ears listening for the signals of the Messiah, the Hep! Hep! Hep! of the Crusaders came like the bay of bloodhounds; and in the presence of those devilish missionaries with sword and firebrand the crouching figure of the reviled Jew turned round erect, heroic, flashing with sublime constancy in the face of torture and death—what would the dingy shops and unbeautiful faces signify to the thrill of contemplative emotion? But the fervour of sympathy with which we contemplate a grandiose martyrdom is feeble compared with the enthusiasm that keeps unslacked where there is no danger, no challenge—nothing but impartial midday falling on commonplace, perhaps half-repulsive, objects which are really the beloved ideas made flesh. (380–381)

Clearly, Deronda's meanderings in Whitechapel fail to achieve detachment. He does not gaze at Jews from a hidden distance; rather, he imagines himself inserted into the scene from another time. As the narrator explains, he is "imagining one's self in quest of a beautiful maiden's relatives." Longingly, in his mind, Deronda aligns himself with the people he hopes to find, and he fantasizes that he has removed both parties—himself and the object of his search—into another time zone. He fails, of course, and remains perched in the present amidst the faces he detests. But in his failure we see his interest in distancing himself from the Jews he has racialized, and his alignment of himself with the noble Jews from Mirah's family with whom he is reunited in his fantasy construction of the Crusades.

On his next visit to Whitechapel Deronda feels "an inward reluctance" (384) and decides as an afterthought not to find out more about Ezra Cohen. Dodging the pawnshop, he enters a bookshop where Deronda finds a Jewish man reading "yesterday's *Times*" (386) dressed in "threadbare clothing" and with a "dead yellowish flatness of the flesh, something like an old ivory carving" (385). The passage continues in similar vein, contorting the man in the shop as the embodiment of Judaism's twin times:

> the thought glanced through Deronda that precisely such a physiognomy as that might possibly have been seen in a prophet of the Exile, or in some New Hebrew poet of the mediaeval time. It was a finely typical Jewish face, wrought into intensity of expression apparently by a strenuous eager experience in which all the satisfaction had been indirect and far off, and perhaps by some bodily suffering also, which involved that absence of ease in the present. . . . It might never have been a particularly handsome face, but it must always have been forcible; and now with its dark, far-off gaze, and yellow pallor in relief on the gloom of the backward shop, one might have imagined one's self coming upon it in some past prison of the Inquisition, which a mob had suddenly burst open; while the look fixed on an incidental customer seemed eager and questioning enough to have been turned on one who might have been a messenger either of delivery or of death. (386)

Readers learn later that this Jewish man "with a typical Jewish face" and his "far-off gaze" is Mordecai, Mirah's brother. For the moment, however, Deronda knows nothing about this man. He imagines the shop as occupying the period of the Inquisition. Again, Deronda distances himself from the struggling, unbeautiful Jewish man while simultaneously inserting himself in his own nostalgic reconstruction of a Jewish past. To say that Deronda draws from an anti-Semitic discourse in this and other passages in order to separate himself from the foreigner does not account for the interior drama playing out in his mind. Here and in other places Deronda longs for sympathetic alignment with the plight of the foreigner. Yet he is repulsed by the vision of the Jewish body sitting before him. If the smack of his related anti-Semitism did not reveal itself so fully, we might miss seeing how his fear of alignment with the foreign Jews, his xenophobia, inspires his tendency toward nostalgic reverie.

The subsequent turn of events awakens the Walter Mitty–like Deronda from his hallucination. Unable to find a price for the book, but curious about Deronda's interest in Jewish history, Mordecai addresses him directly:

> the strange Jew rose from his sitting posture, and Deronda felt a thin hand pressing his arm tightly, while a hoarse, excited voice, not much above a loud whisper, said—'You are perhaps of our race?' Deronda coloured deeply, not liking the grasp, and then answered with a slight shake of the head, 'No.' The grasp was relaxed, the hand withdrawn, the eagerness of the face collapsed into uninterested melancholy, as if some possessing spirit which had leaped

into the eyes and gestures had sunk back again to the inmost recesses of the frame. (387)

This conversation is a near replay of the one in Frankfurt, only with a twist. In Frankfurt Deronda instantaneously detached himself from Kalonymos's touch. Although disturbed by Kalonymos's efforts to claim him, Deronda moves away and ruminates on his insecurities about his unknown past. Here, however, in the East End bookshop Deronda feels shame when he is rebuked by Mordecai. Immediately following this exchange, the narrator offers a forward-looking moment: "The effect of this change on Deronda—he afterwards smiled when he recalled it—was oddly embarrassing and humiliating, as if some high dignitary had found him deficient and given him his *congé*" (387). Deronda's strange reaction suggests that some transition has taken place in his thinking from the earlier Frankfurt scene. He has not merely construed Jewish people as racial others; he has also aligned himself with their plight. Mordecai's dismissal of Deronda awakens the would-be flaneur from his dream-state. And once he is cast off, Deronda can no longer transfer the modern Jewish world into another time zone. He is thereafter trapped in the present where, in his mind, Jews are little more than ugly and vulgar. The narrator leads us toward hope, however, rather than exasperating annoyance at Deronda's misjudgment of foreigners. Mention of his later embarrassment helps to frame this passage as humorous rather than odious.

Deronda is an outsider for dozens of reasons, and yet still he burrows his way into the East End, into their shops, into their economies, and finally, into their homes. His goal is to find their secrets, to connect Mirah to their world, but to do so in a way that will not shame *her*, as he sees it, for *their* shortcomings. Thus he penetrates with ease and trepidation, initially as the flaneur in search of knowledge of an unknown world. To insure that his motives remain undetected, Deronda relies on pretense and acting. First, he feigns interest in the silver clasps from the pawnbroker's window to gain entry into Ezra Cohen's shop. Next, he flatters the shop-keeper's mother, hoping to discern if she is Mirah's mother. And finally, under the pretense of needing to sell a diamond, he finagles his way into their home for Shabbat dinner. In short, Deronda-the-interloper gains entry into the Jewish East End by a series of acts that he believes will allow him to pass in their world. When he arrives at five o'clock to find the shop closed and the Christian servant waiting to let him in, the narrator describes Deronda as looking "surprised at the prettiness of the scene" (394). The house is located behind the shop, and although old, "the large room he now entered was gloomy by daylight" he surmises, but is now "agreeably lit by a fine old brass lamp with seven oil-lights hanging above the snow-white cloth spread on the central table"

(394). Observing the care taken to make the home beautiful for Shabbat, and the well-dressed family, Deronda "was almost ashamed of the supercilious dislike these happy-looking creatures had raised in him by daylight" (394). The narrator continues, "Nothing could be more cordial than the greeting he received, and both mother and grandmother seemed to gather more dignity from being seen on the private hearth, showing hospitality" (394).

Prior to this scene, Deronda found Cohen to be "the most unpoetic Jew he had ever met with in books or life" (391). He faults Cohen by noting that "his phraseology was as little as possible like that of the Old Testament; and no shadow of a Suffering Race distinguished his vulgarity of soul from that of a prosperous pink-and-white huckster of the purest English lineage" (391). But on Shabbat, Deronda's impressions turn. In the moment when Cohen enters the room to say the blessing, "Deronda thought that this pawnbroker proud of his vocation was not utterly prosaic" (396). As Deronda tries to take in the various signs and conversations, the family turns to the covered bread on the table, and as Cohen washes his hands in preparation to break the bread, he yells "Mordecai!" (396). In keeping with his earlier blunders, and in one of the lighter moments in the novel, Deronda wonders, "Can this be part of the religious ceremony?" (396). When a man named Mordecai enters the room, Deronda realizes his error. Deronda may well narrate what he sees in Jewish space, but his interpretations, as we see here, are consistently inaccurate because of what he fails to understand about the space and social world he observes.

As Deronda moves through foreign territory—everywhere from streets to shops, and Synagogues to homes—he is positioned as the foreign inter-loper, entering spaces to which he does not belong. And as he wrestles with his desire to reject Jewish people on the grounds of their vulgarity, Deronda similarly aligns himself with Jewish foreigners. Such passages open up dif-ficult questions concerning Victorian xenophobia and anti-Semitism; about the tendency of wealthy West-enders to understand the world they represent in their slumming narratives or depictions of the all-seeing flaneur; and the problem of categorizing anyone as a foreigner. Surely wanderers may cross lines and enter social spaces, but what they understand or see depends upon their knowledge of the places they visit. In this sense, we might read Deron-da's missteps not as a sign of the hopeless obtuseness of his character, per se, but as a larger statement about print culture's proclivity for marketing the East End from the perspective of a presumed, all-seeing, West End eye.

Paul Newland has argued that "a powerful spatial idea of the East End can be understood to function as a product of the formation and rise of a dis-tinctly English bourgeois self-image."[17] Indeed, Eliot is unusual in granting

---

17. Paul Newland, *The Cultural Construction of London's East End: Urban Iconography, Modernity*

us access to constructions of the East End emanating from acts performed by insiders and outsiders alike. Their differing perspectives, however, change everything about the way readers see Jewish space. While Deronda believes his act will penetrate Jewish space, will grant him access to a foreign world, the insiders in that world unwittingly call him out. More than just comparing the two perspectives on Judaism, in these scenes Eliot presents Jewish space as a product of exchanges between insiders and outsiders. Deronda explores the East End, but he also acts within it. At the same time, he is the audience and an actor in the Jewish dramas that take place before him, which, in turn, are shaped by his presence. Still, his vision is understandably limited. He is at the beginning of a quest to understand his and Mirah's pasts. And so he clings in vain to a fantasy world in his failed effort to remain detached, invisible, and objective.

Conclusion: Nostalgia and Xenophobia

Xenophobia may appear to be simply a reaction of fear or loathing directed toward outsiders, but in *Daniel Deronda* we find a related, reverse problem. Deronda's xenophobia emerges when he imagines how "vulgar Jews" will off-set his perception of Mirah's perfection. Yet, his fear of foreigners intensifies when Kalonymos touches his arm, and Deronda fears that the dingy men he sees in the Juden-gasse may also reflect upon his own identity. Initially this fear provokes him to create an imagined past that will vindicate Mirah's affiliation with Judaism. In effect, he recoups Judaism from its modern form by imaginatively pushing it into a nostalgic, memory space, where it holds a beauty that will allow him to love Mirah and ultimately himself when he discovers his own Jewish ancestry. Thus, instead of loving Mirah because of her association with modern Judaism, Deronda desires her because of her affiliation with what he imagines to be a purer, better, more perfect form of Judaism. His hatred of the ugliness of modern Jews is the result of anti-Semitic prejudice—or of thinking that poverty or modern urban landscapes are signs of Jewish racial degeneracy. Deronda's xenophobia, in contrast, stems from a fear of *alignment* with foreigners. Thus, Deronda's retreats from Kalonymos and Mordecai stem from his fear that he is just like them—a foreigner trying to pass in someone else's world.

According to Svetlana Boym, "At first glance, nostalgia is a longing for a place, but actually it is a yearning for a different time."[18] She adds, "The

---

and the Spatialisation of Englishness (New York: Rodopi, 2008), 20.

18. Svetlana Boym, *The Future of Nostalgia* (New York: Basic Books, 2001), xv. For excellent, related discussions of nostalgia in nineteenth-century culture, see Linda M. Austin, *Nostalgia in*

nostalgic desires to obliterate history and turn it into private or collective mythology, to revisit time like space, refusing to surrender to the irreversibility of time that plagues the human condition."[19] Nicholas Dames adds that "some form of 'nostalgia' has always been with us, . . . it is the nineteenth-century novel that lifts it into the light of art and, starting with Austen's fiction, gives it a distinct cultural purpose: the amelioration or cancellation of the past. The nostalgic moment is the sign of a culture freed from its past, freed from consequences and resonances, prepared for the perfections of the future."[20] However, unlike the novelists Dames recalls, Eliot evokes nostalgia for the purpose of highlighting the insecurities that inspire it. In her made-up past, or what she calls in her opening epigraph to the novel "the make-believe of a beginning," readers encounter a re-creation not just of the events that led to the future, but a re-conceptualization of the way a version of the past might be used to secure boundaries (7). The novel's Zionist projection might even be read as a final stage of that nostalgic impulse, what Dames terms the reach toward "the perfections of the future."[21] In this way, the novel's ending leads us to consider the slippage in Deronda's mind between different moments in time and the uncertain boundaries delineating spaces and peoples.

Irene Tucker has suggested that "George Eliot intends her novel as . . . an affirmation—indeed, a celebration—of the power of geographical locale to shape the most intimate subjective contours of its inhabitants."[22] Deronda's forays into such geographies, or into Jewish city spaces, combined with his growing awareness of Jewish performances taking place there, lead him to see his interpretive missteps. What he understands initially is the cant of epithets and the signs of anti-Semitism's over-determined and offensive racializing lens. Yet, what he learns to see instead, over the course of many chapters, are the limits of that vision. Eliot suggests in the process that Jewish space is no different from other kinds of spaces; for all space is uniquely understood by those who live within it. And those who visit can learn, and will grow once they abandon the divisions between "us" and "them" or once they begin to

---

Translation, 1780–1917 (Charlottesville: University of Virginia Press, 2007); Ann C. Colley, *Nostalgia and Recollection in Victorian Culture* (New York: St. Martin's Press, 1998); and Tamara S. Wagner, *Longing: Narratives of Nostalgia in the British Novel, 1740–1890* (Lewisburg, PA: Bucknell University Press, 2004). Also very important is Susan Stewart, *On Longing: Narratives of the Miniature, the Gigantic, the Souvenir, the Collection* (Durham, NC: Duke University Press, 1993).

19. Boym, *The Future of Nostalgia*, xv.

20. Nicholas Dames, *Amnesiac Selves: Nostalgia, Forgetting, and British Fiction, 1810–1870* (New York: Oxford University Press, 2001), 6.

21. Dames, *Amnesiac Selves*, 6.

22. Irene Tucker, *A Probable State: The Novel, the Contract, and the Jews* (Chicago: University of Chicago Press, 2000), 81.

see how foreignness has less to do with a particular group of people, than with an individual's identity within the context of his or her environment.

Deronda's nostalgic lens, or his invention of a long lost noble Jewish culture, is thus a creation manifested by his xenophobic panic. Uncertainty about his own identity might then be read as a key part of his desire to turn to the past. I have tried to suggest that it also stems from his bonds with other foreigners, with his sense that when he enters Jewish space he gazes not only at foreigners, but at those with whom he shares a common identity *because* of that foreignness. One of Eliot's achievements in the novel is to complicate issues of belonging, to lead us to see how every character in the text is, in one way or another, a foreigner. In the end, we are left with a vision of xenophobia that grows from an inability to reconcile what characters cannot control about their own identities, and the panic they experience upon learning that other people and other pasts have some power to (re)define them.

Works Cited

Anderson, Amanda. *The Powers of Distance: Cosmopolitanism and the Cultivation of Detachment.* Princeton, NJ: Princeton University Press, 2001.

Austin, Linda M. *Nostalgia in Translation, 1780–1917.* Charlottesville: University of Virginia Press, 2007.

Benjamin, Walter. *The Arcades Project.* Translated by Howard Eiland and Kevin McLaughlin. Prepared on the basis of the German volume edited by Rolf Tiedmann. Cambridge, MA: Belknap Press of Harvard University Press, 1999.

Boym, Svetlana. *The Future of Nostalgia.* New York: Basic Books, 2001.

Colley, Ann C. *Nostalgia and Recollection in Victorian Culture.* New York: St. Martin's Press, 1998.

Dames, Nicholas. *Amnesiac Selves: Nostalgia, Forgetting, and British Fiction, 1810–1870.* New York: Oxford University Press, 2001.

Eliot, George. *Daniel Deronda.* Edited by Terrence Cave. London: Penguin, 1995.

Goldberg, David Theo. *Racist Culture: Philosophy and the Politics of Meaning.* Malden, MA: Wiley Blackwell, 1993.

Haight, Gordon S. *George Eliot: A Biography.* Oxford: Oxford University Press, 1968.

Koven, Seth. *Slumming: Sexual and Social Politics in Victorian London.* Princeton, NJ: Princeton University Press, 2006.

Langmuir, Gavin I. *Toward a Definition of Antisemitism.* Berkeley: University of California Press, 1990.

Newland, Paul. *The Cultural Construction of London's East End: Urban Iconography, Modernity and the Spatialisation of Englishness.* New York: Rodopi, 2008.

Nord, Deborah Epstein. *Walking the Victorian Streets: Women, Representation, and the City.* Ithaca, NY: Cornell University Press, 1995.

Röder-Bolton, Gerlinde. *George Eliot in Germany, 1854–55.* Burlington, VT: Ashgate, 2006.

Roemer, Nils. "London and the East End as Spectacles of Urban Tourism." *Jewish Quarterly Review* 99.3 (2009): 416–434.

Stewart, Susan. *On Longing: Narratives of the Miniature, the Gigantic, the Souvenir, the Collection*. Durham, NC: Duke University Press, 1993.

Sudan, Rajani. *Fair Exotics: Xenophobic Subjects in English Literature, 1720–1850*. Philadelphia: University of Pennsylvania Press, 2002.

Tucker, Irene. *A Probable State: The Novel, the Contract, and the Jews*. Chicago: University of Chicago Press, 2000.

Wagner, Tamara S. *Longing: Narratives of Nostalgia in the British Novel, 1740–1890*. Lewisburg, PA: Bucknell University Press, 2004.

Walkowitz, Judith R. *City of Dreadful Delight: Narratives of Sexual Danger in Late-Victorian London*. Foreword by Catherine R. Stimpson. Chicago: University of Chicago Press, 1992.

Wistrich, Robert S. "Introduction: The Devil, The Jews, and Hatred of the 'Other.'" In *Demonizing the Other: Antisemitism, Racism, and Xenophobia*, edited and introduced by Robert S. Wistrich. 1–16. Amsterdam: Harwood Academic Publishers, 1999.

11

Exile London

Anarchism, Immigration, and Xenophobia in Late-Victorian Literature

❧

ELIZABETH CAROLYN MILLER

In late-Victorian Britain the literary figure of the anarchist embodied a range of social, cultural, and racial stereotypes about European immigrants. Literary portrayals of anarchist exiles in 1880s and 1890s London were strikingly common, and in writing by H. G. Wells, Arthur Conan Doyle, Joseph Conrad, and many other authors, nativist apprehension and xenophobia bleed into depictions of London anarchism. At this time anarchism constituted a key faction of radical British politics, and anarchist philosophy had seriously influenced such major writers as William Morris, George Bernard Shaw, and Oscar Wilde.[1] Anarchism could be said to represent a genuine threat to "Englishness" in that it actively opposed the nation state as a political and social formation; as we will see, however, literary accounts of this genuine anarchist threat to Englishness are tinged with xenophobic fears about the dilution of English national identity by way of immigration. The political danger and security risk anarchism appeared to pose was thus projected onto London's entire immigrant population, feeding suspicions about immigrants' supposed predisposition to vice and criminality. At the same time the racialization of

---

1. Benedict Anderson, *Under Three Flags: Anarchism and the Anti-Colonial Imagination* (London: Verso, 2005), 2. Anderson writes of the final decades of the nineteenth century: "Following the collapse of the First International, and Marx's death in 1883, anarchism . . . was the dominant element in the self-consciously internationalist radical Left." Anderson, *Under Three Flags*, 2.

anarchism served to debase the political claims of what was, at the time, a significant social movement.

While anarchism was never as large a movement in England as on the Continent, in the late nineteenth century, there were a few thousand anarchists in London alone.[2] Several anarchist newspapers were based in London, including the *Alarm, Anarchist, Freedom,* and, *Torch,* and there was a regular slate of anarchist lectures and rallies reported in the anarchist press. The London movement comprised a wide range of views—unsurprisingly given its basis in an anti-authoritarian political school—and there were perhaps as many anarchisms as anarchists.[3] But the London movement rested on two core platforms, as Louisa Sarah Bevington describes in her 1895 *An Anarchist Manifesto:* the abolition of private property in favor of communism, and the "paralysation of all existing authoritarian institutions and organizations" in favor of "the rearrangement of relations between men on the basis of voluntary agreements."[4] Anarchists were part of the First International coalition of revolutionary socialist groups, but while Marxist-socialists and state-socialists wanted to centralize power and production in the state, believing that the state was requisite (at least transitionally) to orchestrate social equality, anarchists wanted to do away with the nation state altogether. They believed that the state in any form necessitates violation of individual liberty, and that governmental authority is inherently corrupting. As Bevington wrote, "the very nature of the state prevents anything good coming of it."[5] Anarchists envisioned a future society of small, cooperative collectives operating on the principles of free choice and voluntary association. Under anarchism, the state would not wither away, as Marx predicted it would under communism; it would be smashed.

---

2. As Matthew Thomas notes, "The number of anarchists in Britain was always smaller than anywhere on the continent. An article published in December 1896 suggested that, in London, there were 8,000 anarchists, of whom 2,000 were Russian Jews. Of the English anarchists, it said, 'they number between 3000 and 4000. . . . These figures seem far too high. . . . The anarchists could mobilize 600 people on a working day and upwards of 1,000 on a Sunday. . . . This would seem to indicate a maximum of 2,000 British anarchists in London in 1896, and even this is a generous estimate." Matthew Thomas, "'No-one Telling Us What to Do': Anarchist Schools in Britain, 1890–1916," *Historical Research* 77.197 (August 2004): 406–407. For background on late nineteenth-century British anarchism, see James Joll, *The Anarchists* (London: Methuen, 1979); John Quail, *The Slow Burning Fuse: The Lost History of the British Anarchists* (London: Granada, 1978); H. Oliver, *The International Anarchist Movement in Late Victorian London* (London: Croom Helm, 1983); Haia Shpayer-Makov, "Anarchism in British Public Opinion, 1880–1914," *Victorian Studies* (summer 1988); and Matthew Thomas, *Anarchist Ideas and Counter-Cultures in Britain, 1880–1914* (Aldershot, Hampshire: Ashgate, 2005).

3. Henry Seymour used a variant of this formulation in his pamphlet *The Two Anarchisms,* which describes the differences (and similarities) between mutualist and communist anarchism. *The Two Anarchisms* (London: Proudhon Press, 1894).

4. L. S. Bevington, *An Anarchist Manifesto* (London: Metropolitan Printing Works, 1895), 13.

5. Bevington, *An Anarchist Manifesto,* 4.

London anarchism as a social movement owed a great debt to immigration. Because of Britain's relatively munificent policy toward political exiles, London in the 1880s and 1890s was a haven for continental anarchists expelled from their home countries, especially Russia, Italy, and France.[6] Several internationally prominent anarchists made their home in London at this time, including Peter Kropotkin, an exiled nobleman from Russia who was perhaps the most important anarchist thinker of the age, and Louise Michel, the so-called "Red Virgin" who achieved fame in the Paris Commune of 1871. There were also, however, a great many English-born anarchists, and the number of anarchist émigrés in London was small in relation to the immigrant population as a whole. The presence of anarchist political exiles, then, cannot alone explain the literary preoccupation with foreign anarchists, nor can it explain the note of xenophobic panic that we find in many of these works.

This essay will suggest that literary representations of anarchists became a medium for expressing xenophobic anxiety, and race became a mode of critique employed against anarchism, because anarchism threatened a set of naturalized, ideological connections among nation, race, and politics. Benedict Anderson has argued that the "nation" in its modern form emerged in the late eighteenth century, when it came to be imagined as both "limited" and "sovereign."[7] Borders and boundaries became more critical to defining the nation, whereas in older imaginings the monarch had marked the nation's center and borders were less distinct. In a sense, late nineteenth-century literary depictions of anarchists demonstrate how modern forms of xenophobia rose alongside modern conceptions of the nation: these texts emphasize the importance of protecting national borders against foreigners who would defy the bounds of the nation state. Anarchism was a line of thinking that necessarily challenged the ideal that national borders emerge naturally as an expression of racial or cultural unity; it called into question the mythical link between nation and race that operated to shore up nationalist ideology and cement the state as a political formation. Anarchists threatened not only England, but "Englishness" as a racial and cultural category; in this way they became an apt channel for the expression of anti-immigration sentiment.

---

6. Rudolf Rocker, *The London Years* (London: Anscombe, 1956). The social formation of anarchism in London was achieved partly through London's radical press, which included several Yiddish anarchist and anarchist/socialist papers, such as *Arbeter Fraint* (Workers' Friend), established in 1885, and *Germinal*, established in 1900. Thomas writes that these papers had "a wide readership in proportion to their Yiddish reading public. In 1907 the *Arbeter Fraint* had an average circulation of 2,500 and *Germinal* of 4,000." Matthew Thomas, *Anarchist Ideas*, 38. According to Rocker, the papers were also smuggled into Russia and read there.

7. Anderson, *Imagined Communities: Reflections on the Origin and Spread of Nationalism* (London: Verso, 1991).

A native tradition of English philosophical anarchism, dating back to William Godwin and Percy Bysshe Shelley, had long been a factor in British radical discourse, so anarchism wasn't simply a foreign import.[8] Godwin's *An Enquiry Concerning Political Justice,* first published in 1793, established anarchy as the telos of Enlightenment reason, progress, and tolerance. His work is considered "the first comprehensive argument for philosophical anarchism," but by the end of the nineteenth century, English anarchism was more a product of French and Russian thinkers such as Pierre-Joseph Proudhon and Mikhail Bakunin than of Godwin.[9] Still, elements of Godwin's foundational outlook remained, including his cosmopolitan universalism. A political school that rested hope on the eradication of the state had to be more than just internationalist: it had to imagine a world in which the barriers that internationalism crossed were themselves defunct, in which self and subjectivity were grounded in something other, something more primary, than national borders and national culture. Accordingly, London anarchist newspapers urged readers toward a communitarian ethos irrespective of nation and race. Olivia and Helen Rossetti's anarchist newspaper the *Torch,* for example, called in 1893 for the abolition of "all petty race-hatred and race-pride."[10]

------

8. There are significant differences among national traditions of anarchist thought. Anarchism tends to be a strongly nostalgic philosophy, dependent on a notion of an ideal past, but as John Hutton notes, this operates differently in different contexts: "In Germany and Britain, anarchism drew strength from a nostalgic glorification of the past—especially the Middle Ages—and a horror of industrialization. In Britain, the younger generation of the Rossetti family moved directly from the pseudo-medievalism of the Pre-Raphaelites to anarchism—a transition that paralleled in broad terms that of the socialist William Morris." John Hutton, "Camile Pissarro's *Turpitudes Sociales* and Late-Nineteenth-Century French Anarchist Anti-Feminism," *History Workshop Journal* 24 (1987): 39. Aspects of English anarchism, in other words, emerged from indigenous British currents, while in France, anarchism's "nostalgic, backward-looking aspect . . . can be linked directly to its social base." French anarchism did not recruit primarily among proletarian industrial workers, who tended to align instead with the socialists and the syndicalists, but from "those sectors of the poor most threatened by the gradual industrialization . . . the small shopkeepers, independent workers and artisans" and so on. Hutton, "Camile Pissarro," 40. Hutton describes antifeminist views among French anarchists such as Proudhon, but English anarchism was more egalitarian. For a discussion of women's position in British socialism and anarchism, see Barbara Taylor, *Eve and the New Jerusalem: Socialism and Feminism in the Nineteenth Century* (Cambridge, MA: Harvard University Press, 1993).

9. Robert Graham, ed., *Anarchism: A Documentary History of Libertarian Ideas* (Montreal: Black Rose Books, 2005), 1:12. In discussing Proudhon and Bakunin's contributions to anarchism, Joll notes that Proudhon provided crucial anarchist principles from early on, including the famous slogan "property is theft," while Bakunin "gave later anarchists an example of anarchist fervour in action" and "showed how great was the difference in theory and practice between anarchist doctrine and the communism of Marx, and thus made explicit the split in the international revolutionary movement." James Joll, *The Anarchists* (London: Methuen, 1979), 67.

10. See, for example, the front page of the June 15, 1893 issue. This is not to say that all anarchists, however, lived up to this progressive vision. The Rossettis themselves expressed anti-Semitism in later writings, as I discuss later in the essay. The English anarchist David Nicoll ran an ostensibly

In the late-Victorian socialist movement, by contrast, nationalism and imperialism were highly contentious issues subject to a good deal of disagreement. Socialists such as Karl Pearson, Robert Blatchford, and the Fabian Society (whose members included H. G. Wells and George Bernard Shaw) lined up behind Anglo-centric imperialism amidst the disastrous Boer War in South Africa, a war that whipped the nation into a frenzy of reckless and misguided imperialist militarism.[11] Anarchists, meanwhile, took issue not only with the forcible extension of British political and economic power, but with the imperial dispersion of British cultural values around the world; indeed, many anarchists protested the dispersion of such values *within Britain* via the public education system, which they saw as a primarily ideological institution.[12] As these examples suggest, anarchism challenged core assumptions about Anglo-Saxon identity and Anglo-Saxon superiority in a way that other radical political ideologies did not.

By the end of the century the anarchists had been expelled from the socialist International, as socialists had come to believe that they hurt their cause.[13] Many anarchists advocated a coming revolution to destroy capitalism, but the movement also encompassed some who promoted "propaganda by deed," including assassination, sabotage, or even random violence. In England very few anarchists actually supported indiscriminate terror—the leading anarchist thinkers in London, Peter Kropotkin and Charlotte Wilson, opposed such violence—but it came nonetheless to stigmatize the movement as a whole. Mainstream literary and journalistic writing of the era practically equated anarchism with indiscriminate violence, while at the same time, this kind of political violence was becoming part of daily life: dozens of dynamite bombings and political assassinations were carried out in late-nineteenth-

---

humorous column on the front page of the June 20, 1897 issue of the anarchist paper *Commonweal,* entitled "The Glories of Victoria's Reign" by "Old Smith." The piece begins: "Well, I'm damned, if all the people aint gone raving mad. And what's it all about? The Jubilee! Wot's a blooming Jubilee? I think they ought to call it the 'Jewbilee,' for I am 'anged if if I aint been jewed out of everything" (1). Evidently, some anarchists, despite subscribing to a political ideology that invalidated nation and race as identity categories, openly expressed anti-Semitic stereotypes, suggesting their pervasiveness among many segments of British society.

11. Stanley Pierson, *British Socialists: The Journey from Fantasy to Politics* (Cambridge, MA: Harvard University Press, 1979), 40–41.

12. Anarchist newspapers of the day are notably resistant to public facilities for educating youth. As Thomas notes, "For the anarchists the state system of education was authoritarian in that it fostered nationalistic and deferential behaviour in its pupils and was based on coercion. . . . The anarchists believed that only a libertarian education could foster the kind of free consciousness that would be vital in any radical transformation of society." Matthew Thomas, "No-one," 406.

13. As Joll discusses, Marx and Engels's "Private Circular of the General Council of the International" provided "the clearest statement yet to appear of the doctrinal differences between Marxists and anarchists," laying the groundwork for the anarchists' separation from the International. *The Anarchists,* 88.

century Britain at the hands of Irish nationalists.[14] The sudden rise of such violence deeply influenced political and social debate, and a whole new sub-genre of fiction emerged focusing on this modern problem. But "dynamite fiction," as it is called, is a historically incongruous genre: very few dynamite narratives address or even refer to "the Irish question," while nearly all of the bombings and assassinations in late-Victorian Britain were executed by militant campaigners for Irish independence. Anarchists performed no major political crimes in Britain, yet they appear in dynamite narratives far more frequently than Fenians.[15]

Why was anarchist terror a more popular literary subject than Irish nationalist terror, despite its historical incongruence? Anarchism was a more eccentric ideology, and was perhaps more intriguing or less controversial, but close consideration of literature about anarchism reveals a more subtle explanation for this representational disparity. The Irish dynamite campaign, as a movement, was headquartered in the United States and geared toward the liberation of colonial Ireland; it was a force fundamentally opposed to England, but not necessarily to Englishness, and certainly not to the ideo-logical link between nation and race. As a nationalist movement it rested on the same core beliefs about the primacy of national character that fueled English nationalism, and it actually reinforced the ideological bond between nation and race that anarchism threatened to sever. Anarchism appears in dynamite literature as a danger to this ideological bond both because of its politics and because of foreign permeation via immigration. In a cultural and epistemological moment characterized by social-scientific theories of degen-eration, morbidity, and eugenics, anarchists represented an insidious foe, the racially charged "enemy within," and anarchism became the preferred vehicle for expressing a range of new fears associated with race, immigration, and national intactness.[16] In literary accounts of late-Victorian anarchism, nativ-

---

14. For more on this topic, see Jonathan W. Gantt, "Irish-American Terrorism and Anglo-American Relations, 1881–1885," *Journal of the Gilded Age and Progressive Era* 5.4 (October 2006): 325–357. As Alex Houen describes in *Terrorism in Modern Literature,* the word "terrorism" took on its modern sense in this period, in the context of Russian nihilist and Irish nationalist insurgency. Alex Houen, *Terrorism in Modern Literature* (Oxford: Oxford University Press, 2001).

15. For a discussion of this historical disparity in late-Victorian dynamite narrative, see Barbara Arnett Melchiori, *Terrorism in the Late Victorian Novel* (London: Croom Helm, 1985), or Eileen Sypher, *Wisps of Violence: Producing Public and Private Politics in the Turn-of-the-Century British Novel* (London: Verso, 1993). For more on anarchism and dynamite in late Victorian fiction, see Shpayer-Makov, "A Traitor to His Class: The Anarchist in British Fiction," *Journal of European Stud-ies* 26 (1996): 487–516; or Elizabeth Carolyn Miller, *Framed: The New Woman Criminal in British Culture at the Fin de Siècle* (Ann Arbor: University of Michigan Press, 2008).

16. Max Nordau's blockbuster study *Degeneration,* published in England in 1895, was perhaps the most famous of the era's social-scientific accounts of degeneration in the modern age. For more on late-Victorian degeneration and eugenic theory, see J. Edward Chamberlin and Sander L. Gilman, eds., *Degeneration: The Dark Side of Progress* (New York: Columbia University Press, 1985); William

ist apprehension about intra-European immigration infuses political apprehension about anarchism, and various writers use anarchism to express fears about the racial dilution of Britain. Anarchism as a movement proposed the eradication of nation-states, but these writers render anarchism's threat to English *national* identity as an argument for maintaining an essential English *racial* identity.

H. G. Wells's story, "The Stolen Bacillus" (1894), for example, yokes the threat of anarchism to biological terror and racial degeneration. It begins in a London laboratory, as a bacteriologist exhibits dangerous cholera germs to a visitor. Unbeknownst to the scientist, the visitor is an anarchist, who purloins a vial of live cholera with which he hopes to infect the entire city of London. Wells's story considers various permutations of a new and dangerous "enemy within." The anarchist, gazing at the cholera through a microscope, marvels that a few germs can topple all of London, just as a few anarchists can ravage an entire nation: "Not so very much to see. . . . And yet those little particles, those mere atomies, might multiply and devastate a city! Wonderful!"[17] His fellow anarchists are "fools, blind fools—to use bombs when this kind of thing is attainable" (197). Wells emphasizes that the inward, invisible threat of biological material is more grave and dangerous than the loud, conspicuous spectacle of dynamite; by extension, this associates the biological permeation of London by foreigners, such as the anarchist himself, with the more overt threat posed by terrorism and dynamite. The anarchist plans to infect London's water with cholera: "He had only to make sure of the water supply, and break the little tube into a reservoir. How brilliantly he had planned it" (198). Such images of water and reservoirs in the story repeatedly highlight the interconnected porosity of London, a port city, and the fluidity of transmission among its populace.

After the anarchist accidentally spills the vial on himself, however, he decides instead to drink the cholera and spread it through his own contagion. He walks through the crowd near Waterloo Bridge, "carefully jostling his infected body against as many people as possible" (201). The image of the bridge again stresses connectedness and transmission among the London populace, but in having the anarchist spread cholera via his own "infected body" rather than the water supply, Wells locates the story's danger and contagion squarely in the anarchist's physiology. This is particularly meaningful

---

Greenslade, *Degeneration, Culture, and the Novel, 1880–1940* (Cambridge: Cambridge University Press, 1994); Kelly Hurley, *The Gothic Body: Sexuality, Materialism, and Degeneration at the Fin de Siècle* (Cambridge: Cambridge University Press, 1996); or Daniel Pick, *Faces of Degeneration: A European Disorder, c. 1848–c. 1918* (Cambridge: Cambridge University Press, 1989).

17. H. G. Wells, "The Stolen Bacillus," in *The Short Stories of H. G. Wells* (London: Benn, 1952), 195. Subsequent references to this text are cited parenthetically.

since throughout the story, the anarchist is associated with foreignness and racial degeneration: he has a "morbid," "haggard expression," and a "fitful," "nervous manner" (196). The bacteriologist, endowed with the eye of science, attributes this morbidity to race: he muses on "the ethnology of his visitor. Certainly the man was not a Teutonic type nor a common Latin one. 'A morbid product, anyhow, I am afraid,' said the Bacteriologist to himself" (197). The passage perhaps obliquely implies that the anarchist is Russian, since he is neither "Teutonic" nor "Latin," but only indicates certainly that he is "a morbid product." As John Stokes has written, the term "morbid" at this time "carried a burden of meaning greater than any other derogatory adjective," signifying "the enemy within, an internal threat to the organism."[18] The story's depiction of the anarchist as a "morbid product" of indeterminate racial origin neatly encapsulates the menace the anarchist posed in late nineteenth-century literature: an internal threat to the nation as a racial and biological construct.

The disease that the anarchist hopes to disperse in Wells's story is a virulent strain of "Asiatic cholera," again associating the anarchist with foreignness, racial alterity, and (possibly) Russia. By locating the cholera's origin in Asia, where Britain had considerable colonial interests, the story also subtly associates imperial expansion with the threats posed by immigration and foreign nationals, for English contact with Asia was spurred by British imperial objectives.[19] At the end of "The Stolen Bacillus," however, the anarchist's race or skin color ironically becomes a visible sign of disclosure rather than contagious danger: the bacteriologist's vial, it turns out, doesn't contain Asiatic cholera at all, but a species of bacteria that causes "bright blue" patches to appear on one's skin. The bacteriologist mistook the vial of harmless, bluing bacteria for the vial of Asiatic cholera. Thus, while "The Stolen Bacillus" frighteningly associates anarchism with English deracination and the brand new menace of biological terror, its ending makes the anarchist's inner morbidity visibly evident in a noticeably distinctive skin color: blue. Wells links together various examples of the enemy within—the anarchist, germs, disease—but offers skin color as a means of recognizing internal forces of danger to the nation.

Nation states often depend on a myth of racial unity to naturalize political power and geographical configuration; even in late nineteenth-century

---

18. John Stokes, *In the Nineties* (New York: Harvester, 1989), 26.

19. Wells's "Asiatic cholera" suggests a degree of rhetorical overlap in late-Victorian fiction's representation of European immigrant and colonial immigrant populations. The anarchist in this story is European—perhaps Russian—but the cholera he wields is Asiatic. Fictional accounts of anarchism typically focus on Continental political exiles, since the anarchist movement was strongest on the Continent, but xenophobic rhetoric around Continental immigration often echoed rhetoric against colonial immigration, as other essays in this collection demonstrate.

Britain, at the height of Britain's imperialist efforts to extend its national reach well beyond its ostensible racial reach, a myth of racial superiority and an Anglo-centric sense of cultural ascendancy offered a biology-infused argument for national expansion.[20] Anarchists hoped to destroy the nation state altogether as a framework of social, political, and racial understanding; in this sense, the threat posed by the anarchist is comparable to the threat posed by the immigrant. This is evident in Wells's short story "The Thumbmark," which was published in the *Pall Mall Budget* magazine a few months after "The Stolen Bacillus" appeared in the same venue. "The Thumbmark" also focuses on an anarchist outrage, but unlike "The Stolen Bacillus" it does not illustrate the anarchist's threat to England at large—its anarchist villain blows up the home of a police inspector instead of targeting the populace generally—nor does it emphasize the anarchist's racial morbidity to the same extent as "The Stolen Bacillus." "The Thumbmark" does, however, give its anarchist a name, Chabôt, indicating that he is French. The other characters in the story have Anglo-Saxon names (Smith, Porch, Mason, Wilderspin, and Askin), so the anarchist is marked out by his foreign name and his unwillingness to assimilate with the other students in his chemistry class: "he had been rather conspicuous for a reserve that most of us considered sulky in its quality."[21] Within the story Chabôt's implied racial otherness and immigration status stand stead as a motive for his anarchist attack on the police inspector's house; it is as though there is no need to explain his animosity toward British national authority, represented by the British policeman, since he is a foreigner on alien soil. His motives are obvious and inscrutable at the same time because he is politically and nationally "other."[22] Like "The Stolen Bacillus," the story begins in a scientific laboratory, presenting the microscopic domain of biochemical life as the new front for attacks on England and Englishness.

Wells's triangulation of bacteria, anarchism, and foreign menace has parallels among his contemporaries. Arthur Conan Doyle's 1904 story "The Adventure of the Six Napoleons" describes an "Italian colony" in London like a diseased bacterial colony, a festering breeding-ground for criminals and

---

20. Such a mentality was particularly associated with the "New Imperialism" of the 1890s. See George Stocking, *Victorian Anthropology* (New York: Free Press, 1987).

21. H. G. Wells, "The Thumbmark," in *The Man with a Nose and the Other Uncollected Short Stories of H. G. Wells* (London: Athlone, 1984), 105.

22. Nils Clausson has argued that Wells's failure to explain the anarchist's motive in "The Thumbmark" is a critique of the detective story as a genre, since detective stories typically offer a rational, scientific approach to crime. I would suggest, on the contrary, that within the context of the story, the anarchist's motive essentially *is* his racial otherness. Nils Clausson, "The Anarchist and the Detective: The Science of Detection and the Subversion of Generic Convention in H. G. Wells's 'The Thumbmark,'" *Victorian Newsletter* 112 (fall 2007): 19–32.

degenerates. Part of the Sherlock Holmes series published in the *Strand Magazine,* the story focuses on a seemingly inexplicable rash of crimes in which busts of Napoleon are being systematically smashed. Initially the authorities believe that the criminal must be mentally degenerate, a victim of monomania. Later they theorize that the crime is political and that its perpetrator is an anarchist; a victim in the case says, "No one but an anarchist would go about breaking statues."[23] Both these theories turn out to be wrong, but the twin shadows of degeneracy and anarchy hang over the crime, and are again linked to foreignness and immigration. The perpetrator turns out to be an Italian immigrant named Beppo, who lives in London's "Italian colony." At this time Italy had one of the most active anarchist contingents in Europe: in Italy "the doctrines of Bakunin were more popular than those of Marx" and "in the 1870s, adherence to the International meant in Italy embracing the anarchist cause."[24] In Conan Doyle's story Beppo's vaguely anarchist characterization goes hand in hand with his racially degenerate physique: he is described as a "sharp-featured simian man, with thick eyebrows and a very peculiar projection of the lower part of the face, like the muzzle of a baboon" (811), and as "a lithe, dark figure, as swift and active as an ape" (819). He has a "hideous, sallow face, with writhing, furious features," and snaps at Watson's fingers "like a hungry wolf" (820). Beppo's physical characteristics associate him with theories of primitivism or racial degeneracy: he is foreign and an immigrant, but he is also under-evolved.

By positioning this degenerate, possibly anarchist foreigner in the so-called "Italian colony" of London, Conan Doyle pointedly reminds readers that within the British metropole, there is "a riverside city of a hundred thousand souls, where the tenement houses swelter and reek with the outcasts of Europe" (815). This riverside colony echoes Conan Doyle's depiction of London in *A Study in Scarlet,* the first installment in the Sherlock Holmes series, as "that great cesspool into which all the loungers and idlers of the Empire are irresistibly drained."[25] Conan Doyle was born in Scotland of Irish descent, yet according to David Glover, he was a supporter and member of the British Brother's League, an anti-immigration activist organization.[26] Conan Doyle's political opinions appear to inform his depiction of Beppo and the Italian colony in "The Adventure of the Six Napoleons," for his use of the phrase "outcasts of Europe" ties the story to a key histori-

---

23. Arthur Conan Doyle, "The Adventure of the Six Napoleons," in *Sherlock Holmes: The Complete Novels and Stories* (New York: Bantam, 1986), 1: 814.

24. Joll, *The Anarchists,* 101.

25. Conan Doyle, *A Study in Scarlet,* in *Sherlock Holmes: The Complete Novels and Stories* (New York: Bantam, 1986), 1: 4.

26. David Glover, "Aliens, Anarchists and Detectives: Legislating the Immigrant Body," *New Formations* 32 (1997): 25.

cal debate raging in Britain at the time of its publication: Britain's policy of offering sanctuary to exiled foreigners—literal "outcasts of Europe"—was being reconsidered amid increased terrorism and immigration at the turn of the century. Britain had a tolerant policy regarding political exile, and under the Extradition Act of 1870 liberally extended refuge to many political exiles (including anarchists). Shortly after this story was published, however, the 1905 Aliens Act would severely restrict immigration, reflecting widespread public anxiety about immigration and about potential violence on the part of political exiles.[27]

Representations of anarchist aliens thus engage a host of conflict-ridden contemporary debates about immigration, international relations, and national identity, but within this spectrum of relations, connections between depictions of immigrant Jews and exiled anarchists are particularly common.[28] Such representations stress parallels between anarchist and Jewish immigrants, linking the two groups by accentuating their similarities: both came from the continent, often after expulsion, and tended to form like-minded communities in London; and because anarchists wanted to do away with nation states altogether, the figure of the wandering, nationless Jew transitioned easily to a stereotypical Jewish anarchist. This move tied in with contemporary immigration debates. Xenophobic accounts of Jewish immigrants' intractable resistance to assimilation, which implied that they would never be fully subject to the British state, much less culturally subject to the English nation, linked Jews to state-rejecting anarchists. Yoking the two together fed a climate of anti-immigration sentiment focused on racial and national intactness.

Many critics have noted, for example, that Jack the Ripper was widely reported to be a Jew, and that a Jewish shoemaker was wrongfully arrested in the investigation. The association of Victorian Jews with anarchism engaged many of the same stereotypes at work in the Ripper investigation. Sara Blair has argued that the cultural fantasy of a Jewish Jack the Ripper served as a powerful instrument for an emerging Anglo-Saxonist political ideology, represented by groups such as the Anglo-American League and the Trans-atlantic Society of America, in which Britain and the United States were to draw together politically on the basis of shared racial inheritance: "the Ripper murders occasion a refashioning of the myth of the Jew's debased racial economy as a newly powerful threat to the projects, aspirations, and character

---

27. See Glover, "Aliens, Anarchists and Detectives," for more on the Aliens Act.

28. Shpayer-Makov points out that while anarchist Jews commonly appear in late-Victorian fiction about anarchism, they were typically not afforded central narrative positions: "Only seldom was 'the Jew' chosen to be the all-powerful anarchist criminal, but the reader often found him lurking behind the scenes." Shpayer-Makov, "A Traitor," 319.

of the Anglo-Saxon world."[29] In other words, "Jack as Jew"—the idea of the Jew suspected in the Ripper investigation—shored up not only the ideal of an essential Englishness, defined in opposition to Jack the Ripper, but also the ideal of an essential Anglo-Saxon national character based in race. Anarchism threatened to dismantle the ideological conception of the state as a political formation that emerged naturally from such an identity; "Jack as Jew" propped up this very conception, operating to bind the Anglo-American world into a closer national alliance.[30]

The idea of Jack the Ripper as Jew also chimed with a stereotypical notion that Jews, like anarchists, inhabited an anti-authoritarian stance toward state law and state institutions. Sander Gilman quotes Sir Robert Anderson, the police official in charge of the Jack the Ripper case, as saying, "the conclusion we came to was that [Ripper] and his people were low-class Jews, for it is a remarkable fact that people of that class in the East End will not give up one of their number to Gentile justice."[31] The idea that Jews are a discrete "nation" within the nation, rejecting "Gentile justice" and British law, governed the legal response to the case. A similar depiction of Jews appeared in the same 1904 issue of the *Strand Magazine* that ran Doyle's "Adventure of the Six Napoleons"; in an article entitled "In Alien Land," George Sims describes London's Jewish Ghetto as a completely discrete territory within London, where British sovereignty and British authority no longer hold sway: "a vast area . . . entirely given up to the alien immigrant." Sims invites readers to imagine walking through it: "stop for a moment and gaze at the crowd. . . . Everywhere the Oriental type predominates. . . . You are in London, but you might be in Cairo or Mogador."[32] Sims was an author "renowned for his empathetic evocations of the London poor," but his piece in the *Strand* contributes to a late-Victorian sense that Jewish immigration into London was a threat to Englishness as a national-cultural-racial formation.[33] That a "little Cairo" or "little Mogador" could exist autonomously within Britain's borders suggests national rupture, secession, or colonization;

29. Sara Blair, "Henry James, Jack the Ripper, and the Cosmopolitan Jew: Staging Authorship in *The Tragic Muse*," *ELH* 63.2 (1996): 491.

30. Blair's argument about emergent Anglo-Saxonism helps account for Sherlock Holmes's hope, expressed at the end of "The Noble Bachelor," that Britain and America will reunite "under a flag which shall be a quartering of the Union Jack with the Stars and Stripes." Conan Doyle, "The Noble Bachelor," in *The Adventures of Sherlock Holmes* (Oxford: Oxford University Press, 1993), 241.

31. Sander Gilman, *The Jew's Body* (New York: Routledge, 1991), 115–116.

32. George Sims, "In Alien Land," *Strand Magazine* 27 (1904): 419, 416, 420. The town of Mogador, Morocco, was "the most important point of contact between Moroccan Jews and Europe—above all with England . . . throughout most of the nineteenth century." Daniel Schroeter, "The Town of Mogador (Essaouira) and Aspects of Change in Pre-Colonial Morocco," *British Society for Middle Eastern Studies Bulletin* 6.1 (1979): 30–31.

33. Seth Koven, *Slumming: Sexual and Social Politics in Victorian London* (Princeton, NJ: Princeton University Press, 2004), 140.

this sense transitions easily to representations of anarchists, who openly disdain British borders, institutions, and the notion of the state itself.

Literary depictions of Martial Bourdin—the 26-year-old French immigrant who blew himself up in the 1894 Greenwich Park bombing—engage not only with debates about political sanctuary and immigration from the continent, but with fears that Jewish-anarchist sedition was afoot on London soil. The Greenwich Park bombing was the only terrorist act linked to anarchism that occurred in late Victorian Britain, but the facts of the case remain hazy: Bourdin's bomb killed only himself, and while it is assumed that he intended to blow up the Greenwich Observatory, the bomb actually detonated in a deserted area of the park. Because the Observatory is so unpopulated and impractical a target, many have wondered if he intended to blow up anything at all. At the time of the bombing London anarchists suspected that Bourdin was actually an agent provocateur, paid by the police to whip up public anxiety about anarchist exiles in London. The unemployed Bourdin was apparently out of funds, and his brother-in-law, H. B. Samuels, was thought to be a police spy.[34]

This baffling event would probably have faded into obscurity if Joseph Conrad had not made it the subject of his 1907 novel, *The Secret Agent.* Four years before this work, however, a long account of the bombing appeared in *A Girl among the Anarchists,* an autobiographical novel written by Helen and Olivia Rossetti under the pseudonym Isabel Meredith. The Rossetti sisters, daughters of William Michael Rossetti and nieces of Christina and Dante Gabriel Rossetti, had been editors in their youth of the anarchist newspaper the *Torch,* and *A Girl* describes their experience in the London anarchist movement and their ultimate disillusionment and withdrawal. Recounting the Greenwich bombing from the perspective of anarchist insiders, they categorically assert that the event was a put-up job: "That the whole conspiracy was a got-up affair between [Samuels] and the police was evident."[35] As I have discussed elsewhere, Conrad seems to have been influenced by the Rossettis' novel, though he never acknowledged it.[36] In *The Secret Agent,* the Rossettis' newspaper is even sold in Mr. Verloc's shop.

---

34. For more background on the Bourdin case, see David Mulry, "Popular Accounts of the Greenwich Bombing and Conrad's *The Secret Agent,*" *Rocky Mountain Review of Language and Literature* (fall 2000): 43–64; David Nicoll, *The Greenwich Mystery: Letters from the Dead* (London: David Nicoll, 1898); Hermia Oliver, *The International Anarchist Movement in Late Victorian London* (London: Croom Helm, 1983); John Quail, *The Slow Burning Fuse: The Lost History of the British Anarchists* (London: Granada, 1978); or W. C. H. [Walter Hart], *Confessions of an Anarchist* (London: Grant Richards, 1906).

35. Isabel Meredith, *A Girl among the Anarchists* (Lincoln: University of Nebraska Press, 1992), 71. Subsequent references to this work are cited parenthetically.

36. Ford Maddox Ford was a cousin of the Rossettis and claims he introduced them to Conrad. For more on this and other connections between Conrad and the Rossettis, see my book *Framed.*

The Rossettis and Conrad similarly represent the Greenwich Park bombing as an event predicated upon immigration and racial cosmopolitanism in London, though only the Rossettis specifically emphasize Jewish immigration. The Rossettis describe Samuels, the alleged police spy, as "a mean enough type of the East End sartorial Jew," claiming his "physiognomy" reveals his "low order of intelligence, cunning, and intriguing," his "shifty" character, and his propensity for "petty swindling" (45).[37] The Rossettis interweave two different strains of public anxiety, anarcho-phobia as well as anti-Semitic xenophobia, but in making Samuels a double agent who is traitor to the state as well as to the anarchists, they emphasize a stereotype of Jewish resistance to affiliation such as we also see in the Jack the Ripper case. There, the police believed Jews would never be loyal to the forces of "Gentile justice"; here, appropriately enough since the novel is told from the anarchists' perspective, the Rossettis emphasize the Jew's disloyalty to his anarchist comrades rather than to the police. The information Samuels provides to the police is given out of commercial interests rather than nationalist loyalty; as represented in *A Girl*, Samuels is committed to neither his country nor his comrades.

Later in *A Girl among the Anarchists,* we meet two Jewish anarchists who are loyal comrades in the movement, but the novel still stresses their unique severance from the British nation, even beyond other anarchists. Rebecca Weisman possesses "the foreign Jews' dread of policemen as omnipotent beings" (180), and Mr. Yoski lives in a neighborhood where

> I seemed to be in a foreign country. . . . The shop-signs and advertisements were mostly written in Hebrew. . . . The narrow, dirty street was swarming with inhabitants . . . it would be a euphemism to speak of enjoying the fresh air in such a neighborhood. The house at which I stopped was a six-roomed 'cottage,' but . . . at least 14 persons passed in and out . . . the children clustered round like little animals. (178–179)

Meredith visits this "swarming," ill-smelling locality in an effort to shake a police spy who is trailing her, and she pointedly loses him just before entering the "foreign country."

The Rossettis' depiction of Jewish anarchists resonates with a broader cultural tendency to depict immigrant Jews as a threat to British nationality, both racially and politically. By appealing to this kind of xenophobia, the Rossettis go very much against the cosmopolitan, post-racial principles of anarchist thought and against their own stated ideals before they abandoned

---

37. Just as the Rossettis call themselves "Isabel Meredith," they use pseudonyms for all the characters in their memoir, though most are quite obviously based on real London anarchists. Their name for H. B. Samuels is "Jacob," but I will continue to call him "Samuels" here to avoid confusion.

anarchism and wrote *A Girl among the Anarchists.*[38] Their shift of thinking evident here perhaps prefigures the sisters' later support of Mussolini and Italian Fascism. Indeed, throughout their careers as anarchists, they had strong ties to Italian nationalism due to their grandfather's legacy of Italian republicanism; Gabriele Rossetti had, after all, himself been a political exile in London. In any case, the xenophobia evident in the sisters' depiction of Jewish anarchists mirrors contemporary crime fiction more closely than contemporary anarchist thought.

Conrad's fictionalization of the Greenwich Park bombing doesn't explicitly treat Jewish immigration, but like the Rossettis, Conrad positions the story in a context of London cosmopolitanism and immigration, and like Conan Doyle and Wells, he associates anarchism with biological degeneration. The character Stevie serves as Conrad's version of Martial Bourdin, and he is practically a poster-child for scientific theories of racial degeneracy: he is of French descent, has a "vacant droop of his lower lip," and has his address sewn inside his coat so he won't get lost.[39] His sister and mother describe him with euphemisms like "delicate" or "queer," but another anarchist explicitly associates him with the theories of Cesare Lombroso: "Very good type . . . of that sort of degenerate. It's good enough to glance at the lobes of his ears. If you read Lombroso" (77). Lombroso had influentially argued that criminality was an inborn trait, a kind of fatal degenerate inheritance associated with physical features resembling "primitive" races; he had used this notion of the "born criminal" to account for anarchism in books such as *Gli Anarchici.*[40] *The Secret Agent*'s anarchists—Michaelis (whose principles are actually socialist), Ossipon, Karl Yundt, and the Professor—are all vaguely foreign and degenerate: most of their names sound foreign, and most are physically debilitated. Conrad's version of Bourdin's police-spy brother, Adolph Verloc, has a foreign name, but ties to multiple governments (Russia, France, Britain), as well as to several different revolutionary groups. He "came and went without any very apparent reason. He generally arrived in London (like the

---

38. See my book *Framed* for fuller treatment of the Rossettis and their novel from another angle.

39. Joseph Conrad, *The Secret Agent* (London: Penguin, 1990), 49.

40. While in Conrad's novel the anarchist Ossipon is a "disciple" of Lombroso, in reality Lombroso's theories were inhospitable to anarchist thought, not only because Lombroso considered the anarchist a species of "born criminal" but also because his theories went against the anarchist tendency to attribute human failings to a corrupt social environment. As the anarchist A. Agresti, who would later marry Olivia Rossetti, wrote in an 1894 issue of the *Torch*, "Illustrious Lombroso, you have written a book on the Anarchists . . . we are obliged to point out the mistakes . . . A man's character is formed by his environment, his education, his first impressions, his manner of life . . . Besides, can you define crime? . . . we should like to call your attention to the fact that in the Fiji islands it is considered the correct thing to kill and eat your aged relatives, that in Russia it is a crime to shout 'Long live the Republic;' whilst in France it is a duty." Agresti, "A Criticism of the Anarchists By C. Lombroso," *Torch* 5 (31 October 1894): 4–5.

influenza) from the Continent" (47). Here, immigration, rootlessness, and traffic between nations are forms of contagion, spreading danger and disease to London. Ironically, however, the Greenwich Park bombing turns out in Conrad's novel to have been provoked by officials at the Russian embassy, who sought to scare Britain into legislating stricter rules on political exile for foreign radicals. Britain's refusal to extradite certain Russian political exiles living in London had long been a source of aggravation to the Czarist regime. In a sense, then, Conrad's novel actually subverts xenophobic and anti-immigration rhetoric by suggesting that imperial powers such as Russia are a much greater threat to England than immigrants and radicals, "the enemy within." Still, the novel paints a decidedly sleazy, menacing portrait of London's multi-national political underbelly.

Conrad himself was an immigrant expatriate, but his novel echoes popular suspicions about those deemed insufficiently tethered to national tradition because of political opinions and non-English origins. Similarly, Conan Doyle's family had roots in Ireland, and came to Scotland via immigration. The Rossetti sisters' grandfather came to England from Italy as an exiled republican and Italian nationalist, and Olivia Rossetti herself relocated to Italy before co-authoring *A Girl among the Anarchists* with her sister. These authors' own biographies suggest how international and ethnically diverse Britain already was by the late-nineteenth century, yet the fantasy of a homogenously intact nation—racially, culturally, and politically undivided— nonetheless exerts a strong pull within their work. As I have attempted to demonstrate, these fictional accounts of anarchist terror have a clear historical referent not in their treatment of anarchism, for there were no major anarchist outrages in Victorian Britain, but in their treatment of race, immigration, and the "enemy within." Fictions of exile London, a place characterized by its political radicalism and its polyglot racial character, express and appeal to fears of a nation divided into tiny, autonomous units, a nation that cannot unite into one sovereign body because of its racial, ethnic, and national diversity. The anarchist became a figurative channel for such fears not only because of the presence of foreign anarchist exiles in late Victorian London, but because anarchism threatened the ideological construction of nationhood that anti-immigration activists sought most to preserve: the ideal of the nation as a cultural and racial entity that sustained and upheld the nation as a political entity.

The Aliens Act of 1905 emerged out of widespread public anxiety about immigration, which itself stemmed from xenophobia and from fears about foreign radicals and terrorism; yet ironically, it is more likely that London's status as a haven for continental anarchists in the years leading up to the Aliens Act actually helped shield Britain from anarchist violence. David

Nicoll, a prominent English anarchist, wrote to his comrade Max Nettlau in 1894: "Another Bourdin affair and England will be closed as a refuge to the victims of tyranny on the continent, and men whom I love and admire handed over to death. . . . My dear Nettlau, you do not know the English people. They can understand men using dynamite in the continent, but not here, and their general impression is that Anarchists are a lot of 'bloody foreigners.'"[41] In tune with this letter's perspective, literary depictions of anarchists focus inordinately on race and ethnicity, and are interwoven with anxiety about the influence of foreign racial groups on British culture. These literary representations thus resonate not only with arguments against sanctuary for political exiles, but with arguments against all kinds of immigration.

Works Cited

Agresti, A. "A Criticism of the Anarchists By C. Lombroso." *Torch* 5 (31 October 1894): 4–5.

Anderson, Benedict. *Imagined Communities: Reflections on the Origin and Spread of Nationalism.* Rev. Ed. London: Verso, 1991.

———. *Under Three Flags: Anarchism and the Anti-Colonial Imagination.* London: Verso, 2005.

Bevington, L. S. *An Anarchist Manifesto.* London: Metropolitan Printing Works, 1895.

Blair, Sara. "Henry James, Jack the Ripper, and the Cosmopolitan Jew: Staging Authorship in *The Tragic Muse.*" *ELH* 63.2 (1996): 489–512.

Chamberlin, J. Edward and Sander L. Gilman, eds. *Degeneration: The Dark Side of Progress.* New York: Columbia University Press, 1985.

Clausson, Nils. "The Anarchist and the Detective: The Science of Detection and the Subversion of Generic Convention in H. G. Wells's 'The Thumbmark.'" *Victorian Newsletter* 112 (fall 2007): 19–32.

Conan Doyle, Arthur. "The Adventure of the Six Napoleons," in *Sherlock Holmes: The Complete Novels and Stories.* Vol. 1. New York: Bantam, 1986.

———. "The Noble Bachelor," in *The Adventures of Sherlock Holmes.* Edited by Richard Lancelyn Green. Oxford: Oxford University Press, 1993.

——— *A Study in Scarlet,* in *Sherlock Holmes: The Complete Novels and Stories.* Vol. 1. 1–103. New York: Bantam, 1986.

Conrad, Joseph. *The Secret Agent.* Edited by Martin Seymour Smith. London: Penguin, 1990.

Gantt, Jonathan W. "Irish-American Terrorism and Anglo-American Relations, 1881–1885." *Journal of the Gilded Age and Progressive Era* 5.4 (October 2006): 325–357.

Gilman, Sander. *The Jew's Body.* New York: Routledge, 1991.

Glover, David. "Aliens, Anarchists and Detectives: Legislating the Immigrant Body." *New Formations* 32 (1997): 22–33.

---

41. Letter from Nicoll to Nettlau (27 March 1894), Nettlau Archive, International Institute for Social History, Amsterdam.

Graham, Robert, Editor. *Anarchism: A Documentary History of Libertarian Ideas.* Montreal: Black Rose Books, 2005.

Greenslade, William. *Degeneration, Culture, and the Novel, 1880–1940.* Cambridge: Cambridge University Press, 1994.

Hurley, Kelly. *The Gothic Body: Sexuality, Materialism, and Degeneration at the Fin de Siècle.* Cambridge: Cambridge University Press, 1996.

Houen, Alex. *Terrorism in Modern Literature.* Oxford: Oxford University Press, 2001.

Hutton, John. "Camile Pissarro's *Turpitudes Sociales* and Late-Nineteenth-Century French Anarchist Anti-Feminism." *History Workshop Journal* 24 (1987): 32–61.

Joll, James. *The Anarchists.* 2nd ed. London: Methuen, 1979.

Koven, Seth. *Slumming: Sexual and Social Politics in Victorian London.* Princeton, NJ: Princeton University Press, 2004.

Melchiori, Barbara Arnett. *Terrorism in the Late Victorian Novel.* London: Croom Helm, 1985.

Meredith, Isabel. *A Girl among the Anarchists.* 1903. Reprint, Lincoln: University of Nebraska Press, 1992.

Miller, Elizabeth Carolyn. *Framed: The New Woman Criminal in British Culture at the Fin de Siècle.* Ann Arbor: University of Michigan Press, 2008.

Mulry, David. "Popular Accounts of the Greenwich Bombing and Conrad's *The Secret Agent.*" *Rocky Mountain Review of Language and Literature* (fall 2000): 43–64.

Nicoll, David. "The Glories of Victoria's Reign" by "Old Smith." *Commonweal* (20 June 1897): 1.

———. *The Greenwich Mystery: Letters from the Dead.* London: David Nicoll, 1898.

———. Letter to Nettlau, 27 March 1894, Nettlau Archive, International Institute for Social History.

Oliver, Hermia. *The International Anarchist Movement in Late Victorian London.* London: Croom Helm, 1983.

Pick, Daniel. *Faces of Degeneration: A European Disorder, c. 1848–c. 1918.* Cambridge: Cambridge University Press, 1989.

Pierson, Stanley. *British Socialists: The Journey from Fantasy to Politics.* Cambridge, MA: Harvard University Press, 1979.

Quail, John. *The Slow Burning Fuse: The Lost History of the British Anarchists.* London: Granada, 1978.

Rocker, Rudolf. *The London Years.* Translated by Joseph Leftwich. London: Anscombe, 1956.

Schroeter, Daniel. "The Town of Mogador (Essaouira) and Aspects of Change in Pre-Colonial Morocco." *British Society for Middle Eastern Studies Bulletin* 6.1 (1979): 24–38.

Seymour, Henry. *The Two Anarchisms.* London: Proudhon Press, 1894.

Shpayer-Makov, Haia. "Anarchism in British Public Opinion, 1880–1914." *Victorian Studies* (summer 1988): 487–516.

———. "A Traitor to His Class: The Anarchist in British Fiction." *Journal of European Studies* 26 (1996): 299–325.

Sims, George. "In Alien Land." *Strand Magazine* 27 (1904): 416–423.

Stocking, George. *Victorian Anthropology.* New York: Free Press, 1987.

Stokes, John. *In the Nineties.* New York: Harvester, 1989.

Sypher, Eileen. *Wisps of Violence: Producing Public and Private Politics in the Turn-of-the Century British Novel.* London: Verso, 1993.

Taylor, Barbara. *Eve and the New Jerusalem: Socialism and Feminism in the Nineteenth Century.* Cambridge, MA: Harvard University Press, 1993.

Thomas, Matthew. *Anarchist Ideas and Counter-Cultures in Britain, 1880–1914.* Burlington, VT: Ashgate, 2005.

———. "'No-one Telling Us What to Do': Anarchist Schools in Britain, 1890–1916." *Historical Research* 77.197 (August 2004): 405–436.

W. C. H. [Walter Hart] *Confessions of an Anarchist.* London: Grant Richards, 1911.

Wells, H. G. "The Stolen Bacillus," in *The Short Stories of H. G. Wells.* London: Benn, 1952.

———. "The Thumbmark," in *The Man with a Nose and the Other Uncollected Short Stories of H. G. Wells.* Edited by J. R. Hammond. London: Athlone, 1984.

12

Xenophobia
on the Streets of London

Punch's Campaign against
Italian Organ-Grinders, 1854–1864

⚕

ANNEMARIE McALLISTER

Discourses about English national identity often play with negative ascriptions and are linked to a complex interlocking framework of cultural and social needs; this essay explores dominant discourses about the foreign and the other in the mid-nineteenth century to illuminate some of the sources and effects of xenophobia. It argues that the fear and hatred of those seen as "foreign" are often projections of insecurities and undeclared desires, and that xenophobia is rarely simple. In order to define, re-inscribe, and preserve the construct of the English nation, mainstream Victorian culture demonized "outsiders." Yet some outsiders, or some nations or cultural groups, possess cultural capital, arouse desire, or provoke envy. Nineteenth-century Italian street musicians provide a particularly complex and rich example of the tensions and ambiguities in the perceptions of Italians, built up by ascription and association. Unlike Jewish or Irish objects of disdain, Italians came from the land of the Roman Empire, of Verdi, and of the cultural glories of the Grand Tour. Their struggles for national independence in the mid-nineteenth century gave them added glamour—and yet when on the streets of London they also aroused fear and loathing in a particularly complex and venomous way, as this essay will show.

Italians as Others

Since the publication of Edward Said's *Orientalism* in 1978, it has become almost a commonplace to assert that representations of a foreign culture reveal little about that culture, and much about the preoccupations, needs, and desires of the culture from which the representations originate. Homi Bhabha has explored the fragile identities behind the creation of the other, showing how the stereotyped other reveals the desires and defenses of those involved in the construction.[1] In the case of national identities, those from foreign countries may possess aspects that we would like to imaginatively claim yet fear to acknowledge, as well as aspects against which we can contrast ourselves more obviously. The mid-nineteenth-century reader could draw upon many nationalities for such self-constructions, of course, but I would argue that for the English reader Italians formed a particularly interesting group. Italians could be figured as inheritors of Roman glory, but simultaneously of Roman decadence—unlike the English, who could therefore be cast as the more worthy successors of glory. Italians were symbols of the South (and therefore frequently constructed as lazy, servile, corrupt, and primitive) whereas the English could participate in the Northern stereotype of industry, freedom, honesty, and progress. Often represented as passionate, instinctive, and sexually unbridled, Italians also offered sites for imaginative exploration of alternative lives, as well as a frisson of righteous indignation that they enjoyed apparently pleasant lives despite lacking the Northern virtues.[2] The pages of *Punch* in this period illustrate the pleasures and reassurances gained from the circulation and consumption of one prominent Italian stereotype—the street musician—which was mixed with other constructions of Italian identity.

Stereotypes of Italians

The representation of the Irish in the nineteenth century provides something of a parallel to the more complex representation of Italians, and there have

---

1. Homi Bhabha, *The Location of Culture* (London: Routledge, 1994).

2. I have outlined only some of the most prevalent narratives about Italians circulating at this period (and later, of course). These are explored in Annemarie McAllister, *John Bull's Italian Snakes and Ladders: English Attitudes to Italy in the Mid-Nineteenth Century* (Newcastle: Cambridge Scholars Publishing, 2007); Gian Antonio Stella, *L'orda: quando gli albanesi eravamo noi* (Milano: Rizzoli, 2002); and John Dickie, *Darkest Italy: The Nation and Stereotypes of the Mezzogiorno, 1860–1900* (Basingstoke: Macmillan, 1999).

been seminal studies of Irish stereotyping in written and visual material of this period.[3] However, there has been much less written about the other notable example of a nation commonly represented as dirty, disreputable, and even simian—the Italians. When they focus on Italian stereotypes studies tend to lean heavily on the experiences of immigrants to the United States, or on child musicians. For example, the association with dirt and primitivism in representations of nineteenth- and twentieth-century Italian immigrants to the United States has been explored by Stella, Guglielmo, and Salerno.[4] In *The Little Slaves of the Harp* John Zucchi provides detailed accounts and analysis of child street musicians' experiences in Paris, New York, and London, and Lucio Sponza has set the English campaign against the organ-grinders in a wider context in *Italian Immigrants in Nineteenth-Century Britain: Realities and Images*.[5] Yet the significance of a particular set of *Punch* representations of Italian adult musicians on the streets of London, and its relation to other dominant discourses about the foreign and the other, has nevertheless been little explored. Such images make startling reading, especially against a set of cultural assumptions that frequently associate Italianness with musical excellence, and open up a wider discourse of English fears and desires.

The figure of the Italian has long been open to a broad range of significations in England, one of the most powerful being the ascription of inherent musicality. In the first half of the nineteenth century this could be said to have reached its apex in England, with the high profile of Italian opera: not only were key composers such as Giuseppe Verdi Italian, but so were the vast majority of "star" performers—frequently known by their surnames only, such as Mario and Grisi—and the most famous conductor, Costa. It was 1889 before Covent Garden ceased to translate all operas into Italian, and 1892 before The Royal Opera dropped the modifier "Italian" from its title.[6] Pierre Bourdieu writes in *Distinction* of the "grandiose luxury of the opera-houses" as announcing the sacred character to the high culture into which outsiders strive to be initiates, and of the associated aesthetic stances as "opportunities to experience or assert one's position in social space, as a rank

3. See, for example, L. Perry Curtis, *Apes and Angels: The Irishman in Victorian Caricature* (Washington, DC: Smithsonian Institute Press, 1997) and Michael De Nie, *The Eternal Paddy: Irish Identity and the British Press, 1798–1882* (Madison: University of Wisconsin Press, 2004).

4. Gian Antonio Stella, *L'orda: quando gli albanesi eravamo noi;* and Jennifer Guglielmo and Salvatore Salerno, eds., *Are Italians White? How Race is Made in America* (London: Routledge, 2003).

5. John Zucchi, *The Little Slaves of the Harp: Italian Street Musicians in Nineteenth-Century Paris, London, and New York* (Liverpool: Liverpool University Press, 1999); Lucio Sponza, *Italian Immigrants in Nineteenth-Century Britain: Realities and Images* (Leicester: Leicester University Press, 1988).

6. Nicholas Temperley, "Introduction: The State of Research" in *The Lost Chord: Essays on Victorian Music*, 7–9.

to be upheld or a distance to be kept," and these features are supremely desirable to many in a society that allows social mobility.[7] Bourdieu's concepts of social and cultural capital provide a particularly useful framework to illustrate how "investment" of participation in activities associated with music—and particularly opera—could return dividends in terms of social prestige and validation. As Derek Scott remarks of the second half of the century, "the increase in urban populations and rise of the bourgeoisie brought a need for public demonstrations of social standing, since it was no longer common knowledge who was important."[8] Scott examines attendance at concerts, but his argument can also be applied to familiarity with, as well as attendance at, grand opera. The tunes, plots, scenes, and stars, often mediated through popular illustrated papers such the *Illustrated London News* or *Punch,* circulated as cultural commodities quite apart from the smaller population who actually attended the spectacle.[9]

Opera had become identified with social and cultural status, and preeminently with Italians: for example, many English musicians adopted Italian names, presumably to gain musical glamour, prestige, or authority, such as the native of Rochdale who became "Signor Delavanti" for musical purposes.[10] However, it was attending or being familiar with the opera that conferred the most social and cultural status. Musical performances constructed artists as objects, to be viewed and judged, positioning the English viewer as a superior consumer. Italians involved in high-status cultural productions such as opera were represented as worthy of admiration and note, but this did not extend to their social position. Social boundaries existed for even the most eminent performers: for example, the conductor Costa was blackballed when he applied to join the exclusive Athenaeum club in 1868.[11] Such behavior could be ascribed to the traditional low status of performers, and the resentment at such dominance of Italian cultural capital, but there were, in fact, more complex forces at work.

---

7. Pierre Bourdieu, *Distinction: A Social Critique of the Judgement of Taste* (London: Routledge and Kegan Paul, 1984), 34, 57, 87, 101.

8. Derek Scott, "Music and Social Class in Victorian London," *Urban History,* 29.1 (2002): 63. Subsequent references to this text will be cited parenthetically.

9. For example, *Punch* frequently ran skits or cartoons referring to operatic titles, figures, or plots, and the *Illustrated London News* (*ILN*) covered opera news first in its Music columns, in the season, and some weeks exclusively. Opera scenes and performers provided subject matter for illustrations regularly, and when Covent Garden burned down in 1856, the *ILN* devoted several illustrated pages over two weeks' issues to the story. The majority of readers of these publications would not attend opera, but familiarity and a certain amount of interest was obviously assumed.

10. David Russell, *Popular Music in England, 1840–1914* (Manchester: Manchester University Press, 1997), 34.

11. Cyril Ehrlich, *The Music Profession in Britain Since the Eighteenth Century: A Social History* (Oxford: Oxford University Press, 1985), 42.

Stereotypes of Italians: The Wider Picture

There were powerful myths circulating simultaneously of Italians as primitive, amoral, degenerate, and animalistic—a group clearly set apart from the English. For example, an Italian convicted at the Old Bailey in 1865 was recommended for a reprieve by the judge as "being of a more revengeful nature than others" purely by virtue of his nationality.[12] The Italian had been a signifier for amorality since the first English readings of Machiavelli in the sixteenth century, and this stereotype was sustained by dramatic travel tales such as *English Travellers and Italian Brigands* by W. J. C. Moers in 1866, as well as literary portrayals such as Count Fosco in Wilkie Collins's *The Woman in White* (1859). Gothic romances such as Ann Radcliffe's *The Mysteries of Udolpho* (1794) and *The Italian* (1797) had emphasized the violence and passionate nature of Italians, and this residual cultural construct was firmly inscribed for the Victorians. This stereotype of intensity and essential animality of Italians as swayed by passion and without rational control could shade into another commonly attributed feature—their low level of civilization and their consequent poverty and dirt. This put them on the level of animals, with which they were frequently pictured. Despite the urban nature of much Italian life, popular representations of Italians usually featured them in a rural setting with donkeys, goats, or oxen, and with bare feet.[13] Even pictures of Italians gaily dancing the tarantella emphasized them as creatures ruled by animal spirits. This could be seen, however, as an enviable situation in many ways, especially at a time when England's own pastoral past was being celebrated in many cultural forms, from paintings at the Royal Academy such as William Collins's "Cottage Hospitality" (1834) to collections of folk songs published as supplements to magazines. Nostalgia for a vanished pastoral England, and an awareness of modern squalor and disease, meant that Italy could also represent a playground, or a place of traditional ease. And it had been, after all, the stage from which the Roman Empire and the Renaissance had influenced the world, as plentiful architectural and artistic remains testified. One way in which to resolve this tension was to separate the country from its inhabitants. Shelley's comment provides a rich example of this disjunction, frequently expressed by other writers on Italy such as Ruskin and Elizabeth Barrett Browning:

> There are two Italies: one composed of the green earth & transparent sea and
> the mighty ruins of antient times, and aerial mountains, & the warm and

---

12. Cited in Martin J. Weiner, "'Homicide and 'Englishness': Criminal Justice and National Identity in Victorian England," *National Identities* 6.3 (2004): 206.

13. See McAllister, *John Bull's Italian Snakes and Ladders,* chapters 2 and 6.

radiant atmosphere which is interfused through all things. The other consists of the Italians of the present day, their works and ways. The one is the most sublime & lovely contemplation that can be conceived by the imagination of man: the other the most degraded[,] disgusted and odious.[14]

However, present-day Italians were appearing in English headlines as heroes, or at least as honorable victims, in the campaign to unite Italy as a nation, the *Risorgimento*. Giuseppe Garibaldi was the most famous, but Giuseppe Mazzini, the republican patriot, based himself in England from 1837 until 1868, and was highly visible in English public life as he was an active journalist and promoter of the Italian cause. He enlisted such figures as Carlyle and Dickens, and became a public hero when his correspondence was spied on by the Home Secretary.[15] But when such indicators of social or cultural importance were absent, the more negative myths served as the context for viewing Italians on the streets, the organ-grinders.

Italians on the Streets: Creating a Nuisance

Significantly, the growth in the mid-nineteenth century of the property-owning middle classes fueled the imperative to separate oneself from disorder and dirt, locating it outside in the street and even making it "foreign." As Jenni Calder remarks, "[t]o have an interior environment that enabled such things to be forgotten was a priority of middle-class aspiration."[16] Moreover, as John Picker notes, the creative professionals who wrote, composed, or drew for their living (and created the world shown in *Punch*) were without a formal, separate workplace as marker of their status. Noise pollution presented a very real threat to their concentration and therefore livelihood, but the infiltration of street music challenged their lives on a deeper level. Picker writes about the professional insecurity of such workers (almost invariably men), and the corollary that "those aspiring to respectability needed to fight aggressively to mark their territory as professionals, as industrious intellectuals."[17] In addition to professional anxieties, middle-class males had the task of constructing themselves as respectable "English gentlemen," which again involved a

---

14. Percy Bysshe Shelley, unpublished letter, 1818, quoted in Wolfgang Kemp, *The Desire of My Eyes: The Life and Work of John Ruskin,* 152.

15. See McAllister, *John Bull's Italian Snakes and Ladders,* 202–203. The classic study on Mazzini in England is William Roberts, *Prophet in Exile: Joseph Mazzini in England, 1837–1868* (London: Peter Lang, 1989).

16. Jenni Calder, *The Victorian Home* (London: Batsford, 1977), 15.

17. John Picker, "The Soundproof Study: Victorian Professionals, Work Space, and Urban Noise," *Victorian Studies* 43.3 (1999): 435.

separation from all varieties of male behavior that could be construed as the opposite.[18]

The fragility of masculinity and social status was such that it had to be remade in almost every context, from one's own hearth to street confrontations. In such a situation, uncertainty was raised about boundaries of all kinds, and therefore much of the mid-nineteenth-century discourse about the organ-grinders explores liminal spaces—or that contested boundary between the hard-won home space and uncontrollable outside and other spaces (depicted in cartoons as pavement). In infringing upon this space, the Italians, by their very national positioning, were made to serve as a repository for negative and feared qualities. For example, their very links with the world of music which could confer social and cultural capital, as demonstrated by opera composers, conductors, and singers, posited alternative values to those of the solidly—or stolidly—middle-class John Bull. This is of particular significance with the Victorian soundscape, where notions of aurality and the value and acceptability of public sounds were open to negotiation in a shifting cultural climate. "Noise" may be considered as sound in an inappropriate context or at an inappropriate level, and significant factors are surely taste and boundaries: one person's music is another's noise, like Mary Douglas's definition of dirt as being matter that is considered to be in the wrong place.[19] The question arises: why the sound of a street organ, not inherently offensive, was felt to be so threatening? Emily Cockayne's study concludes that the term "noise" was often used imprecisely, and could be applied to sounds pleasant or unpleasant, being largely synonymous with "sound," but that "noisy" sounds "irritated the hearer because they were loud, clamorous, importune, irregular, intrusive, disturbing, distracting, inexplicable or shocking."[20] The portable organ's classification as noisy cannot be separated from its low cultural value, linked to its availability to all: perhaps this is a good example of the process Bourdieu describes as "petit-bourgeois aestheticism . . . [which] . . . defines itself against the 'aesthetic' of the working classes, refusing their favourite subjects."[21] Derek Scott points to a movement away from popular music in the mid-nineteenth century; he explains that "in the first half of the century, popular music had been acceptable in the 'best

18. The classic study is by Robin Gilmour, *The Idea of the Gentleman in the Victorian Novel* (London: George Allen and Unwin, 1981). There has also been important work on this area by John Tosh in works such as *A Man's Place: Masculinity and the Middle-Class Home in Victorian England* (New Haven, CT and London: Yale University Press, 1999).

19. Mary Douglas, *Purity and Danger: An Analysis of the Concepts of Pollution and Taboo* (London: Routledge and Kegan Paul, 1966).

20. Emily Cockayne, "Cacophony, or vile scrapers on vile instruments: bad music in early modern English towns," *Urban History* 29.1 (2002): 36.

21. Pierre Bourdieu, *Distinction,* 58.

of homes,' but from now on the message of 'high art' was that there was a 'better class of music' and another kind (soon to be seen as degenerate) that appealed to 'the masses'" (64). But there is also the territorial perspective, in which sound entering one's space performs an act of hostility: according to Jacques Attali, noise is "experienced as destruction, disorder, dirt, pollution, an aggression against code-structuring messages. In all cultures, it is associated with the idea of the weapon, blasphemy, plague."[22] As for the householders being confronted with such a plague, Eric Hobsbawm compares the recently socially mobile in the mid-1800s to members of Alcoholics Anonymous, "precariously balanced on the plateau of respectability."[23] Challenges to order and social position, which the organ-grinders represented, interrogated the status and power of the unwilling hearer as well as their notions of what it meant to be English, drawing on some of the powerful mythology of ascribed Italian qualities.

Organ Grinders and Xenophobia in *Punch:* The Growing Hostility

Punch began in 1841 as a radical comic paper in the tradition of the *Charivari* in France (from 1832). Hence *Punch* mainly ridiculed and punctured English insularity and complacency, rather than trading in foreign stereotypes. However, when the ownership and editorial board changed, a movement to foreign targets enabled the paper to survive financially. By 1843 *Punch* was relying on mild xenophobia for laughs, with a cartoon of disreputable foreigners waiting outside a tannery with a sign outside saying "Foreign skins cleaned here" (IV: 118).[24] *Punch* never achieved the high sales of the penny papers or those addressed to a more popular market: its cultural, historical, and political references (including those to Italian opera) suggest that readers were assumed to be from the educated middle class and, indeed, Richard Altick has described it as "addressed to an upper- and middle-class audience."[25] This ensured its influence, as the legislators and intelligentsia would be sure to see its pages, and *Punch* addresses the reader as not only the voice of sanity and reason, but the voice of the country. The English constitution was frequently celebrated as a source of power and stability,

---

22. Jacques Attali, *Noise: The Political Economy of Music* (Manchester: Manchester University Press, 1985), 27.

23. Eric Hobsbawm, *The Age of Capital, 1848–1875* (London: Abacus, 1997), 276.

24. All *Punch* citations will be cited parenthetically in the text.

25. Richard Altick, *The English Common Reader: A Social History of the Mass Reading Public, 1800–1900* (Chicago: University of Chicago Press, 1963), 358.

most especially in times of threatened social or political unrest, and in 1848, with revolutionary activity igniting most of Europe and threatening England, many cartoons showed John Bull keeping his balance, sailing a boat, and even making a pudding with more success than the crowned heads of Europe. Anxiety about revolution at home often required the externalization or projection of such forces so that the reader might remain secure, and in 1849 *Punch* soothed the anxieties of its readers with the comforting message, "There is No Place Like Home" (see figure 12.1). The central part of a larger illustration shows John Bull with his family, safe, and well fed; while the perimeter depicts the revolutionary chaos of the rest of the world. One of the most prominent ruffians, shown chasing the Pope away at the top of the page, is clearly Italian by his high-crowned hat—a well-known marker of Italianness—and a bestial stance, with a hand wielding a knife and a huge jaw. Anxiety about potential revolution, still very powerful at this point, required the externalization, or projection, of such forces so that John Bull might be secure. And of course there is the psychological mechanism contributing to xenophobia—that we project our shared and secret fears onto an "out" group, which then becomes a repository for all those aspects impossible to acknowledge in ourselves. As Linda Colley remarks in *Britons,* "once confronted with an obviously alien 'Them,' an otherwise diverse community can become a reassuring 'Us.'"[26] To find examples of such a group on one's own doorstep, and to be unable to control them, is to risk contamination as well as external threat.

In 1849 there was also a feature on *The Begging Profession* using Italian musical terms to satirize the techniques of "professional" foreign beggars and seeming to identify the two—and yet such was the fluidity and complexity of "Italian" as a signifier that later on in the same year a poem could appear lauding Mazzini as a brave patriot (*Punch* 16: 25, 35). Mazzini, a gifted publicist for the Italian cause in England, had recently failed to sustain the brief 1848 Roman revolution, but his advocacy of revolution was against Papal and Austrian forces, and sufficiently far away, perhaps, to enable *Punch* readers to construct him as no immediate danger to their pockets or property. There is also a mention in 1849 of "those unfortunate dogs, the Italian organ boys" (*Punch* 17: 54). *Punch* appears compassionate towards the children, and waxes indignant about the exploitation of the boys in two brief articles, but at the end of 1849 there is a spoof letter on *The Organ and Monkey Nuisance,* which is a sign of things to come. The writer signs himself, "The father of a family," and constructs himself as the protector of his family's space, which

---

26. Linda Colley, *Britons: Forging the Nation, 1707–1837* (New Haven, CT and London: Yale University Press, 1992), 6. Also see Allan Christensen, *Nineteenth Century Narratives of Contagion: 'Our feverish contact'* (London: Routledge, 2005) on contemporary fears of contagion.

Figure 12.1 "There is No Place Like Home," *Punch* 16 (1849): 27

clearly extends outside the house in this case. The postscript links the literal disturbance with the disturbing of society's boundaries, "Couldn't the Alien Act be put into place against these Italian imps? They are far more mischievous than any Socialist" (*Punch* 17: 244). The Removal of Aliens Act, introduced in 1848 as a reaction to the wave of revolutions sweeping Europe, was actually something of a paper tiger: it enabled the government to exile alien citizens considered dangerous, but this power was never exercised, and its duration was stated in the Act as one year only. In the absence of direct political confrontation, the place of revolutionaries could be filled by boys with their irruption into private space, threatening hard-won leisure by their noise.

The "imps" who played street organs were not judged to pose too great a threat, but with the Crimean war in 1854, and the threat of conscription for Englishmen, *Punch*'s jingoism produced the startling cartoon shown in figure 12.2, "Foreign Enlistment" by John Leech. The boys have become fully grown men; this is significant because organ-grinders continue to be represented as adult males only for the next ten years of *Punch* cartoons. These

Figure 12.2 "Foreign Enlistment," *Punch* 27 (1854): 262

men bear signs that can be read as signifying degeneracy; they are shorter by a head than the soldier accompanying them, and their faces are shadowed so that they look rather grimy. They can be recognized as organ-grinders by their barrel organs, of course, and as Italian by their characteristically "Italian" hats, but the faces are most interesting. They all have beards. Although the beard became fashionable for young English men a few years later (and was duly satirized by *Punch*) it was still associated with foreigners at this point. The beards, however, fail to hide completely the most significant feature of all—the men's jutting, prognathous jaws.

The early nineteenth-century "sciences" of phrenology and physiognomy read jaw formation and facial angles as well as skull shape as signs that various races were higher or lower on the evolutionary scale. The more developed the jaw, forehead, and cheekbones, the nearer to brute beasts, was the theory, and the Irish, for example, were commonly portrayed with ape-like, jutting jaws.[27] The discovery of Neanderthal man in 1856 gave further impetus to these beliefs, which were later to be developed into Edward Tylor's *Primitive Culture,* published in 1871. Tylor developed a scale that located "the educated world of England and America" at one end of a continuum, with "savage tribes" at the other. Between these poles, examples were given of the Australian [Aboriginal], Tahitian, Aztec, Chinese, and Italian "races" in this "ascending order of culture."[28] The minute differences between Europeans were scrutinized to make a point which, surely, had more to do with nationalism and xenophobia. Italians were almost but not quite as civilized as the English. To attribute elements of savage nature to a specific group of outsiders positions oneself as having risen above this, and is, of course, very comforting in an age of uncertainty about the relationship between man— or the gentleman—and nature. It renders "scientific" a traditional projection mechanism. Darwin had advanced a theory that singing had developed from animal mating calls and certainly street singing was characterized as animal-like, in these images.[29] So the construction of Italian street musicians as adult, none-too-clean, and sharing facial characteristics with their

---

27. Ironically, Cesare Lombroso, the Italian anthropologist, was later to identify similarly prognathous features as the mark of inherited criminality in his 1876 paper, subsequently published in *L'uomo delinquente* (1896–1897, Rome) translated in part as the book *Criminal Man,* produced by his daughter G. L. Ferrero (New York and London: Putnam, 1911). In the Italian peninsula this stereotype was, in turn, applied to Southern Italians.

28. Tylor, *Primitive Culture* (London: no publisher given, 1871), 23–24. George W. Stocking *Victorian Anthropology* (London: Macmillan, 1987) is a classic text that remains an excellent summary of nineteenth-century racial anthropological theories and gives context for Tylor's views on Italians.

29. Alisa Clapp-Itnyre, *Angelic Airs, Subversive Songs: Music as Social Discourse in the Victorian Novel* (Athens: Ohio University Press, 2002), 22.

monkeys might well have fulfilled many needs for the *Punch* reader. Such representations offered externalization and containment of potentially dangerous contagions, as well as establishing the reader as socially, hygienically, and morally superior. At the time that this image appeared in *Punch* it was also full of reports on the appalling pollution in the Thames, and locating the omnipresent dirt in others was a way of firmly establishing English cleanliness and godliness.

After this there were no positive portrayals of organ-grinders in *Punch* for a period of ten years. Hostility to foreigners usurping English rights and pavements appeared in article headings like "An Influx of Foreign Rascals" as well as in poems about the musicians. A typical example demands that "All the wretches who go about grinding / And prevent us our business from minding / Should to justice be brought for the crime" (*Punch* 21: 240). The "crime" mentioned here is simply that of intruding into work or leisure, but is transformed to the worst possible, in an article in the same year, "The organs murder sleep with the same organised hostility, and in the neighbourhood of the Haymarket, about ten o'clock, the hideous chorus of yells arising from so many musical murders being all perpetrated at the same time, must be heard to be fully appreciated" (*Punch* 21: 141). The itinerant Italians' murder of music leads to the conceit of music as a murder weapon, firmly dissociating the grinders' activity from more sanctioned forms of musical activity. It is hard to believe that all such street musicians would have been so raucous and untalented, or their repertoire so murderous, although there are few records of such transitory performances. Mayhew quotes an organ-grinder, "You must have some opera tunes for the gentlemen, and some for the poor people, and they like the dancing tune." We are then given slightly more detail about his current repertoire, "Two are from opera, one is a song, one a waltz, one is a hornpipe, one is polka, and the other two is dancing tunes. One is from *I Lombardi* of Verdi."[30] Picker also uses Verdi in his description of the grinders' repertoire as a continuum "from the prison song in *Il Trovatore* to 'Rule Britannia'" (444). Yet despite such links with high-status opera, these musicians were damned—their low status as performers was further undermined by their ascribed embodiment of dirt, poverty, and animality, and they represented the lowest possible strand of society. Thus, class concerns were embedded in the public reception of their music, whether opera or "dancing tunes."

Punch representations are concerned more with boundary maintenance, the construction of class and urban "rights" to space, and an outlet for profound hostilities. These extended more widely than those of the few householders (such as *Punch* contributors, particularly the artist John Leech) who

---

30. Henry Mayhew, *London Labour and the London Poor* (London: Griffin, 1861), 3: 175.

worked from home. Although Leech died of a heart condition and overwork in 1864, a myth arose that he had been killed by the torments of such noise. Undoubtedly, the frequent and intrusive melodies were a nuisance to those whose place of work was also their home. But this campaign seems to have tapped into a much larger reservoir of animosity felt by middle-class readers towards the street performers who dared to assert their power to infringe the liminal space and challenge the physical boundaries that embodied class distinctions.

In 1857 the campaign against the organ-grinders intensified, with a letter from an imaginary grouch signing himself "Old Morose," boasting of tricking the "Organ-Fiend" by a vigilante group—of householders, of course:

> We privately hire three or four smart sharp *gamins,* glad to earn an honest shilling, to keep watch. An organ comes, and they fly to the fellow, and while one or two dance, and chaff, and amuse him, another slips out a sharp knife and quietly cuts the strap that holds up the organ. Next minute the whole lot have vanished, and the brown beast is left perfectly helpless. (*Punch* 33: 33)

This lawless behavior is sanctioned, as it is against the enemies of property, and the English *gamins* (although interestingly referred to by a French term) are contrasted to the foreign adult. He is only a "fellow" or, even more interestingly, a "brown beast." It is as though his exotic skin and origin has denied him humanity, or placed him in a position inferior to the English children. In the iconic significance of the humble organ grinder, we see illustrated George Mosse's concept of the countertype, the outsider who symbolizes physical and moral disorder and degeneration to enable the construction of the stereotype of modern masculinity.[31]

Italians were also guilty by association with the current threat of a revival of the English Roman Catholic establishment. The despised and feared Cardinal Wiseman, at the head of this movement, is shown loitering on the street with an organ to emphasize the link, illustrating contemporary anxieties over the power of such a "primitive" religion to seduce and unman the English and reduce them to the status of superstitious beggars. And in a spoof article about recruitment for the Chinese war we are told that the army wants "frightfully ill-looking young men and so will send an army of Italian organ-grinders" with "monstrous noses and horrid squints" (*Punch* 33: 207). The illustration shows their hairy, dirty, and rather subhuman appearance that is obviously calculated to have a repellent value worth considerable weaponry.

---

31. George Mosse, *The Image of Man* (Oxford: Oxford University Press, 1996).

"Italian Persecution": The Campaign Intensifies

By 1858 *Punch* readers had come to expect that in dramatic accounts of *Italian Persecution,* the persecution alluded to was neither that of Italian freedom fighters chained in cells, nor peasants butchered by Austrian forces, as the politically astute reader might assume, but that of organ-grinders plaguing the victimized English householder (*Punch* 34: 176). Like much humor, the title relies on this central paradox. It is a short play, a mock-drama form, used frequently by *Punch.* The contrast between the actual atrocities in Naples covered by *Punch* in other pages of the same issue, and this minor fracas is sobering, and reinforces the significance of the apparently innocuous organ-grinder. *Italian Persecution* was set in "a quiet street in London," in which the Paterfamilias attempts to defend his territory where "a Mother is tending a sick boy." But the organ-grinder defies him with "extreme insolence" and makes an equal claim to the territory of the street, standing his ground impudently (see figure 12.3, untitled). The Paterfamilias is almost ludicrously respectable; tightly buttoned up in his suit complete with top hat, he uses authoritative language such as "Be off!" and "By Jove, you scoundrel!" But the villainous-looking organist, complete with prognathous jaw and simian appearance, refuses to respect the bourgeois authority system. "Ha! ha! P'lice," he cries, "Where you find P'lice?" His shadow falls threateningly upon the steps of the householder's very property. The policeman is away romancing the kitchen maid, but once he is found he can do little. Threatened, the organ-grinder "Suddenly begins to blubber, and appeals to the bystanders for mercy to a poor refugee." Eventually, "the howling brute is driven off" and the hapless Paterfamilias is called a tyrant by onlookers. Verbally and visually, this article perfectly catches the note of outraged indignation felt by the (perhaps aspiring) gentleman who finds that sympathy is being given, unfairly, to animal-like foreigners. His home, his castle, is threatened—and the police will not provide him with protection. There is an almost vigilante mood about this, underlined by *Punch*'s conviction that readers will share the indignation of the householder and draw the implicit conclusion that he should be able to take the law into his own hands against such bestial parasites. There were to be more insulting portrayals of an organ-grinder in the next few years, but none that related them so closely to their middle-class victims. This text, however, serves as an iconic example of what can only be described as a campaign, in which *Punch* joined with other opinion-formers to focus middle-class fears and odium onto the Italian musicians.

There were debates about vagrancy and street entertainers in both Houses of Parliament in 1858 and, scorning impartiality, *Punch* headed its reports

Figure 12.3 Untitled, *Punch* 34 *(1858)*: 176

of debate with titles such as "Our Organ-Grinding Tyrants."[32] But as events
in the Italian peninsula were coming to a head, and as reports circulated of
brave deeds and stirring actions, for much of 1859 and 1860 *Punch* found
it more appropriate to eulogize Liberty, attack Papal power, and represent
Italy as a weak, feminized, and in need of help.[33] This provided a comfortable, powerful, position for the readers. Italy was moving towards a copy
of the English constitutional monarchy, under the leadership of the anglo-
phile Count Camillo Cavour and of course Garibaldi, who was frequently
presented as brave, fairish in hair and complexion, and, according to the
Illustrated London News on June 25, 1859, "having the calm manner and
appearance of an English gentleman officer." Garibaldi is a fascinating study,
as he was re-made as a quasi-Englishman, recuperating desired qualities such
as bravery for the English reader whilst being differentiated from the previously popular Mazzini, who was not only a revolutionary, but a man depicted
with dark hair and a swarthy complexion.[34] When dark and swarthy organ-

---

32. See Picker's excellent summary of social attitudes to organ grinders gives details of the wide
range of sources, not just *Punch,* in which they were vilified. John Picker, "The Soundproof Study."

33. Maura O'Connor, in *The Romance of Italy and the English Political Imagination* (Basingstoke:
Macmillan, 1998), discusses the feminization of Italy, particularly in chapters 2 and 3.

34. See Lucy Riall, *Garibaldi: Invention of a Hero* (New Haven, CT: Yale University Press,
2007).

grinders featured again in *Punch,* early in 1859, they were once more the safe repository for all that was feared and scorned. An organ-grinder is shown a foot upon the pavement, but the military Punch defends his space with a raised bayonet. There are more organ-grinders lurking in the street, whilst a policeman is shirking his duty of protecting the householder's rights.

Even when *Punch* commented on the political maneuvering of France and Austria in an 1859 comic poem called "The Italian Quadrille," it saw fit to illustrate this with an organ-grinder (see figure 12.4). In this case his jaw is even more pronounced, his gait is more brutish—and he has even grown a tail. This is the most extreme illustration in the series, and it is almost a relief to have the point made explicitly after the increasingly simian hints in earlier representations. It would surely have been perceived by some readers as contentious at such a climactic stage of Italy's struggle, given the popular support for the *Risorgimento.* After this nadir, during 1860 at a delicate stage in peninsular fighting and the international negotiations, *Punch* seemed to find a safer standpoint in the manly representations of Garibaldi and a linking of English and Italian nationalism in poems such as *Italy is Free,* referring to the "noble struggle." Or Italy was feminized, for example shown with her cousin John Bull at the Nations Ball in 1861 (*Punch* 40: 131), where Mr Bull and his Queenly companion Victoria induct their timid, weak cousin into the grown-up world of nationhood. But there were still brief, telling references to the degraded or bestial street musicians visible and audible on the streets of England when discussing French / Piedmontese political negotiations: "We are familiar with this style of demeanour as exhibited, in begging, by dirty fellows in high-crowned hats, with white mice and a hurdy-gurdy" (*Punch* 38: 129).

For a short time, all would seem to have gone delightfully quiet in the streets of London, according to *Punch,* but in 1862 two brutal illustrations reintroduced the demonic threat of the organ-grinder. In a reference to the recent popular exhibition of a gorilla, and the anthropological theory referred to above, we find an extremely large monkey leading the grinder (or perhaps they are indistinguishable?) in "One Good Turn Deserves Another" (see figure 12.5). More transgressive and dangerous behavior was shown in a visualization of a recent news report of an attack by an organ-grinder's monkey, where Mr. Punch was again shown as forced to take on the role of policeman (*Punch* 42: 11).

These illustrations seemed to signal open season on the grinders and the intensification of *Punch*'s campaign. It was suggested that a corps of grinders be sent to the American Civil War, a poem was written about the joys of dowsing them with water (*Punch* 41: 78–79), and the Pope was portrayed

THE ITALIAN QUADRILLE.

Cavalier seul by GENERAL GYULAI.
General *Ronde d'hilarité.*

Figure 12.4 "The Italian Quadrille," *Punch* 36 (1859): 226

as another *Popish Organ Nuisance* (*Punch* 42: 167). Here, in a self-referential twist to previous illustrations such as *Italian Persecution,* Palmerston, as householder, berated the French Emperor Louis Napoleon for being derelict in his duty as an international policeman. Events in Italy were frustrating, as there was an Italian state that, however, did not comprise the whole of the peninsula, and *Punch* was full of advice to the Pope to hand over Rome,

ONE GOOD TURN DESERVES ANOTHER.

THE LAZY ORGAN GRINDERS HAVE HAD IT ALL THEIR OWN WAY WITH THE MONKEYS—NOW THEN—CHANGE ABOUT !

Figure 12.5 "One Good Turn Deserves Another," *Punch* 42 (1862), Almanack

and advice to the King and Garibaldi as to how to achieve this. Without any more positive ascriptions, Italians were once more represented as threats by John Leech as "Faust and the Organ-Fiends" (see figure 12.6) in which the devils are legion, with not a police officer in sight. Their only companion, symbolically, is an insect (a louse?) shown below the central figure's staff. In the article accompanying this 1863 illustration, a note of paranoia is detectable. Mr. Punch, losing his sense of humor, becomes positively draconian:

> The law says the street is a highway for passengers which no one may obstruct.
> Let the police be empowered to keep the Organists moving. They will soon

FAUST AND THE ORGAN-FIENDS.

SKETCH FROM A STUDY WINDOW.

Figure 12.6 "Faust and the Organ-Fiends," *Punch* 46 (1863): 53

get tired of that. SIR RICHARD MAYNE is hereby charged with the execution of this decree (*Punch* 45: 53).

In the following year it is suggested that policemen should be provided with tongs for the purpose of taking hold of a nuisance so disgusting as an Italian organ-grinder, "whose clothes are always saturated with dirt, and who, if he wears a collar, has probably a state of things underneath it into which the idea of putting your hands is revolting" (*Punch* 46: 27).

Although there were contemporary references to many other street musicians such as German bands and African performers, no other musicians were singled out in this way. Indeed, the powerful focus on Italians and their dirt seems to be fulfilling an important function. Their animality and interchangeability with their monkeys seems to invalidate any ascribed Italian inherent musicality. In the same year, 1864, Garibaldi visited England, and the public image and rapturous reception of "The Noblest Roman of them All," as *Punch* nominated him (*Punch* 46: 149), acted as a powerful contrast. England might not have a Liberator, and might have been relatively inactive in the *Risorgimento,* but by *Punch*'s insistence on locating dirt and disreputability in Italian organ grinders, the English were enabled to construct themselves in a position of civilized superiority. The valor of Garibaldi and the glamour of the Italian Opera at Covent Garden had their shadow in the despised organ-grinder—and as *Punch* had shown, he was legion.

The Bass Bill and the End of the Campaign

Finally, in 1864, *Punch*'s witch hunt, for no less a term seems appropriate, came to a quasi-victorious end. Michael T. Bass, M.P. for Derby, had first put forward a Bill in 1863, and resubmitted it in May, 1864. His proposed Act was to be "for the Better Regulation of Street Music in the Metropolis," and did not actually mention organ-grinders in its title. However, to increase its chances of being passed, he published *Street Music in the Metropolis* (London: John Murray, 1864), a large volume comprising a collection of letters received from supporters with addresses in the better part of town, articles such as those in *Punch,* and official reports, which did feature many complaints focusing upon the "organ-grinding nuisance." He acknowledged that actual prosecutions had been few, but argued that the current law made it too difficult for the police to arrest street musicians. Bass had influential supporters: Dickens wrote a letter, which was co-signed by twenty eight "cultural workers" such as Tennyson and, of course, John Leech. The mathematician and inventor Charles Babbage had also been active, both in writing and in bringing prosecutions, to an obsessive degree.[35] Until July, when the Bill was passed, *Punch* issues sounded a note of near hysteria, suggesting "packs" to "hunt down" the "varmints" (*Punch* 46: 251; 222), and nominating them as "fiends" in almost each one of the many other references. In figure 12.7 (also by Leech) the title hammers home the point: "Three Cheers for Bass and

---

35. See Picker, "The Soundproof Study," 437; and Sponza, *Italian Immigrants in Nineteenth-Century Britain,* 175–177.

Figure 12.7 "Three Cheers for Bass and his Barrel of Beer, and out with the Foreign Ruffian and his Barrel-Organ!" *Punch* 46 (1864): 222.

his Barrel of Beer, and out with the Foreign Ruffian and his Barrel-Organ!" Bass, with a proudly non-prognathous facial profile, is shown driving a simian rascal over the cliffs down into the sea at the right, symbolically knocking him and his barrel organ over with a different kind of barrel, one filled with good English beer (he was from the brewing family). In fact, the main changes implemented by the eventual Street Music (Metropolis) Act[36] were merely that a police officer or a servant, in addition to a householder, could now ask the musician to leave without claiming illness or other reasonable cause, and that now the street musicians were liable to a 40 shillings fine or three days' imprisonment if they refused to move on. However, for this last action to be taken, the original complainant had to come to a later hearing to identify them; this would seem to create even more inconvenience for householders and was unlikely to have been popular. The Street Music Act

---

36. Sponza, *Italian Immigrants in Nineteenth-Century Britain,* 177–179, gives a full account of the passage and eventual form of this act.

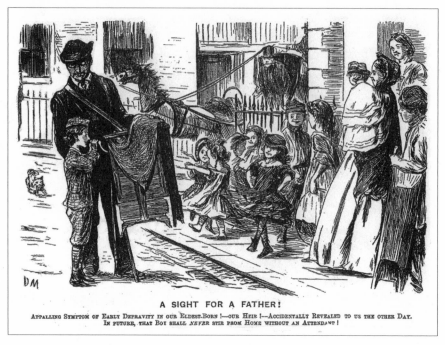

A SIGHT FOR A FATHER!

Appalling Symptom of Early Depravity in our Eldest-Born !—our Heir !—Accidentally Revealed to us the other Day.
In future, that Boy shall *never* stir from Home without an Attendant !

Figure 12.8 "A Sight For a Father!" *Punch* 48 (1865): 250

was rarely invoked, and in any case was not a particularly swinging measure, but *Punch* constructed it as a huge victory for the forces of order, liberty, and cleanliness. Although the organ-grinders did not disappear from the streets, they immediately became almost invisible on *Punch*'s pages. In the next year a poem, *A Song of the Streets* enumerated the many nuisances to be found, but "the organs, that distract your mind/ With their 'dem'd low perpetual grind'" only appear after forty-one lines, towards the end (*Punch* 48: 112), and when there was a poem on *The Grinders* it turned out to be on the Sheffield steel trade with not a mention of fiends or nuisances (*Punch* 49: 193). An illustration from 1865, "A Sight for a Father!" dramatizes the change in *Punch*'s perception of the organ-grinder after his symbolic defeat of the year before (see figure 12.8). He looks well groomed, and differs radically from his earlier brothers in that he does not participate in the exaggerated visual conventions of caricature—but then of course he is, significantly, standing in the roadway, not on the pavement.

There were many other nationalities of refugees in England, many of them street entertainers. As their music drifted into English dwellings, they would all have provided a threat of some kind to the attempts of bourgeois householders to establish their worthiness, their propriety, the boundaries of their properties, and their lives. As Bass himself pointed out with great vigor, the musicians were "not to be found in the alleys and courts, but in the squares and handsome streets."[37] However, he refers to these musicians in the same sentence as "the brass bands and the organs, the Savoyards and the German vagrants"—and indeed mentions German bands as frequently as Italian organ-grinders. But, as Picker remarks, "Italian organ-grinders came to be seen as the repulsive source of most noise in the city."[38] Sponza describes the Italian organ-grinders as "a sort of litmus paper," but only as revealing "the degree of social and ideological polarization and antagonism of Victorian London."[39] Reading the pages of *Punch* one is struck by the overwhelming use of the Italian street musicians as a symbol. An organ, even a portable one such as depicted in these illustrations, can certainly produce a powerful sound. But of course Italians inhabited a particularly contested cultural area. They were dashing revolutionaries, winning their liberty; they were the inheritors of Rome, Dante, and Michelangelo; they were sensuous, exciting, musical, handsome, and therefore represented a possible threat to the self-esteem of an Englishman. So other strands of discourse about them were necessary. The bourgeoisie could constitute Italy as a place of peasants, whose much-vaunted cultural superiority stood revealed as a sham—a degenerate animal-like race who used street music as a weapon for blackmail and legitimized crime. This is the arena in which the war of the organ-grinders and *Punch* was played out.

And then they were rehabilitated. The symbolic victory of The Street Music Act allowing *Punch* to quit the field with honor and the changing political and social context provided less dramatic images of Italians and they clearly presented less of a challenge. Once Italians had accepted England's superiority, symbolized by their adoption of English-pattern constitutional monarchy in the 1860s, they could be safely patronized, and even adopted as honorary Englishmen, like Garibaldi. Italians faded from public view somewhat after the dramatic events of the *Risorgimento,* losing much of their exotic signification. *Punch,* once it had won a small but significant victory, moved to another, existing, target, the un-musical Irish, treating them in a similar, if less complex, manner. But the uniting of music and animality in these images from *Punch* provides several interesting insights into the processes by which the rich, and potentially destabilizing, possibilities of Italians gave rise to a xenophobic episode in English cultural history.

---

37. Michael Thomas Bass, *Street Music in the Metropolis* (London: John Murray, 1864), 97.
38. Picker, "The Soundproof Study," 432.
39. Sponza, *Italian Immigrants in Nineteenth-Century Britain,* 179.

Works Cited

Altick, Richard. *The English Common Reader: A Social History of the Mass Reading Public, 1800–1900*. Chicago: University of Chicago Press, 1963.

Attali, Jacques. *Noise: The Political Economy of Music*. Translated by Brian Massumi. Manchester: Manchester University Press, 1985.

Bass, Michael Thomas. *Street Music in the Metropolis*. London: John Murray, 1864.

Bhabha, Homi. *The Location of Culture*. London: Routledge, 1994.

Bourdieu, Pierre. *Distinction: A Social Critique of the Judgement of Taste*. Translated by Richard Nice. London: Routledge and Kegan Paul, 1984.

Calder, Jenni. *The Victorian Home*. London: Batsford, 1977.

Clapp-Itnyre, Alisa. *Angelic Airs, Subversive Songs: Music as Social Discourse in the Victorian Novel*. Athens: Ohio University Press, 2002.

Cockayne, Emily. "Cacophony, or Vile Scrapers on Vile Instruments: Bad Music in Early Modern English Towns." *Urban History* 29.1 (2002): 35–47.

Colley, Linda. *Britons: Forging the Nation, 1707–1837*. New Haven, CT, and London: Yale University Press, 1992.

Curtis, L. Perry. *Apes and Angels: The Irishman in Victorian Caricature*. 2nd ed. Washington, DC: Smithsonian Institute Press, 1997.

De Nie, Michael. *The Eternal Paddy: Irish Identity and the British Press, 1798-1882*. Madison: University of Wisconsin Press, 2004.

Dickie, John. *Darkest Italy: The Nation and Stereotypes of the Mezzogiorno, 1860–1900*. Basingstoke: Macmillan, 1999.

Douglas, Mary. *Purity and Danger: An Analysis of the Concepts of Pollution and Taboo*. London: Routledge and Kegan Paul, 1966.

Ehrlich, Cyril. *The Music Profession in Britain Since the Eighteenth Century: A Social History*. Oxford: Oxford University Press, 1985.

Gilmour, Robin. *The Idea of the Gentleman in the Victorian Novel*. London: George Allen and Unwin, 1981.

Guglielmo, Jennifer and Salvatore Salerno, eds. *Are Italians White? How Race Is Made in America*. London: Routledge, 2003.

Hobsbawm, Eric. *The Age of Capital, 1848–1875*. London: Abacus, 1997.

Lombroso, Cesare. *Criminal Man*. Produced by G. L. Ferrero. New York and London: Putnam, 1911.

Mayhew, Henry. *London Labour and the London Poor*. 3 vols. London: Griffin, 1861.

McAllister, Annemarie. *John Bull's Italian Snakes and Ladders: English Attitudes to Italy in the Mid-Nineteenth Century*. Newcastle: Cambridge Scholars Publishing, 2007.

Mosse, George. *The Image of Man*. Oxford: Oxford University Press, 1996.

O'Connor, Maura. *The Romance of Italy and the English Political Imagination*. Basingstoke: Macmillan, 1998.

Picker, John. "The Soundproof Study: Victorian Professionals, Work Space, and Urban Noise." *Victorian Studies* 42.3 (1999): 427–453.

Riall, Lucy. *Garibaldi: Invention of a Hero*. New Haven, CT: Yale University Press, 2007.

Russell, David. *Popular Music in England, 1840–1914*. 2nd ed. Manchester: Manchester University Press, 1997.

Scott, Derek. "Music and Social Class in Victorian London." *Urban History* 29.11 (2002): 60–73.

Shelley, Percy Bysshe. Unpublished letter, 1818, quoted in Wolfgang Kemp, *The Desire of My Eyes: The Life and Work of John Ruskin,* Translated by Jan van Heurck. London: HarperCollins, 1991.

Sponza, Lucio. *Italian Immigrants in Nineteenth-Century Britain: Realities and Images.* Leicester: Leicester University Press, 1988.

Stella, Gian Antonio. *L'orda: quando gli albanesi eravamo noi.* Milano: Rizzoli, 2002.

Stocking, George W. *Victorian Anthropology.* London: Macmillan, 1987.

Temperley, Nicholas. "Introduction: The State of Research." In *The Lost Chord: Essays on Victorian Music,* edited by Nicholas Temperley. 2–16. Bloomington: Indiana University Press, 1989.

Tylor, Edward. *Primitive Culture.* London: n.p., 1881.

Weiner, Martin J. "'Homicide and Englishness': Criminal Justice and National Identity in Victorian England." *National Identities* 6.3 (2004): 203–213.

Zucchi, John. *The Little Slaves of the Harp. Italian Street Musicians in Nineteenth-Century Paris, London and New York.* Liverpool: Liverpool University Press, 1999.

13

"You know not of what you speak"

Language, Identity, and Xenophobia in
Richard Marsh's *The Beetle: A Mystery* (1897)

❦

MINNA VUOHELAINEN

"A sense of loathing": The Rhetoric of Xenophobia

In the first book of Richard Marsh's bestselling gothic novel *The Beetle: A Mystery* (1897),[1] the unemployed and homeless clerk Robert Holt is assaulted by a monstrous foreign presence, the eponymous Beetle. Holt describes his ordeal thus:

> It was as though something in my mental organisation had been stricken by a sudden paralysis. It may seem childish to use such language; but I was overwrought, played out; physically speaking, at my last counter; and, in an instant, without the slightest warning, I was conscious of a very curious sensation, the like of which I had never felt before, and the like of which I pray that I never may feel again,—a sensation of panic fear. I remained rooted to the spot on which I stood, not daring to move, fearing to draw my breath. . . . My heart was palpitating in my bosom; I could hear it beat. I was trembling so that I could scarcely stand. I was overwhelmed by a fresh flood of terror. I stared in front of me with eyes in which, had it been light, would have been

---

1. For the publication history of the novel, see Minna Vuohelainen, "Introduction" in *The Beetle: A Mystery*, xii–xvi.

seen the frenzy of unreasoning fear. My ears were strained so that I listened with an acuteness of tension which was painful.[2]

Existing scholarly accounts of this novel have focused mainly on Marsh's depiction of gender ambiguity and sadistic sexuality and, to a lesser extent, on his imperialist and Orientalist agenda and engagement with fin-de-siècle London.[3] The novel certainly supports such readings. The Beetle, a being of ambiguous ethnicity and gender and of considerable mesmeric powers, comes to London on a mission of revenge against a politician who has in his youth offended the forces of Isis in Egypt. The "remarkable tale" (207) that results from this "invasion" (17) is told, respectively, by multiple narrative voices belonging to figures representative of modernity: the unemployed clerk, Robert Holt; the upper-class scientist and inventor, Sydney Atherton; the potential New Woman, Marjorie Lindon; and the aristocratic detective, Augustus Champnell whose narrative also contains a first-person account by the rising politician, Paul Lessingham. Their narratives articulate fin-de-siècle anxieties concerning racial, cultural, and national identity.

However, Holt's sensations of "shrinking, horror, [and] nausea" (16) and of "loathing" (34), provoked by contact with the alien monster, also mark *The Beetle* as using a xenophobic discourse that, in many respects, reflects contemporary medical debates on phobias, or chronic, irrational fears. This essay will explore how a phobic reaction to the alien is articulated in the novel through the use and loss of the command of language. As a split narrative, *The Beetle* is a fragmented text riddled with troubling silences, absences, and tenuous connections between episodes and events. Thus, the very shape of the novel calls attention to the importance of language and the written record in defining and interpreting the chaos brought about by foreign invasion. This essay seeks to understand the xenophobic rhetoric in the

---

2. Richard Marsh, *The Beetle: A Mystery* (Kansas City, MO: Valancourt, 2008), 14–15. All subsequent citations refer to this edition and appear in the body of the text.

3. Rhys Garnett, "*Dracula* and *The Beetle:* Imperial and Sexual Guilt and Fear in Late Victorian Fantasy" in *Science Fiction Roots and Branches: Contemporary Critical Approaches;* Judith Halberstam, "Gothic Nation: *The Beetle* by Richard Marsh" in *Fictions of Unease: The Gothic from Otranto to* The X-Files; Kelly Hurley, "'The Inner Chambers of All Nameless Sin': *The Beetle,* Gothic Female Sexuality, and Oriental Barbarism" in *Virginal Sexuality and Textuality in Victorian Literature;* Victoria Margree, "'Both in Men's Clothing': Gender, Sovereignty and Insecurity in Richard Marsh's *The Beetle,*" *Critical Survey* 19.2 (2007); Minna Vuohelainen, "'Oh to Get Out of that Room!': Outcast London and the Gothic Twist in the Popular Fiction of Richard Marsh" in *Victorian Space(s): Leeds Centre Working Papers in Victorian Studies* VIII; Julian Wolfreys, "Introduction" in Richard Marsh, *The Beetle,* ed. Julian Wolfreys; and "The Hieroglyphic Other: *The Beetle,* London, and the Abyssal Subject" in *A Mighty Mass of Brick and Smoke: Victorian and Edwardian Representations of London.*

novel through an analysis of how command, loss, and absence of language function in formulating a phobic commentary on the alien invader. Command of language is, arguably, central to the definition of Britishness in the novel. Throughout the novel, however, the alien monster places the British characters' ability to use language under threat, reducing them to irrational, xenophobic inarticulacy. As will be argued here, this threat to language represents anxieties over the possibility of an annihilation of British identity by the foreign presence—an interpretation that accords well with contemporary philological views on the centrality of language to thought, identity, and nationhood. Hence, the Beetle's presence in London poses a threat not only to the individual, but also more generally to British culture, including established boundaries of gender, class, and national identity.[4]

Fin-de-siècle medical accounts define phobia as "morbid fear" or "a symptom of nervous disease"[5] that occurs "due to insanity or a diseased brain."[6] "[C]losely analogous to obsessions and imperative ideas," phobias could "best be explained by postulating the existence of *loci minor resistentiæ* in neuropathic brains which do not offer normal resistance to nervous currents and therefore find themselves in a state of constant excitation and irritation."[7] Phobias were seen to affect certain subject groups, including "[w]eakly constituted, sickly, ailing, highly imaginative persons"; "those weakened by repeated or great loss of blood [or] general sickness"; "women during the periods of catamenia, pregnancy, confinement, of secretion of milk, and excretion of lochia"; "children, adolescents, and adults whose education has been neglected, [or] whose mental education has been conducted on false principles"; "those whose mental irritability is increased by mental or bodily stimuli," for example "drink" or "onanism, masturbation, and other sexual excesses"; "those who are already mentally depressed"; mentally anxious "professional men"; and "in general students and others who overtax their mental powers."[8] Thus, pre-existing mental or physical weaknesses were seen as likely to predispose a person to states of fear. The symptoms caused by such morbid fears were seen to include physical sensations such as "cold

---

4. It should be noted here that while the gender and sexuality of the monster contribute to its loathsomeness, no attempt will be made here to explore these related issues, which have been extensively discussed by the critics listed in footnote 3 above.

5. B. Ball, "On Claustrophobia," *British Medical Journal* (6 September 1879): 371 (comment by Dr. G. M. Beard).

6. Josiah Morse, *The Psychology and Neurology of Fear* (Worcester, MA: Clark University Press, 1907), 37.

7. Morse, *The Psychology and Neurology of Fear*, 44.

8. M. Roth, *A Few Notes on Fear and Fright, and the Diseases They Cause and Cure; also on the Means of Preventing and Curing the Effects of These Emotions* (London and Manchester: Henry Turner, 1872), 7–8.

perspiration," "tremor of lips and chin," "pallid, startled, staring, flickering" countenance, "oppression of the chest," "irregular, interrupted" pulse, "nausea," and "[w]eak, heavy, shaking, collapsed, powerless, and paralytic" limbs.[9] Of particular interest are the psychological effects of states of fear, which include sensations of "anxiety and pressure" in the brain, "the regular functions [of which] are interrupted"; "loss of memory and recollection" and "loss of speech"; "a succession of recurring periods of unconsciousness, alternating very rapidly with intervals of consciousness"; and "almost a perfect cessation of the function of the will, and a momentary general paralysis of all action."[10] These symptoms very closely mirror those experienced by Holt, a homeless tramp who is "overwrought, played out; physically speaking, at [his] last counter" (14–15). While the word "phobia" is never mentioned in the novel, *The Beetle* uses a linguistic register closely allied to medical discourses on phobia to articulate its characters' reactions to the alien presence.

Sensations of "abject terror" (80) among characters in the novel are related to the Beetle's foreign origins which, it is implied, render the monster particularly loathsome, indeed animalistic and parasitic. It could, then, be argued that the characters' phobic reactions sparked by the Beetle are specifically the result of xenophobia. The word "xenophobia" did not enter the English language until 1909, but its antecedents were present in the nineteenth century in expressions of Germanophobia, Francophobia, Anglophobia, and, most commonly, Russophobia.[11] These terms articulated in a concise way a set of fears and anxieties inspired by a specific cultural or national grouping. The later, related term, xenophobia, by contrast, is much less definite in its all-embracing irrational fear of *all* foreigners. Thus, xenophobia is arguably tied to the imperial and migrational conditions of the fin de siècle which, as discussed below, witnessed increasing contact between the British and a number of foreign peoples. The designation "phobia" arguably defines such fears as irrational and morbid, suggesting that a phobic reaction to foreign cultures might be read as pathological rather than natural. In Marsh's novel, the "paroxysm of fear" (172) and "antipathy" inspired by contact with the alien are indeed recognized as representative of "a rooted, and, apparently, illogical dislike" (174); yet the novel's British protagonists cannot escape from their "nauseous consciousness of the presence of something evil" (42). Arguably, if phobic reactions are to be read as signs of irrationality or disease, their true origin lies not with the alien presence, but within the British psyche.

---

9. Roth, *A Few Notes,* 2–3.

10. Roth, *A Few Notes,* 2–4.

11. The first recorded use of "Anglophobia" occurred in 1793, of "Russophobia" in 1836, of "Francophobia" in 1870, and of "Germanophobia" in 1887. *Oxford English Dictionary Online.* Accessed June 30, 2011.

While the British characters describe the foreigner as monstrous, the narrative subtly undermines their authority by emphasizing the irrationality of the phobic impulse.

"So unnatural, so inhuman": Invasion Gothic and Xenophobia

The Beetle fits, in many ways, Patrick Brantlinger's concept of imperial gothic, or a mixture of gothic and male adventure romance, in which civilization is placed at risk of contagion from primitive, atavistic forces. In these tales, Brantlinger adds, the dark side of human nature is revealed in a collision of the modern with the archaic.[12] As noted above, the events in *The Beetle* are triggered by Paul Lessingham's encounter with a dangerous but alluring priestess of Isis in Egypt: Lessingham is lured into the native quarters of Cairo and there drugged and abducted by the mesmeric Oriental woman who reduces him to helplessness while engaging in "orgies of nameless horrors" (213) that appear to involve the violation and sacrifice of white women. For Lessingham, the Oriental woman is something less than human: "so unnatural, so inhuman" is she that he contemplates "destroy[ing] her with as little sense of moral turpitude as if she had been some noxious insect" (211). Eventually, Lessingham attempts to strangle his captor, who indeed turns into a gigantic scarab at the point of death, disturbing his mental balance and giving him an understandable "antipathy to beetles" (174). Lessingham's encounter with the alien results, then, in a phobic conflation of the foreign with the parasitic.

This preamble to the novel, dated twenty years before the main thrust of the narrative, is buried towards the end of the text. The majority of *The Beetle,* in fact, takes place in contemporary London that has suffered an invasion from an obnoxious representative of Isis, possibly the priestess herself. The reduction to irrationality and the challenge to modernity that Brantlinger associates with imperial gothic here take place in "the heart of civilised London" (266), not some far corner of the Empire. Hence, this essay will propose that *The Beetle* stands as an example not of *imperial* gothic but of what will tentatively be called *invasion* gothic. This brand of gothic will here be defined as a mixture of urban gothic and fashionable invasion narrative, articulated in an essentially xenophobic discourse. Invasion gothic sees British identity, security, and superiority placed under threat from a foreign, often supernatural, monster, which reveals insecurities, anxieties, and

---

12. Patrick Brantlinger, *Rule of Darkness: British Literature and Imperialism, 1830–1914* (Ithaca and London: Cornell University Press, 1988), 227–230.

phobic responses already latent within the British nation; these preexisting weaknesses, which arguably amount to a disease, predispose Britain to a foreign invasion.[13] While, then, the events are rooted abroad, their outcome is played out in the Western world; specifically, in the imperial metropolis of London, which suffers a frightful invasion from an alien force. This characteristic mixture of supernatural, foreign invasion and native weakness within a dark, menacing, but contemporary London is articulated by a phobic, gothic rhetoric.

As H. L. Malchow notes, nineteenth-century gothic and racial discourses were closely connected and greatly influenced one another.[14] Like all gothic fiction, invasion gothic draws on contemporary developments, in particular the extensive debate over what was known at the fin-de-siècle as the "Alien Question." The end of the nineteenth century witnessed increasing contacts between the British and people of other ethnic origins. Both within the growing Empire and at home, the British were increasingly brought into day-to-day contact with imperial subject peoples and immigrants from Eastern Europe, Africa, and Asia. By the 1880s, large numbers of Eastern European Jews had settled in London's East End, and their presence provoked an extensive debate over Britain's immigration policy.[15] These "undesirable aliens" were seen as a threat to the host nation, on whom they were seen to prey financially and sexually. "Isn't there some superstition about evil befalling whoever shelters a homeless stranger?" Marjorie Lindon wonders in Marsh's novel (130) in an echo of the contemporary fear of racial miscegenation. Various branches of anthropology—racial, cultural, criminal, sexual—were developed in response to such ethnic mixing, with knowledge of other cultures, peoples, or modes of behavior as their chief goal. In the wake of evolutionary biology, the new "Science of Man" placed peoples and cultures on an evolutionary ladder that appeared to indicate a teleological progression from "primitive" culture towards white European civilization. Anthropology could be used reassuringly to classify different cultures, and taxonomies of skin color, facial features, and cultural habit were formulated to determine each group's place on the evolutionary ladder.[16] Such taxonomies were connected,

13. Other examples of invasion gothic texts from this period would include Marsh's novels *The Goddess: A Demon* (1900) and *The Joss: A Reversion* (1901); Bram Stoker's *Dracula* (1897); George Du Maurier's *Trilby* (1894); Marie Corelli's *The Sorrows of Satan* (1895); and Arthur Machen's *The Great God Pan* (1894).

14. H. L. Malchow, *Gothic Images of Race in Nineteenth-Century Britain* (Stanford, CA: Stanford University Press, 1996), 5.

15. David Feldman, *Englishmen and Jews: Social Relations and Political Culture* (New Haven, CT and London: Yale University Press, 1994); "The Importance of Being English: Jewish Immigration and the Decay of Liberal England" in *Metropolis: London Histories and Representations since 1800*.

16. Kenan Malik, *The Meaning of Race: Race, History and Culture in Western Society* (Houndmills and London: Macmillan, 1996), 87.

on the one hand, to the imperialist rhetoric of the mission to "civilize" supposedly more backward peoples; on the other, they presented the worrying possibility that racial miscegenation at home might result in the degeneration of the white British "race." Arguably, xenophobic reactions to other cultures could be seen to mirror such anthropological classifications, with the defining characteristic of each nation reduced to the military or cultural threat it was perceived to pose.

Furthermore, Kenan Malik notes that in the nineteenth century the "notion of race" could also be evoked to discuss "differences *within* a particular society," so that "[w]hat we would now consider to be class or social distinctions were seen as racial ones."[17] Malik argues that "[t]he very process by which nationhood was constructed in Europe . . . revealed the internal divisions within the nation."[18] Thus, indigenous class distinctions split the home culture itself into various "races," which, when mingling with immigrants, might produce yet another racial grouping. In their pursuit of the Beetle, the upper-class characters in Marsh's novel come to realize that London is a city of ethnic tribes: their dealings with East End slum-dwellers are seriously hampered by their inability to communicate effectively with their own countrymen whose Cockney accents are incompatible with upper-class English accents, and whom they regard with evident suspicion as culturally and racially alien. Yet the novel also recognizes indigenous Londoners' xenophobic reactions to foreigners. For these lower-class Cockneys, the Beetle is a "Harab" (272), "a dirty foreigner, who [goes] about in a bed-gown through the public streets" (246) and speaks in "that queer foreign way them Harab parties 'as of talkin'" (280). Marsh's ironic commentary highlights the ignorance, prejudices, and faulty use of the English language of the lowest class of Londoners, setting them up as a race apart from the classes above them.

The bulk of Marsh's novel, significantly, takes place in contemporary London, a monster city of six million people where social problems were magnified by the fin-de-siècle. London produces the conditions that enable the Beetle's invasion, while simultaneously facilitating a xenophobic reaction in a population already predisposed, according to contemporary commentators, to nervous ailments and irrational fears. The phobic experience was for contemporary medical men intimately connected to the very condition of modernity itself. Modern urban existence—with its noise, anonymity, and hectic pace—was seen as conducive to nervous illnesses, including phobias.[19] Marsh's novel begins with scenes that condemn Britain for its lack

---

17. Malik, *The Meaning of Race*, 81.
18. Malik, *The Meaning of Race*, 81.
19. Frederick William Alexander, "'Claustrophobia': Cause and Cure (Reprinted from the *Medical Times*)" (London: n.p., 1925), 1–2.

of care for its own citizens, particularly in the city.[20] A nameless and home-less tramp curses Britain as "a—fine country" (9) at the very beginning of the novel, which also sees Holt as "a stranger" (10) within an environment in which he should be at home. Instead the imperial metropolis, a melting pot of migrants, accommodates foreign presences, even ones as objectionable as the Beetle; its busy streets and remote suburbs provide such undesirables with the anonymity and seclusion they require; it supplies discontented and vulnerable victims for them to prey upon; and its extensive system of public transport allows them to traverse the city with impunity. Modern London offers no protection from the alien presence, in many ways appearing to aid the monster's invasion.

"Providence does sometimes write a man's character in his face": Language, Character, and Knowledge

While nineteenth-century fears over racial degeneration have been well rehearsed,[21] the threat of linguistic degeneration is relatively unexplored in gothic criticism. Hans Aarsleff notes that studies of ethnography and anthropology were often connected with the study of language in the nine-teenth century.[22] At the end of the eighteenth century Sir William Jones argued that it was impossible to know a people without understanding their language,[23] and during the Romantic period philologists asserted that the character of the people, including a record of its knowledge, beliefs, and superstitions, was articulated through the vernacular.[24] In accordance with anthropological procedures, August von Schlegel's early-nineteenth-century linguistic system placed languages in an order of supposed superiority, with Western, "isolating" languages (such as English) at the top of the tree, fol-lowed by inferior, "inflecting" and "agglutinating" languages (such as Ara-bic and the languages of the ancient Near East, respectively).[25] Gwyneth Tyson Roberts argues that according to this teleological system of language

20. Margree, "'Both in Men's Clothing,'" 64.

21. See, for example, William Greenslade, *Degeneration, Culture and the Novel, 1880–1940* (Cambridge: Cambridge University Press, 1994); Daniel Pick, *Faces of Degeneration: A European Disorder, c. 1848–1918* (Cambridge: Cambridge University Press, 1993).

22. Hans Aarsleff, *The Study of Language in England, 1780–1860* (Minneapolis: University of Minnesota Press and London: Athlone Press, 1983), 207–208.

23. Aarsleff, *The Study of Language,* 126.

24. Aarsleff, *The Study of Language,* 144–147.

25. Gwyneth Tyson Roberts, "'Under the Hatches': English Parliamentary Commissioners' Views of the People and Language of Mid-Nineteenth-Century Wales" in *The Expansion of England: Race, Ethnicity and Cultural History,* 178.

development, "a 'highly-developed' language was a clear marker of a 'highly-developed' society, and a 'highly-developed' society would of course have a 'highly-developed' language."[26] Nineteenth-century language study, thus, agreed with contemporary anthropology in suggesting a progression from primitive to more sophisticated society and culture, with the English language, the British set of cultural values, and the British "race" at the top of the evolutionary ladder. Thus, Richard Chenevix Trench had argued in 1851 that language was a "faithful . . . record of the good and of the evil which in time past have been working in the minds and hearts of men."[27] He termed language "a moral barometer, which indicates and permanently marks the rise or fall of a nation's life," and argued that "[t]o study a people's language will be to study *them,* and to study them at best advantage: there where they represent themselves to us under fewest disguises, most nearly as they are."[28] Trench went on to equate the study of language with "the love of our country expressing itself in one particular direction," since "a clear, a strong, an harmonious, a noble language" was a sure marker of "a glorious past" and "a glorious future."[29]

In accordance with such views, *The Beetle* is a novel in which the ability to command language and knowledge determines a person's character, intelligence, and moral fortitude. The ability to speak forcefully, eloquently, and clearly, and a command of the knowledge available in the English language, define in the novel the best of British manhood, and thus of Britishness itself: as Marjorie remarks, "no satisfaction [is] to be got out of a speechless man" (167). Thus, Paul Lessingham, a reforming Member of Parliament, is known as a fine orator and "speaks with an Apostle's tongue" (99). "Adept with words" (145), Lessingham "owes his success in the political arena in no slight measure to the adroitness which is born of his invulnerable presence of mind" (41–42). His "practical, statesmanlike speech[es]" (93) show evidence of "knowledge, charity, and sympathy" (155) and of "incontestable" "aptness," "readiness," and "grace" (93). The novel abounds with descriptions of Lessingham's "calm, airy" (42) and "silvern tones" (220); "short and crisp" sentences (92); and "clear and calm, not exactly musical, yet distinctly pleasant" voice (92). Moreover, Lessingham's oratory is distinctly English; as Atherton explains,

> It was very far from being an "oration" in the American sense; it had little or nothing of the fire and fury of the French Tribune; it was marked neither

---

26. Roberts, "'Under the Hatches,'" 179.
27. Aarsleff, *The Study of Language,* 240.
28. Aarsleff, *The Study of Language,* 240–241.
29. Aarsleff, *The Study of Language,* 245–246.

by the ponderosity nor the sentiment of the eloquent German; yet it was as satisfying as are the efforts of either of the three. (92)

Sydney Atherton, the "genius" inventor, "the fame of [whose] inventions is in the mouths of all men," deals with up-to-date scientific knowledge, which he uses for the benefit of his country (162). Atherton is "a person of whom [. . .] many men and women join in speaking well" due to his "discoveries" and "inventions" (88), and observers are "struck by something pleasant in his voice, and some quality as of sunshine in his handsome face" (49). Augustus Champnell, the private detective, is in command of the minutest of details but also, importantly, of the ability to keep a secret. A "speechifying" (157) New Woman figure, the "sharp-tongued" (137) Marjorie Lindon speaks on public platforms and her writing is, like her personality, "unusual, bold, decided" (53). Robert Holt, whose previous employment as a clerk makes him an expert scribe, possesses the "voice [. . .] of an educated man" (177) and recounts his "curious story" "with a simple directness which was close akin to eloquence" (177) that proves that he has "not made an ill-use of the opportunities which [he has] had to improve [his], originally, modest education" (45).

The chief British characters in the novel are, thus, positively defined by their associations with language, writing, oratory, and the command of facts, whether through learning, invention, or personal observation. Britishness is here associated with measured linguistic expression, which itself is associated with knowledge, culture, and order. Indeed, key scenes in the novel take place in Atherton's laboratory and in Lessingham's study, "a fine, spacious apartment, evidently intended rather for work than for show," with "three separate writing-tables, . . . all covered with an orderly array of manuscripts and papers"; "a typewriter," "piles of books, portfolios, and official-looking documents," and walls "lined with shelves, full as they could hold with books" complete the picture of Lessingham as a man of knowledge (39). Importantly, in its respective ways, this knowledge is harnessed in the service of Britain—whether in Atherton's military inventions, in Lessingham's political reforms, or in Champnell's efforts to prevent crime—and language is thus associated with the good of the nation.

Predictably, then, contact with the alien results in attempts at classification according to well-established Orientalist taxonomies as the characters endeavor to use their knowledge to determine the exact nature of the Beetle. Holt's initial description of the Beetle as an ancient Asiatic mummy is conditioned by his inherent subscription to British conventions of Orientalist classification: "There was not a hair upon his face or head, but, to make up for it, the skin, which was a saffron yellow, was an amazing mass of wrinkles" (19).

Next, however, we are told that the monster is animalistic, though the size of its nose also directs the reader to consider racial stereotypes of Jews as well as the sharp, shriveled features of the mummy: "The cranium, and, indeed, the whole skull, was so small as to be disagreeably suggestive of something animal. The nose, on the other hand, was abnormally large" and "resembled the beak of some bird of prey" (19). The next set of facial characteristics classifies the creature not only as Negroid, but also as deformed: "The mouth, with its blubber lips, came immediately underneath the nose, and chin, to all intents and purposes, there was none" (19). Finally, Holt returns to his earlier classification of the creature as Asiatic, although the emphasis on its powerful eyes also reminds the reader of the Jewish evil eye: "so marked a feature of the man were his eyes, that, ere long, it seemed to me that he was nothing but eyes. . . . They held me enchained, helpless, spell-bound" (19). In opposition to the British protagonists, the monster's voice is distinctly "disagreeable" (18) and "rasping" like "a rusty saw" (51) or "a rusty steam engine" (246). What is more, the speech of this "inspired maniac" (113) is "an inarticulate torrent . . . not a little suggestive of insanity" (28) and "more resembling yelps and snarls than anything more human,—like some savage beast nursing its pent-up rage" (53). Holt repeatedly comments on the monster's "markedly foreign" accent (28) and "guttural tones" with "a reminiscence of some foreign land" (21). Thus, the Beetle is distinguished from the British characters as much by its speech as by its appearance, and both are directly equated with foreign moral and racial degeneracy in the novel.

In the end, Holt is unable to arrive at a stable classification as he concludes that he "had no doubt it was a foreigner" (18). We have here the first sign that Holt's language is failing him and giving way to an irrational phobic reaction to the alien. It could be argued that instead of showing repulsion towards the representative of a particular culture, Holt gives voice to a xenophobic prejudice towards the foreign *in general*. While Holt may not be familiar with different cultures, Atherton is known as something of "a specialist on questions of ancient superstitions and extinct religions" (76). However, this educated man is similarly at a loss over the Beetle's ethnicity: "he wore a burnoose,—the yellow, grimy-looking article of the Arab of the Soudan" (69), Atherton explains, agreeing with Holt that the "fellow was oriental to the finger-tips,—that much was certain" (106). Beyond this, however, Atherton, too, fails to classify the Beetle in a statement remarkable for its negativity:

> In spite of a pretty wide personal knowledge of oriental people I could not make up my mind as to the exact part of the east from which he came. He was hardly an Arab, he was not a fellah,—he was not, unless I erred, a Moham-

medan at all. There was something about him which was distinctly not Mussulmanic. So far as looks were concerned, he was not a flattering example of his race, whatever his race might be. (106)

Despite the wealth of descriptive detail in Atherton's and Holt's accounts, their attempts at classification prove inconclusive as well-rehearsed Orientalist discourse fails to establish the Beetle's exact provenance and character. The Beetle is here defined by what it is *not*, by its intangible "foreignness." Unable to determine his opponent's ethnic makeup, Atherton, like Holt, is content to label the Beetle as a degenerate foreign monster, concluding by associating the Oriental's "uncommonly disagreeable" (149) appearance with a moral degeneracy: "If it is true that, now and again, Providence does write a man's character on his face, then there can't be the slightest shred of a doubt that a curious one's been written on his" (72). Western knowledge, articulated through scientific discourse, is challenged by the Beetle's liminality and hybridity, associated in the novel with the monster's foreign origins. "You know not of what you speak!" (115), the Beetle warns Atherton, who is indeed forced to concede defeat: not only is Western knowledge of the "Papyri, hieroglyphics, and so on, which remain" of ancient Eastern civilization "very far from being exhaustive" (76), but also Atherton is forced to admit that "civilisation was once more proved to be a failure" in the "game of bluff" he had played with the monster (121). This failure of supposedly objective scientific knowledge leads in the novel to xenophobic responses to the alien. Arguably, then, there is a direct connection between Orientalist discourse and expressions of xenophobia, as the narrative establishes the inadequacy of racial and scientific taxonomies in defining and containing the foreign presence.

"Speechless":
Phobic Inarticulacy, Linguistic Collapse, and Identity

It is not simply Western knowledge of the Orient, articulated through the English language, that fails in the novel: it is the English language itself. When brought into direct contact with the alien presence, first in the Beetle's native Egypt and later in London, the English language suffers a breakdown which can be interpreted as a reduction to xenophobic inarticulacy and even muteness. While the presence of the foreign monster is the immediate cause of this breakdown, the narrative implies that its roots extend to preexisting weaknesses within the British psyche. Faced with the Beetle, Holt, Lessingham, and Marjorie all lose their command of language and are reduced to

varying states of chronic inarticulacy in keeping with the contemporary medical men who identified "loss of speech" as one symptom of phobia.[30] Holt,
due to his deficient physical state, is reduced to "[s]hrieking like some lost
spirit" (17) as a result of contact with the monster. Under the Beetle's spell,
Holt speaks either "in a sort of tremulous falsetto" (189) or in "a queer, hollow, croaking voice" (130) "which [he] should not have recognised as [his]"
(48). Holt's voice, containing an "almost more than human agony" (171),
is indicative of his horrible experience. Lessingham, too, retreats from the
vicinity of the monster in inchoate panic, "clutching at" his "bookshelves"
"as if seeking for support" (43) from this vestige of knowledge and certainty
in an attempt to regain his composure.[31] Contact with the monster destroys
Lessingham's habitual "inpenetrability" (41), and his "suavity and courtesy"
(42). Not only does "[h]is voice falter" (215) as he "stumble[s] in the telling"
(211) of his story and is reduced to "a miserable weakling" (220), but he now
speaks "in a harsh, broken voice which no one who had heard him speak
on a public platform, or in the House of Commons, would have recognised
as his" (265). So extreme is Lessingham's linguistic collapse that he utters "a
stream of inchoate abuse" in "frenzied, choking accents" (43), "mumble[s]
to himself aloud" (48), "shriek[s]" (81) and "gibber[s],—like some frenzied
animal" (148). Marjorie's budding speechifying, too, is brought to an end
by the Beetle. "Her voice . . . but an echo of itself" (134), she finds that she
has "lost the control of [her] tongue" and "stammer[s]" (171) as "the words
wouldn't come. . . . [Her] longings wouldn't shape themselves into words,
and [her] tongue was palsied" (133–134). These failed attempts to use language and speech convey a xenophobic experience: the British protagonists
are rendered unable to communicate in an effective way, and their advanced
knowledge base fails repeatedly throughout the novel as contact with the
unknown exposes latent weaknesses within the nation. Their previous eloquence and self-assurance give way to what philologists had termed a "language of action," a basic form of communication consisting of inarticulate
gestures, interjections and signs,[32] in keeping with such accepted symptoms
of phobic behavior as sensations of anxiety, loss of speech, and failure of
willpower.[33]

So extreme is this failure of language that, as Kelly Hurley observes, *The
Beetle* can be read as a novel of silences. At several points throughout the
text, language fails the characters to such an extent that their consciousness,

---

30. Roth, *A Few Notes*, 2.
31. I am indebted to Dominic Bignell for this insight.
32. Aarsleff, *The Study of Language*, 21.
33. Roth, *A Few Notes*, 2–4.

too, fails. Hurley attributes these silences to a narrative "coyness"[34] which made it impossible for Marsh to depict scenes of rape and sexual violence involving men and women alike.[35] Thus, Holt passes out into "oblivion" (54) as the Beetle assaults him; Marjorie writes about her ordeal repeatedly but always stops at the point of her encounter with the monster as "oblivion" "come[s] to [her] aid" and she "swoon[s]" (175); and Lessingham allows "a curtain . . . to descend" as "a period of oblivion" obscures his experiences in Egypt (210). However, the ellipses and silences which punctuate the novel are also instances in which language utterly fails to explain the events. Characters attempt to describe and understand the alien presence, but words fail them and they are forced to employ such empty phrases as "unimaginable agony," "speechless torture," and "nameless terrors" (266) caused by "that Nameless Thing" (120); or they refer to "two unspeakable months" (213) of "nameless agonies and degradations" in "some indescribable den of horror" (269). The English language, it is implied, does not contain words to describe the experience of contact with the alien presence. The characters' silences and gaps in the plotline define the narrative, and the muteness provoked by the Beetle is at its center. The characters' phobic discourse within the invasion text is, then, essentially inarticulate and inconclusive.

This failure of language is equated in the text with a challenge to Western knowledge, the loss of national and cultural identity, and, ultimately, the destruction of Western civilization itself: the English characters' linguistic regression implies a degeneration of the entire nation, resulting from internal weaknesses, defined through its command of the vernacular. In the late eighteenth century, influential philologists such as Horne Tooke had argued that the study of language was in fact "the natural history of understanding, of thought, of mind" because language was central to thought, thought was embedded in language, and, indeed, that language *was* thought.[36] Faced with the monster, some of the British characters lose their ability to use the English language, their instrument of making sense of the world; in the process, their ability to think independently and thus their British identity are placed under threat. Like immigrants in contemporary xenophobic discourse, the Beetle in Marsh's invasion text is represented as a parasite exploiting both real and perceived weaknesses within British culture. Nineteenth-century anxieties about class, gender, and morality are most clearly embodied in the Beetle's victims—an unemployed, emasculate clerk, a "New Woman" regarded as "a thing of horror" (157), and a radical politician with

---

34. Hurley, "'The Inner Chambers of All Nameless Sin,'" 206.

35. It is, of course, also a common gothic device to invite the readers to fill in such gaps with the worst violation their minds can conjure.

36. Aarsleff, *The Study of Language*, 14, 19.

a past. However, the body politic itself is presented as inherently flawed in the novel due to the linguistic failure of a host of inarticulate politicians. One of Marjorie Lindon's three suitors, the parliamentarian Percy Woodville, is notorious for his lack of oratorical powers and has "to have [his] speeches written for [him]" (90). Woodville does not "know what to speak about" and "can't speak anyhow" (96), and his notes take the form of "hieroglyphics, but what they meant, or what they did there anyhow, it was [impossible to] tell" (61–62). The elderly Mr Lindon, a senior Member of Parliament, is unable to form a coherent sentence without beginning to "stutter and stammer" (95), "puffing and stewing . . . at the top of his voice" (124). What is more, the "language which he habitually employs" is described as "unbecoming to a gentleman," especially one of "high breeding" (168).

Given such weaknesses within British society, the underlying fear in the novel is that contact with the alien may strip the English characters, already somehow lacking in quintessentially British characteristics and physical and mental stamina, of their national and cultural identity. This collapse is represented in the novel as a total loss of linguistic independence and, thus, of self-expression. For Holt, speech is associated "with the power to show that there still was in [him] something of a man" (32). As the unfortunate tramp falls into the Beetle's clutches, he admits that "something was going from [him],—the capacity, as it were, to be [him]self" (22). The monster's "sentences, in some strange, indescribable way, seemed, as they came from his lips, to warp [Holt's] limbs; to enwrap themselves about [him]; to confine [him], tighter and tighter, within, as it were, swaddling clothes; to make [him] more and more helpless" (32). Holt explains,

> There was this odd thing about the words I uttered, that they came from me, not in response to my will power, but in response to his. It was not I who willed that I should speak; it was he. What he willed that I should say, I said. Just that, and nothing more. For the time I was no longer a man; my manhood was merged in his. I was, in the extremest sense, an example of passive obedience. (20)

Holt is unmanned by the monster's invasion: "something entered into me," Holt explains, "and forced itself from between my lips, so that I said, in a low, hissing voice, which I vow was never mine, 'THE BEETLE!'" (42).

If, as philologists argued, the character of a people was represented in the vernacular, then the loss of language erases the British characters' cultural identity and replaces it with a markedly foreign register. Under the Beetle's spell, both Marjorie and Holt are taken to be "of weak intellect": "They said nothing, except at the seeming instigation of the Arab, but when spoken to stared and gaped like lunatics" (264). Holt, "speechless" (19), acts in "a silence which was supernatural . . .;—not a word issued from those rigid lips" (65). Indeed, Lessingham is forced to wonder what Holt's nationality may be, since he is speechless and dressed in an Eastern cape: "You look English," he says, "is it possible that you are not English? What are you then . . .? Your face is English" (45). Lessingham is himself thrown "into a state approximating to a paralysis both of mind and body" (218) and loses his memory, language, and identity following his "agony of fear" (218). He describes his collapse into "a state of semi-imbecility" and "a species of aphasia": "For days together I was speechless, and could remember nothing,—not even my own name" (216). The monster appropriates its victims' British identity, arguably most clearly articulated through their command of the English language. The Beetle's invasion is, thus, associated with the removal of the victims' original linguistic and cultural identity and the substitution of something alien and essentially loathsome.

The Beetle, by contrast, is able to communicate its wishes very clearly indeed in its appropriation of the English vernacular and, by implication, of British culture. A native speaker of what is in the novel condescendingly termed "the *patois* of the Rue de Rabagas," an imaginary Cairene street, and equated with "gibberish" (45), the Beetle also speaks English; indeed, Lessingham comments on his encounter with the Egyptian priestess that "[a]ll languages seemed to be the same to her. She sang in French and Italian, German and English,—in tongues with which I was unfamiliar" (209), perhaps as a result of frequent engagement with European imperialism. It is true that several of the characters comment on the monster's "queer foreign twang" (105) and "queer lingo" (255), dismissing its speech as "a sort of a kind of English" (246) and its writing as "straggling, characterless caligraphy" [*sic*] not unlike "the composition of a servant girl" (244). Yet, in spite of the Beetle's foreign accent and appearance, the monster is able to navigate contemporary London with ease, hailing cabs, purchasing railway tickets, renting houses and taking rooms both in writing and in speech. Indeed, the monster's "yells and screeches, squawks and screams" (248) are in marked contrast to the British characters' increasingly halting tones and muteness. The Beetle's language is associated with physical and mental violence, violation, and command, leading those who come into contact with it to stand "in expectation of a physical assault" (29). In the novel, this form of communication proves stronger than the British characters' supposedly superior tones. The polite, polished expression associated with Britishness is, thus, shown to be feeble when confronted with the Beetle, and in the novel this fragility is equated with degeneration and disease within the British nation.

Like Stoker's Dracula, the Beetle is able to appropriate English culture through a command of the English language.[37] In the mouth of the Beetle and its victims, words become spells, the most powerful of which is "the spell of two words," "THE BEETLE!" (34). This curse is repeated throughout the novel and always followed by a descent into chaos and destruction of certainty. The Beetle also communicates very effectively without words through telepathy and gestures.[38] Holt comments on the monster's apparent access to his thoughts, which it "seemed to experience not the slightest difficulty in deciphering" (52), while Atherton struggles to understand the Beetle's sign language: "raising his hands he lowered them, palms downward, with a gesture which was peculiarly oriental" (107). While able to write in English, the monster also uses a form of communication reminiscent of Egyptian hieroglyphic writing when it sends Lessingham a "dexterously done" "photogravure" (80) or pictorial "representation" (218) of a beetle, not unlike "a cartouch" (114), which provokes his phobic attack. These alternative modes of communication represent a challenge to the established conventions of speaking and of recording speech in the West and suggest, again, the monster's ability to appropriate the English language and all that it symbolizes in the novel, and to offer a markedly foreign substitute.

The novel concludes with the narrative of the aristocratic detective, Augustus Champnell. Unlike a typical detective narrative, this final fragment is inconclusive. Instead of providing the certainty and ready answers one expects from detective fiction, Champnell can offer the reader only a startling lack of conclusions and certainties. His narrative is punctuated by negatives, just as the novel itself has been punctuated by silences and ellipses. The very nature of the fragmented split narrative, Champnell's final statement of the case, is brought into question as the detective reveals that Holt's narrative was in fact not his but "compiled from the statements which Holt made to Atherton, and to Miss Lindon." Marjorie, by contrast, "told, and re-told, and re-told again, the story" of her ordeal in writing but "she would never speak of what she had written" (295). While the resulting text presents a gathering together of fragments, it is, finally, inherently flawed. Champnell is here forced to agree with the Beetle's accusation that the British characters "know not of what [they] speak" (115). The fragmented, inconclusive nature of the invasion text confirms the essential inarticulacy of the characters' phobic discourses, at the center of which there is a linguistic vacuum. The phobic experience of contact with the foreign has permanently compromised the

---

37. For a reading of Count Dracula as an invader, see Stephen Arata, "The Occidental Tourist: *Dracula* and the Anxiety of Reverse Colonization," *Victorian Studies* 33.4 (summer 1990).

38. For a discussion of telepathy in the novel, see Roger Luckhurst, *The Invention of Telepathy* (Oxford: Oxford University Press, 2002), 208–210.

British characters' ability to synthesize information in coherent language, shaking their belief in the omnipotence of Western science and knowledge and challenging their assumptions of the stability of national and cultural identity.

Works Cited

Aarsleff, Hans. *The Study of Language in England, 1780–1860.* Minneapolis: University of Minnesota Press; London: Athlone Press, 1983.

Alexander, Frederick William. "'*Claustrophobia': Cause and Cure (Reprinted from the Medical Times).*" London: n.p., 1925.

Arata, Stephen. "The Occidental Tourist: *Dracula* and the Anxiety of Reverse Colonisation." *Victorian Studies* 33 (1990): 621–645.

Ball, B. "On Claustrophobia." *British Medical Journal,* 6 September 1879, 371.

Brantlinger, Patrick. *Rule of Darkness: British Literature and Imperialism, 1830–1914.* Ithaca, NY, and London: Cornell University Press, 1988.

Garnett, Rhys. "*Dracula* and *The Beetle:* Imperial and Sexual Guilt and Fear in Late Victorian Fantasy." In *Science Fiction Roots and Branches: Contemporary Critical Approaches,* edited by Rhys Garnett and R. J. Ellis. 30–54. Houndmills: Macmillan, 1990.

Feldman, David. *Englishmen and Jews: Social Relations and Political Culture.* New Haven, CT, and London: Yale University Press, 1994.

———. "The Importance of Being English: Jewish Immigration and the Decay of Liberal England." In *Metropolis: London. Histories and Representations since 1800,* edited by David Feldman and Gareth Stedman Jones. 56–84. London and New York: Routledge, 1989.

Greenslade, William. *Degeneration, Culture and the Novel, 1880–1940.* Cambridge: Cambridge University Press, 1994.

Halberstam, Judith. "Gothic Nation: *The Beetle* by Richard Marsh." In *Fictions of Unease: The Gothic from* Otranto *to* The X-Files, edited by Andrew Smith, Diane Mason, and William Hughes. 100–118. Bath: Sulis Press, 2002.

Hurley, Kelly. *The Gothic Body: Sexuality, Materialism, and Degeneration at the Fin de Siècle.* Cambridge: Cambridge University Press, 1996.

———. "'The Inner Chambers of All Nameless Sin:' *The Beetle,* Gothic Female Sexuality, and Oriental Barbarism." In *Virginal Sexuality and Textuality in Victorian Literature,* edited by Lloyd Davis. 193–213. Albany: State University of New York Press, 1993.

Luckhurst, Roger. *The Invention of Telepathy.* Oxford: Oxford University Press, 2002.

Malchow, H. L. *Gothic Images of Race in Nineteenth-Century Britain.* Stanford, CA: Stanford University Press, 1996.

Malik, Kenan. *The Meaning of Race: Race, History and Culture in Western Society.* Houndmills and London: Macmillan, 1996.

Margree, Victoria. "'Both in Men's Clothing': Gender, Sovereignty and Insecurity in Richard Marsh's *The Beetle.*" *Critical Survey* 19.2 (2007): 63–81.

Marsh, Richard. *The Beetle: A Mystery.* Edited by Minna Vuohelainen. Kansas City, MO: Valancourt, 2008.

Morse, Josiah. *The Psychology and Neurology of Fear.* Worcester, MA: Clark University Press, 1907.

Pick, Daniel. *Faces of Degeneration: A European Disorder, c. 1848–1918.* Cambridge: Cambridge University Press, 1993.

Roberts, Gwyneth Tyson. "'Under the Hatches': English Parliamentary Commissioners' Views of the People and Language of Mid-Nineteenth-Century Wales." In *The Expansion of England: Race, Ethnicity and Cultural History,* edited by Bill Schwarz. 171–197. London and New York: Routledge, 1996.

Roth, M. *A Few Notes on Fear and Fright, and the Diseases They Cause and Cure; also on the Means of Preventing and Curing the Effects of These Emotions.* London and Manchester: Henry Turner, [1872].

Vuohelainen, Minna. "Introduction." In Richard Marsh, *The Beetle: A Mystery,* edited by Minna Vuohelainen. vii–xxx. Kansas City, MO: Valancourt, 2008.

———. "'Oh to Get Out of that Room!': Outcast London and the Gothic Twist in the Popular Fiction of Richard Marsh." In *Victorian Space(s): Leeds Centre Working Papers in Victorian Studies* VIII, edited by Karen Sayer. 115–126. Leeds: Trinity and All Saints, University of Leeds, 2006.

Wolfreys, Julian. "The Hieroglyphic Other: *The Beetle,* London, and the Abyssal Subject." In *A Mighty Mass of Brick and Smoke: Victorian and Edwardian Representations of London,* edited by Lawrence Phillips. 169–192. Amsterdam: Rodopi, 2007.

———. "Introduction." In Richard Marsh, *The Beetle: A Mystery,* edited by Julian Wolfreys. 9–34. Peterborough, ON: Broadview, 2004.

14

Dracula's Blood
of Many Brave Races

❧

THOMAS McLEAN

In Victorian narratives, mixed blood is a familiar sign of trouble. One need not turn to texts with colonial settings to see the difficulties faced by characters whose parents are not both English. In *Silas Marner*, little Eppie barely survives the death of her opium-addicted Irish mother; in *Felix Holt*, Esther Lyon must overcome the pride she inherits from the French mother she never knew. Aurora Leigh describes her Italian mother more favorably, but Aurora's position between two nations as different as Britain and Italy makes it always a struggle for her to fit either. Adèle Varens—even if she isn't Rochester's daughter—is a constant reminder of his gaudy, cross-channel amours. Stormy Eustacia Vye (like her Corfiote father) attempts to hide her ancestry by taking her mother's last name. Fewer male protagonists suffer the trope of miscegenation, but their positions in Victorian society are made similarly ambivalent. Will Ladislaw, whose grandfather was Polish, endures the slander of Middlemarchers who identify him by a variety of racial epithets. Daniel Deronda embraces his Jewish ancestry and abandons England. Amy Foster's son seems unlikely to learn much about his Carpathian father.

To succeed in Victorian Britain, these narratives suggest, one must conceal or deny one's mixed ancestry. The exception that proves the rule comes from Transylvania: "We Szekelys have a right to be proud, for in our veins flows the blood of many brave races who fought as the lion fights, for lordship."[1]

---

1. Bram Stoker, *Dracula* (New York: Penguin, 1993), 42. Subsequent references to this text will be cited parenthetically.

If early readers were in any doubt about the dangers of visiting the Austro-Hungarian Empire—or better, selling British property to a Transylvanian nobleman—Dracula's open pride in the mixture of blood flowing through his veins would have reassured their phobic impulses. Dracula is the antithesis of the trueborn Englishman; or, as I argue below, the Eastern European immigrant, of avowed mixed ancestry and military background, is the antithesis of the educated, well-traveled Anglo Saxon. The irony, of course, is that English blood is as mixed as Transylvanian, and from the same causes: war, empire, and immigration. But this irony was probably lost on most early readers of Stoker's 1897 novel.

Dracula compresses into its pages a century of continental immigration to Britain, and in so doing offers insights into the considerable shift in mood towards those immigrants, in particular those from Eastern Europe. Reading Bram Stoker's novel as a nightmare of foreign immigration allows the reader to identify Transylvania not simply as a region of the British unconscious or as a stand-in for the British colonies, but as a specific place in Europe; and to place its eponymous character not only in the realms of Gothic literature, but also among the foreign revolutionaries who escaped to Britain during the nineteenth century. In the first half of this essay I examine nineteenth-century immigration to Britain from other parts of Europe, in particular the increasing number of political refugees who arrived in London after the revolutions of 1848—refugees whose radical affiliations and failed uprisings encouraged xenophobic feelings among their new British neighbors. Then I turn to Stoker's text in order to place the nationalist warrior Count Dracula within this continental context. While recent scholars have productively read *Dracula* as a record of Britain's anti-Semitic or colonial fears, close attention to the novel connects the title character more persuasively to the complicated politics of nineteenth-century Eastern Europe—a context that, until recently, has been ignored in *Dracula* studies.[2] By considering Stoker's Count

---

2. Scholars working in this national vein owe a debt to Patrick Brantlinger, *Rule of Darkness: British Literature and Imperialism, 1830–1914* (Ithaca and London: Cornell University Press, 1988), and to Stephen Arata, *Fictions of Loss in the Victorian Fin de Siècle* (Cambridge: Cambridge University Press, 1996). Recent investigations focused on Eastern Europe include Eleni Coundouriotis, "*Dracula* and the Idea of Europe," *Connotations* 9.2 (1999/2000): 143–159; Carol A. Senf, "A Response to "*Dracula* and the Idea of Europe," *Connotations* 10.1 (2000/2001): 47–58; and Jason Dittmer, "*Dracula* and the Cultural Construction of Europe," *Connotations* 12.2–3 (2002/2003): 233–248. Coundouriotis considers *Dracula* in the context of the Eastern Question and the Turkish massacres of Bulgarian Christians in 1876; her respondents expand her argument in fruitful ways. See also Matthew Gibson, *Dracula and the Eastern Question: British and French Vampire Narratives of the Nineteenth-Century Near East* (Basingstoke: Palgrave Macmillan, 2006). Gibson considers *Dracula* in light of the 1878 Berlin Treaty and sees Stoker as a supporter of both Turkish and Austrian rule over their Balkan neighbors. For a reading of Dracula as Russian agent, see Jimmie E. Cain, *Bram Stoker and Russophobia: Evidence of the British Fear of Russia in* Dracula *and* The Lady of the Shroud

among the historical military figures who found exile in nineteenth-century Britain, passages and plot developments take on new meaning. I foreground this important, new context, but I also suggest that Dracula might best be read as the threat of all that is foreign to the apparently pure blood of the novel's protagonists. Dracula's ethnicity associates him foremost with Eastern Europe, but Stoker actually associates the Count with a remarkable variety of nations and peoples, from China and South America to Scotland and Ireland. Scholars often overlook this fact, and in doing so they fail to engage directly with the novel's representations of late-Victorian xenophobia. And yet this may be what is most significant about the Count: his association not with older anti-Semitic or anti-Irish stereotypes, but with emerging xenophobic attitudes. Limiting our analysis of *Dracula* to a single nation or ethnicity ignores the fact that late-Victorian fears were not centered on a single group; rather they encompassed almost any group that wasn't British. By giving his villain a global geography of metonyms, Stoker identifies an important cultural shift and critiques the hypocritical society that endorses such xenophobic feelings.

Representing Exile in Victorian Britain

Describing the characteristics of a vampire, Professor Van Helsing tells his companions, "He cannot go where he lists . . . [h]e may not enter anywhere at the first, unless there be some one of the household who bid him come; though afterwards he can come as he please" (308). It is not surprising then that Dracula should choose London: for much of the eighteenth and nineteenth centuries, Britain had one of the most liberal immigration policies in all Europe. Though concerns over immigration reached a peak in the 1890s, the presence of foreigners was a long-standing fact of British society. Britain's position as a major naval trading power and its expanding colonial empire meant that foreign visitors were a familiar sight in commercial centers like London, Bristol, and Manchester even in the mid-eighteenth century. The era's first large-scale influx of foreigners occurred in the 1790s, when revolution brought between ten and twenty thousand French refugees to Britain. Though most historians describe these émigrés as ultra-royalist aristocrats, Kirsty Carpenter suggests that the French community in London represented a much greater variety of economic and social backgrounds. These refugees had a considerable impact on London life, setting up schools and churches

(Jefferson, NC, and London: McFarland & Co., 2006). My own concerns are less with either the Eastern Question or Stoker's personal politics and more with the nineteenth-century history of Eastern European immigration to Britain.

throughout the city, but most never intended to remain in Britain, and more than two-thirds returned home after the Peace of Amiens in 1802.[3]

Still, a considerable number of French remained, and through the first half of the nineteenth century other continental refugees, particularly from Italy, Poland, and Hungary, joined them. The earliest refugees tended to be aristocracy, but a growing number were political exiles.[4] The best-known refugee at mid-century was probably Giuseppe Mazzini, who wrote and published numerous articles in English and was befriended by Thomas Carlyle, Algernon Swinburne, and other literary figures. Ironically, Mazzini became a household name only after it was discovered in 1844 that British government officials were illegally opening his mail and forwarding information to the Austrian government. Mazzini's popularity grew immensely, and literary representations of Italians, such as *Little Dorrit*'s Cavaletto and *The Woman in White*'s Professor Pesca, reflect the British public's mid-century sympathy towards Italy. Mazzini's popularity was eventually overshadowed by that of Giuseppe Garibaldi, whose more pragmatic politics led to Italian unification.[5]

If representations of Italian political exiles grew more positive as the century passed, the opposite could be said of Poles and Hungarians. Early in the century many British poets, including Lord Byron, S. T. Coleridge, and John Keats, had praised the Polish patriot Tadeusz Kościuszko, prompting one critic in 1910 to note that "no alien before or since has been more belauded by our writers."[6] After the Russo-Polish War of 1830–1831, writers and politicians called for British involvement on behalf of the Poles. Labor groups and political committees assisted Polish refugees in finding work in cities like Hull and Glasgow. British journals described sympathetically the later Polish revolts of 1846 and 1848, but the British public apparently grew tired of Russian victories and new Polish arrivals. As William Thackeray's narrator in *The Newcomes* (1853) records, "Polish chieftains were at this

3. Kirsty Carpenter, *Refugees of the French Revolution: Émigrés in London, 1789–1802* (New York: St. Martin's Press, 1999). Regarding the number of émigrés, see 39–43. The Treaty of Amiens, signed in March 1802, halted armed conflict between the United Kingdom and France. The peace collapsed in May 1803.

4. For a useful overview of nineteenth-century national movements, their leaders, and their exiles, see Adam Zamoyski, *Holy Madness: Romantics, Patriots and Revolutionaries, 1776–1871* (London: Weidenfeld & Nicolson, 1999). For a sustained analysis of Polish refugees in nineteenth-century British literature and culture, see Thomas McLean, *The Other East and Nineteenth-Century British Literature: Imagining Poland and the Russian Empire* (Basingstoke: Palgrave Macmillan, 2011).

5. Harry W. Rudman, *Italian Nationalism and English Letters: Figures of the Risorgimento and Victorian Men of Letters* (London: Allen & Unwin Ltd, 1940). For a more recent consideration of Italy in the Victorian imaginary, see Matthew Reynolds, *Realms of Verse, 1830–1879: English Poetry in a Time of Nation-Building* (Oxford: Oxford University Press, 2001).

6. John Collings Squire, *Books in General by Solomon Eagle* (New York: Knopf, 1920), 126.

time so common in London, that nobody (except one noble member for Marylebone, and, once a year, the Lord Mayor) took any interest in them."[7] Charles Lever's *The Dodd Family Abroad* (1854) includes a minor Polish villain, Count Koratinsky, who "commanded the cavalry at Ostrolenca, and, it is said, rode down the Russian Guard, and sabred the Imperial Cuirassiers to a man." Sounding like a much-later literary Count, Koratinsky brags that he "has the blood of three monarchies in his veins [and] has twice touched the crown of his native land." But Koratinsky is finally a figure of ridicule: he makes off with James Dodd's umbrella and cloak and disappears from the plot, inspiring the following diatribe from James's father: "we hear a great deal of talk about the partition of Poland . . . but I am convinced that the greatest evil of that nefarious act lies in having thrown all these Polish fellows broadcast over Europe. I wish it was a kingdom to-morrow, if they'd only consent to stay there."[8] Anthony Trollope's novel *The Claverings* (1867) features yet another aristocratic Polish villain, the dissipated Count Pateroff, who fails in his attempts to blackmail the British female protagonist into marriage.[9]

Hungarian refugees made up a smaller community, but their influence was considerable, thanks to Lajos Kossuth, a minor noble of similar popular standing to Mazzini. Defeated by the Austrians, Kossuth came to Britain in 1851, where great crowds welcomed him. He spent much time traveling in Britain and the United States, raising money and planning future uprisings in Hungary against Austrian rule. In 1867 Kossuth broke with many compatriots who accepted the Austro-Hungarian Compromise and published his famous "Cassandra Letter" in 1872, expressing his fears for the future of Hungary. Though the compromise gave new powers to the Hungarians, it did not grant them sovereignty, and Kossuth lived the rest of his life in Italian exile.

Kossuth and Hungarian nationalism were often tied to Polish nationalism (many Poles had fought for Hungary in 1848 against Austria), and the two communities organized public events together in order to keep their nations in the British public eye. But unlike Italy, enthusiasm for Poland and

---

7. William Thackeray, *The Newcomes: Memoirs of a Most Respectable Family,* 97. The "noble member for Marylebone" was Lord Dudley Coutts Stuart, who also supported the exiled Hungarian leader Lajos Kossuth.

8. Charles Lever, *The Dodd Family Abroad,* 15, 56. In Lever's 1844 novel *Arthur O'Leary,* a Polish Count and his wife dupe the protagonist while in Brussels.

9. Anthony Trollope, *The Claverings.* Pateroff ushers in the most memorable and ethnically mixed villains of Trollope's mature fiction: Joseph Emilius of *The Eustace Diamonds* (1873) and *Phineas Redux* (1876), the Bohemian Jew of Polish origins who murders with a French-made bludgeon; and the even less identifiable Augustus Melmotte of *The Way We Live Now* (1875) and Ferdinand Lopez of *The Prime Minister* (1876).

Hungary waned. Italy remained a desired commodity in Victorian Britain: it was considered distinguished to speak Italian, Roman and Renaissance culture were widely admired, and many Britons had first-hand experience of Italy by way of the Grand Tour. Neither Poland nor Hungary could boast such attributes, and the results were later literary representations like Count Koratinsky, Count Pateroff, and Count Dracula. One of the most familiar claims for both nations was that each had been Europe's bulwark during the height of the Ottoman Empire. But in the 1850s Turkey was an ally, and in any case, the independence of neither Poland nor Hungary seemed likely to settle the European chessboard.

General sympathy towards revolutionary leaders began to decline after the failed revolutions of 1848. Mazzini's involvement with revolutionary schemes in Italy and his unwillingness to deal with King Emmanuel of Piedmont tarnished his reputation among moderates. Kossuth's fame faded as well, and his reputation was injured by his involvement in a plan to print revolutionary banknotes in England and a rocket-making enterprise in Rotherhithe.[10] After the Austro-Hungarian Compromise he rarely appeared as a public figure. The prestige of all émigrés in Britain was gravely damaged in 1858, when Felice Orsini attempted to murder Napoleon III in Paris. The Emperor escaped unhurt, but dozens were injured or killed, and France was quick to point out that Orsini had planned his attack in Britain, the only nation that from 1823 until the end of the century did not expel refugees. Orsini was caught and tried in Britain, but he was finally allowed to go free. Bernard Porter argues that this was Britain's way to declare itself outside the influences of European despots, but it also must have affected British public opinion towards later refugees.[11]

Meanwhile, other national developments turned British public opinion even further against political refugees. The first was a growing fear in Britain of invasion. The strengthening and consolidation of Germany under Otto von Bismarck—one of the motivations for the Austro-Hungarian Compromise—inspired numerous invasion novels, most famously Sir George Chesney's 1871 *Battle of Dorking* and H. G. Wells's 1898 *War of the Worlds*. A second development was the growth in Europe of anarchist, Fenian, and Nihilist organizations. The invention of dynamite in the 1860s allowed fringe anarchists to terrorize Londoners in the 1880s and 1890s. As Barbara Melchiori notes, "infernal machines" hidden in bags and boxes around London became a familiar feature of newspaper articles and fictional tales at the turn of the century. Actual attacks on the underground and government

10. Bernard Porter, *The Refugee Question in Mid-Victorian Politics* (Cambridge: Cambridge University Press, 1979), 202, 145.

11. Porter, *The Refugee Question in Mid-Victorian Politics,* 170–199.

offices occurred frequently, many of them connected with French or Irish anarchists.[12]

An anxious situation in Britain was made worse when great numbers of immigrants from Eastern Europe and Russia arrived in the 1890s. Most of these immigrants were Jews, escaping poverty, political uncertainty, and the pogroms that began in Russia in 1881 after the assassination of Czar Alexander II by Nihilist revolutionaries.[13] Jules Zanger writes that "these new Jews pouring in from the East appeared to be nothing like the distinguished, highly civilized, Sephardic philosopher-idealists created by Disraeli in *Tancred* and George Eliot in *Daniel Deronda*. . . . The response to their presence was both hostile and fearful."[14]

All these developments—the failure of revolution in Eastern Europe, the fear of invasion in Britain, the increase of immigrants from unfamiliar parts of the continent, and the public perception that great revolutionary leaders of the past like Kościuszko, Mazzini, and Kossuth had degenerated at century's end into terrorists, fraudulent counts, and Jewish immigrants—created an ideal atmosphere for Stoker's vampire warrior. As I argue below, Dracula combines the most popular nineteenth-century representations of the Eastern European exile: the courageous freedom fighter, defending the frontiers of Europe, and the obscure, fin-de-siècle foreigner, contaminating British culture.

Dracula the Revolutionary

In the opening pages of *Dracula,* Jonathan Harker's descriptions of Budapest evoke the familiar stereotypes of British travel beyond Western Europe: "we were leaving the West and entering the East; the most Western of splendid bridges over the Danube, which is here of noble width and depth, took us

---

12. Barbara Melchiori, *Terrorism in the Late Victorian Novel* (London and Dover, NH: Croom Helm, 1985), 1–32.

13. Raymond P. Scheindlin, *A Short History of the Jewish People from Legendary Times to Modern Statehood* (Oxford: Oxford University Press, 1998), 181.

14. Jules Zanger, "A Sympathetic Vibration: Dracula and the Jews," *English Literature in Transition* 34.1 (1991): 34. For other readings linking Dracula and Jewish immigrants, see Judith Halberstam, *Skin Shows: Gothic Horror and the Technology of Monsters* (Durham, NC, and London: Duke University Press, 1995), 86–106; H. L. Malchow, *Gothic Images of Race in Nineteenth-Century Britain* (Stanford, CA: Stanford University Press, 1996), 148–166; and Carol Margaret Davison, *Anti-Semitism and British Gothic Literature* (Basingstoke and New York: Palgrave Macmillan, 2004), 120–157. Clearly there are powerful and disturbing connections between Victorian characterizations of the immigrant Jew and Stoker's portrait of Dracula. Yet as Zanger himself admits, "Count Dracula . . . is uncompromisingly aristocratic and autocratic, a lord and commander of armies; it is difficult to think of anyone less like the stereotype of the Jew." Zanger, "A Sympathetic Vibration."

among the traditions of Turkish rule" (7). The foreignness of Budapest is confirmed by the sight of some Slovaks, who, on the British stage "would be set down at once as some old Oriental band of brigands," and in Harker's observation on train travel: "It seems to me that the further East you go the more unpunctual are the trains. What ought they to be in China?" (10, 9). The association between Dracula and the East continues in Britain: it is no surprise that the Count should choose to arrive at the eastern port of Whitby. At Dracula's English property in Purfleet (suitably east of London), Dr Seward is astonished by "a big bat, which was flapping its silent and ghostly way to the west . . . as if it knew where it was bound for or had some intention of its own" (143). Even the distribution of the Count's boxes in London imitates the cartographic position of Eastern Europe: "He was now fixed on the far east of the northern shore, on the east of the southern shore, and on the south. The north and west were surely never meant to be left out of his diabolical scheme" (336–337).

But if Harker and company are quick to Orientalize Dracula and his environs, Bram Stoker seems to have had a more nuanced cognitive engagement with Eastern Europe. His father-in-law, Lieutenant-Colonel James Balcombe, was a distinguished veteran of the Crimean War.[15] His brother George had served as a medical officer in the 1877–1878 Russo-Turkish War and authored a memoir of his experiences.[16] In 1890 Stoker met the Jewish Hungarian scholar Arminius Vámbéry, who "had been to Central Asia, following after centuries the track of Marco Polo and was full of experiences fascinating to hear." They met again two years later, when Vámbéry received an honorary degree at Dublin University: "He soared above all the speakers, making one of the finest speeches I have ever heard. Be sure that he spoke loudly against Russian aggression—a subject to which he had largely devoted himself."[17] Vámbéry enters the pages of *Dracula* as a consultant and friend of Van Helsing (whose unique style of English perhaps owes something to the Hungarian scholar).[18] In 1892 Stoker's close friend Hall Caine traveled

---

15. Paul Murray, *From the Shadow of Dracula: A Life of Bram Stoker* (London: Jonathan Cape, 2004), 77.

16. George Stoker, *With "The Unspeakables"; Or, Two Years' Campaigning in European and Asiatic Turkey* (London: Chapman & Hall, 1878). According to David Glover, George's memoir "contains many of the features that later graced Stoker's 1897 novel." See *Vampires, Mummies, and Liberals: Bram Stoker and the Politics of Popular Fiction* (Durham, NC, and London: Duke University Press, 1996), 33.

17. Bram Stoker, *Personal Reminiscences of Henry Irving*, 2 vols. (London: W. Heinemann, 1906), 1: 371–372.

18. A sample from Stoker's *Personal Reminiscences:* "I asked him if when in Thibet he never felt any fear. He answered:

Fear of death—no; but I am afraid of torture. I protected myself against that, however!

to the Russian border on behalf of the London Russo-Jewish Committee to investigate Jewish persecution.[19] At about this same time Stoker also became acquainted with two Russians from opposite ends of the political spectrum: Sergius Stepniak, the Russian Nihilist exile who told Stoker about "the state of affairs in Russia" and the difficult lives of political exiles in Siberia; and, in California, the bear-hunting Prince Nicholas Galitzin.[20] More generally, the "Eastern Question"—the question of control over the territories of the failing Ottoman Empire—was a major concern of British foreign policy throughout Stoker's lifetime. Significantly, when Stoker returned to Transylvania in his 1909 novel *The Lady of the Shroud,* the seeming vampire figure, Lady Teuta, turns out to be a courageous nationalist leader. She marries the English protagonist, and together they rule over a confederation of Balkan states that stands against the oppressive threats of Turkey, Russia, and Austria-Hungary.[21] All of these examples suggest that the Victorians in general knew more about Eastern Europe than we give them credit for knowing, and that Bram Stoker in particular was surrounded by friends, family, and acquaintances who understood much of the history, politics, and conflicts of these lands.

Furthermore, as Stephen Arata notes, Stoker's "Eastern" villain does not conform to stereotypes of the East.[22] Count Dracula is well read, cultured, and reliable: all attributes that separate him from colonial or Eastern stereotypes but connect him firmly with earlier, aristocratic immigrants. Dracula describes in detail his own descent from freedom fighters: "Is it a wonder that we were a conquering race; that we were proud; that when the Magyar, the Lombard, the Avar, the Bulgar, or the Turk poured his thousands on our frontiers, we drove them back?" (42). The Count is particularly proud of his

---

However did you manage that?
I had always a poison pill fastened here, where the lappet of my coat now is. This I could always reach with my mouth in case my hands were tied. I knew they could not torture me, and then I did not care! (1: 371).

19. Vivien Allen, *Hall Caine: Portrait of a Victorian Romancer* (Sheffield: Sheffield Academic Press, 1997), 214–222.

20. Stoker, *Reminiscences,* 2: 53–58.

21. Glover has noted how Stoker reemployed narrative details from his 1890 novel *The Snake's Pass* (set in Ireland) in *The Lady of the Shroud* (51–57). The central national concern of *Shroud*—how a smaller nation or ethnic community in Europe can survive among expansionist neighbors—has obvious significance for Stoker's homeland. In fact comparisons between Ireland and various Eastern European nations were often employed in the Victorian Era. For examples, see Thomas McLean, "Arms and the Circassian Woman: Frances Browne's 'The Star of Attéghéi,'" *Victorian Poetry* 41.3 (2003): 299–301; Murray, *From the Shadows of Dracula,* 194–196; and Maria Todorova, *Imagining the Balkans* (Oxford: Oxford University Press, 2009), 100–101. While this association potentially supports an "Irish" reading of *Dracula,* I want to call attention here to Stoker's longstanding interest in Eastern Europe.

22. Arata, *Fictions of Loss,* 123.

race's victories over the Turks: "to us for centuries was trusted the guarding of the frontier of Turkey-land" (42–43). His use of a passive verb almost lets the reader ignore who entrusted Dracula with such a position: Western Europe. For Victorian readers, the best-known defenders of Europe from eastern invasion were the Poles and Hungarians; many writers and poets argued for Polish sovereignty by reminding readers of John Sobieski's 1683 epoch-making victory over the Turks at Vienna.[23] Like the Poles and Hungarians, who at different times fought Russia, Austria, and Turkey, the Székelys struggle against a number of different oppressors, "for," avers the Count, "our spirit would not brook that we were not free" (43). Dracula speaks of Transylvania as "the whirlpool of European races" and assures Harker that "there is hardly a foot of soil in all this region that has not been enriched by the blood of men, patriots or invaders" (42, 33). The Count's elaborate account is supported by Van Helsing's (and Stoker's) friend Arminius, who admits the Draculas were once "a great and noble race" (309).

It is worth noting that Dracula does not live in Romania; he is a resident of Hungary, and more specifically the Austro-Hungarian Empire. Transylvania became part of Romania only after the First World War. Furthermore, though Romanians were Transylvania's largest ethnic group, Dracula is not Romanian but Székely, a Hungarian minority in Transylvania. It may be, as Vesna Goldsworthy suggests, that Stoker was simply employing an ethnic identity "even more exotic" than Romanian for the sake of his Anglophone readers.[24] In any case, Dracula appears in the novel as a once great leader who now lives under another empire. It is significant that Dracula belittles the ruling families of both Austria and Russia and condemns the present political situation of his land: "the Szekelys . . . can boast a record that mushroom growths like the Hapsburgs and Romanoffs can never reach. The warlike days are over. Blood is too precious a thing in these days of dishonourable peace" (43). Besides hinting at the sanguinary events to come, this passage reminds the careful reader that Austria and Russia together put down Hungary's 1848–1849 revolution—hence Dracula's particular mockery of their ruling families. It then refers to the 1867 Austro-Hungarian Compromise—the agreement that enabled the "dishonourable peace" that Dracula laments.

---

23. "What was Austria to Poland that Poland should be generous to her in her time of need? Had Austria deserved so well of Poland? . . . But Sobieski was magnanimous. If there was any leading idea and purpose of his life, it was to shatter the power of the Turks, to clear Europe of them and drive them back to Asia." [Joseph Neuberg], "Poland: Her History and Prospects," *Westminster Review* (January 1855): 139. William Wordsworth, Thomas Campbell, and Alfred Tennyson were among the many British poets who invoked Sobieski's victory.

24. Vesna Goldsworthy, *Inventing Ruritania: The Imperialism of the Imagination* (New Haven, CT, and London: Yale University Press, 1998), 82. Arata suggests that Stoker follows Emily Gerard in identifying the Székelys as Romanian (*Fictions of Loss,* 116).

As noted above, many Hungarian freedom fighters accepted this compromise, but others, including Kossuth, did not. Clearly Dracula is of the latter party.

If Dracula's rhetoric in Transylvania brings to mind frustrated freedom fighters like Kossuth, his actions in England conjure up later, decadent images of the Eastern European exile. Dracula's arrival in Britain coincides with the enormous immigration of Russian and Eastern European Jews who, like Dracula, would have arrived at ports like Whitby on Russian vessels. Once in England, Dracula attacks society not (as he would have in Transylvania) by assembling an army of conquest, but rather in guerilla fashion.[25] He follows in the footsteps of Count Fosco, Count Pateroff, and Joseph Emilius in furthering his plans by gaining control of rich, married women. He relies on the mentally unstable but politically astute Renfield[26] to invite him in—after all, who but a mad man would assist a foreign terrorist? He even imitates the Fenians and Nihilists who hid explosives in bags and boxes around London when he surreptitiously distributes his sacred boxes of earth throughout the city. Interestingly, Stoker described an incident that perhaps inspired Dracula's methods: in the *Reminiscences,* Stoker relates the care with which a ship owned by Czar Alexander II (the *Livadia*) was checked for infernal machines: "[t]hese machines were exploded by clockwork set for a certain time, and were made in such fashion as would not excite suspicion. Some were in the form of irregularly shaped lumps of coal. The first thing to be done was therefore to take out all the coal which had already been put in."[27] Like the workers digging through the Czar's coal, Van Helsing and company are in a race against time to locate Dracula's boxes of earth.

Dracula's decadent and revolutionary origins are further emphasized through the efficacy of Catholic objects. During his visit to Hungary, Jonathan Harker initially finds distasteful a crucifix that a peasant gives him: "as an English Churchman, I have been taught to regard such things as in some measure idolatrous" (12). He soon learns its usefulness in combating foreign threats. Later Van Helsing uses Catholic wafers to limit Dracula's movements. Catholicism symbolizes the old religions of Europe and separates the continent from Britain, but it is also the religion connected with the most revolutionary countries of nineteenth-century Europe: Ireland, France, Italy, and Poland. Though Van Helsing says that vampires fear all things sacred, it is significant that he must import the Catholic wafers from the continent.[28]

---

25. As Van Helsing notes, "We have on our side power of combination—a power denied to the vampire kind" (306).

26. See Renfield's remarks on the United States and the Monroe Doctrine (313).

27. Bram Stoker, *Reminiscences,* 2: 49. Stoker's notes concerning the Russian schooner "Dimetry" are the obvious source for the *Demeter* and its cargo (Stoker, *Dracula,* 513); perhaps the *Livadia* suggested to Stoker the dangers of even the most mundane cargo.

28. He also imports (from Haarlem) the garlic used to defend Lucy (171, 177).

Just as it requires the Catholic, continental Van Helsing to understand and explain Dracula, so a Catholic, continental weapon is required to defeat him.

Like the political exile, Dracula must be invited to live elsewhere. More important, he cannot return on his own to his homeland. As Mina notes, Dracula "must be *brought back* by someone" (451, original emphasis). Many famous nineteenth-century political exiles, including Kościuszko and Kossuth, waited for a change in government that would allow them to return home honorably. But they only returned to their homelands, like Dracula, in caskets.

Fearing the Foreigner

Dracula can succeed only by total assimilation into his newly adopted culture, even down to the accent: "a stranger in a strange land, he is no one; men know him not—and to know not is to care not for. I am content if I am like the rest, so that no man stops if he see me, or pause in his speaking if he hear my words, to say, "Ha, ha! A stranger!" (31–32). Arata points to this passage as evidence of the most alarming aspect of Dracula's journey to England: "The truly disturbing notion is not that Dracula impersonates Harker, but that he does it so well. Here indeed is the nub: Dracula can 'pass.'"[29] It is this skill that makes possible the "reverse colonization" Arata so convincingly describes. And yet Dracula never quite succeeds in becoming British. In London he chooses the urbane but un-English alias De Ville, and when he attempts to take passage on the *Czarina Catherine*—wearing an absurd combination of black suit and straw hat—the Captain tells the Count "he doesn't want no Frenchmen—with bloom upon them and also with blood—in his ship" (409). A vampire in London may be able to "appear at will," "direct the elements" and "command all the meaner things," but he cannot hide his foreignness (304–305).

This suggests a weakness in Arata's argument, and perhaps my own. Arata sees in Dracula a threat either from the colonies or from another imperial power in Europe, like Russia or Germany. In the preceding pages, I've argued for the revolutionary exiles of Poland and Hungary as more likely sources for Stoker's characterization of Count Dracula. But in Stoker's novel the threat of the vampire is not limited to a single nation or territory. As Van Helsing tells his companions, the vampire "is known everywhere that men have been. In old Greece, in old Rome; he flourish in Germany all over, in France, in India, even in the Chersonese; and in China . . . He have follow

---

29. Arata, *Fictions of Loss,* 124.

the wake of the berserker Icelander, the devil-begotten Hun, the Slav, the Saxon, the Magyar" (307). Furthermore those objects and creatures associated with Dracula defy categorization as "colonial," or as coming from a particular part of the world; they can be categorized only as foreign. It is true that Van Helsing compares Dracula to "[y]our man-eater, as they of India call the tiger who has once taste blood of the human," and that Harker and Morris hunt Dracula with kukri and bowie knives (412, 483). This suggests that the protagonists *perceive* Dracula as an eastern threat. But Dracula's metonyms are international. He arrives and departs England on Russian vessels, the *Demeter* (a Greek goddess) and the *Czarina Catherine.* He makes use of a Norwegian wolf taken from the zoo, and takes the form of a South American bat to pursue his victims. Jonathan and Mina first spot the Count in London "outside Giuliano's," the premises of an Italian jeweler (222). He purchases his Piccadilly home under the French pseudonym De Ville. His return to Eastern Europe is made possible through the services of the Scottish sea captain Donelson, the Jew Hildesheim, and the Slav Petrof Skinsky (448–449). Slovaks and gypsies carry Dracula back towards his castle.

There are a number of sympathetic portraits of foreigners in Stoker's novel. Transylvanian peasants attempt to keep Harker away from Castle Dracula, and the kindly Hungarian Sister Agatha nurses him back to health in Budapest. Most significantly, Van Helsing's friend Arminius aids in the gathering of knowledge about Dracula. But these minor figures remain safely in their homelands. Unlike, say, *The Woman in White,* where the benevolent Professor Pesca balances the evil Count Fosco, there is no Eastern European character in Britain to balance the threat of Dracula or to encourage the reader to feel sympathetically towards Transylvanians abroad. The novel suggests that foreign travel is allowable only to the British, and even for them is potentially dangerous.

The seeming exceptions are the Dutch Van Helsing and the American Quincey Morris. Noting that Van Helsing's English is "much worse than Dracula's," Michael Kane sees an important distinction between the British visits of the two personages: "whereas Dracula has perfected his English in order to settle down and blend in with the native community . . . Van Helsing is clearly a foreigner with no designs on immigration and integration, who will return home after a short visit."[30] The same cannot be said necessarily for Quincey Morris, who first appears in the novel as one of Lucy's suitors. Arata sees Morris, representative of the ascendant imperial power across the ocean, as a second threat to British authority, and his death as symbolic

---

30. Michael Kane, "Insiders/Outsiders: Conrad's *The Nigger of the 'Narcissus'* and Bram Stoker's *Dracula,*" *Modern Language Review* 92.1 (1997): 20.

end to that threat.[31] Both arguments are insightful, but neither explains why these foreigners are allowed to infuse their blood into Lucy's body. I would suggest that the relationship of each man's nation to Britain allows for their participation in hunting down Dracula and in giving their blood to a British woman. Van Helsing's Holland was the home of William III, whose Glorious Revolution in 1688 rescued Britain from the Stuarts and continental Catholicism. Morris's United States is Britain's legitimate descendant.

The combined forces of Britain past, present, and future expel the unwanted immigrant from their island. But if Dracula is defeated, mixed blood triumphs. Mina's child Quincey becomes the offspring not only of herself and Jonathan but also of Dracula, since the Count earlier forces Mina to drink his own blood. As Arata notes, "Through Roumania, the English race invigorates itself by incorporating those racial qualities needed to reverse its own decline."[32] Dracula predicts a similar conclusion during the scene of Mina's blood drinking, when he tells Mina, "They should have kept their energies for use closer to home. Whilst they played wits against me—against me who commanded nations, and intrigued for them, and fought for them, hundreds of years before they were born—I was countermining them. And you, their best beloved one, are now to me, flesh of my flesh; blood of my blood; kin of my kin" (370). Dracula's "them" refers to Van Helsing and company, but he could just as easily have been referring to the modern Western powers who for centuries relied on Poland and Hungary to contain the threat of Eastern invasion, but who also insisted on regarding those nations as distant, mysterious, other.

It is tempting to think of the residual Székely blood in Quincey's veins as a wonderfully perverse slip on Stoker's part. But perhaps Stoker knew what he was doing. I've already noted Stoker's own complex relationship with the people and politics of Eastern Europe, and his sympathetic portrayal of continental figures like Arminius and Sister Agatha. But it is also significant that Stoker goes out of his way to suggest that the United Kingdom is as ethnically mixed a land as Transylvania. He does so by setting parts of his novel in Whitby and Exeter, places invaded by the Danes;[33] by showcasing a rich variety of dialects—the Whitbian Swales, the Cockney zookeeper Bilder, the Scottish captain Donelson, the Texan Morris; and by giving his heroines surnames with connotations Irish (Westenra) and Scottish (Murray). No wonder that Dracula desires "to go through the crowded streets" of London, "to be in the midst of the whirl and rush of humanity" (31). The

---

31. Arata, *Fictions of Loss,* 129.

32. Arata, *Fictions of Loss,* 129.

33. Mina notes that Whitby Abbey was "sacked by the Danes" (85); Exeter had earlier been a Roman settlement.

"whirl and rush" of London echo the Transylvanian "whirlpool" of races and suggest that Britain's own history makes it fertile ground for Dracula's plans. In Van Helsing's imperfect English, "He find out the place of all the world most of promise for him" (412). Rather than read *Dracula* as evidence of Stoker's own xenophobia, perhaps we should read it as an honest admission that encounters between different peoples in Europe have always resulted in war, distrust, and misunderstanding; that the surest way to unite the older disparate elements of a nation is by introducing a newer disparate element. In the wake of increased 1890s immigration, the 1905 Aliens Act made it far more difficult for Eastern Europeans to find a new home in Britain. But eight years earlier Dracula had already left his mark, adding his own to "the blood of many brave races" that was already racing through Quincey Harker's veins (42).

Works Cited

Allen, Vivien. *Hall Caine: Portrait of a Victorian Romancer.* Sheffield: Sheffield Academic Press, 1997.

Arata, Stephen. *Fictions of Loss in the Victorian Fin de Siècle.* Cambridge: Cambridge University Press, 1996.

Brantlinger, Patrick. *Rule of Darkness: British Literature and Imperialism, 1830–1914.* Ithaca, NY, and London: Cornell University Press, 1988.

Cain, Jimmie E. *Bram Stoker and Russophobia: Evidence of the British Fear of Russia in* Dracula *and* The Lady of the Shroud. Jefferson, NC, and London: McFarland, 2006.

Carpenter, Kirsty. *Refugees of the French Revolution: Émigrés in London, 1789–1802.* New York: St. Martin's Press, 1999.

Coundouriotis, Eleni. "*Dracula* and the Idea of Europe." *Connotations* 9.2 (1999/2000): 143–159.

Davison, Carol Margaret. *Anti-Semitism and British Gothic Literature.* Basingstoke and New York: Palgrave Macmillan, 2004.

Dittmer, Jason. "*Dracula* and the Cultural Construction of Europe." *Connotations* 12.2–3 (2002/2003): 233–248.

Gibson, Matthew. *Dracula and the Eastern Question: British and French Vampire Narratives of the Nineteenth-Century Near East.* Basingstoke and New York: Palgrave Macmillan, 2006.

Glover, David. *Vampires, Mummies, and Liberals: Bram Stoker and the Politics of Popular Fiction.* Durham, NC, and London: Duke University Press, 1996.

Goldsworthy, Vesna. *Inventing Ruritania: The Imperialism of the Imagination.* New Haven, CT, and London: Yale University Press, 1998.

Halberstam, Judith. *Skin Shows: Gothic Horror and the Technology of Monsters.* Durham, NC, and London: Duke University Press, 1995.

Kane, Michael. "Insiders/Outsiders: Conrad's *The Nigger of the 'Narcissus'* and Bram Stoker's *Dracula.*" *Modern Language Review* 92.1 (1997): 1–21.

Lever, Charles. *The Dodd Family Abroad.* London: Chapman & Hall, 1854.

Malchow, H. L. *Gothic Images of Race in Nineteenth-Century Britain.* Stanford, CA: Stanford University Press, 1996.

McLean, Thomas. "Arms and the Circassian Woman: Frances Browne's 'The Star of Attéghéi.'" *Victorian Poetry* 41.3 (2003): 295–318.

McLean, Thomas. *The Other East and Nineteenth-Century British Literature: Imagining Poland and the Russian Empire.* Basingstoke: Palgrave Macmillan, 2011.

Melchiori, Barbara. *Terrorism in the Late Victorian Novel.* London and Dover, NH: Croom Helm, 1985.

Murray, Paul. *From the Shadow of Dracula: A Life of Bram Stoker.* London: Jonathan Cape, 2004.

[Neuberg, Joseph]. "Poland: Her History and Prospects." *Westminster Review* (January 1855): 114–154.

Porter, Bernard. *The Refugee Question in Mid-Victorian Politics.* Cambridge: Cambridge University Press, 1979.

Ragussis, Michael. *Figures of Conversion: "The Jewish Question" & English National Identity.* Durham, NC, and London: Duke University Press, 1995.

Reynolds, Matthew. *Realms of Verse, 1830–1879: English Poetry in a Time of Nation-Building.* Oxford: Oxford University Press, 2001.

Rudman, Harry W. *Italian Nationalism and English Letters: Figures of the Risorgimento and Victorian Men of Letters.* London: Allen & Unwin, 1940.

Scheindlin, Raymond P. *A Short History of the Jewish People from Legendary Times to Modern Statehood.* Oxford: Oxford University Press, 1998.

Senf, Carol A. "A Response to 'Dracula and the Idea of Europe.'" *Connotations* 10.1 (2000/2001): 47–58.

Squire, John Collings. *Books in General by Solomon Eagle.* New York: Knopf, 1920.

Stoker, Bram. *Dracula.* 1897. Edited by Maurice Hindle. New York: Penguin, 1993.

———. *Personal Reminiscences of Henry Irving.* 2 vols. London: W. Heinemann, 1906.

Stoker, George. *With "The Unspeakables"; Or, Two Years' Campaigning in European and Asiatic Turkey.* London: Chapman & Hall, 1878.

Thackeray, William. *The Newcomes: Memoirs of a Most Respectable Family.* Edited by Andrew Sanders. Oxford: Oxford University Press, 1995.

Todorova, Maria. *Imagining the Balkans.* Updated edition. Oxford: Oxford University Press, 2009.

Trollope, Anthony. *The Claverings.* Edited by David Skilton. Oxford: Oxford University Press, 1991.

Wolff, Larry. *Inventing Eastern Europe: The Map of Civilization on the Mind of the Enlightenment.* Stanford, CA: Stanford University Press, 1994.

Zamoyski, Adam. *Holy Madness: Romantics, Patriots and Revolutionaries, 1776–1871.* London: Weidenfeld & Nicolson, 1999.

Zanger, Jules. "A Sympathetic Vibration: Dracula and the Jews." *English Literature in Transition* 34.1 (1991): 33–44.

Afterword

Fear and Loathing

Victorian Xenophobia

❦

ANNE J. KERSHEN

While it is true, as a number of the contributors to this book have pointed out, that a precise word—xenophobia—to describe aversion to, or fear of (justified or not), those who are strange or foreign, only entered the English language in the first decade of the twentieth century, negative reactions to the presence and activities of outsiders in England have a much longer history. However, before taking the "long view" of English xenophobia, it is necessary to mark out the word's parameters, as well as highlighting other words that indicate indigene revulsion and abhorrence directed towards those who are "other" in terms of religion, race, and nationality. The *Shorter Oxford English Dictionary* defines xenophobia as "A deep antipathy to foreigners and foreign things."[1] If used precisely the word does not infer racial inferiority, rather it indicates an emotion or pattern of behavior that is in response to a real, or imagined, threat to home, job, national identity, and culture.

Theories that some races are inherently inferior to others found increasing credence in central Europe in the latter decades of the nineteenth century. The word "racism" to define belief in racial supremacy is recorded as first being used in the mid-1930s, but it was not until after the Second World War that the term was generally adopted (*Shorter OED*, 2446). In England

---

1. *Shorter Oxford English Dictionary,* 3688. Subsequent references to this text will be cited parenthetically.

its common usage coincided with the large scale entry of African-Caribbean and South East Asian migrants in the 1950s, following the passage of the British Nationality Act in 1948.[2] In spite of the difference in meanings, it is not uncommon for the word xenophobia to be used to describe what are, or were, racist patterns of behavior, while accusations of racism are made about those who, in reality, are more accurately, xenophobes. In addition, as will become apparent, there are occasions when the two can be used in tandem.

One of the earliest manifestations of xenophobia based on religious aversion was anti-Jewishness. Though this sentiment predates the birth of Christ, it made its first appearance in England following the arrival of Jews from northern France who had traveled to England in the wake of William of Normandy. Labeled as "murderers of Christ," Jews represented the epitome of otherness and threat. In addition to religious antipathy, as usurers and merchants it is little wonder that they became prime targets for verbal and physical attack.[3] In medieval England and beyond, anti-Jewishness was an inevitable adjunct of Christianity. From the twelfth century onwards Jews were diabolized by commentators and in cartoons. This linkage with the devil is a thread that can be traced through the centuries.[4] As late as the 1940s Jewish evacuees in East Anglia reported that local children looked under their hair for the stubs of horns they believed were the mark of a Jew.[5] Anti-Jewish sentiment has not been the only form of religious antipathy to emerge in England. Anti-Catholicism began in the reign of Henry VIII, was manifest after the Fire of London in 1665[6] and exploded into violence with the Gordon Riots of 1780. Aversion to Islam, and thus to Muslims, can be traced back to the Crusades and the wars raged against the infidels in order to

---

2. Under the provisions of the Act, citizens of the New Commonwealth enjoyed relatively free access to the United Kingdom and almost identical rights to United Kingdom citizens, including entitlement to take up employment on arrival.

3. In 1144, the body of a young boy who had died a violent death was discovered in the woods near Norwich. Rumor quickly spread that the Jews had killed him in order to use his blood to make the Passover unleavened bread. This became known as the blood libel, the first of a number of such accusations. Only the intervention of the King saved the Jews of Norwich from the violence of the populace. Forty-six years later, on 17 March 1190, following a series of attacks on their homes, the Jews of York took shelter in the city's castle. When the castle was besieged by a mob, those taking sanctuary decided to take their own lives rather than be forced to convert. The following morning the few that were left, believing they could depart in safety, were murdered. The York Massacre heralded a century of discrimination. By 1290 a Jewish presence seemed an anomaly when the King was fighting the infidels in the Holy Land. In July of that year, the 15,000-strong Jewish population was expelled from England.

4. In 1753, at the height of the furor over the Jew Bill, a cartoon was published that showed a Jew in the foreground, masquerading as the devil and clutching money bags.

5. Tony Kushner, *The Persistence of Prejudice: Anti-Semitism in Britain in the Second World War* (Manchester: Manchester University Press, 1989), 69.

6. English Catholics and suspected Huguenot crypto-Catholics were rumored to have started the fire.

regain the Holy Land for Christianity. However, recognition of this antipathy as a phobia is a much more recent phenomenon, first recognized in Britain in the 1980s, and the subject of a report published by the Runnymede Trust in 1997.[7] It was only after 9/11 and the reactionary concern over the growth of Islam in the West that the term Islamophobia was commonly adopted to describe "hatred or fear of Islam or Muslims, particularly as a political force" (*Shorter OED* 1429).

Xenophobia and tolerance do, at times, appear side by side. This was the case in the late-seventeenth century when Huguenots fleeing persecution in France took refuge in England. For though the Calvinists were welcomed by the English monarch, Charles II, who established a charity to help support indigent French refugees, there were those who felt threatened by the presence of men and women whom they feared might be crypto-Catholics. Other xenophobes condemned the refugees for undercutting wages; for importing new technology that advanced the weaving of silk and took jobs away from English weavers; and even for the sound of their "croaking" voices. Some blamed the Huguenots for starting the fire of London.[8] The deeds and words of the diarist Samuel Pepys best sum up the anomalies. For while he wrote, "we do naturally all . . . hate the French," he also donated money to the Huguenot cause.[9] It was not only Huguenots in the seventeenth and eighteenth centuries that were subjected to xenophobic attacks because of their (alleged) economic threat. Fifteenth-century Dutch brewers also were harassed because of the profits they made as a result of their monopoly of the beer brewing trade. When the rumor was spread that beer brewed by the Dutch was poisonous, a number of Dutch-owned breweries were attacked.[10] Medieval Dutch immigrants were not the only ones to be accused of endangering English lives with tainted food. Lucio Sponza has shown how, in Victorian England, at the height of late-nineteenth-century jingoism, Italian penny ice-cream men were accused of being out to "poison the children" with their products made in unsanitary conditions. The subtext was clear; the Italians were undermining the future of the British nation.[11]

During the last half of the nineteenth century theories of racial science began to take a hold in Central Europe. In 1873 a disillusioned German journalist, Wilhelm Marr, produced a pamphlet, *Jews Victory over Teutonism*,

---

7. *Islamophobia—A Challenge to Us All*, no author (London: Runnymede Trust, 1997).

8. Anne J. Kershen, *Strangers, Aliens and Asians: Huguenots, Jews and Bangladeshis in Spitalfields, 1660–2000* (Abingdon: Routledge, 2005), 193.

9. Kershen, *Strangers, Aliens and Asians*, 198.

10. Lien Bich Luu, "Dutch and Their Beer Brewing in England, 1400–1700" in *Food in the Migrant Experience*, 106.

11. Lucio Sponza, "Italian Penny Ice-Men in Victorian London" in *Food in the Migrant Experience*, 36.

which examined Jewish racial qualities and their impact on the German people. He was convinced that unless Jews were removed from society they would become more powerful than the German nation. It is Marr who is credited with having invented, and used in his publication, the word anti-Semitism to describe Jew hatred.[12] In England too, racist ideology was taking over from forms of xenophobia based on religious otherness. Benjamin Disraeli's Balkan policy was considered by Goldwin Smith to be a direct result of the Prime Minister's racial origins. Smith highlighted such a theory in an article entitled, "Can Jews be Patriots?" which appeared in 1878.[13] As the century drew to its close, established Anglo-Jewry became a target for certain writers and social commentators who considered assimilated Jews to be a political and social threat to the nation.[14]

However, it was the mass influx of Eastern European Jews who arrived in England from the mid-1870s onwards that aroused a powerful negative reaction, and which led to the introduction of a series of words to describe the new, secular, xenophobia. The term anti-Semitism was one rarely heard in Britain until after the First World War, the pejorative designation selected to describe Eastern European Jewish immigrants who were "taking the jobs and homes of Englishmen," was "alien" while those who opposed them were "anti-alienists" and their discriminatory practices, "anti-alienism." The goal of the anti-alienists was to restrict, or ideally ban, the entry of pauper aliens (Eastern European Jews) not because of their religious difference from Anglicism, but because of the threat they posed to the identity of the indigenous population, particularly those living in the East End of London where, by 1901, it was estimated at least 100,000 aliens had settled. Though the use of the word alien might be considered a euphemism for Jew, the language of criticism and condemnation was not. Racial supremacists were convinced that the pauper aliens in England were of inferior stock. In the words of the Member of Parliament for Bow and Bromley (in the East End of London), "England was being made a human ash pit for the refuse population of the world."[15] The alien nature of the immigrants was further emphasized by the Rev. S. G. Reaney, an East End clergyman, who was convinced that East-

---

12. Lucy Dawidowicz, *The War Against the Jews: 1939–1945* (London: Weidenfeld and Nicholson, 1975), 34. The pamphlet went through twelve editions between 1873 and 1879, and it is possible that for this reason the date given for the first use of "antisemitism" is frequently 1879, rather than 1873.

13. Goldwin Smith, "Can Jews be Patriots?" in *Nineteenth Century* (London: C. Kegan Paul, 1878), 878–899.

14. Colin Holmes, *Anti-Semitism in British Society, 1876–1939* (London: Edward Arnold, 1979), 77; Todd Endelman, *The Jews of Britain, 1656–2000* (Los Angeles and London: University of California Press, 2002), 151–156.

15. *East End News*, 1888, London, qtd. in Kershen, *Strangers*, 202.

ern European Jews' otherness was non-negotiable. He highlighted the fact
that their faces were "so un-English and the sound of the speech so utterly
foreign . . . In face, instinct, language and character their children are aliens
and still exiles. They seldom really become citizens."[16] The aliens were condemned for their unsanitary habits, for their wage undercutting, for their
exploitation of the housing shortage, yet rarely for their religious practices.
Anti-alienism, as it emerged in late-nineteenth-century England, was a fusion
of Marr's form of intellectual anti-Semitism and indigenous xenophobia galvanized by concern for jobs and housing. Yet, even here, centuries old anti-
Jewishness was detectable, for though few referred to the alien as "Jew," a
Stepney member of the British Brothers League demanded in 1903 that "no
more Jews be brought into the country."[17] With the passage of the Aliens Act
in 1905, the anti-alienists achieved only a measure of success, for though the
Act did control pauper immigrant entry, it left the door open for refugees
seeking sanctuary from religious and political persecution as well as for those
who could prove they had sufficient funds to support themselves and their
families.[18]

Even after the First World War the alien threat persisted. The legacy of
wartime xenophobia and the belief that all Jews were Bolshies were powerful
forces behind the passage of the Aliens Restriction Act of 1919 and the Aliens
Order of 1920, which imposed far harsher controls on alien immigrant entry
than had previously operated in peace time.[19] Jews remained the objective
of xenophobes and racists throughout the 1930s and 1940s. As founder and
leader of the British Union of Fascists, Oswald Mosley targeted both the "big
Jews and the little Jews," in his fascist campaigns in the 1930s. More recently,
anti-Semitism has been manifest on the terraces at football matches, in the
desecration of gravestones in Jewish cemeteries, and on certain university
campuses.

Though the alien Jew was still considered to be a possible danger to the
stability of the state, the post-World War One legislation embraced other
"aliens"—in particular, foreign (black) seamen working in British ports and

---

16. Arnold White, *The Destitute Alien in Great Britain* (London: Sonnenschein and Co., 1892),
20.

17. The British Brothers League was founded in 1901 in East London with the specific intent
of achieving a ban on alien (Eastern European Jewish) immigration. It was a precursor to the fascist
organizations of the 1930s. The remark of the member of the League is a quote from Colin Holmes,
Anti-Semitism in British Society, 1876–1939 (New York: Holmes & Meier Publishers, 1979), 96.

18. The right to refuge was abolished under emergency wartime legislation in 1914. It was not
until the Geneva Convention in 1951 that England again opened its doors to refugees.

19. During the war, Jews with German sounding names had come under attack by those seeking
out the enemy alien. The violence and outcome of the Russian revolution in 1917 was allied to the
mistaken belief that all Jews were Bolsheviks and as such were a threat to the sovereign state.

on British merchant ships. When the war ended so did the need for black seamen recruited from the British Empire. Where the Empire black seaman had been valued as a significant aid to the war effort, he rapidly became the subject of discrimination, perceived as taking the jobs of deserving white English seamen. By the summer of 1919 riots broke out in the port of Liverpool as British sailors protested violently against non-white seamen. The outcome was a clause in the 1920 Aliens Order which required that alien (non-white) employment on British ships be curtailed. In 1925 this was formalized as The Special Restriction Order which obliged seamen to register in accordance with provisions made under the 1920 Act. In effect, this meant that seamen wishing to work on His Majesty's ships had to provide evidence that they were British or British Empire born. This was not a simple procedure, as the majority of those born overseas rarely had the necessary documentation. As a result, many lost their jobs. In the event the Order never achieved parliamentary ratification, for though supported by trade unionists, it faced opposition from the India Office and certain politicians who felt uneasy about its racist implications. Within a decade the Order was withdrawn. It was, however, one of the earliest examples of twentieth-century institutionalized racism.

Antipathy to the "black presence" was not a phenomenon of the twentieth century. In 1596 Queen Elizabeth I ordered the expulsion of the blackmoores, demanding that "those kind of people should be sent from the land."[20] Reasons given for the antipathy towards the resident Africans vary from the fact that they were considered heathen and bestial, to the intensity of their blackness which contrasted with the "whiteness [of the virgin Queen] which stood for purity, virtue, beauty and benefice," and which emphasized the "filthy, base, ugly and evil" otherness of the black man.[21] This sixteenth-century example is illustrative of the way in which the demarcation line between xenophobia and racism becomes blurred.

Gradation by skin color was one of the fundamental tools of the new science of race. Categorization of otherness was by color, by facial characteristics, and by voice. Jews and those of Mediterranean appearance, such as Italians and Greeks, were considered lesser white, forced to work their passage of integration if they wished to achieve parity with their Anglo Saxon counterparts. The Irish were not exempt from scientific racialization; the percep-

---

20. The National Archives, "Black Presence: Asian and Black History in Britain from 1500 to 1850," www.nationalarchives.gov.uk/pathways/blackhistory/early_times/elizabeth.htm. Accessed 15 December 2010.

21. Douglas Lorimer, *Colour, Class and the Victorians: English Attitudes to the Negro in the Mid-Nineteenth Century* (Leicester: Leicester University Press, 1978), 19; and Peter Fryer, *Staying Power: The History of Black People in Britain* (London: Pluto, 1984), 10.

tion of their facial characteristics and voices frequently labeled them as the "white blacks."[22] But it has been incomers from the New Commonwealth, particularly those who arrived in England after 1948, who have been the recipients of some of the most violent and foul racist attacks to take place in England.

Racial discrimination in the form of a color bar was nothing new to post-War England. Before and during the War, some hotels and clubs in London operated a ban on black people, while the arrival of black American servicemen in 1942, though welcomed by some, was feared by others. In the 1950s, as New Commonwealth immigration gathered pace, the impact of colored immigrants on the nation was an issue that aroused concern across the political spectrum.[23] Matters came to a head in 1958 when riots broke out in Nottingham and Notting Hill in West London, the latter an area inhabited by poor whites and African Caribbeans. At the end of August, following a confrontation between immigrants and white youths on a "nigger hunt," fighting ensued for a number of days. At the same time, further north in Nottingham, tensions between blacks and whites were also erupting into violence.[24] Yet again, tensions driven by fear produced immigration controls. The Commonwealth Immigrants Act of 1962 was directed specifically at those who had been given freedom of entry under the 1948 act. Initially, it did little to slow down the arrival of migrants from South East Asia who poured in before the Act was implemented. Nor did it quell discrimination against non-whites. In spite of the Race Relations Acts brought in the 1960s and 1970s, in the workplace, in housing allocation, and on the streets, racism persisted.

While it was predominantly African-Caribbean immigrants who came under attack from racists in the 1950s, by the late 1960s the emphasis had changed. It was now immigrants from Pakistan who became the butt of the racist xenophobes. Initially, the early Pakistani immigrants were not viewed as a threat. They were sojourners, remaining in England to earn enough money to enable them to go home as "rich men of high status." However, as so often is the case with economic migrants, the dream becomes a myth of return and the sojourner a settler. Realizing that their future now lay in England, the men began to send for wives and children, or for new, young brides and the temporary bachelor enclaves of young Bangladeshis[25] transformed into

22. Bronwen Walter, "'Shamrocks Growing Out of their Mouths': Language and the Racialisation of the Irish in Britain" in *Language, Labour and Migration,* 60.

23. Colin Holmes, *John Bull's Island* (London: Macmillan, 1998), 258–259.

24. See Randall Hansen, *Citizenship and Migration in Post-war Britain: The Institutional Origins of a Multicultural Nation* (Oxford: Oxford University Press, 2000), 80–82.

25. The majority of the immigrants from Pakistan came from the eastern side of the country, a region that, after a long and bloody civil war, became the independent nation state of Bangladesh

family communities. Community signaled permanency. Permanent settlement meant not only the proximity of an alien culture, but also the outsider need for housing, schooling, and medical support. All of these imposed
strains on local and national resources. Where once there had been a tolerant benevolence towards the Bengalis, whose ancestors had first arrived in
the East End in the late eighteenth century, there was now antagonism that
translated into physical attacks. In the 1970s and 1980s these became an
almost weekly occurrence in and around Brick Lane. It was here, in the London Borough of Tower Hamlets, that the first incidence of "Paki-bashing"
was recorded. Not only had a new form of violence emerged on the streets
of London, but to accompany it came a new term to describe that specific
manifestation of xenophobic racism.

Supported by the National Front, racism in East London assumed a
nightmarish mantle. Between March and May 1976, thirty cases of assaults
on young Asians were recorded in Brick Lane, while a total of five Bengalis died in the racial violence.[26] It was not only the male members of the
immigrant population who were targeted; women and children also were
terrified to leave their homes as, when they did they were verbally and
physically assaulted by white youths. The two areas of tension were housing and racial nationalism. According to local racists, the immigrants were
pushing white families out of the area to make way for "coloured people."
In order to remove the Bengalis from what they considered should remain
all white estates, stones were thrown through windows, and excrement and
petrol bombs put through letter boxes. Attacks on homes and persons continued throughout the 1970s, 80s and into the mid- 90s.[27] In spite of this,
by the late 1990s the Bangladeshi community of East London had become
established and, to an extent, accepted. The National Front no longer ran
amok up and down Brick Lane, and the levels of racial violence declined.
Tragically, this has not been true of England as a whole. In the summer of
2001 racist-inspired riots broke out in a number of northern cities.[28] One of
main causes of the riots was the segregated nature of the Asian and White
communities that created tensions between the two groups who believed
they had little in common. As commentators sought to learn from the ashes
of the riots, a new phrase entered the lexicon of multicultural England—
"community cohesion."[29] While old tensions ebb, new ones flow. These are

in 1971. Therefore, though many of the men were Pakistani when they settled, from 1971 onwards
they considered themselves Bengali.

26. *Guardian* (London) 6 June 1977 (no author).

27. Kershen, *Strangers,* 211–217.

28. These included Oldham, Bradford, Burnley, and Leeds.

29. The concept of community cohesion is that people from different backgrounds living in
proximity share a common sense of belonging, recognize difference, and work for the common good.

now visible between the established Bangladeshi communities, and recently arrived immigrants from Eastern Europe. The former now adopt the language of the traditional xenophobe, claiming that the new arrivals are "taking their jobs and homes," the latter, unused to people of darker skin, manifest a racist antipathy. As one young Polish student explained, "I know I shouldn't say it but I don't like black people."[30]

Taking the long view has clearly shown that while the terminology may be that of the twentieth century, the emotions and resulting actions have a much longer history. In some cases they are the outcome of ignorance; at other times intellectual obsession and scientific fixation. As I suggested at the outset of this Afterword, xenophobia and racism have two separate and specific meanings, yet at times there is no doubting they can be used as a binary to describe certain patterns of behavior. The attacks on the long-resident German community at the onset of the First World War were galvanized by fear of an enemy within, but there is no suggestion that the attackers considered their targets to be inferior beings. In contrast, the harassment of Bengalis may have originated from the local population's fear that the incomers were receiving priority treatment, but in the hands of the white supremacists this natural concern was soon massaged into a racial issue.

An examination of the semantics of xenophobia and racism has demonstrated that specificity of victim requires specificity of terminology, thus we arrive at anti-Jewishness; anti-Semitism; Islamophobia and Paki-bashing— words used to describe emotions and patterns of behavior directed towards particular groups throughout history. Terms instantly recognizable as tools of those with a particular fear and/or hatred of those deemed other. This book has explored the application and interpretation of reactions to the figure of the other in the Victorian era; a period of history when British empire and industry were at their height, and when a British identity achieved maturity.[31] As a sense of "Englishness" grew[32] so did a heightened awareness of those who were different by nature of culture, color, creed, language, and nationality. It was at the end of Victoria's rule that "xenophobia," as a word to describe the reactive emotion to otherness, was formalized. No coincidence that this followed the end of the Boer War and the passage of the Aliens Act of 1905. Both served to highlight the threatening other; one on the other side of the world, one embedded within the capital itself. A study of xenophobia and racism illustrates that throughout history it has been

---

30. Conversation between the author and a young Polish student, 19 October 2010, in Oswestry, Shropshire.

31. Linda Colley, *Britons: Forging the Nation, 1707–1837* (London: Vintage, 1996).

32. At the height of industry and empire, Englishness and Britishness were synonymous. See Anne J. Kershen, *A Question of Identity* (Aldershot: Ashgate, 1998), 5–6.

human nature to fear that which is strange and foreign. It should also advocate that the only way to overcome the negativity of this emotion is through knowledge and understanding of that which is, and those who are, other. Something this book goes a considerable distance towards achieving.

Works Cited

Colley, Linda. *Britons: Forging the Nation, 1707–1837.* London: Vintage, 1996.

Dawidowicz, Lucy. *The War Against the Jews: 1939–1945.* London: Weidenfeld and Nicholson, 1975.

Endelman, Todd. *The Jews of Britain, 1656–2000.* Los Angeles and London: University of California Press, 2002.

Fryer, Peter. *Staying Power: The History of Black People in Britain.* London: Pluto, 1984.

Guardian (London), 6 June 1977.

Hansen, Randall. *Citizenship and Migration in Post-war Britain: The Institutional Origins of a Multicultural Nation.* Oxford: Oxford University Press, 2000.

Holmes, Colin. *Anti-Semitism in British Society, 1876–1939.* London: Edward Arnold, 1979.

———. *John Bull's Island.* London: Macmillan, 1998.

Islamophobia—A Challenge for Us All. London: Runnymede Trust, 1997.

Kershen, Anne J. *A Question of Identity.* Aldershot: Ashgate, 1998.

———. *Strangers, Aliens and Asians: Huguenots, Jews and Bangladeshis in Spitalfields, 1660–2000.* Abingdon: Routledge, 2005.

Kushner, Tony. *The Persistence of Prejudice: Anti-Semitism in Britain in the Second World War.* Manchester: Manchester University Press, 1989.

Lorimer, Douglas. *Colour, Class and the Victorians: English Attitudes to the Negro in the Mid-Nineteenth Century.* Leicester: Leicester University Press, 1978.

Luu, Lien Bich. "Dutch and Their Beer Brewing in England, 1400–1700." In *Food in the Migrant Experience,* edited by Anne J. Kershen. 101–133. Aldershot: Ashgate, 2002.

The National Archives. "Black Presence: Asian and Black history in Britain from 1500 to 1850." www.nationalarchives.gov.uk/pathways/blackhistory/early_times/elizabeth.htm. Accessed 15 December 2010.

Shorter Oxford English Dictionary. Oxford: Oxford University Press, 2002.

Smith, Goldwin. "Can Jews be Patriots?" In *Nineteenth Century.* London: C. Kegan Paul, 1878. 878–899.

Sponza, Lucio. "Italian Penny Ice-Men in Victorian London." In *Food in the Migrant Experience,* edited by Anne J. Kershen. 17–41. Aldershot: Ashgate, 2002.

Walter, Bronwen. "'Shamrocks Growing Out of their Mouths': Language and the Racialisation of the Irish in Britain." In *Language, Labour and Migration,* edited by Anne J. Kershen. 57–73. Aldershot: Ashgate, 2000.

White, Arnold. *The Destitute Alien in Great Britain.* London: Sonnenschein, 1892.

Contributors

MARIA K. BACHMAN is Professor of English at Coastal Carolina University. She is editor of *Reality's Dark Light: The Sensational Wilkie Collins* (University of Tennessee Press, 2006) and has edited critical editions of Wilkie Collins's *Blind Love* (Broadview Press, 2004) and *The Woman in White* (Broadview Press, 2006). She is currently working on a book-length monograph, *We Read, Therefore We Are: Embodied Consciousness and the Novel.*

CHARLOTTE BOYCE is a Senior Lecturer in English Literature at the University of Portsmouth. Her research interests are focused on nineteenth-century representations of food, cooking, and domesticity, and she is currently completing a book-length monograph on the Victorian dining-room.

PATRICK BRANTLINGER is the Rudy Professor Emeritus of English at Indiana University, Bloomington. His books include *The Spirit of Reform: British Literature and Politics, 1830–1900* (1977); *Bread and Circuses: Theories of Mass Culture as Social Decay* (1983); *Rule of Darkness: British Literature and Imperialism, 1830–1914* (1988); *Crusoe's Footprints: Cultural Studies in Britain and America* (1990); *Fictions of State: Culture and Credit in Britain, 1694–1994* (1996); *The Reading Lesson: The Threat of Mass Literacy in Nineteenth-Century British Fiction* (1998); and *Who Killed Shakespeare? What's Happened to English since the Radical Sixties* (2001).

JENNIFER HAYWARD is Professor of English at the College of Wooster. She is the author of *Consuming Fictions: Active Audiences and Serial Fictions from Dickens to Soaps*, as well as editor of *Maria Graham's Journal of a Residence in Chile*. She has also published articles on women's travel writing, colonialism, and African-American literature.

HEIDI KAUFMAN is Associate Professor of English at the University of Oregon and co-editor of the interdisciplinary journal *Nineteenth Century Studies*. She is the author of *English Origins, Jewish Discourse, and the Nineteenth-Century British Novel: Reflections on a Nested Nation* (Penn State Press, 2009) and co-editor of *An Uncomfortable Authority: Maria Edgeworth and Her Contexts* (University of Delaware Press, 2004). Currently, she is at work on two projects focusing on nineteenth-century East End material and print culture.

ANNE KERSHEN was Barnet Shine Senior Research Fellow in the Department of Politics at Queen Mary University of London from 1990 until her retirement in 2011. She founded the Centre for the Study of Migration at Queen Mary University of London in 1995 and was its Director until 2011. She is now an Honorary Senior Research Fellow at the Centre for the Study of Migration at Queen Mary and also an Honorary Senior Research Associate at University College London. She is the author of *Strangers, Aliens and Asians: Huguenots, Jews and Bangladeshis in Spitalfields 1660–2000* (Taylor and Francis [Routledge], 2005); *Uniting the Tailors* (Frank Cass, 1995); and *Tradition and Change A History of Reform Judaism in Britain 1840—1995* (Vallentine Mitchell, 1995). She has also edited *Food in the Migrant Experience* (Ashgate, 2002); *Language, Labour and Migration* (Ashgate, 2000); *A Question of Identity* (Ashgate, 1998); and *London the Promised Land? The Migrant Experience in a Capital City* (Avebury, 1997). She has published numerous journal articles and has acted as advisor to, and appeared on, radio and television on the subject of migration in London.

ANNEMARIE McALLISTER is a Lecturer at the University of Central Lancashire and the author of *John Bull's Italian Snakes and Ladders: English Attitudes to Italy in the Mid-nineteenth Century* (Cambridge Scholars, 2007). She continues to write on representations of Italians but also now works on the history of Temperance in the UK, particularly the children's movement, the Band of Hope.

THOMAS McLEAN is a Senior Lecturer in English at the University of Otago. He is editor of *Further Letters of Joanna Baillie* (Fairleigh Dickinson, 2010) and author of *The Other East and Nineteenth-Century British Literature: Imagining Poland and the Russian Empire* (Palgrave, 2012).

ELIZABETH CAROLYN MILLER is Associate Professor of English at the University of California Davis. She is the author of two books, *Framed: The New Woman Criminal in British Culture at the Fin de Siècle* (University of Michigan Press, 2008) and *Slow Print: Literary Radicalism and Late Victorian Print Culture* (Stanford University Press, 2013). Her articles have appeared in such journals as *Feminist Studies, Literature Compass, Modernism/modernity,* and *Victorian Literature and Culture.*

THOMAS PRASCH is Professor and Chair in the Department of History at Washburn University, Topeka. His recent publications include "Eating the World: London in 1851" (*Victorian Literature and Culture,* 2008), "Mirror Images: John Thomson's Photographs of East Asia" in *A Century of Travels in China: Critical Essays on Travel Writing from the 1840s to the 1940s* (Hong Kong University Press, 2007), and various entries on nineteenth-century international exhibitions in *Encyclopedia of World's Fairs and Expositions* (McFarland, 2008).

JAY D. SLOAN is Assistant Professor English at Kent State University, Stark. His research interests are focused on Victorian constructions of masculinity, particularly on the alternative masculinities formulated in the work of the Pre-Raphaelite poet and painter, Dante Gabriel Rossetti.

JOY SPERLING is Professor of Art History at Denison University She has published in the areas of nineteenth-century American and British art, modern art, and new art, including *Famous Works of Art in Popular Culture* (Greenwood Press, 2003) and *Jude Tallichet* (Sara Meltzer Gallery, 2010). Her current book project is titled *Independent Women and the Spectacle of the Southwest: Visually Enchanting the Land of Enchantment in Modern America.*

RAJANI SUDAN is Associate Professor of English at Southern Methodist University. She is the author of *Fair Exotics: Xenophobic Subjects in English Literature* (University of Pennsylvania Press, 2002) and is currently completing *Mud, Mortar, and Other Technologies of Empire,* a book-length study of the non-European origins of the Enlightenment.

MARLENE TROMP is Professor of English and Women and Gender Studies and Dean at Arizona State University's New College of Interdisciplinary Arts and Sciences. She is the author of *Altered States: Sex, Nation, Drugs, and Self-Transformation in Victorian Spiritualism* (SUNY Press, 2006), and *The Private Rod: Sexual Violence, Marriage, and the Law in Victorian England* (University Press of Virginia, 2000). She has also edited or co-edited and contributed to *Victorian Freaks: The Social Context of Freakery in the Nineteenth Century* (The Ohio State University Press, 2007) and *Mary Elizabeth Braddon: Beyond Sensation* (SUNY Press, 2000). She has two other books under review, *Abstracting Economics,* a volume she edited with Daniel Bivona, and *Force of Habit: Life and Death on the Titanic.* She is presently at work on a new book, *Intimate Murder: Sex and Death in Nineteenth-Century Britain,* which explores deadly violence in intimate relationships.

MINNA VUOHELAINEN is Senior Lecturer in English Literature at Edge Hill University. Her research is focused on fin-de-siècle popular fiction and print culture. She has published a number of articles on Richard Marsh and has edited his fiction, including *The Beetle,* for Valancourt Books. She is currently working on a monograph on Marsh's professional practice as a popular author.

Index